THE INVESTIGATION OF WHITE-COLLAR CRIME

A Manual for Law Enforcement Agencies

APRIL 1977

PROJECT STAFF: Herbert Edelhertz, Project Director
Ezra Stotland
Marilyn Walsh
Milton Weinberg

PROJECT MONITORS: James O. Golden, Director
Enforcement Program Division
Office of Regional Operations

Stephen W. Cooley, Chief
Organized Crime Desk
Office of Regional Operations

This manual was prepared for the Enforcement Program Division, Office of Regional Operations, Law Enforcement Assistance Administration, U.S. Department of Justice, under Grant Number 76-TA-99-0011 awarded to the Battelle Law and Justice Study Center. Points of view or opinions stated herein are those of the authors and do not necessarily represent the official position or policies of the U.S. Department of Justice.

Books for Business
New York-Hong Kong

The Investigation of the White-Collar Crime:
A Manual for Law Enforcement Agencies

by
Law Enforcement Assistance Administration
U. S. Department of Justice

The Seventh Basic Investigative Technique:
Analyzing Financial Transactions in the
Investigation of Organized Crime and White Collar
Crime Targets

by
Richard A. Nossen, Consultant

ISBN: 0-89499-145-0

Reprinted from the 1977 edition

Books for Business
New York - Hong Kong
http://www.BusinessBooksInternational.com

ACKNOWLEDGMENTS

This Manual builds upon the broad-ranging and intensive experience of numerous investigators and their agencies, a good portion of which has been organized in specialized manuals, in internal agency documents which reflect agency policies and practices, and in the extensive knowledge of individual investigators who provide a wealth of information and advice if one takes the trouble to ask. It would have been impossible to under- take or to complete this task without access to the work of those who have developed written materials in the past, and without the help and advice of those actually currently engaged in law enforcement in the area of white-collar crime. We know that we have overlooked the contributions of many, since even a cursory review of the text of this Manual tells us that we have forgotten where we heard this particularly valuable piece of advice, or that specific admonition to beware of a serious investigative pitfall --- and we hope that the sources of such experience will forgive us for inadvertently omitting recognition of their contributions.

This Manual had its genesis in discussions with James Golden, Director of the Enforcement Program Division, Office of Regional Operations, L.E.A.A., and with Stephen Cooley, Chief of the Organized Crime Desk of that Division, who recognized the need for and the potential benefits to the law enforcement community of the pulling-together of white-collar crime investigative experience in terms of common problems and approaches. Their unfailing interest and participation in this effort constituted a positive contri- bution, and together with Jay Marshall and Katherine Landen of their staff they were constantly alert to facilitate every aspect of this work.

While we examined many prior sources in preparation of this Manual, we would be remiss if we did not note the special helpfulness of Richard D. Latham, Director of Enforcement, Texas State Securities Board, who kindly made available an advance draft of his Midwest Enforcement Manual; of Charles A. Miller, former Director, Office of Criminal Investigation, U.S. Postal Inspection Service, who over many years contributed to the education of this project's director and whose "Economic Crime: A Prosecutor's Hornbook" prepared for the National District Attorneys Association was a most valuable resource; and of Richard A. Nossen, formerly of the Intelligence Division of the U.S. Internal Revenue Service, whose advice was invaluable and whose handbook on financial investigations is an appendix to this Manual.

In the course of gathering information we visited with many local, state and federal agencies, and should make special note of the following:

In Federal agencies: to William Erxleben, Director, Region X, U.S. Federal Trade Commission; Jack Bookey, Director, Region X, U.S. Securities and Exchange Commission, to William Haye, of the Region X office of the U.S. Department of Housing and Urban Development and Clark Blight of his staff.

In State agencies: to Vern Hoy, Director of the Arizona Department of Public Safety and to Bill Bayley, Sgt. Ray Lambertson, and Lt. James Chilcoat of his staff; to Clark Mears in the Public Corruption Section of the Office of the Attorney General in Oregon; to Nicholas A. Dotoli, Chief Investigator in the New Jersey State Enforcement Bureau and members of his staff; to Lts. Lawrence Reece and Lawrence Birch of the Special Investigations Unit of the Michigan State Police and to Victor J. de Wolf, Earl Miller, Patrick Devlin, and Robert Pickel of the Michigan Attorney General's Organized Crime Unit; to Sam Papich and William Tarangelo of the Governor's Anti-Organized Crime Division in New Mexico and to Harvey Fruman of that state's Attorney General's Office; and to Craig Beek and Tom Ruxlow of the Criminal Investigations Bureau of the Iowa Department of Public Safety.

We were greatly assisted by local prosecutors and members of their staffs We owe special thanks to the following: in Nassau County, N.Y., to Milton Lipson, Charles Padgett, and Robert Clarey; in King County (Seattle), Washington, to Gene Anderson and Michael Cohen; in San Diego, California, to James Lorenz and Lawrence K. Wilson, Lyle Strand, William Bergmeister, and Robert Fellmuth of his staff; in Genessee County (Flint), Michigan, to Prosecutor Robert Leonard and George C. Steeh, Edwyna Anderson, Bob McFadden, Bruck Smock, Barbara Menear, and Sheldon Siegel of his staff; in the District of Columbia, to Robert S. Ogren, Chief of the Fraud Unit in the U.S. Attorney's Office; and to Joseph P. Paone of the Prosecutor's Office in Albequerque, New Mexico. Charles Ehlert, formerly director of Seattle's municipal Consumer Protection Bureau, was of great help in orienting us to the investigative issues and problems of agencies such as his.

Many local police agencies deeply involved in investigation of white-collar crimes, gave generously of their time, advice, and internal technique documentation. Special mention should be made of the cooperation of the Bunco-Forgery Division of the Los Angeles Police Department, directed by Captain Thomas Sena, whose staff advised us and in some cases critiqued preliminary drafts of sections of this Manual --- Lt. William Mossman; Sgts. Elmer Owens, Jack Stiff (ret.), Carl Hughett, Gordon McDevitt, John Olsen, William Lietz, Robert Nieto, Art Ramirez, Daniel Binstein (ret.); and to Officers Ray Madrid, George Nielson, J. Black, and D.A. Bowers; and finally to Lt. A. Romero who is conducting a unique consumer outreach program in the Los Angeles Police Department. In Seattle, Lt. Jerry Anderson and Sgt. James Whelan were most helpful, as were Sgts. Donald M. McCathran and Earl Gould in the District of Columbia.

Members of the Battelle staff made their own invaluable contributions. Roma St. James was project coordinator/secretary/schedule keeper/draftsperson of charts and tables --- without whose efforts none of us could have worked as effectively. The work of Dr. Michael Brintnall on organization of prosecutive and investigative functions of white-collar crime units, completed while a member of the Battelle staff prior to this project, was of great value to this effort. Harvey Chamberlain assisted us in the earlier stages of the

project in collecting and organizing data; Deborah Berger is responsible
for extensive searches of the literature and the structuring of this
Manual's organized bibliography; and Sheldon Arenberg, a Battelle consultant
prepared the Link Network Diagram - Chapter II. It should be noted that among
the authors of this Manual, principal responsibilities were as follows:
Dr. Ezra Stotland for sections on organization and training; Dr. Marilyn
Walsh for sections on intelligence and evaluation; and Milton Weinberg for
sections on conduct of white-collar crime investigations and computers.

Herbert Edelhertz
Project Director

GUIDE TO THIS MANUAL

This Manual was developed for the use of those who investigate white-collar crime and related abuses, and to assist those who supervise and must interact with investigators in this field. It was not addressed to any specialized audience within these groups, but rather to meet general interests in white-collar crime investigation which cut across such specialized lines.

The world of white-collar crime enforcement is a broad one, transcending lines of geography, organizations, and subject matter jurisdiction. On the federal level there are widespread white-collar crime investigative efforts which cut across subject matter lines (as in the U.S. Department of Justice and its Federal Bureau of Investigation, and the U.S. Postal Inspection Service), and efforts which are far more specialized, such as are to be found in the U.S. Securities and Exchange Commission and in every department and agency with purchasing, program or revenue responsibilities such as the Department of Defense, the Department of Housing and Urban Development, and the Internal Revenue Service. The work of each of these also results in civil, regulatory, or administrative cases, in the same way as outcomes of investigations by the Federal Trade Commission.

On the state government level investigators are similarly active in state police agencies, offices of attorneys general, state revenue departments, state bureaus of investigation, and state regulatory agencies, enforcing criminal and civil laws dealing with white-collar crime and related abuses. These agencies deal with such matters as consumer fraud, investor protection, environmental protection, public corruption, regulatory violations, government procurement, and organized crime.

On county and municipal levels, police, sheriffs' offices, local revenue departments, consumer protection offices, local license departments, prosecutors' offices, departments of weights and measures --- all these and many more which operate in great numbers of organizational frameworks, deal with all of the variations of white-collar crimes and related abuses.

Private organizations --- for public service reasons or in support of their own economic interests --- more and more are to be found investigating white-collar crime and related abuses in order to protect the internal integrity of their member operations, to deter white-collar crime, and as a basis for supporting civil remedies or referring cases to public agencies which have criminal investigative and prosecutive jurisdiction.

It is obvious that each of these types of agencies, organizations, and governmental units can use its own specialized, detailed manual to guide its investigators and to assist those who supervise or cooperate with them. Some may, for example, have special powers such as subpoena power or the right to inspect the books and records of regulated entities or licensees; most would not. Many such agencies and organizations have prepared their own manuals which address their own problems in great detail. This Manual does not purport to fill such specialized needs. Rather it explores common problems in organizing and operating white-collar crime investigative units, in investigating white-collar crimes and related abuses, and in making sure that the products of investigation are most likely to be used appropriately by prosecutors and litigating attorneys who ultimately determine whether a case will go forward and how it will be presented. Hopefully the approach adopted in this Manual will fill two key needs: (1) to generally orient new organizations as to what must be done to successfully set up and operate an organization which investigates white-collar crime; and (2) to provide an inventory of strategies, tactics, and techniques both for new organizations and for already established investigative organizations, which will help them to enhance the comprehensiveness of their operations --- and to improve them.

This Manual has been structured to achieve its purpose, as described above, by being usable in two ways: first, as a narrative description which can be read in its entirety to develop a total picture of white-collar crime investigative issues and methods; and second, as a reference or resource document from which portions can be selectively taken to answer specific questions or provide guidance as to particular problems. To make it usable in these two distinct ways, some issues were necessarily discussed in more than one portion of the Manual, although from different perspectives.

The organization of this Manual goes from the general to the specific. First it deals with the basic issue of what white-collar crime is, why it is a proper area for law enforcement efforts, and what its impact is on individuals, business, and the general community. As part of this discussion, white-collar crime elements, characteristics, offender motivations, relationships to other crime areas, and remedies are discussed at some length --- for the light they shed on both the justifications for and proper methods of responding to these crimes and the abuses related to them. From there the Manual goes on to discuss the kinds of organizations and organizational activities which have been found to be required to effectively deal with white-collar crime, and factors such as the form of organizational units, interfaces of unit activity within agencies and externally, personnel selection, and the role of intelligence in a white-collar crime enforcement effort.

Having thus set the stage for action, the elements of white-collar crime are then analyzed for the purpose of showing how the investigator can identify and target the kinds of information and evidence he will need in order to construct his case. Once this is done it becomes relevant to go into detail as to how the investigator should proceed to obtain this information and evidence, for example by searches for documentation, finding and interviewing victims and witnesses, and interrogation of suspects. Also included in this section of the Manual is a discussion of computers, both as a tool used by the white-collar criminal in committing his crimes and as an investigative resource for use by the investigator to unravel and prove a case.

The main part of the Manual concludes with a discussion of evaluation of white-collar crime efforts, not merely as a basis for judging success or failure but, more importantly, as an aid to setting goals and priorities, as a source of information for guiding and steering agency or unit operations, and as a basis for resource allocation and budget justification.

The Appendices are added for the purpose of providing more specific forms of expertise and assistance with respect to such matters as training investigators, readily identifying the sources of information needed in white-collar crime investigations, following financial trails, and directing the reader (by use of a selected glossary of white-collar crimes numerically keyed to an organized bibliography) to sources of further information on white-collar crime issues, victims, and specific offenses.

From this description of the structure of the Manual it should be obvious that it is not an encyclopedia designed to answer all questions or convey all available knowledge in the field, but rather one resource to assist the reader to master the issues and techniques which are important to white-collar crime investigation. Individual agencies should prepare their own manuals, addressing their own subject matter and jurisdictional issues, as additions to or incorporating materials in this Manual. With increasing attention to white-collar crime in the media and in the community at large, we should anticipate that this will be only the first of a series of manuals, training aids, and research products to support this vital law enforcement effort.

TABLE OF CONTENTS

Page

TABLE OF CONTENTS (continued)

TABLE OF CONTENTS (continued)

X11

TABLE OF CONTENTS (continued)

Page

TABLE OF CONTENTS (continued)

TABLE OF CONTENTS (continued)

CHAPTER I

INTRODUCTION

A. WHITE-COLLAR CRIME IS CRIME

Law enforcement agencies and the publics they serve often consider "crime" only in terms of acts of violence, threats of violence, and overt thefts. These common crimes have immediate and observable impact on victims. From the point of view of law enforcement agencies, such common crimes compel their priority attention because:

- The offender is easily perceived to be dangerous to the personal safety of members of the community.

- The victims know they have suffered harm.

- The wrongful acts fall into familiar categories of crime.

- The consequences of the wrongful acts, to both victims and society, are clear.

- The acts to be investigated are relatively simple.

- It is easily confirmed and highly probable that a prosecutable crime has been committed.

- The more serious the harm to the victim, the more likely it is that prosecution will result.

- There is substantial possibility that conviction will be followed by incarceration or, at the least, direct or close supervision of the offender.

When white-collar crime is called to the attention of law enforcement agencies the issues are rarely so easily perceived, although the human and financial costs may be greater than in the case of many common crimes. It is usual, after all, that a victim will physically recover from an assault, but the impact of fraud may continue for the lifetime of the victim; and white-collar crime has a corrosive and corruptive effect on our society by souring our trust in one another, and in the business, social, and political institutions and networks which are so essential to our lives.

The human impact of white-collar crime was movingly described in one newspaper account:

Beyond the cash he stole, [the offender's] crime lies in smashing the delicate pattern of an elderly person's life. . . . A lifetime of thrift, of small hard-won advances and setbacks painfully overcome left [the victim] with a tiny niche in the world. Now she finds herself computing on the backs of envelopes the money she has left against the years she might live. "I'm using up my savings and I'm worried about running out of money," she said. "How many years will I have something to take care of me?"[1]

Its contemporary significance as <u>real crime</u> was forcefully stated by a leading jurist, who said:

> In our complex society the accountant's certificate and the lawyer's opinion can be instruments for inflicting pecuniary loss more potent than the chisel or crowbar . . .[2]

It is nevertheless the fact that law enforcement authorities are often reluctant to undertake investigations and prosecutions. This reluctance stems from instinctive understanding, on the part of law enforcement professionals, that:

- The wrongful acts do not always fall into familiar categories of crime.

- There are usually available alternative or civil remedies.

- It is difficult to decide whether the alleged wrongful acts constitute a crime without further, and frequently extensive, investigation.

- Victim cooperation may sometimes be less than wholehearted.

- The alleged offender can be "allowed to walk the streets" since he inflicts no physical injuries on his victims.

- The alleged offender will also often be involved in legitimate activity and doesn't regard himself as a criminal.

- Investigation may be relatively complex and time-consuming, as compared to investigation of common crimes.

- The more serious the harm to victims, the more complex and difficult the investigation is likely to be.

- Investigators anticipate difficulty in persuading prosecutors that charges should be filed.

- There is common perception that those convicted of white-collar crimes receive lenient or only nominal punishment.

---

[1]Saar, "Crime in the Suites Held Epidemic," <u>Washington Post</u>, April 13, 1975, at p. A-1.

[2]<u>United States v. Benjamin</u>, 328 F. 2d 854 (1964).

Because these problems are real, they should be openly recognized and dealt with. Any traditional law enforcement agency which is involved in criminal enforcement and does not face up to these problems is bound to fail--or at the least may be condemned to only half-hearted success. Facing up to these problems means, in the first instance, that a law enforcement agency recognize that its duty is enforcement against criminal activity in the fullest sense of the term. White-collar criminals are thieves: they steal money, they steal opportunity, they pollute our society. They are not just legitimate businessmen who have "crossed into" a gray area of "sharp" business practice. Indeed they may be criminal businessmen, organized syndicate criminals, or fences, who are pursuing their primary criminal activities in gray areas between legitimate and illegal business. The impacts of their activities directly affect:

- Individual and business victims who are directly swindled.

- The public-at-large who are indirectly taxed through higher prices on goods purchased.

- Honest businessmen who are unable to compete with white-collar criminals.

- Local, state, and national governments who are defrauded.

- The disadvantaged, programs for whom are looted and often discredited.

In recent years there has been heightened consciousness of the importance of white-collar crime and the threats it presents at every level of our society. At every level of government and in every arena of our society--political, law enforcement, the academic world--white-collar crime is discussed. There is talk not only about the harm it does, but also about the fact that the criminal justice system unfairly singles out poor street offenders as objects of enforcement while ignoring or leniently treating the upper-class, white-collar criminal.

This increased level of attention has been accompanied by some increases in resources available to combat white-collar crime and related abuses--though these increases in the level of resources have not been proportionate to the rising clamor for enforcement. Through direct grants from the Law Enforcement Assistance Administration and block grants in the states, through municipally funded consumer protection offices and state attorneys' general offices, through local district attorney's offices and police departments, and through public interest groups and business trade associations--new efforts have been and are being launched against white-collar crime. Of central importance to the success of law enforcement efforts to combat white-collar crime and related abuses is the development of a body of expertise on the subject--not only at prosecutive levels, but down the line where crimes are detected, where victims are seen, where cases are investigated. The prosecutors and the litigators and the juries and the judges have their essential roles, but their performance depends upon and will largely reflect the persistence and the skill with which investigators find and develop cases to help victims and punish offenders.

B. <u>DEFINITION OF WHITE-COLLAR CRIME</u>

White-collar crime is stealing--but not so plain and not so simple. It is clever theft, like that committed by a pickpocket, but is far more clever--because it operates in a manner which throws a smokescreen over the crime, either to hide the fact that there has been a crime at all, or to delay its discovery, or to insulate the receiver of the loot. And because the stealing is artful, proving criminal intent is usually made difficult by greater confusions than where a common thief is apprehended. The tools of crime are paper, pens, printing presses, advertising, glib talk, and even exploitation of government programs intended to protect the public from deception.[3]

Confusion as to the criminal nature of white-collar crime is also the result of a variety of remedies which flow from confusion as to intent. If a pickpocket is apprehended--though he too operates through deception--there is just one legal remedy, which is criminal prosecution. He is or is not prosecuted. However, where white-collar crime is involved, there are large numbers of alternate remedies--mediation, civil litigation, regulatory or administration action. This confusion makes it all the more important that investigative agencies and their personnel have a clear working definition of white-collar crime, and a basis for considering white-collar criminal acts in relationship to available remedies--so that these acts may be dealt with by maximum use of all available remedies and so that nothing inadvertently "falls between the cracks."

One useful and widely accepted definition of white-collar crime is:

. . . *an illegal act or series of illegal acts committed by nonphysical means and by concealment or guile, to obtain money or property, to avoid the payment or loss of money or property, or to obtain business or personal advantage.*[4]

The term *illegal acts* should be considered to include misrepresentations by omission or otherwise, which deprives a victim or government agency of information necessary to protect himself, herself, or itself.

---

[3]See section, "Reliance by Offender on Ignorance or Carelessness of the Victim," at p. 23.

[4]Herbert Edelhertz, <u>The Nature, Impact, and Prosecution of White-Collar Crime</u>, U.S. Department of Justice, L.E.A.A. (U.S. Government Printing Office, 1970), p. 3. This definition was described as a "good working definition" in the Attorney General's First Annual Report on Federal Law Enforcement and Criminal Justice System Assistance Activities (Washington, D.C.: U.S. Government Printing Office, 1972), p. 161.

This definition has achieved substantial acceptance, primarily because it defines "white-collar crime" in terms of the nature and character of the wrongful activity involved rather than the social or economic character of the offender.[5] It is quite different from the definition offered by Professor Edwin H. Sutherland, who is largely responsible for coining the term "white-collar crime," and who said that ". . . white-collar crime may be defined approximately as a crime committed by a person of respectability and high social status in the course of his occupation," and also that these crimes are violations of law by persons in the "upper socioeconomic class."[6]

Whatever the theoretical value of the Sutherland definition may be, it is an unreal basis for practical law enforcement. If it were to be accepted literally, embezzlement by a bank president would be "white-collar crime," but embezzlement by a low-paid bank clerk would not be; or an organized-crime figure running a bankruptcy scam could not be labeled as committing a white-collar crime because he did not have "respectability and high social status."

"White-collar crime" is not a very good descriptive term because it is confined, in the minds of many, to business or upper-class crime. Those involved in law enforcement should focus on the nature and character of the activity of those being investigated rather than on the character, occupation, education level, or social status of the suspect.

Those involved in criminal activity may pursue the same or related illicit goals by a combination of white-collar and non-white-collar crime. If the subject of an investigation is a corporate executive who takes a bribe to give a contract to a supplier and physically assaults or threatens violence against a fellow worker who might expose him there are several separate crimes stemming from the same activity, both white-collar and common crimes. Likewise, if an organized crime figure uses force and the fear of force to compel an otherwise legitimate businessman to participate in a bankruptcy fraud, there will be white-collar and common crime violations. In such instances, the investigator has several approaches—and can take one or all of them.

The important point to keep in mind is that some wrongful activity, or some aspects of a wrongful pattern of activity are committed by the use of guile and deception, and that there are statutes, methods of analysis, and techniques of investigation which will be particularly appropriate and effective in dealing with them. Familiarity with these statutes, remedies, and techniques should therefore be part of the

------

[5]See Walter C. Reckless, The Crime Problem, 4th ed. (New York: Appleton-Century-Crofts, 1973), pp. 315-333); Martin R. Haskell and Lewis Yablonsky, Criminology: Crime and Criminality (Rand McNally: Chicago, 1974), pp. 13-14, 150; Charles E. O'Hara, Fundamentals of Criminal Investigation, 4th ed. (Springfield, Ill.: Charles C. Thomas, 1976), pp. 902-906).

[6]Edwin H. Sutherland, White-Collar Crime (New York: Dryden Press, 1949), p. 9.

arsenal of all law enforcement agencies and their personnel. *White-collar crime is crime and not just some specially designated activity which is classified as crime because some legislators want to punish activity they don't like.*

It is important that personnel in law enforcement agencies recognize (whether they are employed in public or private agencies) that white-collar crime activity cannot be narrowly considered only in light of its potential for criminal prosecution. This is why, in this manual and elsewhere, we refer to "white-collar crime and related abuses." The very same activity may well be treated as a criminal violation, or as the basis for a civil claim, or as the basis for some civil or regulatory action.[7] For example, in a matter involving government procurement where there is doubt whether it can be proved beyond a reasonable doubt that there has been a false claim, there might still be enough proof for a civil fraud case or for administrative disqualification of the contractor. For another example, it should be noted that a violation of exactly the same section of the Federal Securities Act of 1933, dealing with fraud in the sale of securities, can be the basis for a criminal prosecution, or an injunctive action by the S.E.C., or a private civil action, or all three.

With this background, and keeping in mind that the above definition applies both to criminal violations and related abuses, in considering a case for investigation we should examine particular aspects of the definition for their implications in determining (i) whether there is a white-collar crime situation, and (ii) whether a case properly falls within the jurisdiction of the white-collar crime unit. This latter point, that of jurisdiction, is important not in the bureaucratic sense of who has the power and responsibility to deal with a case. More important, analysis of a case along the lines of this definition can help to determine whether the white-collar crime aspect of a particular suspicious activity is sufficiently present or dominant to make the case most workable by a unit trained, equipped, and oriented to deal with white-collar crime matters or by application of the techniques and approaches referred to in this manual.

The particular aspects of the above definition which are most useful are that a white-collar crime is:

- *Committed by non-physical means,*

- *Using guile and deception.*

In white-collar crime the victim will not know that he or it is being taken. In executing the plan the offender will not simply take something, even surreptitiously like the pickpocket or shoplifter. There will be some plan to procure victim cooperation in the taking.

White-collar crimes are not committed by force or threats. Extortion, therefore, is not white-collar crime, since it involves the threat

---

[7]Edelhertz, op. cit., Note 4, pp. 21-22.

of force or some other harmful action. The weapon in white-collar crime is, as has been pointed out above, the fountain pen, the advertisement, the glib sales pitch, etc. It should be recognized, however, that there may be white-collar crimes committed in conjunction with other crimes, where the situation will have to be more closely analyzed, e.g., where a loan shark pressures his victim (not a white-collar crime) to embezzle from his employer (a white-collar crime).

- *To obtain money or property or to obtain business or personal advantage.*

The objectives of the white-collar crime operator often go well beyond simply obtaining money or property from a victim--though this is all that will be involved in most frauds or con games. In many instances the objective will be to avoid paying something (such as taxes), or to avoid loss of property (as in the case of a bankrupt who hides assets from his creditors). Sometimes it will be to get an edge on a competitor (as in the case of a supplier who bribes a purchasing officer so that he gets the business instead of a competitor), or even to accomplish some legitimate objective by wrongful means (as in the case with some debt collection agencies who pretend that they are official law enforcement agencies enforcing collection procedures).

This, or any other definition of white-collar crime must, therefore, be broadly defined to cover a range of criminal activities, and also related abuses which may not be attractive for criminal prosecution but which nevertheless compels some civil, regulatory, or administrative response. Working with and understanding such a definition will assist the investigator in determining whether a case warrants further action, and in deciding who can most appropriately take responsibility for such action.

C. REASONS TO COMBAT WHITE-COLLAR CRIME

Law enforcement agencies and private law enforcement groups should be concerned about and should combat white-collar crime for these reasons:[8]

- These crimes and related abuses are within the subject matter jurisdiction of public agencies.

- Individual victims are being abused and must have remedies.

- The integrity of our society and its institutions must be protected.

---

[8]These are reasons, in general, for combatting white-collar crime, but specific kinds of agencies, such as police or trade associations, will have additional and more specific reasons for focusing on particular white-collar crimes or related abuses, or for providing particular kinds of remedies.

- White-collar crimes are often related to other criminal operations, such as organized crime, fencing, public corruption, etc.[9] Such unlawful operations may be particularly vulnerable to white-collar crime investigation and prosecution.

It is important to focus on these reasons for enforcement against white-collar crime because there are so many reasons advanced by law enforcement agencies and personnel for avoiding responsibility for dealing with white-collar crime problems.

D. REASONS ADVANCED TO AVOID DEALING WITH WHITE-COLLAR CRIME

There are very real problems which any public or private agency must face in launching or maintaining investigative or other law enforcement efforts directed against white-collar crime. It would hardly benefit any agency, or its citizen constituency, to gloss over these difficulties or to pretend that they do not exist. These difficulties, such as the costs in resources of money and manpower, competing demands for such resources, difficulties in "selling" a case to a prosecutor, alleged leniency of the courts in sentencing white-collar offenders--all these cannot be argued away and can only be answered by developing a sense of understanding of the importance of this law enforcement mission and by considering the range of options which might be made available to cope with these difficulties.

Other arguments against law enforcement involvement in the white-collar crime field are less grounded in reality, and appear to be rationalizations for inaction rather than reasons for non-involvement. These should be given short shrift when advanced. They fall into two general groupings, those related to subject matter jurisdiction and to victim character or characteristics. It is to these we now turn.

1. Rationalizations Related to Subject Matter

Rationalizations against taking action in the white-collar crime area that are related to subject matter usually stem from a lack of clear perception of agency mission. These are most commonly advanced by criminal law enforcement agencies which almost invariably turn away white-collar crime cases with such excuses as (i) they are more properly private disputes, appropriate only for private civil litigation, (ii) they are disputes for which other remedies appear to be available, such as consumer mediation agencies, Better Business Bureaus, etc., or (iii) "we have no jurisdiction."

Law enforcement agencies, whether their principal focus is on criminal or non-criminal enforcement, should recognize that any wrongful

---

[9]See the section, "Relationship between White-Collar Crime and Other Law Enforcement Areas," at pp. 18-21.

activity, such as merchandising frauds for example, will have both
criminal and non-criminal enforcement implications. It will often be
the case that a complaint is more appropriate for mediation or civil
action than for criminal investigation and prosecution, and should be
referred elsewhere--but each such complaint or referral should be carefully scrutinized to determine whether it should not be handled by the
agency which first received it, or whether referral elsewhere will truly
be the most appropriate way to help the victim and to enforce the law.

Subject matter rationalizations are particularly troublesome in two
situations: (i) where personnel making such rationalizations lack
knowledge of the broad range of other services in their communities and
simply take the easy way out by saying, "it's a private matter," etc.,
which leaves complainants with no remedies; and (ii) in communities
where there are not a number of specialized agencies to which victims
can be referred, such as consumer protection agencies, ombudsmen, etc.
Passing the buck where there is some basis for action is bad enough; it
is even worse where the victims are left with nowhere to turn.

2. Rationalizations Related to Victim Character

The easiest "out" of white-collar crime enforcement is to regard
the victim as the party at fault, because he was gullible and should
have known better, or because his own greed involved him in his predicament, or because all the victim is interested in is getting his
money back--which presumably means he will not maintain a cooperative
attitude during investigation or prosecution.

Every investigator working in the field of white-collar crime has
seen victims who are gullible, or greedy, or who have no staying power.
But this is true of victims in any criminal justice area--and is rarely
advanced in other areas as a rationalization for not meeting law enforcement responsibilities. Fraud and other white-collar crime operators should not have a license to steal from those who are less alert,
or wary, or even greedy.

Terms such as "gullible," "greedy," etc. are also relative terms.
Fraud artists are specialists in the business of deceit, who have
developed great skill in exploiting the trust and the needs of others.
Many victims are old, ill, and otherwise disadvantaged. They run the
entire gamut from the proverbial man who "buys the Brooklyn Bridge," to
sophisticated investors who are taken, notwithstanding highly professional and well-meant advice from their attorneys, accountants, and
independent investment advisors. When asked, white-collar crime investigators can even point to people in their own organizations, and
members of their families who were victims of frauds--particularly in
merchandising fields. It is not "greed" when a retired person on a
limited income seeks to get a bargain price for a home repair, or to
supplement his or her income by taking money from a bank where it earns
5% interest and putting it in "guaranteed" mortgage participations at
9%. And there is no reason to believe that a fraud victim is any more
interested in getting his or her money back than is the victim of a
holdup--though the amounts are likely to be considerably larger and more
significant to the fraud victim.

In a market place where we rely on the expertise of others, such as television and auto repairmen, and where we buy merchandise in closed packages, one does not have to be stupid to be swindled. The old rule of *caveat emptor* (let the buyer beware) lost its justification when the makers of goods started packaging their products and erecting barriers of distributors and retailers between themselves and ultimate buyers. And the fraud operator will frequently pick on those least likely to have anyone to turn to for advice, as targets for exploitation. The plain and simple fact is that white-collar crime operators cast broad nets which catch victims who have a variety of motives and capabilities—and who deserve protection.

When the "victim" is a large institution, public or private, there is often a desire to seek an "out," on the rationalization that the institution's procedures are sloppy, that it opened itself wide to fraud, that it has attorneys to pursue the matter civilly, that the institution can afford it, etc. This rationalization is often easy to adopt because many such institutions are less than fully cooperative, and will often work to cover up the fact that they have been defrauded in order to preserve their reputations, or to guard against political consequences (if public institutions) or against litigation (i.e., against officers or directors of corporations who might be held liable for negligence).

There is often very legitimate agency concern about being used as collection agencies, e.g., by credit card companies, or distaste at being called in after the victim has used the threat of such referral to intimidate the thief into making restitution.[10] Such considerations are, of course, valid issues to be considered in deciding whether to proceed with an investigation or prosecution—but law enforcement agencies should not use them as an "out" to avoid responsibility.

E. IMPACT OF WHITE-COLLAR CRIME

Agencies involved in or contemplating enforcement activity against white-collar crime must have a comprehensive and clear view of the impact and cost of white-collar crime for four basic reasons: (i) to develop agency objectives by identification of the range and level of activities to be combatted, (ii) to infuse their personnel with a sense of the worthwhileness of the mission, in both human and simple dollars and cents terms, (iii) to provide a basis for evaluating performance in terms of service to victims and potential victims, and (iv) to provide a basis for budget justification for agencies and sub-agency units engaged in combatting white-collar crime.

The costs of white-collar crime investigation and follow-up litigation or prosecution are substantial, both in absolute dollar terms and in terms of the demands placed on law enforcement agencies which are

---

[10]This would be a violation of law in most jurisdictions, "compounding a felony," but is often very difficult to prove.

already harassed by many other demands for manpower and resources. The essential question is, however, whether these costs are worthwhile and should be borne, and whether particular law enforcement agencies should assume the burdens as well as the opportunity to grapple with the challenges of this significant law enforcement activity. There must be a balancing of the costs of combatting white-collar crime against its cost to the community.

The costs or impacts of white-collar crime can be considered either in terms of dollars or in terms of the effects of such crime on individual victims, communities, and government. Obviously these costs cannot be precisely measured--in fact, the best we can do is to describe the kinds of costs and make some very rough guesses about their magnitude.

Dollar costs are obviously staggering. In 1974 the Chamber of Commerce of the United States, after surveying various sources, came up with a figure of approximately $41 billion annually, not taking into account the cost to the public of price-fixing illegalities and industrial espionage.[11] Quite clearly figures of this magnitude dwarf into insignificance the total dollar costs of common crimes. While it would be irresponsible to argue that an armed robbery in a grocery store should be compared with a merchandising fraud, for example, in strictly dollar terms--personal trauma cannot be measured in dollars, either for victims of armed robbery or consumer fraud--it is certainly relevant to consider such comparisons as justifications for raising the level of response to white-collar crimes while maintaining or even increasing attention to common crimes. More important, the dollar costs of white-collar crime are reflective of a whole range of special costs to victims-human and societal costs.

These human and societal costs (only sometimes measurable in dollars) should be considered both with respect to categories of victims and the ways in which these victims are affected. While there are many overlaps in these categories, they can be generally divided into (1) Individual Victims, (2) Business Victims, (3) Communities as Victims, and (4) Governments as Victims. These are discussed in very general terms below.[12] The list of impacts or consequences is meant to be illustrative only, and not exhaustive.[13]

---

[11]White-Collar Crime: Everyone's Problem, Everyone's Loss, publication of the Chamber of Commerce of the United States (1974), pp. 4-6.

[12]Victim groups can constitute an important part of a white-collar crime enforcement effort around which a unit can be organized, goals set, and the effort evaluated. See Chapter VI, Evaluation of a White-Collar Crime Effort, at pp. 214-225.

[13]For a more detailed list of white-collar crimes, see the later discussion at pp. 27-30.

1. Individual Victims

Individuals are being victimized by white-collar crime in ways which directly deprive them with respect to their (i) human needs, i.e., those things necessary to their existence, (ii) aspirations, i.e., their seeking for improvement in the quality of their lives, and (iii) property, i.e., their money or other assets.

(a) Human Needs. Consumer frauds undercut the ability of individuals to use their assets to meet basic needs in the areas of food, shelter, transportation, and employment. Most people have little economic leeway to make duplicate purchases to meet such needs. The elderly, minorities, and the poor are particularly affected--every loss means additional deprivation for them.

With respect to food, for example, poor people victimized by being cheated on weights and measures or food quality frauds will literally have less food for the table, not to mention erosion of trust in the "system." With respect to shelter, a home improvement fraud may not only deprive the victim of dollars, but may also cause the victim to lose a home because of maintenance costs; "block-busting" by unscrupulous real estate speculators will simultaneously deprive victims of their homes and incite racial fears and antagonisms; landlord and tenant violations cheat tenants out of heat, services, and rental deposits. The auto repair fraud may deprive a victim of his car, possibly making employment difficult because of lack of transportation. The looting of an insurance company by corporate officers may expose a policy holder to claims, without any protection, wiping him out--and at the same time leaving a disabled claimant with no way to obtain full compensation for his injury.

Beyond elemental needs, there are needs which affect the quality of life. The poor, for example, have few entertainment outlets other than television, which can be affected by TV repair frauds. Consumer frauds in the sale of toys can affect both the safety of children and provide them with unwholesome messages about the trustworthiness of society at a very early and impressionable age.

Anti-trust or price-fixing violations raise the prices of goods, commodities, and services (including medical services and funeral services which often impoverish the poor) to every sector of the population

One white-collar crime can expose the victim to additional and continued victimization. Thus the victim, burdened by debts as a result of merchandising or other schemes, is an easier prey for the operator of a debt consolidation scheme or the con artist who promises a financial solution through a phony work-at-home scheme.

(b) Human Aspirations. We all aspire to improve ourselves, with respect to our occupations, our appearance, our relationship to others, and our hopes for our children. These aspirations make us all targets for the white-collar thief--who not only takes money, but makes the victim something less than he or she was before.

Victim hopes for improvement in employment are dashed and frustrated by phony trade and occupational schools, correspondence courses, talent schools and agencies. The lonely, and particularly the elderly, are cheated in lonely hearts club frauds and perpetual dance courses which have been known to financially destroy even relatively well-off aged persons. Misrepresented medical and health nostrums promise much, deliver nothing, but often deceive victims beyond the opportunity to get qualified medical help till it is too late--a problem which particularly afflicts the elderly who suffer from chronic ailments such as arthritis.

Self-employment opportunities are misrepresented, dashing hopes for a business of one's own--through franchise frauds, pyramid schemes, vending machine frauds, etc.

(c) <u>Property Frauds</u>. Some people have extensive property or money for investment, some have a "nest egg" which is their economic cushion, and others have no more than some very small amount, or their homes, to keep them at some marginal level of existence. These assets are a prime target for the white-collar thief.

One large class of frauds involves investments of victim's "surplus monies." These investment frauds are based on many kinds of misrepre-sentations. Stocks, bonds, and other investment interests are peddled by promises of great returns, assurances of security and worth of in-vestments, and substantial tax advantages. These frauds may involve interests in land, cattle, or commodities. The Ponzi scheme, where old investors are paid off from the investments of newer ones, must in-evitably collapse. Variations afflict the less affluent, such as interests in so-called "guaranteed" mortgage participations, looting of state-chartered savings and loan institutions which are not federally insured and purport to carry deposit insurance--but where the private insurer may merely be a shell. Land misrepresented as having a dual purpose--retirement home site and investment--is peddled by energetic and glib sales techniques to unwary buyers.

The particularly gullible are taken by grifters who steal their savings through such schemes as the "pidgeon drop" which is a familiar form of con to every police department.

These property frauds may be no more than an inconvenience to the well-to-do, but they seriously impact the lives of others. Often the investment lost is all that stands between the victim and charity or welfare, and if the victim is middle-aged or retired there is usually no opportunity to replace the loss through hard work and saving.

2. <u>Business Victims</u>

Business enterprises suffer from white-collar crime in three ways: (i) as the direct victims of fraud, (ii) by being placed at a competi-tive disadvantage, and (iii) as indirect victims through public loss of trust in business institutions.

(a) <u>Business as Direct Victims</u>. Business enterprises suffer con-sequences from white-collar crime which range from relatively minor financial losses, up to and including massive financial hemorrhaging which cause their insolvency and destruction. The most serious of these consequences stem from the activities of employees or other insiders, who frequently act in concert with outside confederates.

The most common white-collar crime against business is embezzlement, a form of theft which is very familiar to the law enforcement community. Amounts may be small in some instances, and in others large enough to collapse businesses in which embezzlers are employed. Rivaling embezzlement in impact, though not in law enforcement statistics, is commercial bribery--where business employees or officers take bribes from those who sell goods or services to their employers, or bankers who make loans to those who give them bribes or other incentives. Insider dealings will also involve conflicts of interest, for example where a corporate officer or employee causes his company to enter into contractual relationships with outside firms in which he has an ownership interest, or where a banker causes his bank to lend money to an enterprise in which he has an ownership interest. These and similar insider operations are, in essence, ways in which the assets of a business can be looted. Pension funds, which are really enterprises set up to manage beneficiaries' funds on a businesslike basis, are sometimes similarly looted through the device of making risky investments in return for special kickbacks and participations in potential profits.

Businesses are also the direct victims of a host of white-collar thefts by outsiders which, in total, probably rob our economy of billions of dollars. Common examples would be fake insurance claims, credit card frauds, and the occasional gigantic swindle involving many tens of millions of dollars--such as the Equity Funding case in which several of the nation's major insurance companies were sold fraudulently concocted insurance contracts. With the onset of electronic transfers of funds, both nationally and internationally, the way has been opened to massive thefts--one New York bank, for example, avoided losses in the millions in such an electronic transfer only by the accident of an unclear transmission which triggered a very routine and nonsuspicious *request for a repeat of the original message.* Many business frauds are, of course, on a much smaller scale. Rip-offs such as advanced fee schemes, false directory advertising bills, and padded employee expense accounts, cumulatively cost the business community vast sums of money.

The increasing dominance of computers in our business systems has greatly increased the potential impacts of fraud, since it is now possible for white-collar thieves to stage and keep track of vast numbers of fraudulent transactions almost instantaneously, since computer programming techniques have given thieves the capability to simultaneously generate both fraudulent book entries and back-up concealment systems. Few computer frauds of any magnitude have been discovered by routine internal audits; most have come to light by accident, by nervous scheme participants, or by a scheme developing to a scale beyond that of the participants' capacity to control.

Such direct losses to the business community do not come only out of business profits. In many instances they actually have caused the destruction of businesses, contributed to multi-million dollar insolvencies and reorganizations. In all cases these white-collar thefts represent costs of doing business (both the thefts themselves and the costs of guarding against and detecting them) which are ultimately passed on as additions to the prices of the goods and services consumers buy.

Finally, the increasing sophistication of organized criminal syndicates makes businesses vulnerable to mixed white-collar crime/extortion assaults. Organized criminal groups have demonstrated the ability to get their hooks into legitimate businesses or employees of such businesses through such avenues as loan-sharking, enforced collection of gambling debts, and purchases of businesses, and have used such control to execute traditional white-collar schemes such as bankruptcy frauds (scams), and the marketing of stolen securities through the device of using them as loan collateral at banks.

(b) Business Victimization Through Restriction of Competition. The area of anti-trust violations, price-fixing, and restraint of trade represents a major area in which damage is inflicted on the business community and, as a consequence, on the public who are the customers of the business community. Where suppliers of goods and services are able to control their markets, it is inevitable that many will be placed at a competitive disadvantage because they will be unable to seek new business in the marketplace by offering better services or lower prices. Retailers and wholesalers will be unable to shop for lower prices, and will be at a competitive disadvantage if their suppliers give lower prices to favored customers through such devices as kickbacks, rebates, and phony advertising or promotional allowances. In many instances such practices are subject to criminal sanctions; in all cases they are unlawful--and the overall dollar costs of these violations may well equal that of all other white-collar crimes and related abuses combined.

In most instances the consequences of such unlawful activity are strictly economic, confined to rising costs, elimination or hobbling of business competitors, and retarding innovation and development of new and efficient services. In other cases, where organized criminal syndicates combine white-collar crimes with strong-arm tactics, actual physical harm to people and physical damage to property will occur.

(c) Damage to the Reputation of Business. The business community's reputation is important on four levels: within the individual enterprises; among customers; in relationships with other businesses; and in the general community (politically).

Within individual enterprises the existence of white-collar criminal activity, even on a relatively petty level (such as padding of expense accounts) tends to undercut the overall integrity of an enterprise and to encourage other illegal activity--such as commercial bribery or pilferage--and will substantially contribute to poor administration of the businesses so affected. There is no way to measure the impact of this, but it is clearly a significant cost. Internal corruption, as well as negligence in dealing with it, have led to increases in the frequency of large-scale stockholder suits against directors and officers of corporations who are charged with conflict of interest or incompetence. Such litigation may produce difficulties in acquiring the services of well qualified corporate directors, geometrically increasing premiums for liability insurance to protect officers and directors, and a more pervasive erosion of stockholder confidence in officers and directors generally.

Many white-collar crimes and related abuses, such as commercial bribery, misrepresentations concerning the quality and utility of merchandise, the true costs of installment payments, or the serviceability of products, result in cynicism (often justified) about business ethics. This cynicism reflects on and harms not only those who engage in wrongful practices but also their honest competitors who are not guilty of such practices. These honest competitors must suffer the costs of anticipating and responding to the suspicions of the marketplace. Disclosures of past abusive practice may also seriously affect the future of a business trying to "go straight." For example, a company which manufactures airliners and is exposed for payment of bribes to airline executives will have a special and costly burden in making subsequent sales, because prospective purchasing agents will not want to be suspected as being bribe takers.

Business enterprises operate in relationship not only to their customers, but also in relationship to suppliers, to organizations (e.g., bankers, underwriters, factors) who provide financing and credit. Any activity which indicates lack of integrity and control, such as substantial commercial bribery or a large-scale internal computer fraud, must undercut the confidence of others in such an enterprise and obligate the firm to additional expenses tied to auditing, internal investigation, and management changes to meet such problems.

Many of the greatest costs of white-collar crime to business are those which business suffers in the community at large. The perception of wide-scale consumer fraud in ghetto areas, for example, is believed to have been a significant factor in the urban riots of the 1960s.[14] Concerns as to business credit practices led to development of "Truth-In-Lending" legislation, and undercutting of the "holder in due course" doctrine so important to financing of legitimate commercial transactions. Other disclosures have led to state legislative and congressional investigations and, for example, to ever more stringent restriction and control of business financing through detailed state and federal regulatory monitoring of sales of securities. These necessary regulatory steps were the natural consequence of white-collar crime and related abuses. Their costly consequences to current legitimate business operations (and through business, to the customers of business) reflect both past abuses and also the fear of such abuses and law violations in the future.

---

[14]"Violence in the City--An End or a Beginning?", publication of the Governor's Commission on the Los Angeles Riots (Los Angeles: Office of the Governor, 1965), p. 62.

3. Governments as Victims

Local, state, and federal governments are white-collar crime victims in these ways: (i) with respect to collection of revenue, (ii) by procurement frauds and corruption of government, and (iii) by wrongful exploitation of government programs.

(a) Collection of Revenue. Every governmental entity, whether the township, city, county, state, or federal government, is supported by taxes--which may be levied against income, real or personal property, sales and payroll taxes, excise taxes on items such as cigarettes[15] or fuel, or be based on license fees.[16] To the extent that these governments are cheated in the collection of such taxes, the taxpaying public as a whole must make up the difference--either through increased taxes or through loss of the opportunity to have taxes lowered. The dollar costs, running into billions, must be considered also against the backdrop of necessary services which cannot be provided or must be curtailed--since taxpayers already perceive themselves to be heavily burdened by current levels of taxation.

(b) Procurement Frauds. Governments purchase billions of dollars worth of goods and services every week. Investigations, audits, and prosecutions make it clear that very substantial portions of this procurement process are tainted by favoritism and corruption, through influencing or bribing of public officials, claims for payment where goods and services are not delivered, and through collusion among contractors and suppliers to frustrate competitive bidding processes by setting prices and determining amongst themselves who will share the public's business. Such fraud, or commercial bribery, may operate across national or international lines as well as at the level of local school districts which may be starved for revenue while board members or administrators take kickbacks from sellers of school supplies.

(c) Corruption of Government. Beyond the procurement process impacts described above, white-collar crimes involving bribery and corruption affect numerous other government processes, and have the effects of increasing citizen costs for services and of frustrating public objectives. For example, collusively or corruptly negotiated waste collection and disposal contracts, which set prices and give route monopolies to contractors, may not only result in higher prices to businesses and individuals, but may mean poorer service or subsidization of organized criminal syndicates. Favoritism and corruption with respect to zoning ordinances, franchises to conduct businesses on public property

---

[15]See Michael D. Maltz, et al., Combatting Cigarette Smuggling, U.S. Department of Justice, LEAA (January 1976), pp. 1-4.

[16]Some elaborate schemes involving the theft of license fees have already been uncovered. See, e.g., John T. McQuiston, "Embezzlement of $250,000 Found in Auto Registration Fees on S.I.," New York Times, December 7, 1976, p. 45.

(for example, refreshment stands or restaurants in parks or other facilities, distribution of irrigation water), preferential agreements at low prices to extract publicly owned resources (such as timber or minerals) not only deprive the public of revenue but also of the opportunity to develop their communities and manage their resources to best advantage.

(d) <u>Wrongful Exploitation of Government Programs</u>. Program frauds are an aspect of white-collar crime corruption of governmental processes which merit special attention, particularly when we are considering the impact of fraud--for beyond dollar costs there are very real intangible costs of program frauds which must be considered literally in terms of human suffering and deprivations.

It is public policy to provide support and help to those who for one reason or another are disadvantaged, or who have some special needs. This is true at local, state, and federal levels. Hence we have large numbers of welfare programs to provide the needy with subsistence and shelter, medical programs to assist the needy and the elderly, housing programs to provide decent shelter to veterans and those at different income levels, subsidies to encourage farming, food stamp programs, and employment and training programs for the disadvantaged. When such programs are exploited by false claims for benefits, by false claims for medical or other services provided, by housing frauds, by creation of nonexistent "employees" or beneficiaries to whom salary checks are issued--all this not only costs taxpayers money but also cuts off public support from such programs, depriving eligible beneficiaries of jobs or other benefits, greatly increasing public audit costs and red tape which lowers the level of services provided--and in some cases may actually destroy such programs.

* * * * *

These impacts of white-collar crime should be continuously considered by agencies which combat white-collar crime because they are crucial to making decisions on which cases to investigate and prosecute, in setting priorities among them, in budget justifications, and in evaluation of agency performance.

F. <u>RELATIONSHIP BETWEEN WHITE-COLLAR CRIME AND OTHER LAW ENFORCEMENT AREAS</u>

The tools, techniques, and approaches of white-collar crime investigation and prosecution represent a major alternative approach with respect to a number of other enforcement areas. There are many areas of wrongful activity, or enforcement areas of public concern, where white-collar crimes and related abuses may take place---either alone or in combination with other illegal or wrongful activity. In this section we address the relationship between white-collar crime and (1) organized crime, and (2) general compliance enforcement.

1. <u>Organized Crime</u>

Criminal syndicates are compelled to commit white-collar crimes, even though the commission of other kinds of crimes may be their principal objective. They <u>must</u> commit white-collar crimes in order to conceal their other crimes, and in many instances to realize their gains and complete their crimes. White-collar crimes also represent an attractive source of alternative or additional criminal activity for such syndicates. It is thus important that law enforcement groups combatting organized crime consider examination of possible white-collar crimes---and not be limited to narrower ranges of investigative and prosecutive activity.

(a) <u>Tax Violations</u>. Income received from illegitimate channels cannot normally be declared as income. It therefore follows that those deriving considerable income from illicit activities are extremely likely to commit tax violations at federal, state, and local levels. Such violations will usually involve income taxes, but will often involve other taxes such as local and state sales taxes, gross business taxes, inventory taxes, and excise taxes on cigarettes, liquor, or fuel. In such instances escaping apprehension for illicit activity compels commission of white-collar crime by such individuals. Further, the necessity to safeguard and invest the proceeds of other crimes compounds the problem for these offenders, since declarations of income legitimately earned on investment of criminal proceeds will open up the possibility that their prior criminal activities will be exposed.[17]

(b) <u>Completing Other Criminal Activity</u>. Where property is stolen, whether by force as in the case of hijacking, or by deception as is often the case with respect to stolen securities, it must usually be marketed in what are ultimately legitimate business channels if profits are to be realized. In order to do this, some fraudulent means must be used to establish what looks like legitimate title to property. Often, of course, this is a service provided by the fence. Kinds of activity involved, for example, might be such things as: false declarations of ownership or origin in connection with exports or other regulated shipments, false statements to banks in connection with use of stolen securities as collateral for loans, falsifications in applications for issuance of title papers and registrations for stolen vehicles, or false entries in books or records of financial institutions in connection with "write-offs" of "uncollectible" loans.

(c) <u>White-Collar Crime as Chosen Field of Organized Crime Activity</u>. Organized criminal groups normally have opportunities and incentives to move into white-collar crime through power obtained over businessmen or their employees who get into debt through gambling, dealing with loan sharks, or intentional purchases of stolen goods from fences. This has led to such crimes as major bankruptcy frauds[18] and embezzlement of

---

[17]Another method of concealing illicit gains is to invest or "wash" such gains in legitimate investments. See the discussion below of infiltration of legitimate business at p. 20.

[18]For a good description of such a fraud, see Edward J. DeFranco, <u>Anatomy of a Scam: A Case Study of a Planned Bankruptcy by Organized Crime</u>, U.S. Department of Justice, LEAA, NILE/CJ (Washington, D.C.: U.S. Government Printing Office, November 1973).

large quantities of securities from brokerage houses--probably converted into cash by being used as loan collateral. Organized criminal groups have not been content to wait for targets of opportunity, and have moved forward to initiation of white-collar criminal activities. For example, businesses have been purchased with the intent that they be vehicles for bankruptcy fraud; or clerks have been placed in stock brokerage houses where they gained access to securities.

It should also be noted that even the most blatant of criminal activities, such as those involved in gambling and narcotics, will involve restraints of trade to restrict competition--where organized criminal elements can be unwittingly assisted by criminal justice enforcement agencies who apprehend and prosecute less well organized and capable competitors.[19]

(d) <u>Infiltration of Legitimate Business</u>. Organized criminal activities frequently generate cash surpluses which cannot effectively be employed as capital for criminal operations; or criminal syndicates may consciously elect to diversify operations into legitimate business channels. This may occur through setting up of new businesses, investing in existing enterprises, or forcing their way in through other pressures. This is not a new phenomenon. It started long ago in areas such as trucking, restaurants, and vending machines. With the steady growth of experience and exposure to new business opportunities--such criminal elements have entered new fields--even business areas carefully monitored by regulatory agencies such as banking and the securities industry. No business area has immunity from such infiltration.

Special dangers face business competitors of organized criminal groups, since such groups may make well-financed entries into a business area and--if they encounter difficulties--may adopt anticompetitive methods, i.e. "strong-arm tactics," which can be quite uncomfortable to legitimate businessmen accustomed to more usual forms of competition.

(e) <u>Organized Crime--A Summary</u>. Careful observation of organized crime activities with respect to their white-collar crime aspects can be most productive in combatting the business of rackets, because of possible organized crime vulnerability on this front. To exploit this vulnerability, where it is found, particular stress should be placed on techniques such as those which involve tracing of funds, net worth analyses,[20] determination of true ownership of business enterprises, and persistent scrutiny of transfers of property. Most important, however,

---

[19]See Thomas C. Schelling, "Economic Analysis of Organized Crime," Appendix D, <u>Task Force Report: Organized Crime</u>, President's Commission on Law Enforcement and Criminal Justice (Washington, D.C.: U.S. Government Printing Office, 1967), pp. 114-126.

[20]See Richard A. Nossen, <u>The Seventh Basic Investigative Technique, Analyzing Financial Transactions in the Investigation of Organized Crime and White-Collar Crime Targets</u>, included as Appendix D of this document, p. 325 ff.

is alertness to possible alternative white-collar crime violations while other aspects of organized crime activity are being investigated or considered for prosecution.

2.   Compliance Violations

Enforcement against compliance violations is a traditional area of white-collar investigation and prosecution. This can be seen most clearly with respect to enforcement against government procurement frauds, program frauds involving such areas as housing and welfare, and regulatory agency activity with respect to banking and security frauds.

The usefulness of white-collar enforcement techniques should, however, be given increasing attention with respect to newly developing areas of enforcement, such as environmental protection and civil rights. In most instances the available sanctions are civil, and criminal sanctions usually provide for misdemeanor rather than felony prosecutions. In either case, proofs will require techniques of white-collar investigation such as identification of ownership of facilities, following paper trails to determine responsibility for policies and patterns of activity with companies being investigated, and investigations to determine whether false and misleading documentation has been created to cover up patterns of violations. Attempts to avoid laws with respect to public health and safety, environmental protection, and civil rights will necessarily involve guile and deception and coverups--which are the essence of white-collar crime.

G.   THE ELEMENTS OF WHITE-COLLAR CRIME

It is important that the investigator and prosecutor of white-collar crime recognize that these crimes invariably display certain characteristics, and that it is possible to analyze the execution of these schemes and note that these offenders have certain common objectives. This holds true as well for investigations directed at supporting civil, regulatory, or administrative cases. Familiarity with these elements can serve as a general framework for planning and undertaking action to combat white-collar crime; this chapter seeks to provide that general framework. In Chapter IV, this Manual shows how the techniques of white-collar crime investigation can best be used to develop evidence to show the presence of these elements in cases being investigated.[21]

There are five principal elements in white-collar crimes and related abuses. They are:

1.   *Intent* to commit a wrongful act or to achieve a purpose inconsistent with law or public policy.

2.   *Disguise* (of purpose).

---

[21]See Chapter IV, Conducting Investigations of White-Collar Crime, at pp. 121-153.

3. *Reliance* by the offender on ignorance or carelessness of victim.

4. *Voluntary victim action* to assist the offender.

5. *Concealment* of the violation.

While it is not necessary that proof be obtained as to each of these elements in preparation of a white-collar crime case (even though all these elements will be present) it will be necessary to obtain substantial evidence with respect to the first, *intent*, and some evidence with respect to one or more of the other elements. This discussion is not, it must be repeated, a legal analysis of white-collar crime, but rather is a structural analysis designed to assist law enforcement personnel. Each of these elements is defined and discussed below.

1. Intent to Commit a Wrongful Act or to
   Achieve a Purpose Inconsistent
   with Law or Public Policy

In every white-collar crime or related abuse, it is usually clear the offender knows that he or she is involved in an activity which is wrongful or very much in a grey legal area, whether or not the offender has an awareness of a particular statute which is being violated.

This *intent* may be to avoid that which is required by law, such as disclosure of facts which would make a particular transaction undesirable for the victim, or to act to deceive the victim by some explicit and affirmative deceitful conduct.

Intent is usually inferred from the behavior or statements of the subjects of investigation, and from the presence of proof of the remaining four elements discussed below.

2. Disguise of Purpose or Intent

The first element, *intent*, involves the presence of some wrongful purpose or objective. This second element, *disguise of purpose*, involves the character of the offender's conduct or activity in implementing his plan. When a common crime is committed, the wrongful intent is followed by some overt implementing act, such as an armed attack which is clearly observable. In a white-collar crime situation the offender deliberately avoids force or the threat of force. He employs *disguise*, which is the facade of legitimacy with which he covers the actions he undertakes to implement his scheme.

Disguise may be written or verbal. In a bank, for example, the loan officer who creates a fictional borrower complete with promissory note, a purported borrower financial statement, perhaps a false background check on the nonexistent borrower--has created a facade of reality intended to deceive other bank personnel and bank examiners to cause them to believe that they understand the transaction they are approving or reviewing. In white-collar schemes, pieces of paper are not what they appear to be, notwithstanding the fact that they may bear all indications of legitimacy. Verbal *disguise* is usually employed in combination with written materials, as in the case of con games such as a pigeon drop, or a merchandising fraud where an oral sales pitch is deceptively made to induce a signature to a document which imposes obligations on a victim without indicating the misrepresentations made to obtain the signature.

3. Reliance by Offender on Ignorance or Carelessness of the Victim

While *intent* and *disguise*, the first two elements, are clearly elements which originate with and are controlled by the white-collar offender--involving the offender's own objective and chosen method of execution--*reliance . . . on ignorance and carelessness of the victim* is a victim-related element, since it is based upon the offender's perception of victim susceptibility.[22] The offender will not go forward unless he feels he can depend upon the inability of the victim to perceive deception.

In view of the existence of widespread administrative and regulatory protections for consumers and investors, the offender will often have to rely not only on the inability of the proposed victim to pierce his *disguise*, but also on the procedures of such protective agencies to fail to uncover the omissions and misrepresentations which make up this *disguise*. This *reliance* is grounded on the knowledge that regulatory and administrative agencies cannot fully investigate the accuracy and completeness of every piece of paper filed with them. For example, many land sales and securities sales must be preceded by filing of registration statements with state and federal agencies, which purportedly provide full disclosure of facts which buyers should have in order to make their decisions. The seller who is willing to risk criminal or other action if he is subsequently found out, can reasonably depend on being able to file less than a full disclosure. The agency relies on the deterrent power of criminal prosecution, and (unfortunately) most investors assume that the copy of the registration statement they receive is some indication of governmental approval--even though most agencies require that registration statements contain an up-front, bold-faced warning against any such assumption.

In general, as more and more consumer and investor protection activities are set in motion, and as more and more attention is directed against embezzlement, fraud against the government, and other crimes of deception, white-collar offenders may find it easier to depend on the inability of victims to pierce their *disguise*--because the victim is aware that government agencies are watching advertisements, sales literature, and business practices to protect them. To counter against this, and to discourage *victim affirmative action* (the next element to

---

[22]The term *reliance* is not used here in the usual legal sense of victim reliance on a representation.

be discussed, below), education of consumers, investors, businessmen, and government officials--as to the methods and modus operandi of the white-collar offender--is one of the highest crime-prevention priorities in the white-collar crime area.

4. Voluntary Victim Action to Assist the Offender

The successful execution of a white-collar scheme is not a matter fully under the control of the scheme operator. He must induce the victim to *voluntarily* undertake some act for the scheme to be successfully completed.[23] This element is most important for those with detection and enforcement responsibilities. Measures designed to prevent inadvertent victim cooperation may be more important than other deterrent measures.

In a common crime the victim does not willingly cooperate. A man with a gun at his head will comply with a demand that he surrender his wallet, but it is generally both forseeable and predictable that the victim will not resist; the perpetrator thus controls the entire situation. In contrast, in a white-collar crime, the perpetrator employs *disguise* to deceive the victim, and *relies* on his judgment of the inability of the victim to pierce the *disguise*--in order to obtain the *voluntary victim action* (such as signature on a contract or payment of money) which closes the deal.

This *voluntary victim action* may involve the action by the victim who will be defrauded of money or property, but it also may involve an intermediate victim, such as the government agency which accepts a land or securities registration statement for filing and requires the delivery of the registration statement to prospective individual buyers, or the accounts payable officer of a business or government which approves a voucher for payment on the assumption that the facts represented in the voucher are accurate.

5. Concealment of the Violation

When a violent or other common crime is committed, the offender will give very careful consideration to shielding his identity. He will act in the dark, wear a mask, perhaps even kill to prevent the survival of a witness who can point him out in a lineup. In some rare instances such offenders may have concealment of the crime itself among their objectives, such as the rare and mostly fictional instance where a murder is arranged to look like an accident or suicide. More common is the pilferer who steals small amounts which he hopes will not be missed. *Concealment* of the crime itself, from the victim as well as from law enforcement agencies, is always an objective of the white-collar offender as well as an element of the crime itself.

----

[23]The victim's failure to investigate before taking his voluntary action may raise a question as to his judgment, but it is in no way a defense where the suspect can be shown to have had the requisite intent to defraud.

The ideal white-collar crime, from the point of view of the offender, is one which will never be recognized as a crime or wrongful act. A charity fraud is ideal from this point of view: small amounts are taken from large numbers, and no victim has a sufficient interest to pursue the matter even if he suspects he has been defrauded. In antitrust or price-fixing cases, every effort is made by co-conspirators to make the public, regulators, and law enforcement agencies, believe that normal market forces determine the prices they pay, rather than illegal agreements. Some investment frauds are predicated on the perpetrators' assumption that they can use the scheme proceeds to "make a killing" on some speculative investment, square accounts with their victims, and thus prevent the day of reckoning.

Concealment is especially important to the white-collar operator because he operates in the open. He cannot obtain victim cooperation by wearing a mask, and his objectives are only sometimes short-run. Embezzlers often work at their thefts over periods of years, and sometimes decades--making concealment essential. In one major fraud case counsel for the defendant argued that his client had a clean record, was a regular church-goer and pillar of the community. The judge responded: "Who else could have committed this kind of crime? A street criminal?" The operator will often be a respectable member of the community with strong personal, professional, and business ties. *Concealment* is essential to his ability to maintain his position in the community, his ability to repeat his crimes, or both.

The white-collar operator may recognize that he cannot always permanently cover up his crime, and so *concealment* may become an objective of flexible dimensions. If the crime cannot be concealed forever, can it be concealed long enough to amass sufficient funds to finance a short- or long-term foreign haven?[24] Sometimes the scheme itself is based on the expectation that a sufficiently expanding group of victims can be lured into the net, so that the money obtained from later victims will be used in part to keep earlier victims from knowing they have been cheated.[25] These schemes must eventually fail because of the mathematical progression involved, but some such schemes have continued for many years.

In white-collar crimes, *concealment* only sometimes involves hiding one's true identity.[26] More often its purpose is to hide the fact that

---

[24]Some fugitive financiers were able to prolong their Brazilian havens for many years after discovery. Fugitive Robert Vesco has established a sufficiently strong economic base in Costa Rica to withstand the most strenuous efforts of the U.S. Government to extradite him or recapture funds missing and believed to be stolen.

[25]This is called a Ponzi Scheme, named after one of its early famous practitioners.

[26]Exceptions would be small bunco schemes such as the "pigeon drop."

any crime has been committed. It differs from *disguise*, the second element discussed above. The purpose of *disguise* is to consummate the crime; it is part of the manner and means by which the fraud is committed. To the extent that the fraud is a continuing one, *concealment* and *disguise* will overlap, since putting off pursuit and maintenance of the facade of respectability is the manner and means by which repetitions of the fraud may be inflicted on old and new victims. Even where there is no intent to commit further white-collar crimes, however, *concealment* will be a continuing element of the crime. It may result in new crimes to cover up old crimes, i.e., continuous repetitive alteration and falsification of records or, as discussed above, new thefts to pay off old victims.

* * * * *

This Manual stresses the importance of the elements of white-collar crime because full understanding of them will assist the law enforcement professional to analyze a set of incidents to determine whether there is a case for enforcement and to identify the proof needed to make a case,[27] and--perhaps as important--to see the relationship between differing aspects of an investigation or prosecution. Thus, any proof developed on elements of *disguise, reliance, voluntary victim action, and concealment* will tend to support proof of criminal intent. A showing of how the offender procured *victim affirmative action* will in turn help to develop an understanding of the methods used by the offender to develop *disguise* on which he could base *reliance* that the victim would *voluntarily* cooperate with the fraud. Similarly, a focus on the element of *concealment*, and what the offender did to provide for this element, would contribute to proving *intent, disguise, reliance,* and how *voluntary victim action* was procured. A case thus developed will constitute an integrated whole, rather than a series of isolated facts which a jury must be persuaded to knit together; a case thus seen in its initial and fragmentary stage is more likely to be effectively assessed as a candidate for special attention and investigation.

H. WHITE-COLLAR CRIME CLASSIFICATIONS

In most cases of criminal enforcement, considerations of motives is considered helpful in identifying possible suspects for further and more detailed investigation and, subsequently, to convince a court or jury of the guilt of the accused. In the white-collar crime area there is far less need to examine those with possible motives for the purpose of identifying suspects, since the essential question is not likely to be "Who did it?" but rather "What was done?" "With what intent was it done?" and "Is it a crime?" For these latter purposes, questions of the motivation of already identified suspects will be highly important, since motivation will be of analytic significance in determining the possible modus operandi of the suspect, whether he would have employed confederates, his possible defenses--and most important--what evidence must be gathered on the essential element of *intent*.

---

[27] See Chapter IV, Conducting Investigations of White-Collar Crime, pp. 121-153.

A classification of white-collar crimes along lines of motivation should serve as a helpful starting point. The classifications[28] suggested are:

(1) Crimes by persons operating on an individual, *ad hoc* basis, for personal gain in a nonbusiness context (hereinafter referred to as "personal crimes").

(2) Crimes in the course of their occupations by those operating inside businesses, government, or other establishments, or in a professional capacity, in violation of their duty of loyalty and fidelity to employer or client (hereinafter referred to as "abuses of trust").

(3) Crimes incidental to and in furtherance of business operations, but not the central purpose of such business operations (hereinafter referred to as "business crimes").

(4) White-collar crime as a business, or as the central activity of the business (hereinafter referred to as "con games").

Examples of crimes within each of these categories would be the following:[29]

CATEGORIES OF WHITE-COLLAR CRIMES (EXCLUDING ORGANIZED CRIME)

(A) *Crimes by persons operating on an individual, ad hoc basis*

1. Purchases on credit with no intention to pay, or purchases by mail in the name of another.
2. Individual income tax violations.
3. Credit card frauds.
4. Bankruptcy frauds.
5. Home improvement loan frauds.
6. Frauds with respect to social security, unemployment insurance, or welfare.
7. Unorganized or occasional frauds on insurance companies (theft, casualty, health, etc.).
8. Violations of Federal Reserve regulations by pledging stock for further purchases, flouting margin requirements.
9. Unorganized "lonely hearts" appeal by mail.

(B) *Crimes in the course of their occupations by those operating inside business, government, or other establishments, in violation of their duty of loyalty and fidelity to employer or client.*

---

[28]See Edelhertz, op. cit., Note 4, at pp. 19-20 and at Appendix A, pp. 73-75. This classification was also cited with approval by Reckless, op. cit., Note 5 and Haskell and Yablonski, op. cit., Note 5.

[29]This listing of examples is not meant to be all inclusive and is taken from Edelhertz, op. cit., Note 4, at Appendix A, pp. 73-75.

1. Commercial bribery and kickbacks, i.e., by and to buyers, insurance adjusters, contracting officers, quality inspectors, governmental inspectors and auditors, etc.
2. Bank violations by bank officers, employees, and directors.
3. Embezzlement or self-dealing by business or union officers and employees.
4. Securities fraud by insiders trading to their advantage by the use of special knowledge, or causing their firms to take positions in the market to benefit themselves.
5. Employee petty larceny and expense account frauds.
6. Frauds by computer, causing unauthorized payouts.
7. "Sweetheart contracts" entered into by union officers.
8. Embezzlement or self-dealing by attorneys, trustees, and fiduciaries.
9. Fraud against the government.
   (a) Padding of payrolls.
   (b) Conflicts of interest.
   (c) False travel, expense or per diem claims.

(C) *Crimes incidental to and in furtherance of business operations, but not the central purpose of the business*

1. Tax violations.
2. Antitrust violations.
3. Commercial bribery of another's employee, officer or fiduciary (including union officers).
4. Food and drug violations.
5. False weights and measures by retailers.
6. Violations of Truth-in-Lending Act by misrepresentation of credit terms and prices.
7. Submission or publication of false financial statements to obtain credit.
8. Use of fictitious or over-valued collateral.
9. Check-kiting to obtain operating capital on short-term financing.
10. Securities Act violations, i.e., sale of nonregistered securities, to obtain operating capital, false proxy statements, manipulation of market to support corporate credit or access to capital markets, etc.
11. Collusion between physicians and pharmacists to cause the writing of unnecessary prescriptions.
12. Dispensing by pharmacists in violation of law, excluding narcotics traffic.
13. Immigration fraud in support of employment agency operations to provide domestics.
14. Housing code violations by landlords.
15. Deceptive advertising.
16. Fraud against the government:
    (a) False claims.
    (b) False statements:
        (1) to induce contracts
        (2) AID frauds
        (3) Housing frauds
        (4) SBA frauds, such as SBIC bootstrapping, self-dealing, cross-dealing, etc., or obtaining direct loans by use of false financial statements

       (c) Moving contracts in urban renewal.
17. Labor violations (Davis-Bacon Act).
18. Commercial espionage.

(D) *White-collar crime as a business, or as the central activity*

1. Medical or health frauds.
2. Advance fee swindles.
3. Phony contests.
4. Bankruptcy fraud, including schemes devised as salvage operation after insolvency of otherwise legitimate businesses.
5. Securities fraud and commodities fraud.
6. Chain referral schemes.
7. Home improvement schemes.
8. Debt Consolidation schemes.
9. Mortgage milking.
10. Merchandise swindles:
    (a) Gun and coin swindles.
    (b) General merchandise.
    (c) Buying or pyramid clubs.
11. Land frauds.
12. Directory advertising schemes.
13. Charity and religious frauds.
14. Personal improvement schemes:
    (a) Diploma Mills.
    (b) Correspondence Schools.
    (c) Modeling Schools.
15. Fraudulent application for, use and/or sale of credit cards, airline tickets, etc.
16. Insurance frauds
    (a) Phony accident rings.
    (b) Looting of companies by purchase of over-valued assets, phony management contracts, self-dealing with agents, inter-company transfers, etc.
    (c) Frauds by agents writing false policies to obtain advance commissions.
    (d) Issuance of annuities or paidup life insurance, with no consideration, so that they can be used as collateral loans.
    (e) Sales by misrepresentations to military personnel or those otherwise uninsurable.
17. Vanity and song publishing schemes.
18. Ponzi schemes.
19. False security frauds, i.e. Billy Sol Estes or De Angelis type schemes.
20. Purchase of banks, or control thereof, with deliberate intention to loot them.
21. Fraudulent establishing and operation of banks or savings and loan associations.
22. Fraud against the government
    (a) Organized income tax refund swindles, sometimes operated by income tax "counselors."
    (b) AID frauds, i.e. where totally worthless goods shipped.

      (c) F.H.A. frauds.
         (1) Obtaining guarantees of mortgages on multiple family housing far in excess of value of property with foreseeable inevitable foreclosure.
         (2) Home improvement frauds.
23. Executive placement and employment agency frauds.
24. Coupon redemption frauds.
25. Money order swindles.

It should be noted that certain crimes may fall in more than one category, depending on the motive of the offender and on the context in which he commits a violation. Thus tax evasion may be committed by a person with no motive other than to have more money in his pocket, a *personal* crime, but also by the owners of an enterprise trying to retain capital for corporate expansion, a *business* crime. A bankruptcy fraud could be undertaken by a genuine bankrupt seeking to avoid turning some assets over to his creditors, a *personal* crime, but also it could be a *con game*, executed by a scam artist who creates or takes over businesses and then collapses them in order to exploit suppliers who give him credit.

These classifications will also be useful in considering relationships between white-collar crimes and other crimes. For example, a craving for narcotics or the need to meet a gambling or loan shark debt may motivate an offender to commit *abuses of trust*, and embezzle from his employer.

The relationship between these classifications and the elements of white-collar crime discussed previously[30] should also be carefully noted. In the case of *personal* crimes, such as an individual income tax violation, *disguise* will consist principally of omissions, *reliance* is based on automatic *voluntary victim action* (the tax return is accepted for filing), and *concealment* rests not on something necessarily done by the offender but on the offender's ability to *rely* on the statistical odds against an audit of the return or that the auditing process would have difficulty establishing the violation. In abuses of trust situations, where the white-collar offender is an employee or fiduciary who has taken advantage of employer or client there is likely to be a rather elaborate facade involving *disguise* and *concealment*. Where the white-collar offender has committed a crime incidental to and in furtherance of business operations, but where crime is not the central purpose of his business operation (e.g., an antitrust violation), *disguise* and *concealment* will be undertaken in a subtle and sophisticated fashion, all the more so because the offender does not conceive of himself as a criminal and his wrongful acts will be inextricably intertwined with entirely legitimate business operations. In con games, where the white-collar offender has no business other than to use guile and deception to take the money or property of others, *disguise* will be more blatant,

---

[30]See pp. 21-26.

concealment more contrived, and the con artist will be likely to be highly mobile, moving from place to place to find new victims.

* * * * *

These classifications of white-collar crime, based on the motivational structure of offender activity, can be exploited to positively support investigative efforts. As in any criminal offense analysis, the development of a carefully defined motive for the crime will be of great importance in persuading a jury or court. Beyond this, however, consideration of the classification in which an alleged offense falls will assist the investigator to better piece together the particular modus operandi of the crime, to determine where evidence may be found (for example whether in personal or business records), and to identify offender relationships with others amongst whom witnesses may be found. Taken together with consideration of the elements of white-collar crime discussed above, an analytic approach to determining motivational structures of suspects will substantially contribute to successful investigation of white-collar crimes.

CHAPTER II

ORGANIZATION OF AGENCY EFFORTS TO COMBAT
WHITE-COLLAR CRIME

Even most highly competent fraud investigators will be ineffective
in implementing a white-collar crime enforcement effort if investigators
are not properly organized to do their jobs. The ways in which investigators share responsibilities, communicate, cooperate, and supervise
can have a very strong influence on how well they do, separately and
together.

Organization for detection and investigation of white-collar
criminal activity, and related abuses, will of course differ depending
upon resources available and the location and function of the agency
involved. What would be appropriate for a large urban center would not
be fully appropriate for a less populous locality. Different approaches
are necessary, depending on whether investigators primarily focus on
criminal or civil remedies, and on the kind of agency in which the
white-collar effort is located, e.g., police, prosecutor's office, state
attorney general's office, municipal consumer protection office, regulatory agencies, etc. Nonetheless, there are certain general standards
which should be kept in mind and which are discussed below. These
standards should not be regarded as unvarying directives but rather
should be considered as guidelines and as an itemization of issues which
should be taken into account in developing or changing an organization.

In the section after the one immediately below, various types and
aspects of intra- and inter-organization are discussed in the light of
these standards.

A. ORGANIZATIONAL STANDARDS

1. Coordinating Investigative and Legal Skills

This standard may appear obvious, but the point is that both investigative and legal skills need to be brought to bear on each possible
lead or case which is brought to the attention of an agency. Any agency
which moves forward with great investigative skill but without understanding what information is needed to make a legal case, or consideration of legal admissibility of evidence gathered will not only be
ineffective but will, in the long run, become demoralized by frustra-
tions stemming directly from failure to successfully coordinate skills.
On the other hand, prosecutors who do not concern themselves with the
imagination, skill, and difficulty of investigative work will not be
able to effectively marshal the capabilities of investigators to secure
the evidence needed for convictions. This elemental point is sometimes
ignored; investigators and lawyers may recognize but not sufficiently
appreciate the problems the other faces and the ways in which the other
must go about his or her business and may therefore put off dealing with

the other's concerns until evidence has been overlooked, lost, missed, or become legally useless.

2. Setting Explicit Goals and Priorities

There are many possible agency goals for a white-collar crime effort,[31] and the standards an agency may set in achieving those goals can be equally numerous. Maximizing the number of investigations undertaken; setting priorities on the investigation of crimes with maximal impact on the public; maximizing the satisfaction of the citizenry with the agency; maximizing the recovery of dollars and other values to the victims; maximizing the number of prosecutions emerging from investigations; maximizing the number of convictions; increasing the deterrent force of the criminal justice system with respect to certain types of crimes or focusing attention on cases with the greatest political impact on the community--all of these are examples of objectives the agency may set to assist in the achievement of goals by the white-collar crime enforcement unit. General statements of objectives such as "fighting white-collar crime" or "protecting the public" are so broadly encompassing that they may too easily cover many explicit goals and objectives. In addition, enunciated goals, priorities, and policies may not always be compatible with each other. Sometimes approaching one objective will prevent achievement of another. For example, obtaining restitution for a victim may preclude criminal prosecution, and investigating many minor cases may leave an agency without the manpower and other resources to go after major ones.

The organizational impact of these goals is discussed below. Here, the point is that the white-collar crime enforcement goals of an agency should be made as explicit as possible, and clearly understood both by investigative staffs and by the parent organization within which the white-collar investigative activity is housed. Without such clearly delineated goals, investigators will be frustrated to find that they are being rapped for doing the "wrong thing"; communication between investigators and between the investigative unit and other units can break down; anxieties resulting from uncertainty as to responsibilities and the nature of relationships can lead to excessive turnover. There are a number of ways in which goals and priorities can be made explicit-- through policy statements by supervisors, by consensus, or by subdivision of the effort into several subagencies in order to accommodate competing or conflicting goals.

In many instances, the establishment of a set of goals involves the designation of certain specific types of economic crimes as being the immediate targets of the agency, such as securities fraud, land fraud, auto-repair fraud, etc. However, it is important that some of the broader issues involving goals, as described above, be considered even when an agency specializes in dealing with a specific target crime. These broader issues go beyond particular crime issues, and will influence the particular investigative approach and other policies to be

---

[31]Chapter VI, Evaluation of a White-Collar Crime Effort, suggests alternative choices in selecting the goals and overall mission for a white-collar crime unit. See pp. 216-221.

used. For example, if deterrence is the major objective, then the point at which publicity is released will be greatly influenced by this objective, i.e., publicity would be used early and expansively. On the other hand, where criminal convictions are a major priority, publicity would be handled quite differently so as to avoid jeopardizing the case by exposure to the allegation of prejudicial press coverage.

One of the considerations often overlooked in establishing the goals of an agency is the effectiveness of other agencies in the same geographical area. There will frequently be federal, state, or local agencies which have overlapping jurisdiction with the unit, and also are effective in their investigations and prosecutions. Agencies should weigh the strengths and weaknesses of others and use such considerations in setting their own goals and priorities.

3. Sustaining the Motivation of Investigators

Investigative work can be frustrating and tedious. Cases take a long time to develop. New difficulties arise as culprits invent new schemes. There must be painstaking attention to detail. In short, cases take persistence and imagination. Such imaginative persistence will be difficult to sustain if an investigator is simply told that he is expected to be imaginative and persistent. These qualities are so difficult to define concretely in any specific case that a supervisor simply can't "order" a person to give that extra measure of imagination, the extra push, that can make a case. An agency thus needs to be organized in such a way that the individual investigators are very strongly motivated to attain the agency's goals. In addition, the agency's goals and the individual's own goals need to overlap to a high degree.

As suggested above, the more explicit the agency's goals, the easier it becomes for the individual investigators to mesh their personal goals with those of the agency. When the goals overlap, the investigator can measure his progress appropriately and can make decisions in a personally satisfying way. For example, an investigator in a prosecutor's office is more likely to be disappointed by a failure to prosecute than one, e.g., in a municipal consumer protection office, whose investigative report is rejected for criminal prosecution by the prosecutor but which is used to effect restitution or some civil remedy.

To maintain high motivation among investigators there must be clear standards that signal achievement of goals as well as signs that attainment of enunciated goals is possible and has occurred. Thus, if convictions are the goal of the agency, then investigators need to see at least some convictions resulting from their efforts. If deterrence is the goal, they need to see some signs that a given industry is cleaning itself up. If prosecutions are the goal then the investigators need to see some of their cases being taken to court even if some of them do not result in convictions. Able prosecutors know that there is a "right to be in court" where conviction possibilities are marginal but where the wrong cries out for public attention and deterrence of others. Not all goals need to be attained every time, but investigators must have a genuine sense that there is a clear potential for success.

Another factor in sustaining motivation is the respect given investigators by those who use the investigative work product. Investigators should not be used as mere errand boys to find evidence for prosecutors or civil litigators. Prosecutors should refrain from referring only minor investigations to police, keeping all more significant cases for their own, in-house investigators. In the long run such lack of respect and mutual trust will not only undermine the self-esteem and motivation of investigators, but will also make it difficult for any productive relationship to develop between prosecutors and investigators. As indicated above, investigative work is complex, demanding high levels of professional skills, and fully warrants recognition as such.

4. Maintaining Appropriate Emphasis on Criminal Enforcement

Among the potential alternative options which an agency might have for resolution of its investigations are civil remedies and criminal prosecutions. Agencies will be organized and managed quite differently depending on which of these alternatives is given priority, or depending on the mix of these options employed. Historically, offices of attorneys general, consumer protection agencies, various state licensing agencies, and many federal regulatory agencies, have been limited by law to invoking civil remedies (injunctions, actions for money damages on behalf of victims, etc.) or mediating between the wrongdoers and the wronged. In many such agencies the civil or mediation route is the option of choice even where there is criminal jurisdiction. The civil or mediation approach is frequently selected because investigators are not sufficiently trained in the criminal aspects of white-collar crime. However, there can be little doubt that a better balance of emphasis among enforcement alternatives needs to be attained, so that the most appropriate action is chosen.

In addition to the solely legal and impact reasons for choosing between civil and criminal action, motivational and therefore organizational issues also need to be considered. If the agency is part of a police department, then the criminal alternative may be the only acceptable option to most investigators. Even investigators not in law enforcement may become oriented toward criminal rather than civil actions, for a variety of reasons. Some may have worked previously in other law enforcement agencies; some may become morally outraged at the wrongdoers; some may lose confidence in the deterrent value of civil remedies; some react to the discrepancy in society's reaction to street criminals and white-collar criminals; some perceive themselves to be lawmen, law enforcement officers, rather than negotiators or mediators. These quite legitimate motivations need to be fully recognized by decision makers within agencies and in related organizations, such as prosecutors' offices. Even where civil or mediation remedies are indicated, as in most consumer fraud cases, there is need for some capacity for and orientation toward recourse to criminal prosecutions where appropriate. Without this, motivation among investigators may drop to the point that both the quantity and quality of investigations may deteriorate. In addition, it should always be clearly understood, even in agencies least oriented to the criminal remedy, that where there is prima facie evidence that a criminal statute has been violated, they have not only the right but the obligation to transmit investigative results to prosecuting agencies for enforcement consideration.

5. Contributing to Appropriate Sentences in Criminal Cases

If a major objective of an agency involved in white-collar crime enforcement is to make possible and support criminal prosecutions, then the sentences stemming from resulting convictions need to be consistent with the severity of the crime. Where such sentences appear trivial or grossly lenient, the motivation of those engaged in the effort, both prosecutors and investigators, is likely to deteriorate. Often they will feel that they have given seeming "centuries" of time and energy to investigations and subsequent prosecutions and will wonder whether their efforts were not in vain. While investigators have no role in meting out sentences, there are ways in which they can assist courts in appropriately sentencing white-collar offenders. One way of doing this is to uncover far more victims than are minimally required for prosecution purposes, so the judge can be presented with the totality of the offender's activity when he reviews this information in a presentencing report. They can provide information about other wrongful but non-prosecutable activities of the wrongdoer which are appropriate for inclusion in the presentence report. Any information that can assist the court in choosing an appropriate sentence should be diligently sought by a white-collar crime unit. Working through prosecutors, investigators can provide input to sentencing recommendations and suggest appropriate court-imposed conditions on probationary portions of sentences.

6. Gaining Public Confidence

All white-collar crime efforts are ultimately dependent on the public if they are to succeed. They need the public to submit complaints, to stand up as witnesses, to support the funding of agency efforts, and to give full respect and credit to the agency and its personnel when a job is well done. Both the white-collar crime unit and its parent agency should be organized and managed to generate this public support. More than a public relations capability is needed. Units and agencies must be organized and managed so that the public can legitimately and reliably have confidence in them. Thus, the way citizen complainants and informants are treated, the ways in which victims are handled, the kinds of publicity generated by prosecutors, the kinds of proactive warnings given the public about current fraud activities which threaten it, all influence the degree of confidence of the public.

Some white-collar victims need special attention, even beyond what they would require because of the dollar volume of their losses. Minorities, poor people in general, old or disabled people, may all fall into these categories. Such groups generally sustain dollar losses much less well than other people, making the human impact of crimes against them greater than some other high-dollar-volume frauds. They are less likely to be knowledgeable about who can help them, and can easily lose confidence in our public institutions. Increasingly, these groups are in a position to provide informant, witness, and political support for fraud agencies.

7. Facilitating Community Cooperation
   with Law Enforcement

One of the most important secondary benefits that can result from
white-collar crime investigation and prosecution also concerns the public directly. Anti-white-collar crime efforts, if organized properly,
can also enhance the efforts to control street crime in a number of
ways. This consideration is most important in the case of police agencies. Citizens who have received satisfaction from law enforcement with
respect to white-collar crime are probably far more likely to report
street crime, to be stand-up complaining witnesses, and generally to
cooperate with police in their ordinary work. In fact, it is likely
that the citizen's entire attitude toward government could be improved
by satisfactory contacts with anti-white-collar crime enforcement efforts,
since he will recognize that the agency is attempting to "establish
justice" no matter what the status of the wrongdoer.

Potential gains from anti-white-collar crime efforts are much more
likely to be attained if the entire agency is organized for these ends.
The section below on communication with the public[32] discusses how
subgroups of the citizenry which are especially suspicious of law enforcement can be reached through storefront operations, through liaison of
investigators with patrol officers, or through appropriate publicity
regarding prosecutions. Some of these organizational procedures which
increase public confidence in the agency can also increase the potentiality of helping to control street crime. This latter potentiality is
likely to be realized by integrating law enforcement personnel in police
agencies, such as patrol officers and detectives, with the anti-white-
collar crime effort, as just suggested. These personnel can then be the
same ones to whom the public would turn with respect to street crimes.

8. Deterrence of Additional White-Collar Crime

Since most white-collar crimes are carefully organized schemes
perpetrated by experienced individuals who often benefit from the technical advice of professionals such as accountants and attorneys, there
is good reason to believe that investigative efforts, even alone, can
have substantial deterrent effect. This is because investigative
efforts are likely to "chill" the environment in which white-collar
crime operations are planned or under way, making accountants and attorneys not only more reluctant to provide assistance but also encouraging
their natural instincts to provide strong cautions to their clients.

To maximize this deterrent effect, the anti-white-collar crime effort
must be well organized and managed. Questions of which type of offense
to focus on, the amount and type of publicity given convictions, relationships with trade associations, the degree of specialization within
the agency, special attention to support of probation departments'
presentence report-writing activity, all will have an influence on the
deterrent effectiveness of the agency. The evaluation of the agency's

---

[32]See pp. 58-64. See also "Relationships with Police Patrol," at
pp. 48-53.

performance in the white-collar crime area, then, cannot solely be on the number of arrests and convictions if deterrence is one of its major objectives.

9. Sustaining Flexibility of Investigative
   Approaches

One of the most dangerous characteristics of white-collar criminals is their great ingenuity in fleecing the public in what appear to be "brand new" ways. The ways are usually variations of old and traditional schemes, but the number of variations is almost limitless. Accordingly, agencies need to be organized and managed so as to be alert to new variations of white-collar crime-which may be discerned from such things as changing patterns of complaints, media advertising, frauds reported from other jurisdictions, etc.

If a unit specializes so much that only certain types of schemes are responded to effectively, this very fact almost invites the sophisticated crook to move into the agency's areas of nonspecialization. In a process of Darwinian competition, only those crooks may survive who specialize in the areas the effort overlooks. Some sophisticated operators may sense the limitations of the agency and capitalize on them. This problem does not demand that each agency maintain a full staff of investigators expert in every variety of scheme, but what is necessary is that each agency provide some way for analyzing and detecting new scheme variations and having resources available in-house or in other cooperating agencies to respond to them. For example, a particularly imaginative investigator might specialize in analyzing and coping with unusual and seemingly new fraud situations.

The agency will want to devote special attention to keeping its contacts and level of communication with other agencies open, even when it may appear that there is no immediate need to do so. When a new scheme variation develops, resources (particularly know-how) in these cooperating agencies can be mobilized to cope with it.

10. Effective and Efficient Exchange of Information
    among Investigators, Investigative Agencies,
    and Related Units

As just mentioned, the great and increasing variety of white-collar crime schemes requires that law enforcement have an equivalent variety of sources of information and prosecutorial ability. The effective flow of information among investigators within an agency, and among investigators in different agencies therefore is very important. Jealousies and rivalries among investigators and among investigative and prosecutorial agencies need to be reduced and if possible eliminated. Mistrust among agencies needs to be minimized; any possible grounds for such mistrust must be frankly and openly examined and dealt with. Unless information can flow among investigators and agencies, white-collar criminals have a great advantage.

Furthermore, because white-collar criminals develop their schemes on a regional, national, or even international basis, investigators and agencies need to be organized and managed to keep the channels of information open across jurisdictional lines. Thus, investigative agencies should be organized and managed to exchange information with patrol officers, with state, local, and federal law enforcement agencies and with local, state, and federal regulatory agencies, with organized crime squads, with private investigative organizations and trade associations. Giving each investigator a list of agencies to call upon to gain certain information is not enough. Specific organizational procedures need to be used to accomplish this goal. Maintaining close personal contact with individuals in other agencies, organizing and attending meetings, helping and cooperating when assistance is requested, setting up computerized pools of information, are examples of organizational policies that can be important in keeping the channels of communication open.

Organizational flexibility will also make it possible to truly cooperate and share investigative responsibilities with respect to multi-jurisdictional crimes. Agencies which contribute to an investigation should always be given full recognition and credit, unless they wish it otherwise.

11. Resisting Pressure to Weaken General
     or Specific Investigative Thrusts

Especially in cases in which white-collar crimes are committed by businesses which are otherwise legitimate, an agency which investigates white-collar crime may be subjected to direct or indirect pressures to modify its operations. Such pressure is usually quite subtle in form, but may be especially strong if some other agency of government is implicated in a fraudulent scheme. The investigative agency needs to be organized and managed so it can successfully resist such pressures. Even an implication of a small shift in efforts as a result of such pressure can undermine the credibility of all of the agency's efforts and the morale of its staff.

It should be recognized that pressures against a specific investigation may be concealed within more general policy positions. For example, "new priorities" may be established shifting white-collar crime investigators and resources to some other area of investigation or to another agency function, or the decision may be made that an investigation would "best be handled" if turned over to another unit within or outside the agency. Alternatively, the unit may be distracted from its work by a barrage of "fire-fighting" requests for assistance which may effectively undermine an ongoing probe. It should also be recognized that real and troublesome pressures can be truly independent of particular investigations. For example, legitimate businessmen within a community may become uneasy and attempt to exert pressure if there is a major effort against business crimes because they may believe it undercuts public confidence in the business community. This latter pressure must also be resisted, notwithstanding some legitimate concerns it may represent.

An agency which succumbs to such pressures will soon find that the cooperation it receives from the public and from other agencies which

40

are aware of the situation will be severely undermined. Units combatting white-collar crime must be organized to maximize the professional security and pride of their personnel; leadership of the parent agency must support the effort against even subtle or indirect threats to its integrity. The flow of information among agencies not only contributes to effective investigation, but also tends to keep each agency under scrutiny, to provide investigators with outside support should there be subtle or covert pressures to undercut particular investigative activities.

B. WITHIN-AGENCY ORGANIZATION

In the section below, the general standards that were set forth above will be applied to various facets of agency organization and activity. Some of the standards apply much more to some facets of the organization than to others, and more to some types of organizations, e.g., police, etc. The above standards will not necessarily be cited explicitly but should be obvious in the discussion. (In this discussion, the term "unit" is used to designate a part of or an element of an agency.)

1. Goals and Priorities

Other things being equal, it is generally desirable to set up a special unit to combat white-collar crime and related abuses. Because of the problems of traditional concentration of law enforcement on non-white-collar type crimes, there would be great difficulty in mobilizing resources to fight white-collar crime within units which have other responsibilities, such as burglary investigation, or which are part of a general assignment detective squad. The other areas of responsibility, the other goals, both because of their legitimacy and their traditional place in law enforcement, are highly likely to take priority. In some instances, even street bunco and forgery squads should be separated from anti-white-collar crime units. In many instances, simple embezzlements can be best handled by traditional general assignment detectives. Another reason for having specialized anti-white-collar crime units where the size of the overall agency makes such specialization feasible, is that their clear designation gives them a professional status, an identity, which is important for the sense of professionalism of the investigators.

A unit which is housed within a law enforcement parent agency, such as a police department, has in general a better chance to pursue criminal prosecution as a major objective. Even if such a law enforcement unit deals with consumer problems it is more likely to recognize the potential of such activities as subjects for criminal investigation and prosecution, in contrast to units within non-law enforcement parent agencies which are more likely to downplay criminal referral or prosecution in favor of civil or administrative action, or mediation. This is not to say that all non-police agencies lack orientation to criminal enforcement. Many have shown themselves able to maintain a reasonable balance between the two routes. Nevertheless, police agencies, local, state and federal, by their very nature are more oriented to considering the criminal remedy.

If a unit determines that criminal prosecution is its main objective, it can still retain civil, administrative, or even mediation remedies for situations where criminal actions are not feasible or wise. Obviously, any priority attached to the criminal approach needs to be made explicit and should be adhered to diligently. If it is not, and the unit lapses into more easily attained civil remedies or mediation alternatives, the investigators may lose motivation. But, if the unit makes the use of civil and administrative remedies explicit as second best alternatives, (putting priorities in clear perspective) investigative momentum in the criminal sector is more likely to be maintained. Some investigators may be so oriented to criminal prosecutions that they may not fully understand the value of civil and administrative actions, but experience with victims and observation of the power of civil and administrative remedies can reduce this problem. In fact, experienced investigators should develop great skill at judging when to work toward one enforcement objective rather than another.

When a unit puts a priority on investigations leading to criminal prosecution, it should be made crystal clear that resulting prosecutions do not necessarily have to be felony cases. In some instances, a series of misdemeanor prosecutions can be very effective if they are directed at a given industry, wrong-doer, or group of wrong-doers, such as a group of automobile repair defrauders. A series of misdemeanor convictions may very well deter further criminal activities. Careful organization of information on harm done to victims, properly presented to a court on sentencing, can result in sentencing for misdemeanors which will be as severe as might be anticipated in the case of a felony-- insofar as _actual_ rather than _potential_ sentences are concerned. Further more, in some jurisdictions, conviction on a misdemeanor constitutes a prior conviction for consideration in subsequent cases involving the same defendants.

In order to accomplish its ends, however, the unit needs to articulate its goals and to so organize its work that the investigators do not see themselves as engaged in trivial activities and are not viewed by others as doing so. For example, a squad within the unit might be given the task of cleaning up a given industry, and thus find great satisfaction in using a variety of remedial actions and sanctions when they see the impact of these activities.

Another choice that needs to be made concerns how the unit's resources should be allocated between proactive and reactive approaches. The proactive approach is that which involves an affirmative search for violations; the reactive approach involves waiting for someone to complain about a specific violation. If the unit is by tradition reactive in nature, then more personnel and resources should be placed in complaint handling or referral receiving efforts of the unit. If the unit places greater priority on proactive efforts, such as decoy operations, or scrutiny of newspaper advertisements for possible consumer frauds, relatively more resources should be assigned to investigative work.

After these general types of policy decisions are made about the unit, then specific, high priority, target crimes can be designated--such as land fraud, consumer fraud, etc. However, these target crimes may have to be changed from time to time as the pattern of crime changes, as deterrence becomes effective in certain industries or business areas, or as the economic and social systems change. As pointed out in this manual's chapter on evaluation,[33] both the community and the patterns of crime must be constantly monitored to determine whether and how new target crimes or overall goals need to be established.

While target crimes can be designated, no investigative unit can ignore a possible criminal violation coming to its attention simply because it is not a pre-designated target. Some "non-targets" will be too important in and of themselves to be ignored, and may therefore compel changes or realignment of goals and objectives.

One factor which needs to be considered in making judgments about goals and specific target offenses is that some types of crimes need to be dealt with on a more or less regular basis because there are needs and pressures in the community to do so. If the unit does not work on these crimes, its budgetary and legislative support may tend to weaken. This type of crime may, for example, be a consumer fraud of a given type, or a welfare fraud. The agency also needs to have the capability and freedom to move against other types of crime which are emerging and which it judges to be important to react to. Thus, some balance needs to be maintained between responses to novel or special criminal activities and those given to on-going enforcement responsibilities. The more careful the attention and planning which the unit gives to its "bread and butter" cases, the better able it will be to direct resources to new and challenging areas of interest.

Another major factor in determining and establishing the overall goals and specific target crimes of a white-collar crime effort is the availability and effectiveness of other agencies which are concerned with the same crimes. In many instances it might be better to refer a matter to another agency for investigation, because it has overlapping jurisdiction and either specializes or is in a better position to allocate resources to the task. However, in deciding which types of cases to refer, it is important to evaluate the goals of the other agency to see if their objectives are in fact similar to those of the unit in question. For example, is the other agency also oriented to law enforcement, or to mediation activity? Furthermore, even if their goals are similar, a question must be asked about their comparative effectiveness in attaining these goals.

2. Maintaining a Civil/Criminal Remedy Balance
   in Consumer Protection Agencies

Consumer protection units tend in general to focus on civil or mediation remedies, rather than criminal enforcement. There are many

---

[33]See Chapter VI, Evaluation of a White-Collar Crime Effort, at pp. 216-221.

good reasons for this approach. There should, however, be a reasonable balance between the two approaches, to maintain maximum flexibility in coping with white-collar crime and related abuses. In order to maintain a better balance among the various approaches, it may be important to have local authorities adopt a stance involving more criminal prosecution. This can be implemented by encouraging referral of cases from those agencies which either lack criminal authority, or concentrate on civil or mediation remedies, to those which prefer to or have demonstrated competence in criminal law enforcement. As noted above, this will be facilitated if due credit is given to the referring agency for successful outcomes.

Where local jurisdictions do establish consumer protection units, there are ways of organizing them to help to maintain the balance between civil and criminal remedies where they are part of larger organizations which have criminal jurisdiction.

First, the unit might be better titled *consumer fraud unit*. The title would not only bespeak its objectives; these objectives would also be communicated to the public, to the potential wrongdoers, and, perhaps most importantly, to investigators who work in law enforcement agencies which are explicitly oriented to invoking criminal sanctions.

Second, a better balance between criminal and civil sanctions can be achieved by a sound evaluation strategy. Thus, where a priority is placed on criminal prosecutions, a unit should not be evaluated solely on the basis of the dollar volume of return to victims, since it is in general easier to accrue funds for victims through civil remedies, leaving culprits free to victimize others and treat enforcement problems as just another cost of doing business. Third, and a related point, is that criminal enforcement priorities will be undercut if investigators relate too exclusively to white-collar crime victims in their work. Such a relationship can easily create a situation in which helping particular victims becomes so paramount a consideration that other objectives such as deterrence or the protection of other potential victims is ignored. Investigators in agencies for which the criminal sanction is important need to interact with other investigators, with criminally-oriented prosecutors, etc., to prevent an over-identification with immediate victim concerns. Thus the white-collar unit should not be separated physically from other, more criminally oriented staff personnel who may be part of the parent agency; they all should be in the same building if possible, even on the same floor.

Fourth, the complaint handlers and investigators should be specially trained to be sensitive to the possibilities of criminal involvement. Investigators need to work closely with criminally oriented investigators or prosecutors, so that they can retain and develop skills in criminal investigation. The decision in the unit as to whether to go criminal or civil needs to be made very early, because tactics focused on mediation or civil action may as a legal or practical matter make it difficult or legally impossible to later switch directions and move toward criminal prosecution. It should be clear, however, that if in the course of an investigation new evidence, i.e., new in either character or volume, starts to develop the switch of emphasis is often both possible and desirable. The difference between a civil case and a good criminal case is often no more than the number of times a given misrepresentation is made.

The consumer unit needs to have an effective way of processing complaints so that patterns of offenses will be noticed and will trigger criminal investigation at the earliest possible time. It is often difficult for criminally oriented investigators, especially those in another agency, to take over in cases already substantially investigated by civilly oriented investigators.

3. Task Assignment, Expertise, and Motivation

In very small units, such as those with two or three investigators, the issue of specialization hardly exists; their personnel will usually have to be generalists. However, in larger agencies and units, investigators can be generalists, taking on all sorts of investigations, or they can specialize. There is a very great advantage to well conceived and organized specialization of investigators' assignments in large units which serve populous jurisdictions. The obvious one is that the development of expertise increases the breadth and depth of an investigator's knowledge of a type of crime. Specialists become walking repositories of great volumes of information and ideas about investigations. Second, individual investigators may often possess specialized information about a particular line of business because of previous experience. In fact, in the recruitment of investigators, the possession of such specialized information may well be one basis for selecting unit personnel. Third, individual investigators will often have a particularly negative feeling about certain types of white-collar criminals, sometimes because of the investigator's identification with a special class of victims, such as minority groups, widows, or elderly people. Obviously, such involvement can motivate the investigator to very high levels of activity and be a sound basis for encouraging specialization. Lack of passion is not necessarily advantageous in white-collar crime investigations. Finally, the investigator-expert will be recognized by his fellow investigators for his special capabilities and the respect he gains thereby can raise his motivation even more.

The professional pride that investigators can develop in their expertise and the other satisfactions they find in their work have many additional benefits beyond those conferred on particular investigative efforts. The investigator can gain a great deal of intrinsic satisfaction from his own work. He can gain satisfaction from the sheer exercise of his skills, such as from confrontations with white-collar criminals as their images of themselves as "just sharp businessmen" are shattered when the investigator succeeds in making a case; from the satisfaction of doing justice for the victims with whom he identifies; and, in cases in which undercover work is done, e.g.; by use of decoys, from perceiving that he or she is well able to cope with criminals whose stock-in-trade is the cleverness with which they operate. The significance of these motives should be recognized when cases are assigned to investigators. These satisfactions may become so great that the investigator may be quite content to make a career out of white-collar crime investigation. Nevertheless, and particularly in police agencies, the white-collar crime investigator should be very much a part of the regular force, clearly in the line of general upward mobility. Movement between white-collar units and other police units serves both to bring in fresh blood and to assist in detection and referral to the unit by spreading expertise department-wide. Being in the line of upward mobility can also serve to attract ambitious and able recruits, and to ensure that higher ranks will ultimately include officials with the knowledge both of how to support and to supervise white-collar crime enforcement units.

Specialization can also be a characteristic of sub-units. There may be specialized groups of investigators in very large law enforcement agencies; a land fraud group, a consumer fraud group, etc., depending on the size and nature of the agency or larger unit. However, it is very important that specialization not become so great that the unit loses its capacity to respond to new types of schemes. In fact, if the amount of specialization becomes so great as to be notorious, white-collar criminals may simply move into the areas of nonspecialization. Accordingly, the unit needs to be organized to provide for some capability to make such responses to new scheme variations. If at all possible, investigators who are particularly oriented to take on new challenges should be assigned to a kind of special assignments role--to take on the new and different types of schemes. Such special assignment investigators should not, however, be exempted from taking on cases in one of the more "regular" areas when the backlog in one of these areas is excessive. In some instances, it may be necessary to shift specialist investigators into new areas because of the magnitude or complexity of the new schemes.

If the unit is part of a police department, then the interchange of personnel between the unit and the rest of the department as described above can help to bring new skills into the unit and increase the sensitivity of the rest of the department to white-collar schemes when they see them. However, in some units, it is very important that the response to new schemes not be so great that resources are removed excessively from areas which provide the bread-and-butter cases, the cases which generate support from the public and from administrative and political entities outside the agencies. Bread-and-butter cases are those which are continually confronted such as consumer frauds or medical frauds, e.g., in contrast to a pyramiding scheme which might occur only periodically although with devastating impact.

New cases should be assigned as much as possible to investigators on the basis of their own expertise. If a given investigator has started to work on a given type of case, or has started on a given case or culprit, all additional information regarding these cases should be referred to him or her, even if the case or culprit has been "quiet" for a long time, even years.

4. Leadership and Management

One major implication of the need to respect the professionalism of investigators is that the supervisor of the unit should be supportive and helpful, rather than closely directive in his approach. The supervisor should assign cases to his investigators, and hold them accountable for their performance, but not for the details of their day-to-day work. When and if investigators encounter problem situations which they find difficult to handle, they should feel free to turn to the supervisor for help or guidance, but for the most part the decision to ask for help should be left up to the investigators.

One of the supervisor's main jobs is to protect the unit from outside interference and to foster its interests as a group of professionals within the total organizational environment. This will be easier if investigators have civil service protection. This protection might in some instances be given to all but the highest level personnel in an agency or unit, the highest level being often necessarily and properly an appointive position, since appointment by an elected official is a prime mechanism for keeping an agency responsive to the general public.

5. <u>Communication and Physical Arrangements</u>

As is emphasized throughout this manual, the effective processing of information is essential for a white-collar crime enforcement effort. The very way in which the unit is physically organized can greatly affect efficient information processing. The traditional open room arrangement of police detective squads is often most desirable, since investigators are more likely to share information and ideas under such conditions. Keeping the noise level down is less important than fostering the communication that occurs in such a common room, if only from overhearing one another working. This type of communication also has some secondary benefits, such as one investigator's learning something about another's area of expertise. In that way, he can more readily funnel information, complaints, etc. directly to the most appropriate investigator. And, if there need to be transfers of assignments, such transfers become easier to make. If investigators need to team up to work some cases, this open communication facilitates the development of such teams, be they short term or long term. Investigators can learn about one another's contacts and informants, so that when appropriate, one investigator can ask another to gain information through the latter's contacts. The supervisor can observe what his investigators are doing without being intrusive, and he is readily available to provide help and guidance if it is needed.

The sharing of information and mutual helpfulness are facilitated by the avoidance of the use of the number of arrests as an evaluative criterion for investigator performance. If there is no pressure to generate arrests or other quantifiable data, then the investigators will not be destructively competitive with one another. On the contrary, their helpfulness to one another can be evaluated positively by the supervisor.

In larger units in which the sheer numbers of investigators makes the free flow of communication among investigators difficult, regular staff meetings may be needed. These meetings may involve the total staff of the effort, or small subgroups of the unit. At these meetings, cases can be discussed, as well as overall unit or agency problems. These meetings should not be set aside simply because they are time consuming--the flow of information is too important.

C. RELATIONSHIPS WITH OTHER PARTS OF PARENT AGENCY

1. Relationships with Other Investigative Units

Other investigative units within the parent agency may have some overlapping concerns with the white-collar crime unit. Such units might be an organized crime unit, forgery squad, street bunco, or even some general assignment squads. There are cases which fall into more than one enforcement area. For example, bankruptcy frauds are often per- petrated by organized crime figures; forgeries will often be involved in white-collar crime. It is important, therefore, that information be shared between and among these units. Rather than depend solely on formal information processing, it would be better if there were regular meetings between the supervisors of the white-collar crime unit and the supervisors of each of the other units, joined by investigators handling cases which might overlap. In these meetings, the subtleties, the nuances, and the complexity of cases can be communicated. These meet- ings can lead to a sharing of information, a communication of expertise and new insights, a transfer of cases, or the development of ad hoc teams to work on a case jointly. If any of the cooperative units (i.e., the non-white-collar unit) is evaluated on a quantitative basis, such as number of arrests, it would be preferable to have the other unit take credit for arrests in cases with overlapping involvements. In that way, the chance of future cooperation with the white-collar crime unit is enhanced. Since the white-collar crime unit, hopefully, is not evalu- ated on the basis of mere numbers of investigations and cases, it can gain credit simply by cooperating with the other unit if there are overall affirmative investigative and prosecutive outcomes.

Detective units which are assigned to divisions within a large police department or even to precincts will often run into white-collar crime cases, especially consumer-related problems. These detectives may be able to handle some of the less time-consuming cases themselves. However, more complex cases require more time or more access to cen- tralized records than may be available to them, and they should be on notice that they can ask their supervisor to transfer the case to a white-collar crime unit working out of the central headquarters. Clearly, the white-collar crime unit should encourage this flow of cases, even when some seem relatively unimportant, since the flow itself can serve important informational functions for them; and later on they may need the divisional detectives' help.

In some areas the relationships between white-collar crime and other sophisticated crimes, such as organized crime and fencing, will raise the issue of whether there should be a merging of units. Since many of the techniques and expertise of investigation are quite similar, this may be a highly desirable option for agencies in some jurisdic- tions. If adopted, care should be taken to ensure that white-collar crime priorities, such as consumer fraud, are not downgraded because of the glamor and insatiable resource demands of these other enforcement programs.

2. Relationships with Police Patrol

The potentiality of patrol divisions as a resource for white-collar crime units is far greater than is sometimes assumed. Patrol officers are out in the community and therefore have access to information, witnesses, and other evidence of white-collar crimes which might not otherwise come to the attention of an investigative unit. On the other hand, these potential resources will not be developed without special effort, since patrol officers are generally not sensitive to white-collar crime, nor are there normally any professional benefits they can obtain by developing such sensitivity.

Recently, more police departments have involved police legal advisors in the day-to-day functioning of patrol divisions. They have been assigned to work closely with precincts or have been assigned to work full time for operational units. Since they can have a strong influence on the way that patrol officers react to white-collar crime matters, they should receive special training in white-collar crime issues, and should be involved in the training programs described in this manual.[34] In addition, any training or programs developed for patrol officers should involve these police legal advisors.

The ways that patrol can participate in an enforcement effort against white-collar crime can be divided into a number of categories: (1) contribution to intelligence information, (2) referrals, (3) field interview reports suggesting white-collar crime, (4) citing or arresting for crimes, and (5) participation in special target programs. Each of these will be discussed in turn.

(a) Intelligence.[35] If patrol officers have been appropriately trained and informed, they can acquire information which may not be enough for even a preliminary investigation but which might be useful for investigators to pursue. For example, they may notice that the types of goods loaded or unloaded from a given business establishment begins to change drastically with no apparent reason, suggesting a bankruptcy fraud (or a fencing operation); or they may notice new businesses which suddenly announce close-out sales or close-out sales which go on indefinitely. In one jurisdiction police noted a steady turnover of used cars in a private driveway, suggesting an odometer roll-back operation. In some of these cases, even the patrol officer

---

[34] See Appendix A, Training for White-Collar Crime Enforcement, at pp. 237-238.

[35] For further discussion of the role of intelligence in white-collar crime enforcement, see Chapter III, The Use of Intelligence in White-Collar Crime Enforcement, pp. 98-120.

will have enough basis for making an investigation himself, but the same information may be even more useful to an investigator. The officer himself should be able to make the determination that the information suggests the possibility of white-collar crime, rather than having this determination made by some intermediary between himself and the white-collar crime unit in his department. He should indicate this on his report, so that his supervisor can then send copies of it on to the person in charge of the intelligence efforts of the white-collar crime unit. In this way, the greatest degree of direct communication can be established between the patrol officer and the unit, without the intervention of other administrators and staff people who may not be highly sensitive to the problems of white-collar crime and thus may not fully appreciate the importance of forwarding the information on to the white-collar crime unit.

(b) Referrals. Angered victims often turn to police officers for assistance, since they are the closest representatives of governmental authority available. One traditional response of patrol officers has been to treat these complaints as purely civil, with officers referring the citizens to private lawyers. However, in many instances the complained-of activity may well be criminal in nature, which would be apparent only to an investigator who is alert to white-collar crime issues, and who, for example, has other information which establishes a pattern of complaints. Patrol officers should therefore have a directory of governmental agencies, to which they can refer citizens. The information in such a directory should be organized according to the types of complaints from citizens, rather than in terms of the agencies. The officer receives information from the citizen in the form of a complaint, and he should be able to look up the type of complaint in the directory. Under the complaint category can be listed the agency or agencies to which the citizens should be referred. The information about the agency should be as specific as possible, telephone numbers, addresses, etc. For example, the victim of a burglary may complain to an officer that a door-to-door salesman sold him a burglar alarm that was supposed to ring in the police department. The officer could refer him to the consumer affairs office of the city, or to the fraud squad of his department. A street acquaintance of the officer might complain that some clothes he ordered through the mail are long delayed in being sent; the officer can refer him to postal inspectors. Preparation of such a directory should be a priority task for a white-collar unit, whether within or outside the police department.

However, there are several considerations involved in the use of patrol officer referrals. First, many citizens, especially but not only the poor, uneducated, and minorities, are reluctant to call public agencies with such complaints. They may feel that the referral is the beginning of a bureaucratic run-around; their confidence in these agencies may be minimal; or they may feel that they will be unable to communicate properly. Therefore, the officer may have to call the agency for them, either initiating a telephone call and putting the citizen on the line, or by making the whole call himself. If the agency is close by, he might take them there. If possible, he might wait until the call or visit is well underway so as to be sure that the citizen follows through, or can be referred to an alternate agency if the first is not appropriate.

Another consideration concerns the patrol officer's relationships with the total community, including local businessmen. Since criminal culpability is usually not clear at the complaint stage, an officer may unnecessarily jeopardize his good relations with the local community if he gives even the appearance of making criminal accusations prematurely. By servicing citizens through referrals to the white-collar unit, the officer may avoid this problem. Such referrals are also useful when the officer suspects that he is being used as a "collection agency" to frighten a deadbeat into paying, or in other ways being used as a substitute for private legal actions. Referrals take the officer out of that line of fire, without resort to the standard reaction of "see your lawyer." For people not of great means, lawyers may be a luxury, so that referral to small claims court or to public legal services might be a genuine service by the officer. Such referrals should be logged by the officer, so that investigators later might have a better record to work with if they pursue an investigation. They might find it easier to get leads for approaching other agencies to reach victims, develop patterns, etc.

(c) <u>Field Reports Concerning White-Collar Crime</u>. In some instances, a citizen report may clearly give the officer some reason to believe that a white-collar crime has been committed, but neither citations nor arrests are fully justified or they may not be appropriate. In many instances, such rapid action will be counter-productive to an investigation; there is only rarely danger that the subject of a white-collar crime investigation will disappear while a case is being put together --- as where an itinerant home repair operator flees with the victim's money when the job is only half done. More often the citizen will be reporting some on-going activity which will remain in place long enough for an active white-collar crime unit to respond with appropriate action.

In some instances white-collar crime activity may surface in the course of more conventional police activity. An officer may be called to a place of business either by the businessman or by a customer because of a disturbance or a fight between the two. One or another of the parties may be accusing the other of theft, but the officer may assume without further investigation that the reason for the quarrel is strictly a civil matter and he may therefore just try to deal with the fight as a street crime. However, the reason for the fight may, in fact, be a white-collar criminal act by one of the parties. The officer should at least consider investigating or reporting this possibility as well as dealing with the disturbance of the peace or assault. He may be overlooking a serious problem if he does not.

The patrol officer should be especially alert to the possibility of white-collar crime where there have been a number of disturbances in the same business, with citizens always accusing the business operator of theft or fraud. The officer in that case should not only make a preliminary investigation, but he should include in his report full information about the previous disturbances, including the names of the citizens involved, so that the white-collar investigator can follow through. The officer should carefully collect all records and papers, being careful not to smear over fingerprints on the paper. If some defective piece of property is involved, and there is some chance that the property would be used, etc., before it could be acquired as evidence, then the officer should make arrangements to obtain it. This might be in the case of auto repair frauds, TV repair frauds, etc. The officer might be in a better position to obtain statements and documents than an investigator at a later date because of the danger of losing papers, "using up" the evidence, failing memories, or unavailable witnesses. In short, the officer can often act as the preliminary investigator on the case.

(d) Citations and Arrests. In some police departments, the patrol officer may have enough knowledge of white-collar crime to recognize a probable case, but he may not have the expertise to make the complete investigation, or he may be pressed by his superiors not to spend a great deal of time on such cases; or he may simply not have the time. The time pressure problem may, in fact, be less than initially supposed because most complaints about white-collar crime occur during weekday working hours rather than on Friday and Saturday nights, times when patrol officers are at their peak work loads. In any case, if for any reason the patrol officer comes upon what he believes to be a white-collar crime violation and is not able to make a full report, he should be able to call a white-collar crime investigator from his department to come out and make the report. The patrol officer's superior should be informed by the investigator of the patrolman's action so that the patrolman can get full credit. The investigator should also note the patrol officer's action in his own log. Any information about other disturbances concerning the same person, or other relevant information which will lead to knowledge of additional victims should be gathered at this point.

In some of the cases in which the patrol officer makes out a full report he may also have legal justification to issue a citation or even to make an arrest. Such instances are more likely to occur in cases of itinerant door-to-door salesmen, or home repair defrauders, or curbside auto repair defrauders, where, for example, there is criminal jurisdiction arising out of one possible aspect of broader criminal activity, such as soliciting without a license. In some departments the patrol officer may lack the time or expertise to fill out the citation properly or to make a "good arrest." A system should then be set up to dispatch an investigator immediately to the scene to make out the arrest papers and even to do the booking, with the understanding that the patrol officer will get full credit for the actual arrest. Since the investigator is hopefully not evaluated on the basis of the number of arrests, he has everything to gain from such an arrangement--as has his unit.

(e) Participation in Special Programs. An anti-white-collar crime unit can organize a systematic program against certain types of crime in which the patrol officer can participate. These can be programs against fraudulent door-to-door salesmen, home-repair defrauders, etc. Patrol is likely to be the branch of law enforcement which gets the first information about these activities in an area, either by direct observation or citizen report. Patrol officers can be brought into the program by having in-person presentation by white-collar crime investigators at roll-calls. Included in such presentations should be such things as showing of mug shots and handouts of other information, shift and pre-cinct briefings on the specifics of the arrest process for these types of criminals, assurances that patrol officers will receive full credit for arrests they make, even if they are assisted in the arrest by white-collar crime unit personnel. In some cases, one of the supervisors of a precinct or division might be given the responsibility of coordinating efforts between patrol and the investigative units. Such programs, if successful, are likely to go a long way toward interesting patrol offi-cers in the fight against white-collar crimes.

In order to have a patrol division which actively participates in an anti-white-collar crime effort, there are a number of factors to be considered, some of which have been indicated above. First, patrol officers need to be trained in the Police Academy, at roll-calls, and as part of special in-service training programs.[36] Second, as has been repeatedly noted above, patrol officers need to be given full credit for contributions they make, such as arrests. Third, the relationships between street crime and white-collar crime needs not only to be dealt with in training but the tie-in should be explicitly recognized. For example, if a patrol officer is given the name of a burglar by a citizen grateful for some help with respect to a consumer fraud, this should be specially noted in his report. Fourth, the tie between patrol and the white-collar crime investigator needs to be made clear. Recruiting investigators from patrol rather than from other investigative units can strengthen such ties. Having patrol officers work on temporary assign-ment in the investigative unit would also help. And, investigators would need to both feel and show respect for patrol officers by such subtleties as going to a patrol headquarters for a meeting, rather than vice versa, developing patrol officer expertise by in-house orientation as to how to avoid being cheated themselves by current active schemes, giving high priority to investigating crimes in which patrol officers are victims, and by helping law enforcement in general, such as with charity frauds which use the police name as part of the con.

In departments in which neighborhood team policing has been estab-lished, patrol officers are both more likely to learn about white-collar crime and more likely to be able to react effectively. Neighborhood residents would be more likely to develop rapport with the police and report such crimes to them. This acquaintance with the local citizenry and businessmen would also tend to make the patrol officer appreciate the plight of victims. Also, the patrol officer's greater knowledge of the neighborhood helps him sort out the legitimate complaints from the non-legitimate. He is better able to determine when he is being used as a "collection agency"; when the complainant is really the crook; when an accusation against a businessman is misunderstanding or a genuine civil matter. Of course, his very integration in the community may make it difficult for him to become involved in what might be in part just a quarrel between two parties, especially if he has established close ties with one, or is even dependent on one for cooperation with respect to

---

[36]See Appendix A, pp. 237-238.

other types of crime. As indicated above, the use of an effective referral system can help the officer out of the dilemma. Finally, the continual, visible presence in the neighborhood of an officer clearly interested in white-collar violations can act as a reminder to potential white-collar criminals that law enforcement is near at hand and thus contribute to deterring these offenses.

D. RELATIONSHIPS WITH OTHER AGENCIES

1. Geographical Liaison

One of the major characteristics of some white-collar crime and criminals is their geographic mobility. Thus, white-collar crime units need to maintain close liaison with each other across jurisdictional boundaries, within states, and interstate. This liaison can benefit local agencies in a number of ways. One unit may be able to warn another about the movements of particular suspects. Units may be able to alert other units to the particular schemes being used by the criminals even to the point of indicating how best to investigate the cases. Even more detailed information, such as mug shots, MOs, and aliases can be shared. Officers in one jurisdiction can make arrests or serve warrants on criminals wanted in another.

If the scheme itself cuts across several jurisdictions, additional purposes to the liaison can develop. The investigators in each jurisdiction can be helped by information obtained in the other jurisdictions including information necessary to issuance of a search warrant. Victims of a scheme generated in one area may reside in another, so that information from the victims can be obtained only by cross-jurisdictional cooperation. Each jurisdiction may see only a part of the total criminal operation, so that the full significance of each part cannot be noted unless all of the information is pulled together. One of the jurisdictions may need to take the lead because the strongest case can be developed in that jurisdiction. The use of charts can be very helpful with respect to this kind of problem.[37]

In order to have the most effective liaison and cooperation across jurisdictional boundaries it is important to develop networks of personal contacts across these jurisdictions. Investigators tend to share information and cooperate in other ways only with those whom they know and trust. Such personal relationships can best be established by having meetings among investigators. There can be at least two purposes of such meetings: (i) to share intelligence, and (ii) to deal with educational and business issues. In intelligence meetings, the purpose is to share operational intelligence about particular suspects and schemes. In educational and business meetings, the purpose is to convey information about such general topics as the role and functioning of given agencies, new laws, etc., and to conduct such business as applying

---

[37]See the discussion of charts using link network and time flow analyses at pp. 82-88.

for grant money or developing training programs. It is best not to mix these purposes in the same meetings, for reasons discussed below.

(a) <u>Intelligence Meetings</u>. Investigators invited to intelligence meetings should generally be of sufficiently similar background so that trust and communication can be engendered. Thus, private agency investigators or investigators from agencies which strictly avoid criminal remedies should not be invited to the same meeting as investigators from criminally oriented law enforcement agencies, except where there is some special purpose for doing so. These intelligence meetings should be called by one of the law enforcement agencies in the area, one that is trusted and respected by the others, one which has no inclination to monopolize cases.

One very effective model for such a meeting involves simple intelligence sharing efforts in which each of the investigators has an opportunity to tell the others about a new scheme that is developing in his area which he believes might spread. The person conducting the meeting should do so in as informal a manner as possible. Formal agendas and record taking should be avoided. He should have some idea in advance as to which investigators have something particularly important to convey, and should simply call on them to make quick, 12 to 15 minute, business-like presentations. Next, investigators from each jurisdiction represented should be asked during the meeting, by the person conducting it, if they have anything they would like to share. Each of them can inform the others about criminals who are loose in the community, either with or without warrants outstanding; can request information regarding certain suspects or schemes; ask the other investigators to refer victims to him; and bring other investigators up to date on on-going investigations. New investigative techniques can be described. Copies of evidentiary documents can be passed around; by use of overhead or opaque projectors, the group can be shown mug shots, documents, or lists of relevant information. Actual physical evidence can be shown. In some instances where this method is used, cases have actually developed out of these give-and-take discussions.

Such presentations not only foster the sharing of information; they also assist investigators to know one another. They can learn whom they can trust, and where certain types of information are available. Furthermore, white-collar crime investigators can gain considerable psychological support from such presentations, especially if they come from agencies in which they are relatively isolated from other investigators. This support may very well sustain them in the face of difficulties which they may encounter in their home jurisdictions. Such meetings can serve as an important training device for investigators who have only recently been assigned to work on white-collar crime, acting as an additional training forum in which they can learn about techniques of investigation, the characteristics of particular schemes, etc.

After the presentations are over, ample time should be allowed for the investigators to meet informally in small groups so that direct personal contacts can be made, and friendships developed. These informal interchanges are where future cooperation can be planned, current cooperative efforts enhanced, and past efforts reviewed.

Such meetings should be held on a fairly regular basis with the same group of investigators, or, at most, a homogeneous group with respect to professional identity. Informal meeting groups can develop as part of more formal meetings, such as those associated with training programs, conventions, etc.

(b) Educational-Business Meetings. The purpose of such meetings is more general: to convey information about agencies, laws, budgetary problems, develop new programs, etc. Investigators and other cognizant personnel from law enforcement agencies, from private trade associations, from industry-based investigative agencies, such as insurance, from governmental agencies which do not focus on criminal enforcement, should all be invited. Formal presentations in which agency representatives describe their agencies, analyze new case and statutory law, or introduce information about new investigative technologies can all be conducted at such meetings, with a formal agenda, officers, etc. The value of such meetings for effective law enforcement can be greatly enhanced if there are periods set aside in which people from different agencies can mingle informally, get to know one another personally, develop friendships, and develop some possible cooperative work.

There should be no expectation that operational intelligence information can be conveyed in such meetings because the difference among the groups of investigators tends to minimize the degree of trust they can develop, as well as the degree of full understanding of one another when they attempt to communicate about given investigations. On the other hand, at the intelligence meetings described above, time and energy spent on business and educational matters would detract from effective communication regarding on-going investigations and schemes.

2. Agencies With Overlapping Jurisdiction

Within any geographic and subject-matter area there will be federal, state, and local overlapping areas of authority. In some instances both administrative and enforcement agencies may have jurisdiction over the same activity; for example, a state motor vehicle licensing bureau and an auto repair fraud unit may be concerned with the same abuses. Federal state, and local statutes or ordinances may all be applicable to the same wrongful activity, although the definition of the crime may differ. In some states, both the attorney general and local prosecutors will have the power to enforce a given law. Frequently public and private agencies will offer different remedies for the same abusive activity, e.g., mediation, injunctive relief, civil remedies, or criminal prosecution.

The overlap of legal approaches has the potentiality for great weakness in the system and also for great strength, depending on how those with administrative, regulatory, and enforcement responsibilities approach the problem. On the one hand, the danger is that some wrongful activity will either not be dealt with by any of the agencies or will be dealt with by an ineffective agency, or by a strong agency in an ineffective way. A given type of wrongful activity may be held as a low priority target by all of the agencies, because some of them assume that the others are giving it adequate attention. A law enforcement agency may assume erroneously that a given activity can only be dealt with by a civil or administrative agency, while the latter may tend to ignore it.

On the other hand, an overlap of approaches can have a number of benefits. Most important, an overlap gives agencies a chance to back-stop one another, since one agency can deal with activities which another has tended to overlook or not adequately attend to. An agency can discover the gaps in another's operations by monitoring cases which were referred to another agency, by noticing that there are areas of illicit activity which are not being dealt with by the other agency. In the competition for publicity and political stature, agencies can engage in healthy competition with one another for the most significant cases. It is not uncommon for one prosecutorial agency to stir other agencies out of lethargy by prosecuting cases which they should have handled.

In order to facilitate the development of such relationships among agencies in the same geographical area, periodic intelligence or education-business meetings like the ones described for cross-geographical liaison[38] should be held. Such meetings can build trust and communication, but it is very important that the development of such meetings not be perceived to be (or actually be) an effort by one of the agencies to enhance its power. Even if the staff of one agency may feel that they have a legitimate reason for exercising some degree of leadership, they will lose the ability to lead if they do not share cases, leads, and information with other agencies. Local agencies frequently voice the suspicion that federal agencies do not give local agencies information as much as they are expected to give information to the federal agencies. Obviously, such a breakdown of confidence in mutual helpfulness can only help white-collar criminals.

If there is some suspicion that one of the agencies is a security leak, information should no longer be sent to that agency. However, just freezing out the agency does not really solve the problem of the other cooperating agencies. All agencies will suffer if needed information is taken out of circulation. To solve the problem of suspect agencies, a carefully thought through plan should be developed to correct the situation. One possible remedy might be to discreetly approach trusted and powerful personnel in an agency which has legal or administrative power over the suspect agency. This approach should make it clear that there is no conclusive evidence of misconduct, just a suspicion. Thus, an effort to determine the validity of the suspicion can very well work to the benefit of an agency which is wrongfully suspected. If the investigation of the agency should prove the agency at fault, then appropriate administrative or legal remedies are likely to follow.

3. Regional and State Supportive Agencies

All agencies have some limitations on their technical abilities. Some may not have (or have easy access to) investigative accountants, computer experts, auto repair mechanics, legal experts in certain areas,

---

[38]See the earlier discussion of such meetings at pp. 53-55.

product analysts, etc. Some may have limited ability to make contact with agencies in other states, or in some local jurisdictions. Some may simply not have enough investigators for particular important investigations. Accordingly, it is very useful to have regional or state level agencies which can provide such resources to smaller jurisdictions at their request. In some instances, such agencies can encompass an entire metropolitan area, working in a number of cities. In one state, expert accountants of a state level agency are available on request to work with local agencies, but their salary continues to be paid by the state agency. In another state, the state level department of justice can obtain information from agencies in other states that is needed by local agencies in its own state. In some smaller states, it may be wise to house a computer system for storing criminal justice information in an agency at the state level.

In some instances, such state, regional, or metropolitan-center units can have their own investigative capacity and authority. Investigations by these agencies can be initiated at the request of the local agencies if the director or chief of the latter agency judges that such an investigation is beyond the jurisdiction of his own agency. This inability of the local agency to act on these investigations may simply be the result of a lack of resources. However, in some instances, the local agency may be handicapped by a configuration of political or economic power that it is unable to conduct an investigation except at great cost to itself. In these instances, it is extremely valuable to have a state, regional, or metropolitan agency which is sufficiently strong itself to proceed with the investigation without undue costs to itself. Its base of support is likely to be broader; it may have a more secure civil service position; or it may have greater public credibility The local agency can then invite the stronger agency to conduct the investigation.

However, invitations to the state, regional, or metropolitan agency need to be responded to with some caution. It is possible that personnel in the local agency are trying to use the power of the stronger agency in a political or legal battle, or as a way of gaining power for itself. The stronger agency would need to do some scouting of its own before it makes a commitment to conduct an investigation on its own. In some cases, it might decide to sever all public and administrative connections with the local agency when it conducts its investigation. In other cases, the stronger agency would be wise to give partial or even full public credit to the local, inviting agency in order to strengthen it for future investigations and to maintain good relationships between the two agencies.

In some instances, the state, regional, or metropolitan agency may decide to conduct an investigation without being invited by any local agency. Sometimes such interventions are needed because the local agency, for reasons of policy, organization, or even outside pressures and influences is neglecting a particular area of crime or a particular case. Obviously, such intervention needs to be done with great care.

A local investigative agency which is either part of a prosecutor's office or works closely with one can influence a state, regional, or

metropolitan agency into action by initiating investigations and prosecutions in an area that the latter agency has ignored, even if it has
the legal power to deal with it. This same effect of competitive investigations and prosecutions can also, obviously, be achieved with
respect to other local agencies where jurisdiction overlaps with the
local agency in question.

4. Trade Associations

    Some trade and professional associations can be important allies of
investigative units. Some such associations may be so highly interested
in keeping their record clear that they will assist the investigative
agency by providing information. Thus it is valuable for a white-collar
crime unit to maintain close but informal personal ties with trade and
professional associations. Nevertheless, there is always the danger
that some associations will try to get an investigative agency to concentrate on cases of particular concern to them, to the exclusion of the
agency's other enforcement responsibilities. Investigative agencies
which perceive that this may be happening should examine cases given to
them very carefully.

    On the other hand, work with trade or professional associations
offers important benefits with respect to deterrence. The association
can provide a vehicle for communicating information about the policies
and goals of the agency, as well as providing an informal network for
disseminating knowledge about investigations, prosecutions, and convictions. Hopefully, such ties with the trade and professional associations may lead them to set standards and to monitor the conduct of
their own membership.

E. COMMUNICATIONS WITH THE PUBLIC

1. Complaints From the Public

    One of the most important sources of complaints and investigative
leads is the telephone call from the irate citizen-victim, and from more
organized sources such as attorneys or accountants for victims, or trade
associations. Calls from citizens can go directly to the unit, but may
also go through other government agencies or some private ones. In
either case, it is important that the unit have its own phone number.
But, even where a unit deals with the public through some other organization, it should be concerned as to whether the cooperating agencies have
appropriate relationships with the public.

    In jurisdictions which are likely to have a high proportion of victims
who are poor, aged or infirm, unit offices should be easily accesible
to the public; for example, on the ground floor. Victims should not
be forced to go through a bureaucratic referral system before speaking
to an investigator or complaint handler. Many aged, infirm, or poor
people do not use mails readily and may be inhibited with respect to use
of the telephone (they know from experience that they will be asked to
come down, or write a letter anyhow). They should have a convenient way
of making face-to-face contacts with people in the agency.

A basic problem in relating to the public is the conflict between the need to respond fully and appropriately to complaints from the public and the limited number of fully trained personnel available for this task. Obviously, the best solution is to secure funds to hire some investigators. Nevertheless, in some agencies this problem has been resolved by having telephone calls from the community taken by "complaint handlers" who screen the calls, take care of simple consumer problems which appear to be resolvable by mediation, or simply take down some basic information. The primary advantage of the complaint-handler approach is that of economy of resources. However, complaint handlers tend on the whole to be less well trained, less well paid than investigators and lawyers, and are usually somewhat less sensitive to criminal aspects of complaints.

If there are only a very limited number of investigators in an agency (and there usually are), it will be an unwise allocation of resources to have their time taken up with answering calls from the public if the agency is one in which the calls most often turn out to be matters which do not warrant a criminally oriented investigation. This task may be quite demoralizing for highly professional investigators being kept from work they are better qualified to do.

Complaint handlers sometimes are senior law students or other types of students. The advantage of using them is that they are usually highly motivated, have not yet become jaundiced by having heard the same story over and over again, and, since they are working part-time, can better bear the emotional strain of working with the public. A disadvantage is their high turnover rate, which makes training of replacements a problem for the office. Such complaint handlers should report either to an investigator permanently assigned to supervise them; or in some cases a lawyer or legal advisor may be assigned on a rotating basis to help them answer questions.

Some agencies, especially those in police departments or those staffed by former police officers, give investigators direct responsibility for handling calls from the public. A police officer's general role in part entails taking complaints from the public, so that it is simply an extension of this role to have direct contact with the public in a white-collar crime unit.

Although limitation of resources will frequently compel the white-collar crime unit to employ complaint handlers rather than investigators to deal with the public, investigator assignments to this work offers advantages which merit serious consideration. First, the investigator is more likely than the complaint handler to ask probing questions of the citizen and to follow up on leads, hints, and overtones. Thus, the amount and quality of the information gained is greater. Furthermore, an investigator is more likely than a complaint handler to be alert and sensitive to the description of a new type of scheme. A complaint handler is probably less likely to be sensitive to such new possibilities. Since white-collar crimes take so many new forms, this sensitivity is very important.

Second, in an agency with a high degree of communication among investigators because of an open room, a cooperative spirit, staff meetings, etc., all of the investigators will have developed enough expertise in many areas of white-collar crime to be able to handle the initial complaint at least minimally well, even though it might be outside their own area of expertise.

Third, the agency may already have considerable information about a scheme because of victims having called in, and because of general information processing in the agency. If one of the investigators in the office has already opened a relevant investigation, and another investigator takes the call, the latter can readily transfer the call to the former investigator because he will be well aware of other investigations in the agency. The use of an open room in which all of the investigators can hear each other work facilitates this possibility of transferring calls. Having the complaint handlers in the same room with investigators should be avoided because it would create too much noise and confusion.

Fourth, it is more likely on the whole that an investigator will be sensitive to the criminal enforcement potential of a complaint. Complaint handlers are by definition not professional law enforcement personnel and therefore would in general be less inclined to look for criminal involvement. If they have to refer the complaint to an investigator to determine whether there is criminal involvement, the savings in resources is lessened; and many complaint handlers may be inclined to avoid appearing unknowledgeable to both the citizen and the investigators, and may therefore avoid referring the call.

Fifth, the complaining citizen will be much more satisfied in talking with an investigator, especially if the investigator is knowledgeable in the area of the complaint, than in talking with a complaint handler. The investigator is more likely to be able to develop the conversation to generate some very valuable leads, which not only will benefit the investigation but also is likely to be more gratifying to the complaining citizen.

Citizen satisfaction is extremely important for a number of reasons. The great drop in confidence in government in recent years undoubtedly generates some latent scepticism in the citizens who call, and any response by the agency which could be interpreted as routinized, uninterested, or "bureaucratic," will reduce the likelihood of future cooperation with law enforcement in general, and not only with respect to white-collar crime.

If an agency has a high volume of telephone calls from other agencies and the public, it will often be advisable to designate one investigator to handle such calls each day, on a schedule prepared by the supervisor. The advantage of this procedure is that the investigators would not be interrupted in the middle of their work on other cases by these calls. If there is a lack of sufficient funds to hire enough investigators and complaint handlers have to be used, then it becomes very important that they be trained to the highest level of professionalism possible and that they be supervised as closely as possible.

Concern for the satisfaction of the complaining citizen implies that the citizen always be given some sense of closure on his call. He needs to know if his call leads anywhere, whether an investigation is initiated or an on-going one assisted. If no further immediate action is to be taken, the citizen should be told that his complaint is appreciated, that the information he provided may very well be used at a future time if additional relevant information is received. It would be very helpful to send a letter to each citizen indicating what happened to his call, even if his complaint was only placed in a standby active file.

It will often be desirable to have a victim or witness come to the office to make a full statement, to present his records, etc. However, such invitations should not be communicated in such a way that the invitation to come to the office is perceived by the citizen as a substitute for an adequate and satisfactory telephone conversation. Instead, the invitation should be communicated as a natural outgrowth of the telephone conversation. In some cases, the citizen might not be able to come to the office because of infirmity or because of a fear of officialdom and bureaucracy. Such fears are very likely to occur among the poor. The investigator should always be open to interviewing complainants or witnesses in their homes or on some neutral ground, such as a public place.

In some instances units have used the device of sending questionnaires by mail to complainants. These questionnaires are designed to secure relevant information, especially in the cases of potential consumer fraud cases. The use of such questionnaires obviously handicaps the less well educated and greatly reduces the likelihood that they will cooperate with the white-collar crime unit, but under certain circumstances can be most efficient and effective investigative tools.[39]

If an investigation continues for more than two or three weeks, it would be wise to send a one-time interim notice to the complaining witnesses to inform them of the state of the investigation, to the extent legally and practically possible. Since the public may have little idea of how long white-collar crime investigations take, such reassurances that the investigation is proceeding would be very valuable. When cases are closed without a trial involving the complainant, he should be so informed by a letter which gives the general reasons for the closure.

2. Informing the Public

Through the press and the media, the public will be informed of major convictions, and even of investigations. However, press releases, or any statement to the press, should be the responsibility of the press relations officer, if any, of the parent agency, or of the supervisor of

_____

[39]For a fuller discussion of the use of questionnaires, see Chapter IV, pp. 187-192.

investigations. In some instances, it will be valuable to allow the
press and media to know of an on-going investigation, since the publicity may lead additional victims or witnesses to provide additional
useful information. Press coverage of indictments, arrests, convictions, etc. will tend to increase telephone calls and other communication from the public. Much of the information will be useless, but it
is important for the unit to be prepared for this input, some of which
may be valuable. In any case, publicity given even to indictments,
informations, trends, can have a general deterrent effect. The danger
of bad publicity, the possible cost of a trial, etc. might be more than
some white-collar criminals can afford, especially if they are small
businessmen who might commit white-collar crimes as an adjunct to their
business. Obviously, convictions and heavy sentences have the greatest
potential for deterrent effect. Furthermore, they enhance the status of
the agency in the public regard. Good press coverage can also have the
effect of putting pressure on other agencies which have not been very
active in combatting white-collar crimes and related abuses.

Good press coverage of investigations and litigation also serve the
function of warning the public about possible dangers. If the agency
has a pro-active policy, the agency staff can go even further and can
use the press to warn the public independently of any particular scheme.
Reporters will often be interested in writing stories warning of home
repair defrauders, pyramid schemes, gold and silver investment schemes,
especially if they represent current dangers to the public. The agency
can also inform the public directly at crucial points, or get some
private agency or business to do so. Some banks have large posters near
tellers' windows, warning savings account depositors about the dangers
of, for example, con games such as pigeon drops. Investigators themselves should be available to alert the public through talks before
civic groups, students, church groups, and public interest organizations.

One especially useful technique used by a prosecutor is to have a
radio talk show in which staff members take calls from the public and
answer questions about suspected consumer frauds and other white-collar
crime activity. If this technique is adopted, callers should be warned
as they call in not to use names. This technique, if implemented with
patience and care, will educate the general public and the particular
victim, as well as other staff members in the unit who can learn from
listening to the talk show.

3. Storefronts and Other Ways of Reaching
    the Community

One of the major difficulties in fighting white-collar crime, especially consumer fraud, is that parts of the population are either very
reluctant or unable to report their victimization to a government
agency. When a substantial group of such people reside in a community,
the unit should at least consider the possibility of reaching out to the
group and making its representatives readily available to them.[40] This

---

[40]The unit may also wish to make the handling of victimization of
such groups its major mission. See Chapter VI, pp. 216-221.

outreach can take a number of forms: investigators, assistant investigators, or complaint handlers could visit old peoples' homes and organizations for the aged, union halls, fraternal organizations of minority groups, etc. They can make presentations to these groups, explaining what their units are doing, distribute literature to them, and then simply visit the group on a regular basis to take complaint reports.

In order for such outreach efforts to be successful, the outreach workers should be people who understand the client group or are even members of this group, for example, union members, retirees, etc. Furthermore, the outreach effort needs to have the support of the organization through which the target group is being reached. In some instances the organization may initiate the contact. On the other hand, such outreach efforts may lead to a greater influx of complaints than the unit is prepared to handle. Obviously, there needs to be a coordination between the outreach efforts and the ability of the unit to provide satisfactory service to a target population.

One potentially highly effective way of reaching these target populations is to establish storefront offices in specific neighborhoods. Such operations generally stress mediation and civil or administrative remedies but do not necessarily have to do so. In one populous urban area, storefronts were successfully set up by the police department with a great emphasis on criminal remedies. Operations which stress non-criminal remedies can be a most important source of information leading to development of criminal cases.

The success of such storefronts depends on a number of factors. They must be supported by the local community even before they open. Such support can come from local organizations, from local businessmen who do not want their reputation affected by a few predatory businessmen, etc. Support can be generated by using the local newspapers and other media, but this should be done under explicit sponsorship of an organization or person already established and respected by members of the target population. For best effect, the plans with respect to location, staffing, procedures for the storefront should be worked out in collaboration with local organizations or leaders.

A storefront should be located in a well trafficked place within the target neighborhood. It should generally not be located next to a police station, since this might inhibit some citizen-complainants. The appearance of the storefront should blend into the neighborhood. It should not appear to be too official; furnishings should be comfortable, but not "fancy" or "posh"; access to desks, investigators, etc., should be direct and obvious, with no need to wait in anterooms.

As in the case of other outreach efforts, personnel manning these storefronts must be able to readily establish rapport with the people in the neighborhood. Preferably, they should be of the ethnic or other group which predominates in the area. Even more than in other units, investigators in storefront white-collar crime units should be immediately available to the public and should act on cases on the spot. It is more important to follow up on a complaint immediately than to put off the follow-up until a time in which the investigator's efforts can be more effective. The people in the neighborhood need to learn that the investigators are really concerned with their welfare. If the best procedure is to refer the complaint to another agency, the investigator himself should handle the referral (preferably by a telephone call while the complainant is with him) and follow through as much as possible himself. Even though this may be time consuming, this effort will pay off in community support and trust. One storefront which was geared toward serving the local Spanish-speaking community was so successful that it drew others from great distances, well outside the immediate neighborhood in which it operated.

Most of the complaints will not call for criminal remedies. Of course, when the storefront is run by an agency which is strongly oriented toward possible criminal remedies, potential criminal cases are less likely to slip through the cracks.

The storefront should develop its own publicity system, geared to local, community newspapers and media. When its investigations lead to a conviction or other remedy important to the community, the storefront and its staff should get full credit for it.

The storefront staff also needs to maintain communication with the police patrol in the neighborhood. The patrol officers can refer citizens to the storefront--it gives the patrol officers a convenient place to refer the citizens, and if the referral leads to citizen satisfaction, the patrol officer shares in some of the credit. Furthermore, satisfied citizens may occasionally volunteer information about street criminals to investigators who can then pass it along to the appropriate units. However, such intelligence should never be requested from a citizen, since the citizenry might interpret such requests as showing that the true purpose of the storefront is to develop such intelligence information. Such an interpretation can destroy the vital credibility of the storefront and its parent agency.

Storefront staffs should also maintain close communication with other white-collar crime units, so as to refer more complex cases to them and to receive assistance and advice on cases which they handle themselves. These staffs should, whenever possible, be in a position to retain the right to conduct investigations of complaints they receive throughout the geographic jurisdiction of their parent agencies, or to participate in such investigation, even if they have to work in some other unit's geographical area. The reason for this is that the complainants are more likely to be cooperative if their cases are handled by the storefront staff with which they have good rapport.

F. PROSECUTOR-LAWYER-INVESTIGATOR RELATIONSHIPS

Some of the most complex and potentially difficult relationships that investigators have are those with the prosecuting attorneys. Potential difficulties result in part from differences in training, and in objectives. The differences in training are obvious, but the differences in objectives are sometimes subtle. For example, the prosecutor will be concerned with the problem of succeeding in court, where the ultimate disposition may be outside his control, while the investigator may be more interested in simply bringing someone to trial and letting the court determine guilt or innocence. The prosecutor will be concerned about sharing his resources among different kinds of cases, while every investigator is concerned for *his case*. The prosecutor may be more concerned with the legal strength of the evidence than the investigator. The prosecutor may not be fully informed about the intent and nature of the criminal activity in the community. The prosecutor may have a different set of priorities concerning which type of cases to prosecute than the investigator.

The tensions and miscommunication that result from these problems obviously do not assist in facilitating the prosecution of economic criminals. Some ways of minimizing these problems are suggested below.

1. Lawyer-Investigator Teams

Probably the best way to minimize these problems is to have lawyers and investigators be part of a single unit or team. (The term lawyer will be used occasionally in this section because in some instances the lawyer may be assigned exclusively to the investigative unit and may not actually prosecute the case.) Teams can consist of one lawyer and one investigator, or one lawyer and several investigators; working either as a total team or as a series of teams; they can be temporary or ad hoc teams working on a single case or set of cases, or there can be permanent assignments. Differences would depend on the number of personnel available, the nature of white-collar crime in the jurisdiction, the volume of the workload, etc.

The advantages of having teams are, first, that the lawyer and the investigator can exchange information, theories of cases and hunches, as close to the outset of an investigation as possible. In this way, the investigator can start collecting information and evidence in the most effective way from the very beginning of the case. On the other hand, the lawyer can become much more thoroughly familiar with what is often a very complex web of evidence. Team members should have as much direct contact as possible on both a formal and informal basis. For example, they should have adjacent offices; or share one very large office; or they should feel free to telephone each other directly, without having to go through any intermediaries. It is not conducive to effective team functioning to make the lawyer just available for consultation-when-needed. The contact should be regular, informal, and unhurried, so that leads, nuances, and theories can be fully recognized and developed.

It is essential that there be mutual respect among all the team members. The lawyer needs to respect the skills, knowledge, and effectiveness of the investigator, and vice versa. This should not mean that there be any confusion of their respective and different roles and functions, but rather that there be an awareness of their respective responsibilities and a desire on the part of each to give the other that understanding support which will maximize the effectiveness of each in best fulfilling his or her own role. When there is a mutual rapport, the investigator's motivation will be greatly enhanced, leading to better investigative accomplishments.

Teams with investigators as the supervisor, as well as those with the lawyer as supervisor, have both been found to be effective. For example, a group of several investigators, under the direction of one of their number, may have a permanently assigned lawyer as part of their team. Or, the team may consist of investigators under the supervision of a deputy prosecutor. More important than the pecking order of the hierarchy is the amount of respect for competence. Lawyers who respect the competence of the investigator team leader can take direction from him or her.

There are a number of advantages to having teams, in addition to those set forth above. Investigators can learn better about the subtleties of gathering legally viable evidence. They receive steady feedback as to the effectiveness of their performance. They are more likely to avoid false expectations about the evidentiary value of certain types of information. They will be more likely to be directed toward the same goals as the lawyers. They will be less likey to unfairly blame the lawyer for any failure to prosecute or convict. On the other hand, the lawyer will know that he is working effectively toward his goals. He will learn to appreciate the skill involved in investigative work. He may develop some investigative skills himself. Lawyers have gone out to interview witnesses together with investigators in instances in which the interview was important and the information legally complex or subtle.

In white-collar crime prosecutions, investigators and lawyers (particularly where "teams" are involved) will customarily go to court together, the "investigating" lawyer trying the case. One advantage of the teams following all the way through together is that the investigators can bring their frequently greater detailed knowledge to bear on the case and can thus greatly assist the prosecutor. Furthermore, the investigator's motivation in subsequent cases would greatly increase because of the respect that going to court implies and because he can see the end product of his activities (and its pitfalls) more clearly. Furthermore, he gains some depth of knowledge of the law and of the lawyer's objectives. But probably most important, the "team spirit" is greatly enhanced by the follow-through and is thus well worth the cost.

2. Cross-Agency Contacts Between Investigators and Lawyers

In most instances, investigators and lawyers or prosecutors are in different agencies. This separation does not necessarily mean that prosecutors and investigators cannot develop informal teams or even formal teams across agency lines. When an investigator begins to see that he is dealing with a complex of legally difficult cases, he should be able to turn to a prosecutor in the other agency and develop a working relationship with him. This can be done either by going to the supervisor of the prosecutor, or by going directly to a prosecutor, whichever is administratively acceptable to the latter's agency. The supervisor in the investigator's agency should be informed of the procedure, but the investigator, as a professional, should be free to develop teams as he sees fit, and as he is able to interest and persuade others to work with him. Obviously, such teams might become more or less stabilized as the two members learn to work with each other, especially if they develop an expertise in certain types of cases.

When such teams do not develop, and the investigators must present their investigations to the prosecutors to see if they will take the case, the investigator is almost automatically put at a disadvantage by the very fact that he has to assume the role of a salesman trying to get the prosecutor to buy his product. It is important that the investigators have both the skill and self-confidence to make a strong case to lawyers. Such self-confidence can be enhanced by the investigator's knowledge that his supervisor condones his arguing with lawyers.

If a prosecutor declines to take a case, the investigator should be informed of the reasons, preferably in a face-to-face meeting so that the investigator can ask questions and learn from the experience. The investigator should realize that prosecutive evaluation is not an exact science, and that reasonable people can disagree; within the prosecutor's office there may well have been disagreements. Discussion in connection with a declination, if it is conducted with civility and understanding of the participants (disagreements do not have to be papered over) can set the stage for more receptivity the next time around.

3. Selling the Case

The prosecutor who is not part of a team developing white-collar crime cases together with the investigator will have to be persuaded to go forward with the "package" brought to him or her by the investigator. This holds true for proposed civil, administrative, or regulatory action, as well as criminal action. The fact should be faced that this is a sales transaction, though it may appear in many guises.

Like any other product, the case will sell better if it is a good product, if it is well packaged, and if the "salesman" has given adequate thought to needs and capabilities of his market.

(a) The Basic Product. Whether the investigation is complete or not, the investigator should be sure that he has gathered as much evidence as possible, within the limits of his resources, before he goes to the prosecutor. How much work he can be expected to have done depends on what he wants from the prosecutor, and the constraints placed on him by his own organization.

In some cases, the investigator is quite able to present a complete package to the prosecutor, which the prosecutor will be able to reshape and select from to make his own case. While the prosecutor will frequently wish follow-up on some line of investigation, it is important that no *obvious* line of inquiry be omitted without some clear justification. Where there is what purports to be a complete package, the investigator must be able to demonstrate clear awareness of the legal elements of the case, and have admissible, competent, and persuasive evidence on each such point.[41]

---

[41]See Chapter IV, pp. 195-198.

In other instances the investigator will have gone as far as he can go to make a case, and gathered adequate evidence on all but a few crucial aspects of the case. He will look to the prosecutor, who will have recourse to subpoena power through the grand jury or inquiry judge, to "close the circle" by obtaining this missing evidence. In these instances, it will be essential that the investigator have exhausted every other possibility for obtaining evidence on the missing pieces, and that the portions of the investigation which he has completed are more than usually well done.

(b) Packaging the Case. Before the investigator takes the case to the prosecutor he should carefully consider how it will be presented. The best case may be turned down if it is not well presented; relatively weak cases will be accepted and enthusiastically pursued if well presented and if prosecutors are convinced that some victim or public interest will clearly be served by going forward.

Some investigators, e.g., those in the U.S. Postal Investigation Service and the U.S. Securities and Exchange Commission, present their cases in the form of written referral reports, outlining the theory of the investigation and summarizing the evidentiary elements available to successfully conduct the trial. Where this technique is used, such reports may be hand delivered, and followed up by personal visits which will invite the prosecutor to clarify any doubts or questions he may have--and to jog him into taking the time to carefully review what has been offered to him.

In other instances the investigator will rely on an oral presentation, in which he refers to specific investigative reports or items of evidence as necessary. Here there must be greater reliance on personal persuasiveness and organized advocacy. Since prosecutors will frequently postpone their decisions as to whether or not to take a case, this method presents the danger that after the investigator leaves the effect of persuasiveness may wear off, leaving the prosecutor with a mass of paper that has to be painfully digested and organized--always a justification for further delay which in turn increases the likelihood that a case will be declined for prosecution. It is important, therefore, that at least some short written outline of the proposed case be left behind, and that the investigator follow up to answer questions. This same "short outline" will also serve the purpose of helping the investigator to effectively organize his oral presentation.

In cases in which the scheme is quite complex and difficult to communicate, the investigator should consider a visual, diagrammatic presentation to the prosecutor. This can be done by means of a link-network analysis or a time flow analysis,[42] in which the complexities of the scheme can more easily be seen. This diagrammatic presentation should of course be accompanied by either a written or verbal description, or both.

---

[42]These techniques of graphic presentation are discussed below at pp. 82-88.

(c) <u>Knowing the Customer</u>. Before the investigator presents his case he should consider what the prosecutor's own interests are, how much the prosecutor knows about white-collar crime prosecutions, and what competition he must face in securing prosecutive attention.

If the prosecutor has an established office interest in white-collar crime, it will obviously be easier to persuade him to accept a case. It is important to realize that some deputy prosecutors will be more receptive than others to such cases, and therefore it may be possible (particularly in smaller offices) to interest a particular deputy in a case. Even where there is a formal referral channel, once an investigator knows there is a receptive deputy the referral procedure can be facilitated by an informal approach for advice (it should be for genuinely desired advice which helps the investigation) which could set the stage for a later "logical" assignment to the same deputy.

The "market" can be presold by interaction between the white-collar investigative unit and the prosecutor which focuses on general objectives rather than on specific cases. For example, the supervisor of a white-collar investigative unit can make regular calls on the prosecutor or his chief deputy, or the head of a major crime prosecutive unit, to generally advise him about the investigations under way, patterns of victimization in the community, etc.--all of which will help in three ways: (1) when a case is brought in it will not be a cold presentation coming out of nowhere, but at least some interest and appreciation for it will have been built up beforehand, (2) if the prosecutor is simply not going to take some kinds of cases, it is better to know it beforehand, and (3) such interaction will give the investigators a feel for what kinds of white-collar crime cases particularly interest the prosecutor, i.e., will serve to identify products for which there is a specific demand.

In some instances the investigative agency will have a choice of prosecutive agencies to whom a case can be presented. For example, state investigative units may be able to approach their attorneys general, any one of a number of county prosecutors, or even in some jurisdictions (in the case of matters subject to handling as misdemeanors), city attorneys. Sometimes a local investigative agency will wish to present a case to federal authorities, either because of local lack of interest or resources, or because of the investigative agency's lack of confidence in the integrity or courage of a particular local prosecutor.

Knowing the problems of the local prosecutor can also help. White-collar crime cases are time-consuming, and both the white-collar crime investigating unit and the prosecutor should support the other in acquiring resources for this purpose. Finally, the timing of a referral to the prosecutor is most important; for example, white-collar cases can frequently be delayed for a week or two, and it is rarely wise to walk into a prosecutor's office to present a complex case when that office is up to its ears in some major crisis situation which demands all its attention.

4. <u>Going to Court</u>

In many prosecutor's offices, a station system is used, one deputy prosecutor doing the filings, another the arraignments, etc. Such a system might be efficient for ordinary street crime; however, white-collar crime is not prosecuted often enough for the typical criminal deputy prosecutor at each station to become expert on the case. Furthermore, the cases vary tremendously in scheme, type of transaction, etc., so that it is difficult to build up expertise. Thus, in many cases, station-posted deputy prosecutors who are not specialized in white-collar crime or who are not expert in a particular type of white-collar crime will not be able to deal with the case as well as they should. It then falls on the shoulders of the investigator to track the case through the system, explaining the case to each of the deputies involved in the process.

To help reduce the problem of the deputy prosecutor who is not expert in a particular type of white-collar crime, investigators can invite prosecutive staffs to attend their training sessions, or alert the prosecutor to the existence of special training courses being conducted on a statewide, regional, or even national basis. This special training for the prosecutor would be especially useful when the crime involves products or business procedures of considerable technical sophistication, such as computer frauds, stock market transactions, etc. Another way in which prosecutors can acquire more technical knowledge is for them to be heavily involved in the investigative process, working closely with the investigators in this area. Furthermore, a very thoroughly and deeply prepared case can also increase the technical knowledge of the judges during the process of litigation, especially in trials. In fact, the judges, like other people involved in the justice system, may recognize that they too have probably been victimized and therefore may find additional value in acquiring this information. In at least one instance, a judge recessed a trial in order to inquire of an investigator where to take a relative's damaged car for repairs. In another jurisdiction, the investigators presented background technical information (not on any particular investigation or case) to judges during their regular weekly luncheon meetings. In the case of complex schemes, visual, diagrammatic presentations help to communicate the scheme to both judges and to juries. These diagrams can be Link Network Analyses or Time Flow Analyses.[43]

In many cases, especially those involving consumer fraud, expert testimony is needed in court from such people as engineers, chemists, or mechanics. A team of such experts can be developed from a variety of sources: universities, not-for-profit businesses, testing laboratories, police auto mechanic shops, etc. The advantage of using such a team is that they can establish their competency and credibility in court once and be used again and again. Furthermore, they learn how to effectively deliver their testimony and respond to cross-examination. It is important to have experts who can communicate with nonexperts, who are not so accustomed to jargon that they can't talk plain English,[44] and it

---

[43]These techniques of graphic presentation are discussed below at pp. 82-88.

[44]See the discussion about "Finding Experts/Resources," in Chapter IV, at pp. 192-195.

is most important that the investigator be prepared to help identify and recruit these people.

Investigators can provide useful background and related information to help courts make bail and personal recognizance decisions, and to assist the court through probation departments which must prepare pre-sentence reports. Investigators often have information relevant to the questions of whether a defendant will flee the jurisdiction and whether a heavy sentence is called for. Since white-collar criminals often make a fine appearance in court and may have some degree of social prominence, giving the judge and other court personnel such background information becomes especially important.

5. Sharing the Credit

When cases are taken to court, both the prosecutor's office and the agency should receive their fair share of the credit. If both the prosecutor's office and the agency have investigative staffs, the problem becomes more complex. In some cases, the other agency might be willing to turn over incomplete but fruitful investigations to the prosecutor's office, or even to do an investigation jointly. However, such flexibility can continue to exist only if the prosecutor's office does not keep the highly publicized big cases and leave the other agency with the minor cases to investigate, or with cases which are important but which are perceived as trivial.

G. INFORMATION PROCESS FLOW

The degree to which a unit achieves it goals without excessive costs can be greatly affected by the way in which information is dealt with in the unit. How the information is handled affects the quality of decisions to proceed with investigations, to stop them, or refer cases to other agencies; the degree of understanding of the schemes them-selves; the appropriate use of information for the development of cases in the future; the fast recognition of patterns of complaints and of criminal rather than civil involvement; and the effective coordination of activities with other agencies, criminal or civil; etc. Furthermore, information needs to be handled so that supervisors can keep track of work loads; of progress on investigations; and of coordination with other agencies.

In the following sections are described some ways in which informa-tion can be handled effectively. These are only suggestions; obviously, local circumstances can dictate wide deviations.

1. Files

In order to effectively process information, at least the following sets of files are needed:

(a) A File of On-Going Investigations. This file should be organized by suspect, (including business names and AKAs), and should carry the name of the investigator, the date the investigation is opened and the type of complaint. This file system can be as basic as a set of 3 x 5 cards or as sophisticated as a computer. The actual investigative file containing the evidence and notes of on-going investigations is best kept by the investigator on the case. When cases are closed, these working files should be transferred to the unit's files.

(b) <u>A File of Investigator's Workload</u>. This kind of file duplicates the first but is organized by investigator and by case. This file is kept by the supervisor. As part of this file the supervisor should keep the weekly narrative updates of the investigation, to be described below.

(c) <u>A File List of Previous Complaints</u>. This file can be on a 3 x 5 card system, in an on-line computer, or in computer printouts. In either case, the lists should be organized by victim and by suspect, including business names, AKAs. A duplicate 3 x 5 card should be made out for each of the ways of organizing the file.[45]

In addition to the above, each card or computer entry should contain the date of the complaint, the type of complaint (consumer fraud, stock swindles, land fraud, etc.), and the dates of alleged commission of the fraud, and nature of disposition. If the disposition involved a full investigation, the card or computer entry should contain the name of the investigator, the status of the investigation (closed, open); and the number and location of investigative files.

(d) <u>Reports of Non-Investigated Complaints</u>. Actual complaint reports which did not lead to investigations should be organized by suspect and victim and should be referred to in the file of previous complaints. There should be at least one designated individual, such as an executive secretary whose responsibility it is to maintain these files.

2. Information Flow and the Handling of Complaints

In many types of white-collar crimes the investigation process begins with a complaint to law enforcement from someone seeking some form of redress for some problem. Upon examination, the complaint may reflect nothing more than the anger of a victim who has made a bad investment or a bad purchase, or who has a personal motive to cause trouble for another. An initial complaint, which may take a variety of forms ranging between these two extremes, will rarely provide an investigator with a total case, i.e., indications of all of the required elements of a crime. Even the most innocuous complaints may be the first indication of a criminal fraud. Investigators must therefore become familiar with the process of handling complaints whether or not they are themselves directly involved in the process.

---

[45]If an intelligence system is adopted (as suggested in Chapter III), the master card file would perform this function better than an additional 3 x 5 card file. See Chapter III, at pp. 104-116.

In the discussion below the person who receives the complaint from either a citizen or another agency is referred to as the intaker. This person can be an investigator, assistant investigator, or complaint handler. The term "investigator" refers to the individual who will be responsible for investigative follow-up on the complaint. It is important to note that the intaker and investigator can be one and the same person. The terms "intaker" and "investigator" refer to functions, not persons.

In offices in which investigators also serve as intakers and the influx of reports and complainants is of high volume, then the investigators might have a rotating assignment of acting as intakers for a day at a time.

Established policies and procedures for complaint handling, whether formal or informal, exist in practically all law enforcement agencies. Regardless of the particular policies and procedures established in any individual agency, an investigator dealing with complainants should always aim to accomplish two things: (i) obtain full details in matters that have potential for legal action, and (ii) avoid spending time in collecting information which is not pertinent to legal action. The degree of difficulty in achieving an optimum balance between these two aims will usually be influenced by agency policy regarding public services and maintenance of good will. The difficulty is especially great in agencies dealing with consumer fraud, which must provide for sufficient time to insure that complainants feel that the person receiving the complaint is sensitive to their predicament.

When reports are received by the agency, the intaker receives a telephone call, reads a letter or report from a complainant or referring agency, or speaks to a citizen who walks in. The intaker should get as complete and specific information as possible as to what occurred. New staff should be provided with a checklist of information needed, or preferably with intake report forms in sufficient detail to elicit information adequate for intelligent assessment of the complaint and possible follow-up. This latter point should be stressed. Figures 1 and 2 are two examples of complaint forms. The first, Figure 1, is extremely simple and open-ended, leaving much to the skill of the intaker. Figure 2, on the other hand, is better structured--providing the individual taking the complaint or report with clear guidance as to the kinds of information which are needed and the kinds of questions which should be asked to get such information.

Only a small percentage of public complaints might warrant more investigative follow-up than a telephone call or letter, perhaps to the subject or to another public or private agency. The intaker must be able to distinguish such situations from those which might involve a crime, or investigation in support of public or private civil litigation. To do so, in each complaint handling situation he must be able to put into immediate use a sound knowledge of the common elements of white-collar crime and principles of interviewing.

Interviewing and gathering documents from the initial complainants and other victims may not always be sufficient to establish a clear

FIGURE 1

COMPLAINT REPORT FORM

DATE:_____

SOURCE OF COMPLAINT:_____

_____

NATURE OF COMPLAINT:_____

_____

_____

_____

_____

_____

_____

_____

_____

_____

_____

_____

_____

_____

_____

DISPOSITION:_____

_____

INTAKE INVESTIGATOR

75

FIGURE 2

PLEASE PRINT   REQUEST FOR INVESTIGATION AND COMPLAINT

NOTICE: The legal staff of the District Attorney's Office is
not permitted to engage in the private practice of
law or to furnish legal advice in civil matters.   Senior Citizen?   Yes ☐ No ☐   Area..............

VICTIM: Date...

Your Name...   Occupation..

Address...   Phone (Residence).......................................

....   Phone (Business)..

SUSPECT: List name of firm or individual complaint is being made against. Identify salesman or representative dealt with.

1. Name .... Phone...

Address...

2. Name .... Phone...

Date of occurrence.. Amount of Loss......................................

Location of occurrence (City and County)...

Do you have any witnesses?...

....

Have you contacted an attorney?................. Who?..

Are any civil actions (law suits) pending?...

Have you contacted any other agencies?......... Name agency...

Do you know any other victims?...

Are you willing to sign a formal (criminal) complaint and testify in Court regarding this matter?..................

DECLARATION   PLEASE PRINT

Briefly explain the facts upon which you are basing your complaint, including first contact from suspect:

*Attach addition remarks and copies of contracts and correspondence to this form. -- DO NOT WRITE ON REVERSE SIDE.

....
....
....
....
....
....
....

I declare under penalty of perjury that the foregoing is true and correct, and that this declaration was executed at

...., California. ....
                                                                              Signed

DO NOT WRITE BELOW THIS LINE

Initial Screen
Walk In.................. Mail............
IA.......... UNASS....... FLD............
W/O To...........Supr. INV.............
Master #.............................
W.O...........Out Card............
Initial Print Out.................
Assignment Print Out.............
Postcard Mailed....................

Disposition
Type Complaint...........
Disp. Code ....
Inv/Asst.................
Time...................

Criminal ( ) Consumer ( )
Money/Prop Recovered......................
Fines or Damages.........................
SIA.................Supr. INV...........
Data entered........... (W.O. File)......

Data changes.........................
Criminal Files (Fraud)..................
(Records).........(Other)...............

picture of the alleged scheme, or to determine whether the elements of a white-collar crime are present. In some instances it will be clear that there is a danger that the follow-up investigation may be hampered by its premature disclosure to the subject--who might alter his modus operandi to confuse the investigation and prevent collection of evidence, destroy evidence, or take other steps to sidetrack the investigation. Complainants and other victims should, in such cases, be warned against contacting the promotor. In addition, the investigator should keep in mind that if, despite these precautions, word of the investigation prematurely leaks out, he should be alert to attempts by the subject to interfere with the investigation or to corrupt witnesses, and he should collect any evidence with respect to such attempts; this would not only be relevant to his original case but may also provide a basis for additional charges of obstructing justice, suborning perjury, compounding a felony, and similar crimes.

In cases in which there is any possible suspicion that a crime is involved, the intaker and investigator should avoid involvement in mediating a settlement between the complainant and the promoter. A fraudulent promoter will be only too happy to make a few refunds at the urging of the intaker or investigator, partly because these payments may be well within what he would expect to be the costs of doing his business, partly because this puts the intaker or investigator in a compromising position in any follow-up. Furthermore, the agency would be in the position of generating a settlement using the color of authority; i.e., it would be a "collection agency." Some complainants may in fact hope that the unit's involvement will cause the promoter to pay the victim-complainant. This may often be the case when the complaint is made by the victim's lawyer.

Sometimes a victim, after having filed a complaint, will receive an offer of restitution from a fraudulent promoter, even when the complainant does not expect it; and will sometimes notify the investigator that such is the case and ask his advice about whether to take it. The investigator's response in such cases should consider the needs of the victim; the potential weakening of the case in court; the weakening of the motivation of the victim to cooperate as a witness; the vulnerability of the complainant-victim as a witness. The investigator cannot, however, indicate that he would drop the investigation because of promoter's payment.

In some instances, the complainant may indicate that he is bringing a civil suit as well as calling for a criminal investigation. He may then be reluctant to part with some of the relevant documents. The investigator can sometimes obtain copies which are useful for some legal purposes, although he will need the best available evidence in a trial. In some instances the investigator can obtain cooperation by pointing out that the criminal investigation will support a civil case. In any event, the investigator should painstakingly nail down the details of how custody of the evidence will be maintained if he fails to get possession, and should carefully transcribe the contents or detailed substance for his records.

As soon as information is obtained and even while the complainant or reporter is on the telephone or in the office, the intaker should consult the list of on-going investigations. The intakers should have ready access to such a list. If there is already an on-going investigation, the complainant should be so informed. If the investigator already on the case is present in the office and available, the complainant should be directed to that investigator or the telephone call transferred to his line. It is important to have a telephone system which makes such transfers easily accomplished. At the same time the report form should be taken by the intaker to the investigator on the case. If the latter is not available, the citizen or the person from the other agency should be so informed and told that the report has been sent to the appropriate investigator who will contact the citizen or person from the other agency regarding further action. A copy of the complaint should be sent to the person who records complaints and to the individual in charge of unit files.

If the intaker finds that there is no on-going investigation, he should then consult either the card file or computer printout to determine if there have been any other previous complaints and investigations regarding this same suspect. If there have been previous investigations of this suspect the intaker should refer the complainant and the report to the previous investigator, in the same manner as is done with regard to on-going investigations. The previous investigator can then make any further investigation of the new complaint deemed necessary. If the new information appears to make it worthwhile to reopen the case, he can then request permission to reopen the case from the supervising investigator. If the new information does not at that point indicate a reopening of the case, this should be noted on the report, which should then be sent to the person who records the complaints with a copy to the supervisor and the investigator.

If the intaker finds a record of previous complaints regarding the same suspect but no previous investigation, he should so inform the complainant or referring agency, and should indicate that it will take time to determine what action is needed because the current complaint must be considered in light of information previously received and considered. It is important that the complainant be informed so that he does not feel that the unit is neglecting him. The intaker should then refer the report, along with the list of previous complaints to the investigator who is most expert in the type of possible scheme. If he is not certain who the most expert investigator is, the intaker should consult the supervising investigator. Again, all of the recording reports should be made as indicated above.

If the intaker finds no previous complaints, he should then obtain full information in order to preliminarily determine whether the matter should be considered from a criminal standpoint; or if it would be worthwhile to pursue from a civil point of view; or if it is one that could be "adjusted" by mediation between the complainant and the person who is complained about; or if it is a complaint that is apparently groundless. Intakers who are not also investigators should have a checklist of cues, guidelines, or indicators as to when to view a given complaint or report as having criminal aspects. If a matter appears to warrant further investigation, the report should be referred to the most expert investigator in the manner described above. If it appears to be worthy only of mediation, either the intaker or an investigator can follow it through. If the complaint appears groundless, a report should still be made out and filed in a way which facilitates its retrieval because subsequent information may place the complaint in a different, more important light. If only an intaker is involved, he should delegate the classification of the complaint to his supervisor for the record. If an investigator is involved, he should do the classifying.

The advantages of proceeding in this way are, of course, that maximum use is made of previous information; second, decisions as to dispositions of the complaint are made more frequently by the most expert investigator, thus bringing his expertness to bear at some point; and third, the use of previous complaint data maximizes the potentiality for recognition by the investigators of criminal rather than just civil or mediational potentials of a complaint.

In instances in which no investigation for criminal activity appears warranted but civil action seems justified, the complainant should be referred elsewhere, i.e., to the civil side of the prosecutor's office, or to some other governmental agency with appropriate jurisdiction. In some jurisdictions, it may be worthwhile to refer the complainants to local trade groups or to suggest that the complainant see an attorney or seek the aid of publicly-funded legal service agencies

In offices in which the person acting as intaker is a complaint handler or assistant investigator, the supervisor should examine their reports daily to determine whether they are handling the cases properly, and especially to determine if they are overlooking possible criminal aspects of cases that were treated as civil or "adjustive." He should inform the complaint handler or assistant investigator of his evaluation of their performance, regardless of whether it is satisfactory or not; the complaint handlers need to know how well they are doing; giving feedback only with respect to problems will tend to cause difficulties of communication.

3. Information Flow and the Conduct of Preliminary Investigations

When the investigator gets the information from the intaker, he can then make a judgment as to whether he needs to gain any further information in order to decide whether a full investigation is needed, i.e., whether to continue the preliminary investigation. Such "preliminary" investigation should take no more than a brief period of time. After the investigator has what he judges to be enough information to make a decision as to whether to proceed or not with a full investigation, he should then request permission from the supervising investigator to do so. The supervisor can then make a decision in the context of the goals of the office, the resources available, workloads, as indicated by the supervisor's list of each investigator's cases; the pro-active or reactive policy of the agency; other agency policies. The supervisor, in consultation with the investigator, should then assign a level of priority to the case on the basis of the same criteria.

Supervisors must be especially wary of directing too much effort
into reactions to "big" cases, to avoid neglect of other important
tasks, particularly pro-active investigative efforts. A parallel problem can result from receiving a great many "good" referrals from another
agency, public or private, which would then tend to tie up the resources
of the agency.

In the preliminary investigation stage, the investigation should be
given a name or title. If the unit is capable of employing this approach
a decision needs also to be made at this point as to whether the investigation should proceed with a lawyer involved (who may be a lawyer within
the unit or agency, or a prosecutor). This decision should be based on
a number of factors such as the apparent complexity of the case, and the
degree of legal sophistication of the investigator. Of course, teams
can be established after the investigation has been started, if deemed
necessary.

4. Information Flow and the Conduct of Full Investigations
    of Full Investigations

Once the investigation begins, the supervisor of investigations
should not monitor the investigator's or team's work too closely. The
investigator or team should be accorded full professional respect.
Unobtrusive monitoring can be accomplished by an open room arrangement
in which the supervisor can observe all investigators at work; by his
list of current full investigations being conducted by each of his
staff, or by a concise one paragraph narrative report by each investigator or team each week or month on each of his on-going cases. Monthly
reporting is more appropriate for major fraud cases. The report may
often be no more than one or two sentences in length, since the reports
are essentially weekly or monthly logs and are therefore cumulative.
The investigator should indicate if each investigation is active or
inactive. An active investigation is one in which the investigator was
collecting information or was actively working with the prosecutor that
week. The supervisor can thus get an idea of the actual workload and
progress of each investigator, can easily see which cases are open, and
how long each case has been open. By using this system, the supervising
investigator can keep abreast of the caseloads of each of his investigators and keep track of their work. If the supervisor is well qualified, and if he has able and well-motivated investigators working with
him, this level of supervision should be not only adequate but also
highly supportive and effective. To the extent that a supervisor's
investigators fall short of this ideal, he may observe their work a bit
more closely and make suggestions where useful. However, such observa-
tions and suggestions should be carefully tailored to the selective
expertise of the supervisor and the investigator.

(a) Maintenance of Files. The investigator should be responsible
for the organization of his files.

No investigator should simply rely upon file clerks and secretaries
to keep his files for him. A frequent review of each file should be
made to see that it is being kept in an orderly manner, that information
is not misfiled, and to check and see that all of the information in the

file has come to his attention. It is a desirable practice for the investigator to mark the face of each letter, memorandum, and anything other than original copies of evidence to be placed in the file. File clerks should be instructed not to file matters which have not been so marked, but to route the document to the investigator. This practice will prevent matters from reaching the file prior to examination by the investigator.

After a file has become more than an inch thick, it should be broken down into elements, such as correspondence, memoranda, financial records, witness affidavits, etc., to facilitate orderly examination. A thick file in nothing more than ascending date order is difficult for the investigator to manage and very difficult for anyone else to digest. An unorganized file will plague the investigator and those who follow him, and will probably confuse the investigation.

Facts in an investigator's head, not reduced to writing and filed in their proper place, are lost as far as any effective use being made of them. Investigators, after a few years on the job, learn that small details are important and feel the frustration of trying to understand and use disorganized and incomplete files left by their predecessors.

In addition to organizing the file, the limitations of storage space in most investigative units demand first that the files be shorn of duplicate copies of the same document, and of documents that could have no conceivable use in future investigations. It may be useful to assign an experienced secretary the job of periodically cutting down the size of non-active investigative files. Second, it may be more economical to place the investigative documents on microfishe than to secure additional files and space in which to place them. However, when microfishe is used, care should be taken to retain original documents necessary for use in court.

(b) Semi-Annual Summary Reports. The need for semi-annual summary reports was forcefully stated by one investigator as follows:

"An investigator with a substantial work load will soon find cases getting stale, having been pre-empted by more important matters. Therefore, at least semi-annually, an investigator should review all his open files and write a summary report which will bring together all the important facts, express the suspicions he has as to the violations which may have occurred, propose actions necessary to resolve the matter and peg as closely as possible the last day on which the statute of limitations will run and the case die for failure to act.

Efficient investigators can handle many cases at one time and the summary report will help the investigator to properly assess his priorities and not lose track of meritorious older cases.

The summary memorandum is also an excellent way of keeping supervisors advised of the progress being made on cases."[46]

5. Use of Computers and Monitoring for Patterns
    Within and Across Agencies

Card filing or computer filing can be used alternatively to control the flow of information in a unit. However, there are a number of advantages to the use of computers. One of the main advantages is that the computer can greatly assist the investigator with respect to the recognition of patterns of complaints either about a given suspect, or of a given type of white-collar crime. For example, at the end of each week, or month, a computer can produce a list of all the complaints received during that week or month. This list can then be scanned by the supervising investigator to see if there are any such patterns. In some instances, the computer can produce a printout of all of the complaints against a given suspect during a given period, or all of the complaints of a given type.

Information regarding patterns can then be used by the supervising investigator in a number of ways. First, by looking at all complaints of a given type, he may notice a pattern of complaints against a particular suspect which would not be apparent in weekly or monthly unit summaries. Similarly, he may recognize that such a pattern of complaints against a suspect, each one of which may seem worthy only of civil, administrative, or mediation remedies, in toto may strongly suggest the need for a full investigation. Second, the increases or decreases of certain types of complaints revealed by computerized printouts may suggest that resources should be shifted from one type of investigative emphasis to another.

There is a great advantage to the use of one computer by all the agencies in a given geographical area for complaint handling. All of the complaints can be funnelled into one central computer. In that way, there is a greater possibility of recognizing patterns which might not be recognizable by any one of the agencies because the complaints have been received by a variety of agencies. Should such a regional system be used, one of the cooperating agencies could be designated as the one to review the regional computer printout periodically. If a pattern is recognized from the input of several agencies, the reviewing agency can then inform each of these agencies of this fact. Then the agencies could decide among themselves which one or ones should proceed with an investigation if needed. Information could then be shared among the agencies. This procedure of coordinating across agencies is, of course, dependent on the development of a network of formal and informal contacts among the agencies, as described earlier at pp. 38-39. Since there may be legal questions as to multi-agency use of computers, the matter should be checked with agencies' legal counsel.

---

[46]Richard Latham (Director of Enforcement, Texas State Securities Board), draft of manual in preparation for Midwest Securities Administrators (September 1976), at p. 54. Draft kindly supplied by the author

6. Use of Link Network Analyses and Time
    Flow Analyses in the Management
    of Investigations

In many complex schemes, such as those involving the use of many
shell corporations, hidden ownerships, complex transfer of funds, stock
and involved conspiracies, it is very difficult for an investigator or
even a team of investigators to keep track of all information received.
This problem is especially great when more than one unit or agency is
involved in the investigation. There are two techniques for visually
representing these schemes which can help in keeping track of the information, Link Network Diagrams and Time Flow Diagrams.

Link Network diagrams can show the association between events,
persons, organizations, etc., when there is little concern over the
exact sequence in time of the associations. A Time Flow Diagram can be
used in cases in which sequences and times are important to understand.
As mentioned earlier, these diagrams can be used to communicate to
supervisors, prosecutors, judges, and juries. The following examples
will illustrate the use of such a diagram.

(a) Link Network Diagram. To develop a link network analysis, all
of the raw data needs to be assembled and put in some organized form,
such as a report or narrative. The narrative should then be studied
carefully and certain central entities, such as persons, organizations,
or other objects, should be picked as appearing important for the
analysis. Importance is primarily a matter of how many different
people, organizations or other entities a given entity has connections
with. The more different entities a given entity is associated with,
the more important it is.

Next, the diagram itself can be started by taking the most important entity and representing it on a diagram. The other entities are
then drawn in. Persons should be represented by circles, with their
names enclosed. Organizations can be represented by boxes, possibly
enclosing the circles representing members. Entities are then linked by
straight solid lines if there is strong evidence of a relationship
between or among them, such as meetings, transfer of funds, telephone
calls, etc. Dotted lines can be used to represent an hypothesized
relationship for which the evidence is less strong. Arrows can be used
to represent relationships which flow in one direction, for example, A
gave money to B, but not vice versa.

The draft diagram should then be redrawn, avoiding crossed lines
and using straight lines. The diagram should then be used to suggest
some new lines of investigation to point out weak links in the analysis,
and to help communicate the scheme.

Exhibit A below and Figure 3 below illustrate the use of Link
Network Analysis, in narrative and diagrammatic form.

EXHIBIT A

CASE EXAMPLE USING LINK NETWORK ANALYSIS

Recently, in a midwestern state, a classic "rip-off" of a county's welfare assistance program was uncovered. The scheme was conceptually simple; however, the number of people, addresses, and organizations was large; thus requiring a data structure procedure to keep track of the "players."

The originator of the fraud was a welfare case worker, a lady in this case who we will call (fictitiously), Miss Johnson. She was aware that to disperse a check to a needy client, two basic pieces of data were necessary: her approval and the name and address of the client. The latter was computer checked to assure the welfare agency was not sending more than one check to a recipient.

Miss Johnson persuaded each of 15 of her actual clients to submit four additional claims, making sure that each claim was to a different name and address. She approved each (of the 75) and the computer, after "verifying" each claim, promptly forwarded the checks. Each of the actual clients (let's call one of them Smith), picked up the fraudulently acquired checks at the addresses given on the claim. After paying a "fee" to the individual at the mail drop, each fictitious person "endorsed" the checks over to the actual client. Smith cashed his validly derived check at a bank. He cashed the others at a credit jewelery store (let's call the proprietor Ross) for a fee. Ross covered the "fees" as payments on a set of falsely entered debits in his books. He then deposited the checks to his account. When the checks were cleared and returned to the welfare agency, Miss Johnson was informed that all five checks had been paid. She then went out and got her "cut of the action" from Smith.

The investigator and prosecutor soon found it difficult to follow all the details of names, addresses, and cash flow and they assumed that it would be "impossible" for someone hearing the case for the first time to follow it. To facilitate their investigation and presentation, they resorted to a link diagram. Figure 3 is an example, using Smith as the client. Each line on the diagram was supported by documentary or investigative data. The arrows indicate the flow of the checks. In his court presentation the prosecutor used a series of 15 overlays to show the magnitude of Miss Johnson's criminal conduct.

84

FIGURE 3. LINK DIAGRAM DEPICTING AN ACTUAL WELFARE FRAUD CASE

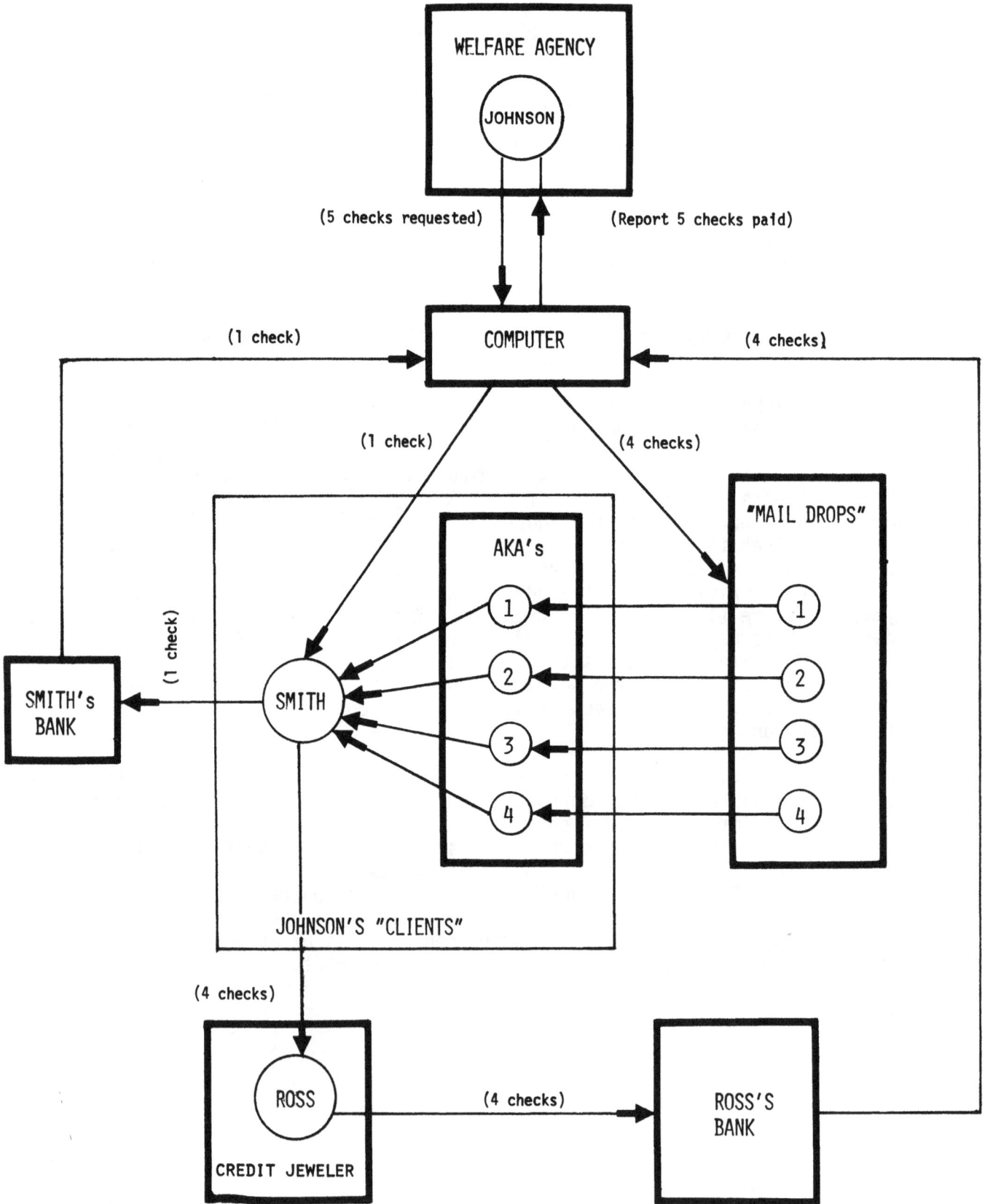

(b) <u>Time Flow Diagram</u>. When it is easier to conceive the scheme as one sequence of events rather than as an on-going process, Time Flow Diagrams can be used instead of Link Network Diagrams. A Time Flow Diagram (or PERT) is a flow chart which diagrammatically shows the sequence of events in a scheme. The scheme is first analysed to identify specific occurrences. The Time Flow Diagram should show the whole scheme as a series of events connected by activities. Each event (or milestone) is represented by a circle; it represents one specific time during implementation of the scheme and it generally describes the start or completion of some activity. The arrows or lines between the events are activities; i.e., the tasks which must be performed in order that the successive events may occur. Thus, an activity is what must happen over a period of time between events. It is the period of time necessary to move from the predecessor event to the successor event. The Time Flow Diagram is illustrated below in Exhibit B and Figure 4.

EXHIBIT B[47]

CASE EXAMPLE USING A TIME FLOW DIAGRAM

On January 15, 1973 the Ace Packing Company, a supplier of meat and poultry to wholesalers and retail markets, found itself short of working capital. John Jones, his father George Jones, and Tom Catlin, the owners of Ace, sought a loan to ease themselves out of difficulties. One of the salesmen employed by Ace, Larry Evans, arranged a loan for them in the amount of $10,000 at an interest rate of 1% per week. The loan was advanced by the Carson Trading Corporation owned by Eileen Warren.

Ace Packing did not succeed in paying off the loan advanced to it by Carson Trading very quickly. As Ace's debt increased, Eileen Warren of Carson Trading insisted upon better financial management of Ace Packing. Her specific demand was that Larry Evans be promoted and made an executive of Ace with broad financial power. The owners of Ace, John and George Jones and Tom Catlin, agreed to this arrangement. Larry Evans was made president of the company with authority to sign all company checks on August 3, 1973.

Once Larry Evans assumed the presidency and control of Ace Packing, the company began to change its business practices. Whereas Ace had normally made purchases averaging $100,000 per week, several months after Evans assumed his new role in the company, Ace began making large purchases on credit totalling $1.3 million in one six-week period. Many of these purchases were made in response to the demands of new customers brought in by Larry Evans. Among these new customers were the C. W. Meat Company, the Alton Food Corporation, and Walden Poultry Supply, all wholesalers of meat and poultry and all owned directly by Eileen Warren or by one of her relatives. The increases in merchandise purchases by Ace Packing occurred in November and the first two weeks of December of 1973, during the holiday season in which large orders for meat and poultry are not considered unusual.

Combined with new purchasing practices, Ace Packing began to engage in new payment practices. Instead of paying for credit purchases within a seven-day payment period, Ace began delaying payment to those from whom it made purchases. When suppliers began to express concern about non-payment or delays in payment, Tom Catlin of Ace made personal calls to reassure them that payment would be forthcoming and inducing them to continue forwarding merchandise ordered. In fact, payments were not forthcoming.

Ace's problems in meeting its purchase obligations resulted from two factors: first, in September 1973 a series of meetings involving

---

[47]This example is based on the actual case described by DeFranco in Anatomy of a Scam, op. cit., Note 18, though shortened and simplified here.

George and John Jones, Tom Catlin, Eileen Warren, and Larry Evans were held at the behest of Larry Evans. At these meetings Eileen Warren agreed to greatly increase the C. W. Meat Company's purchases of Ace products. In addition, an informal agreement was made by which Ace would bill C. W. Meat for meat and poultry at only 1/2 cent per pound over Ace's own costs. Thus, because of these agreements, C.W. Meat's purchases for the month of November constituted 60% of Ace's sales. The second factor affecting Ace's ability to pay for its orders from suppliers was the fact that the company did not use the payments it received (though rarely covering costs) from C. W. Meat to pay supplier-creditors. This resulted in a large bank balance for Ace. In the last week of November 1973, Larry Evans began making cash withdrawals from the Ace account. By December 6th, these withdrawals totalled $735,000.

During this same period C.W. Meat Company began modifying the bills it received from Ace so that C. W. Meat was buying meat and poultry for several cents less per pound than Ace was being billed for this merchandise. Both John Jones and Tom Catlin checked these receipts and accepted reductions in payment prices from C. W. Meat.

Ace Packing maintained a corporate bank account at Royal State Bank. When substantially all of Ace's purchases were going to C. W. Meat, C. W. Meat made payment by check to Ace almost upon receipt of delivery. In the beginning, Ace deposited these checks at Royal State Bank and, immediately after each deposit, withdrew the funds. Royal State Bank subsequently refused to permit withdrawals until checks had actually cleared. On November 22, 1973 at Eileen Warren's suggestion, Evans and John Jones opened another account for Ace Packing at the National Commercial Bank. Both Warren and C. W. Meat maintained accounts at National Commercial. The account at National Commercial was opened with the understanding between Evans and Jones and bank officials that Ace would be allowed to withdraw funds as soon as the C.W. Meat checks were deposited at National Commercial. As it turned out, the only funds ever deposited in the Ace account at National Commercial were those received from C. W. Meat. Joe Nelson, an agent of C. W. Meat, made all of the deposits to the Ace account.

It was at this same time that Evans began making large cash withdrawals from both Ace accounts. With John Jones, he (Evans), made two large withdrawals from the Royal State Bank. Jones assured bank officials that the money was needed to "pay some trade bills." Jones co-signed the checks. At National Commercial Bank, Joe Nelson introduced Evans to a bank officer as a customer of C. W. Meat. On most occasions Nelson was met at National Commercial by Evans when he (Nelson) made deposits to the Ace account. Immediately after these deposits were made, Evans (with Nelson still present) withdrew from the Ace account almost the precise amount that Nelson had deposited.

By mid-December 1973 the supplier-creditors of Ace Packing were forced to file an involuntary petition in bankruptcy against Ace to seek settlement of their claims for non-payment. The bankruptcy of Ace appeared to be precipitated by and result from the large withdrawals from Ace accounts made by Evans. The total withdrawals of $735,000 in cash were never found. The State charges that the Ace bankruptcy was a planned and fraudulent one. The flow of these events is presented diagrammatically in Figure 4.

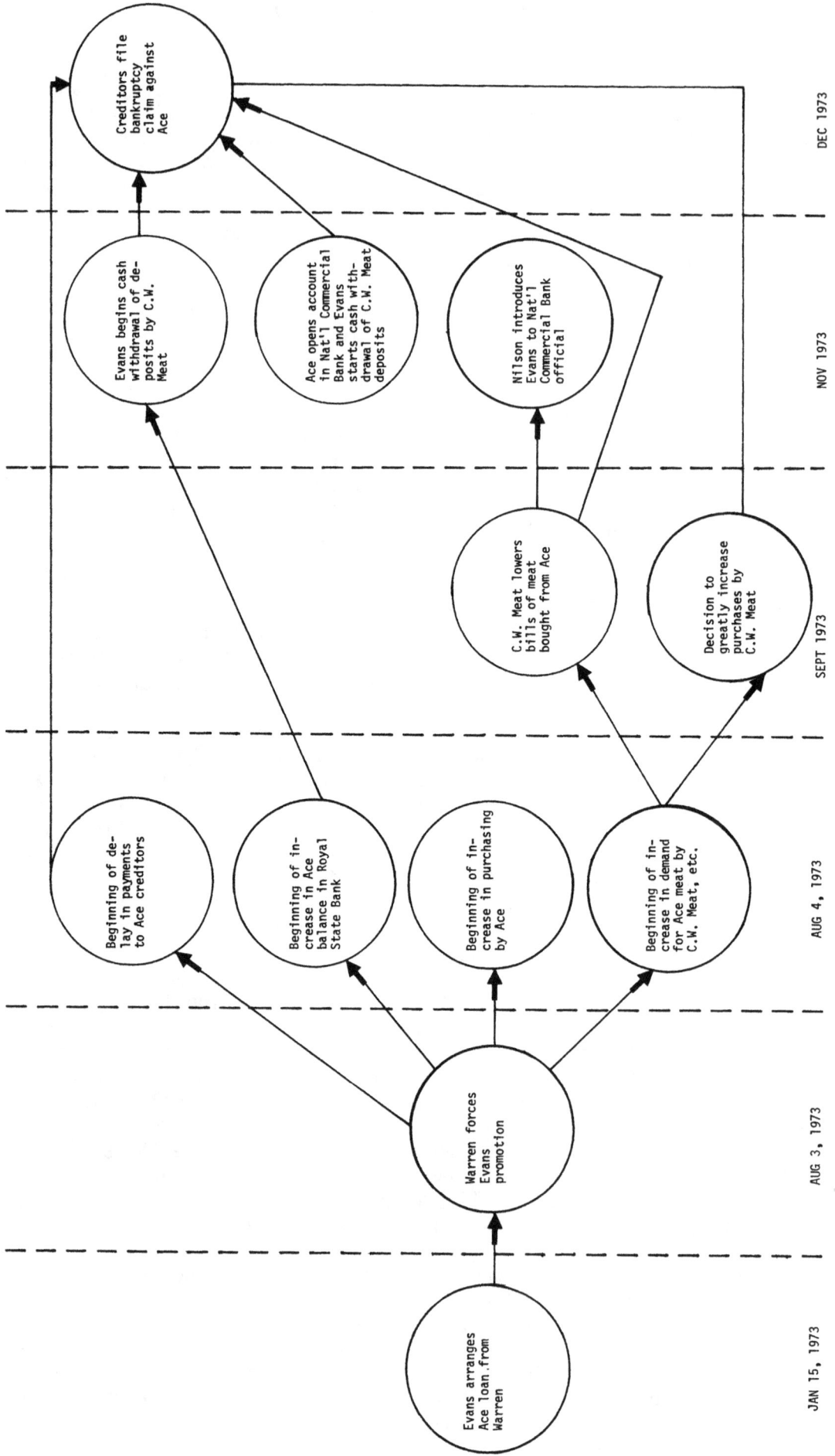

FIGURE 4. DIAGRAM DEPICTING TIME FLOW OF EVENTS IN A BANKRUPTCY FRAUD

88

7. The Flow of Information When Cases Are Closed

Once a full investigation is underway, an investigator or his supervisor may judge that a decision has to be made about whether to continue the investigation. A decision to continue can be made by the investigator himself, but should be subject to the approval of his supervisor. In his weekly log, he should indicate to the supervisor that this is his judgment, and should also give his reasons. If he has been working with a prosecutor as part of a team, the decision should be made jointly. If the team has been formally designated as one, then the supervisor to whom the team reports should have first say.

If a case is closed, notice of this should be placed in the files or in the computer. However, the investigative file should be turned over by the investigator to the unit's storage file of investigations, with its location indicated in the relevant file. The investigative information may be needed at some time in the future.[48] When cases are closed after court action, the investigative file should similarly be placed in the unit's storage files. It is generally desirable to write to the complaining witness or referring agency informing them of the outcome of the case.

H. PERSONNEL SELECTION

White-collar crime units have to face problems which are different from those faced by other types of law enforcement and even other types of investigative units. They must deal with more complex legal and investigative issues, more sophisticated criminals, more intricate and extended investigations, and far more in the way of alternative remedies, i.e., criminal, civil, regulatory, or mediational. Thus, in addition to the usual procedure for recruiting and selecting personnel, there needs to be considerable attention given to the special requirements of white-collar crime investigative units. In this section, these special requirements are discussed, but the usual selection procedures of law enforcement agencies are assumed to be used, such as background checks to ascertain the degree of integrity and the absence of a criminal record; physical examination; evaluations of mental health; and general intelligence. These selection devices should be used not only because of their own importance, but also to enable the unit and its recruits to gain and retain stature in the eyes of other parts of its parent agency, of the public, and of its own personnel. Recruits who meet the normal standards for law enforcement personnel would then view themselves as being full citizens of the parent agency and as being potentially eligible for a higher position in that agency.

Nevertheless, these general selection criteria should be used in conjunction with the special criteria needed to select good investigative candidates. These special criteria for the selection of

---

[48]See Chapter III, at pp. 101-102.

candidates can be divided into four types: motivation; personal attributes; professional investigative experience; and general knowledge and skill. These are discussed in turn below.

1. Motivation

White-collar crime investigations are often complex, long lasting, and frustrating. To overcome all of the obstacles in his or her way, the investigator needs to be highly motivated with respect to this type of crime. Catching a white-collar criminal should be a very important personal goal for the investigator, not just a part of the job. If it is only part of the job and not a personal goal, the investigator will not persist, will run roughshod over details, and will not use his or her imagination to detect new types of schemes. More than in most law enforcement areas, there are excuses and alibis for failure.

The requisite motivation can be generated by the unit itself. It may be so dedicated, its leadership so dynamic, its morale so high that even an originally indifferent investigator may become highly motivated. Daily contact with a group of enthusiastic fellow workers is likely to engender genuine enthusiasm among the new investigators. And such enthusiasm can feed on itself, since it will enhance the chances of successful investigations. Furthermore, as the investigator encounters new types of white-collar crimes and victims on the job or in training, his motivation may be increased.

Nevertheless, the level of motivation of the personnel of a unit can be positively affected if new investigators are selected on the basis of their personal motivation to work on white-collar crime. Self-starters are more likely to be good investigators in this field. This self-starting motivation can stem from a variety of sources. The individual might have been a victim himself, someone close to him might have been a victim, or he might have been a member of an organization which was victimized, such as a police charity. He may have a particular concern for certain types of victims, such as members of minority groups or the elderly. Some patrol officers may have developed particular sensitivity to certain types of victims because they are heavily represented in their patrol area. A person might have worked in a business which was victimized. The extra push that the investigator who is angry from the beginning can provide should be very valuable to an agency.

This personal motivation may frequently lead a person to be particularly concerned with a certain type of crime. Concern for old people could lead to focusing on home repair frauds. Having been a victim of a land fraud can lead to motivation to target in on certain types of suspects. For some units, such delimited goals among investigators may be a great advantage, since the unit may share these goals, and the investigator may make a unique contribution to the unit. However, in other units, such narrow focus may be inappropriate because of the goals of the unit or because the unit needs investigators who can work effectively in a variety of areas. In such instances, a somewhat less "angry' person might sometimes be a better candidate, since he may be more flexible in his goals.[49]

---

[49]Concern for victims, while a highly desirable attribute, should be balanced by recognition of the need to deal appropriately with offender conduct. See p. 43.

In order to determine whether a person has the requisite motivation, the best way would be to interview the candidate in a relaxed setting in which he would be encouraged to talk about his professional goals and aspirations. The candidate can first be asked about his general professional, long-range goals, without any hint in the question about white-collar crime. If he spontaneously talks about his feelings about catching white-collar criminals, if he shows some strong feelings about doing so, if he indicates that his personal experience or experiences of people close to him have given rise to this motivation, this should be regarded as a plus factor. Of course, if the particular direction of his motivation, if the type of crime he is most interested in, is also one in which the agency needs more investigators, then the candidate would be even more desirable.

If the candidate does not affirmatively raise the subject of his interest in white-collar crime, this should not be a disqualifying factor. A candidate's response to discussion of white-collar crime, initiated by the interviewer, should be closely watched to see if he or she responds with eager interest. Once focused on the subject, the good candidate will usually be able to give some indication of personal awareness of the problem, make some reference to a personally known victim, or refer to some aspect of his or her own background or experience which is particularly relevant.

If the candidate does not show any of these signs of personal motivation in this area, then questions should be raised about his or her qualifications. The open questions, such as those described above, are more useful than those which even subtly indicate the type of answer that the interviewer is seeking by mentioning white-collar crime, even indirectly, such as asking why the interviewee is interested in working in the particular agency or unit.

Another related type of question that can be asked in an interview concerns the candidate's reactions to previously held jobs. The interviewer can have a list of the candidate's previous jobs and ask the candidate what the candidate liked and didn't like about each of the jobs. Again, a spontaneous mentioning of anything indicating interest in fighting white-collar crime would be a positive sign. Answers to this question could also be very relevant to the personal attributes which are needed in investigators and which are described below.

2. Personal Attributes

White-collar crime investigators should have special qualities of diligence, patience, and persistence. These qualities are essential since white-collar crime investigations often take a long time to complete, require a tremendous amount of leg work, and are very slow to culminate in actual arrests. A person with a strong need to get results now would make a poor white-collar crime investigator. The person's degree of diligence would best be determined from a person's history both professionally and educationally. An individual who has worked at jobs which require unusual persistence in the face of frustration, who has not grasshoppered around, should be selected. During the personal interview, the candidate should be asked exactly what his responsibilities were in his previous jobs, how much time he spent on certain types of tasks, what types of work he has found most attractive, and what aspects of his previous jobs he found most interesting.

A second quality is that the person should tend to enjoy and value "headwork" in contrast to "muscle work." He needs to have the ability to think through a problem, to be able to sit at a desk reading reports, documents, records; to spend time talking to people; and to spend time just thinking. This quality might take the form of motivation to match wits with the criminal; finding satisfaction in the use of the mind in trying to catch the criminal. It might take the form of a certain flexibility of mind, a kind of suspicious imagination. He should not need to be close to the action, to ride around and interact with citizens on the street, to pursue and catch street criminals. To be precise, a white-collar investigator is not necessarily someone who is more or less intelligent than other law enforcement personnel, but he does need to be someone who is willing and able to sit back and use his mind.

The presence of this quality can be determined in part from the person's work record and reports of the style of his work in his previous jobs. Candidates who have worked in military intelligence, for example, might be specially qualified. Also those have sought to continue their education are highly likely to have the required qualities. Psychological tests might prove very valuable, but should be selected and administered by psychological test experts, including those in the parent agency's personnel department. As mentioned in the section on motivation of candidates, above, they should be asked to indicate their professional goals. Not only will the content and manner of answering this question indicate something about these goals, but will also indicate how much value the candidate places on the needed type of "head work."

A third quality which is in part an outgrowth of the one previously cited is the ability to do detailed paperwork, to search through documents and records for small bits of information, to put bits and pieces of information from separate sources together, to look for information which might be in obscure places, to remember details almost automatically and keep complete and accurate records of detailed information. This ability might be determined from a person's work record, or by the use of tests of clerical ability.

A fourth quality useful for investigators is the ability to communicate with and size up a wide range of people under a wide range of circumstances. The investigator should be one who can deal easily with many different kinds of people, from businessmen and professional people in their own offices, to ghetto residents, to smooth-talking con men, to elderly crime victims. Although some investigators might specialize in dealing with one or more of these types of people, he still needs to be someone who is not easily hoodwinked by them, but at all times has the social adeptness to be able to relate to them in an inoffensive way. He should be someone who can walk into a corporate vice-president's office and meet people there eye-to-eye and not blink. Some of these abilities can be learned, as will be indicated in the section on Training,[50] but it is obvious that an investigator who comes by these qualities "naturally" should be more effective in the long run.

Because of the need for investigators with a variety of backgrounds, white-collar crime units have the most practical of reasons to be "equal opportunity employers." Recruiting qualified candidates from among groups often reflected in the victim populations, e.g., women, blacks, Asian-Americans, Chicanos, Native Americans, as investigators, will make it easier to communicate and work with these groups in white-collar crime enforcement efforts and to relate to groups of victims who might otherwise be overlooked.

3. Background Contacts

As we indicate above,[51] it is important that an investigative agency maintain personal contacts with a range of governmental and private agencies. The formal contact may not be enough to maintain proper communications among the agencies. One way of establishing such personal contacts is simply to recruit people who have worked in or with other agencies. For example, a person who has worked in a military intelligence unit, or the FBI, SEC, or Postal Inspection Service, might be of great value to a local law enforcement agency. A person who has worked in a Better Business Bureau, or a Call-for-Action might have special leads or contacts. A person who has worked in a particularly vulnerable industry like real estate or nursing homes might also be quite useful. Sometimes street detectives who have worked a commercial or similar area might have close contacts with local businessmen, bankers, etc. Such contacts are difficult to build up after the person has started working in an agency, so that recruiting people with such contacts would be very valuable to a unit. People who have retired from these organizations while still having many working years left might be especially desirable candidates.

4. Knowledge and Skill

The special needs and resources of a white-collar crime investigative unit suggest some of the requirements of knowledge and skill among its personnel. Some units may be mandated by law to cover only a narrow range of white-collar crimes, such as securities fraud. Such specialized units need personnel with appropriately focused capabilities. Other units need to have a range or variety of investigative capabilities because of their more general legal jurisdiction over a broad range of white-collar crimes. Such generalist units should be not be hampered by an intractable narrow focusing of their capabilities; unit personnel, either collectively or individually, need to have the knowledge and skill to deal with diverse types of white-collar crime.

---

[50] See Appendix A, Training for White-Collar Crime Enforcement, pp. 261-263

[51] See the earlier discussion, "Relationships with Other Agencies," pp. 53-58.

Both generalist and specialist units need to develop appropriate skills and knowledge among their personnel and can do so in any of the following ways. First, personnel can be selected because of their ability to acquire new knowledge and learn about new businesses; for example, a specialist unit may train its recruits in the area in which they focus. Second, personnel can be sent to training situations to develop this diversity; for example, a generalist agency can select its personnel because they each have knowledge of a variety of business crimes. In this case, each investigator is a wide-ranging specialist. Third, each person recruited can be selected because of a particular special knowledge of a certain industry, business, victim population, white-collar crime area, etc.; a generalist unit can accordingly be made up of specialist investigators.

In many, if not most instances, a person should be selected primarily for his personal attributes, motivations, and the ability to acquire new knowledge rather than primarily for the knowledge of a particular business. If the candidate is a good investigator type, this knowledge can be gained later. However, if knowledgeable candidates already have these personal attributes and abilities, so much the better.

(a) Recruitment of Specialist Investigators. The type of skill and knowledge to be recruited for specialist units is dictated by the explicit goals of the agency. Their areas of specialization can be real estate fraud, consumer fraud, investment fraud, tax fraud, automobile repair fraud, home repair fraud, welfare fraud, medical fraud, etc. Other units may specialize in certain victim target populations, such as the elderly and minority groups. In the latter case they need to know the typical patterns of victimization and special needs of such groups.

Generalist units have, however, a number of issues to consider when they seek to hire specialist investigators. The decisions as to which subject matter areas merit special emphasis should be made partly on the basis of current areas of complaints and referrals, but also on the basis of long-range planning, that is, anticipation that there might be considerable white-collar crime in an area in which only minimal complaints or other reports have yet been received. If the unit has a pro-active philosophy, it might recruit personnel to start looking into such areas. For example, with the increase in the proportion of the population which is retired can come an increase in crimes against the elderly, such as nursing home frauds, retirement land frauds, medical frauds, etc. A unit would need to be ready for these trends even before the criminals start operating in the field,[52] and would therefore start recruiting personnel who have the relevant expertise. These might be medical administrators or real estate regulatory agency personnel, for example.

There is, however, a great danger in recruiting all of the personnel of a generalist unit in this way, because of the very fact

_____

[52]The implications of responding to such trends are discussed in Chapter VI, at pp. 216-221.

mentioned earlier, namely, that white-collar crimes continually appear in new variations. Thus, an office needs to have at least some people who are "born generalists," who have the bent of mind to move into new areas. If an agency has this capacity, it will not be caught flatfooted by a sudden increase in a type of white-collar crime for which it has not been able to prepare by the recruitment of specialized personnel, as suggested above.

It will be helpful to examine the backgrounds of personnel already part of the parent organization, who can be transferred to the investigative unit. Many police officers, for example, have side interests or interests previous to becoming officers which may not be apparent in the usual personnel records. Many will have had business experience, or will have gained a relevant formal education. Police departments have had investigators with building contractor licenses, real estate brokerage licenses, licenses as public accountants, years of experience as auto mechanics, to mention only a few such backgrounds. Some even continue to be active in their fields on a moonlighting basis after they start working in the investigative agencies. Some have gained an education in certain areas, such as B.A. degree in Marketing, or a Master's degree in Business Administration.

There are substantial advantages to recruitment of personnel from within the parent agency. Such personnel can more readily be accepted in the investigative unit; may have personal contacts within the organization and knowledge of it which can be very valuable later. The recruitment process is made much cheaper, since background information has already been accumulated, and evaluation of present performance can be readily obtained. The recruits may have other skills which are useful to the investigative unit. There are, however, some disadvantages: the unit in the parent agency which loses the person may be hurt; the transferred personnel may bring some investigative approaches to the unit which are undesirable, such as proneness to make arrests early in the investigative process, to be careless about paperwork, or to be overly blunt in dealing with people. However, a sufficient concern for the necessary personal attributes as described above should compensate for this disadvantage.

When recruiting from outside the agency, certain types of expertise should be among the required qualifications for the position. In some cases, experience in a specific industry, with a given victim-prone population, such as a minority group, or with a given investigative technique, such as accounting, may be made explicit. Notice of the recruitment might be sent to specialized agencies, such as consumer protection agencies or those working with securities, banking, or housing frauds. Some personnel may have worked in other law enforcement agencies which have special responsibilities, such as the F.D.A., bunco squads, forgery squads, or other police departments.

One potential problem which could be particularly troublesome in a white-collar unit is "moonlighting," because it can create conflicts with respect to the use of time and conflicts of interest. Therefore, in recruiting care should be taken to ensure that potential recruits are not misled on this point.

(b) <u>A Unit Consisting of Generalists</u>. Smaller units, particularly those in less populous jurisdictions, will need to recruit personnel who can investigate a variety of different types of white-collar crime. Such generalist investigators would have many of the personal traits cited above for investigators, but their motivation to catch white-collar criminals, although very high, would not be as narrowly focused as in the case of some specialist investigators. Furthermore, they need to be quick learners who can master new areas of business and of crime rapidly. On occasion, of course, even the specialist investigators need to shift to new areas, but even in large agencies consisting of specialists a few generalists would be valuable to respond to new types of crimes.

The recruiter should therefore most diligently seek to determine the candidate's aptitude for quickly acquiring new information and for its conceptualization; this determination can be based on a number of factors, including but not limited to the candidate's learning record in school and by other tests administered by the parent agency personnel division.

Generalists can be recruited in the same fashion as the specialists, but it is more likely that they will be older and that they will have worked in a variety of investigative agencies, probably in federal or state government. People who have had a career of investigations in a variety of governmental agencies and retired military intelligence or criminal investigative personnel are likely to provide good recruits. Persons retired from other branches of the military are less likely than these groups to be promising candidates. A unit would be likely to find good general investigative skills from among police personnel, homicide, arson and organized crime investigators. Effective investigative journalists often have some of the same skills as good general investigators. Another source would be people with advanced and broad business education, for example, with Master in Business Administration degrees. The unit should be cautious about recruiting people who have had a variety of direct business experience because they may have failed at each enterprise or because they may tend to be restless.

(c) <u>A Unit Consisting of Learners</u>. Units seeking generalists should seek people who can learn quickly, as mentioned above. However, units seeking specialists can also recruit effective learners, since they can acquire knowledge in the same area of agency jurisdiction and also rapidly acquire general investigative skills. Thus, people with a college background or similar adult educational achievement could be recruited not so much for their knowledge, but because of their demonstrated ability to learn. People who have fared well in other educational programs could also be recruited. Certain types of intelligence tests, those designed for adults like the Bellevue-Wechsler Adult Intelligence Scale,[53] could be used to screen recruits.

---

[53]The advice of an agency psychologist should be obtained before *selecting the particular tests to be used*.

In many instances an educational background which does not have any direct and obvious relevance to white-collar crime might in the long run turn out to be quite valuable to the unit. A background in economics, psychology, sociology, etc., could be helpful in dealing with certain types of crime and setting up the planning and evaluation units within the agencies. Training in these areas would be very valuable in setting up and running such units.

(d) <u>Unit Training</u>. All the types of personnel just described could benefit from training, even the specialists mentioned above could benefit from additional training, even if they continue to work in the same area as their specialities. Added training is highly likely to open up new possible approaches to their own areas of specialization.

* * * * *

How much each agency depends on recruitment and how much on training to develop the range of skills needed will obviously depend on the local situation, resources available, etc. However, a blend of all of the approaches described above is probably best in most cases. Such a blend would tend to maximize the range of skills and knowledge available in the agency, thus enabling it to better cope with the numerous varieties of white-collar crime.

III. THE USE OF INTELLIGENCE IN WHITE-COLLAR
CRIME ENFORCEMENT[54]

A. THE FUNCTIONS AND PURPOSE OF INTELLIGENCE

The use of intelligence information, whether through formal or informal processes, is an integral part of any investigative effort. Essentially, intelligence is the process by which new information is added to that already possessed and made available to operational personnel when and where they need it, to educate investigators, to detect crime, trigger investigations, and to positively affect the course and outcome of an investigation. The intelligence process may be limited to the store of knowledge in the heads of individual investigators where information on suspects and their activities is retained and accumulated. Alternatively, the process may be formalized and structured into an intelligence system in which the accumulated knowledge of many individuals is written down, pooled and shared. The latter is by far the more useful model.

The purpose of an intelligence system, then, is to serve investigators as the single, best source of accumulated information on specific offenders and their activities. The underlined words must be stressed. Too often, the intelligence process constitutes little more than an accumulation of information --- a formal dumping ground for disparate bits of data concerning individuals. No matter how formalized, such a process does not represent a bonafide intelligence system, for an intelligence system must be more than an accumulation of information. It must be the best available source of such information. And in order to be so, the system must have three basic characteristics. First, it must establish criteria by which information offered can be evaluated for inclusion. This is to prevent the inclusion of specious and unreliable information which would affect the reliance investigators can place in the system. Second, the system must have a basic organization and analytic structure into which information can be fitted and interpreted. Thus, new information should not merely be added to a system, but rather should be related to that already existing and serve to either augment, supercede, or invalidate previous knowledge. Finally, the system must have a well-defined protocol by which conflicting information is reconciled and out-dated or invalid information is purged. Maintenance and upkeep of an intelligence system must be continuous in order to assure that it remains the most reliable and accurate information source available.

The use of intelligence systems in white-collar crime enforcement is not as well-developed an art as in other enforcement areas. Partially this is because the white-collar offender has not attracted as much attention as have

---

[54]This section specifically focuses on white-collar crime unit intelligence For a more general discussion of operation of intelligence units, see Don R. Harris, Basic Elements of Intelligence, Rev'd. Ed., (Washington, D.C.: U.S. Government Printing Office, 1976).

traditional offenders, but it is also due in part to a misapprehension of the value of intelligence to white-collar crime enforcement. Brief consideration of the basic functions of intelligence, however, will demonstrate its usefulness in the white-collar crime area.

Intelligence has essentially three functions: identification; detection; and education. Each is discussed below.

1. The Identification Function of Intelligence

Probably the most frequent use of intelligence is for the purpose of identifying known and active offenders. By maintaining files that document the personal appearance characteristics, fingerprints and mug shots of such individuals, such systems attempt to quickly identify "whodunit" when particular events occur. In white-collar crime enforcement, however, the question of "whodunit" rarely needs to be asked. "Whodunit" is generally clear. The bigger questions are: what was done? (i.e., was a crime committed, or a civil wrong inflicted, or was there merely the exercise of poor judgment by a victim); to whom was it done? (i.e., how many victims are there, who is the victim); how was it done? (what specific acts, of what character and by whom made the events occur); and where was it done? (the jurisdictional issue). Each of these questions is interrelated to the others. For example, where a white-collar abuse takes place (i.e., whether in the province of federal or local authorities) may make the difference between its being a crime or a civil wrong. The number of victims may determine whether a criminal fraud or civil wrong can be proved, etc.[55]

The major point is that the identification function of intelligence is relatively less important in white-collar crime enforcement, being largely overshadowed by questions of greater significance. Agencies, then, which understand this and which are most familiar only with this function of intelligence are likely to disregard its usefulness in white-collar crime. To do so is to ignore the other functions of intelligence where its greatest promise lies for white-collar crime enforcement efforts.

2. The Detection Function of Intelligence

Closely related to identification is the detection function of intelligence Normally this function occurs as the result of structured surveillance efforts which record the movements and associates of offenders and thereby attempt to anticipate emerging criminal activities, head them off, or provide a basis for going forward in an investigation when anticipated events occur. For example, the reported sighting of two known safe burglars casing a jewelry exchange can result in staking out of the premises with the hope of intercepting the anticipated crime of burglary. Alternatively, the reported sighting, when combined with a subsequent burglary at such location, provides a firm basis for investigation of the crime.

---

[55]See Chapter IV, Conducting Investigations of White-Collar Crime, pp. 128-133.

Because the white-collar offender's activities are not so readily anticipated in detail, there is a tendency to overlook the value of the detection
function of intelligence vis-a-vis the white-collar offender. The mere
sighting of a known land fraud artist at a particular location does not have
the same informative power as in the burglary example described above. However,
such information when combined with a more generalized surveillance of the
economic and business environment may be powerful indeed. Thus newspaper
advertisements telling of fantastic property investments and announcing a
public meeting for interested investors may signal the need for specific
enforcement attention.

Intelligence systems which document the methods and means of white-
collar offenders allow investigators to interpret seemingly unrelated and/or
trivial events in proper perspective. Thus investigative significance can
be given to suspicious activities of unfamiliar subjects, as well as to those
of previously identified intelligence subjects --- a factor of substantial
importance in a crime area where criminals frequently operate through corporate or other business fronts. Investigators can be helped to determine
when altogether proper acts, such as the rental of office space, may really
be preparatory steps in the perpetration of a fraud. And most important,
a basis is provided on which the investigator's gut feelings of suspicion can
be focused, interpreted and acted upon.

3.   The Education Function of Intelligence

The education function of intelligence has two dimensions, those of
continuity and analytic power. Of the two, the continuity dimension is
probably best recognized and understood. It is quite clear, for example,
that a well-developed intelligence system provides a continuity to agency
functioning that would not exist otherwise. Thus, agencies which maintain
effective intelligence systems do not experience major informaton losses
on the death or retirement of active investigators. Instead, their
knowledge, expertise and experience is preserved for the use and benefit of
those who follow. Similarly, new investigators do not have to start at square
one in confronting major offenders, but rather can begin from a solid information base provided by those who preceded them.

The manner in which the education function of intelligence provides
analytic power is less well-appreciated, but is especially important in the
area of white-collar crime enforcement. As has been noted at many points in
this manual, white-collar crime is extremely complex. It cannot be capsulized
in a few statutory definitions nor can its scope and parameters be easily identified and studied. This is because white-collar crime is not a discrete set
of easily described acts but rather a vital and dynamic process by which theft
is subtly perpetrated. The intelligence objective, then, is to capture
the process in the vitality and dynamism of the activities of those known to
perpetrate white-collar crime. If this objective can be achieved it should be
possible not only to better anticipate the course of current activities but
to reconstruct events that have already taken place. Without a composite
source of information, a white-collar enforcement effort is poorly equipped
to face the white-collar offender or to interpret the widely varied schemes he
perpetrates.

4.   The Function and Purpose of Intelligence - A Summary

It is clear that a white-collar crime enforcement effort can benefit from
a sound intelligence system. This is particularly true when the education
and detection functions of intelligence are clearly understood and appreciated.
The discussion following provides guidelines for the design and content of a
white-collar crime intelligence system which can assist in assuring that such
a system conforms to the basic definition of being the single, best source of
accumulated information on white-collar crime.

B.   DESIGNING A WHITE-COLLAR CRIME INTELLIGENCE SYSTEM

The basic rule that should guide the design of a white-collar intelligence
system is that it be arranged for maximum utilization. Two features of a
white-collar intelligence system are likely to affect its use, and thus its
ultimate value. The first of these is the system's design. The simpler the
basic design of a white-collar intelligence system, the easier it is to develop
and maintain it and the more likely it will be to experience constant use.
Overly complex systems discourage use, taking more time to access properly than
the investigator has available, or too much time relative to the perceived
benefits offered.

The second feature relevant to the use a white-collar intelligence system
will receive is the extent to which it is directly and easily accessible to the
investigative effort it is designed to enhance. No matter how well designed
an intelligence system, if it is divorced from the investigative function
benefitting from it, it soon becomes little more than a repository for dust
rather than for vital information. Utilization is positively increased, then,
where an intelligence system is operated and maintained by the unit having
investigative and enforcement responsibility for the subjects about which it
is concerned. A white-collar intelligence effort, if it is to be undertaken
at all, must be made a functional responsibility of the white-collar crime
unit itself rather than integrated as part of a general intelligence function.

Those best able to make decisions about an intelligence system, then, are
its ultimate users. In this sense, textbook blueprints for intelligence files
can only provide ideas, not precise designs that will serve everyone best.
Still, there are some basic decisions that must be made in developing a
system that will affect its ultimate design. These are discussed below.

1.   Investigative versus Intelligence Files

Quite clearly, there is a difference between investigative and intelligence
files. Investigative files represent focused efforts linked to a specific crime
known or believed to have been committed. Intelligence files, on the other
hand, reflect general investigative efforts associated with an offender,
offender group or entity concerning illegal activities known or suspected over
a period of time. Obviously, investigative and intelligence efforts are related
to each other, but rarely are they filed together. Generally, investigative
units --- not just those concerned with white-collar crime --- maintain separate
investigations files both for the entire unit and by each investigator described

earlier.[56] In addition, the investigative work of a unit is filed historically
with separate places for investigations which are past and completed, those
closed, and those which are on-going. Intelligence files are also separately
maintained, generally using an alpha arrangement by the subject's name, but are
not subject to an historical separation through filing. Instead, intelligence
files are kept intact and made subject to update and purging procedures which
insure their maximum utility.

Investigative and intelligence functions cannot be independent of each
other. In fact, the strength of an intelligence system depends upon the
operational relationship it bears to investigative efforts and the extent to
which it is continuously updated to reflect the existence of new investigative
efforts which concern file subjects. An intelligence system divorced from
operational reality of an investigative unit may be a beautiful file, but
have little value. The point to remember is that, while the two efforts are
intertwined, rarely are the two files joined in one and a unit that decides to
develop an intelligence system must expect to have at minimum, two sets of
files.

2.   Who Should Be Subjects of Intelligence Files?

Another decision which will affect the design of an intelligence system
is the determination of who will and who will not be regarded as an
intelligence subject. This determination is critical from both a policy
and a utilization standpoint. With respect to policy, the criteria for entry
to an intelligence file may determine the legal permissibility of the activity
and the degree of privacy to be accorded the files. From a utilization perspective, the size of the file, as determined by the number of subjects, may
affect its value. Thus, too many listings may transform the intelligence files
into a garbage file or telephone book rather than a useful investigative tool.

Several questions should be answered by a unit developing a white-collar
crime intelligence system:

- Will all offenders who have been the subject of an investigation
  be included in the intelligence system?

- Will all offenders who have been the subject of a complaint
  be included in the intelligence system?

- Will offenders who have not been the subject of official
  action by the unit be included in the intelligence system?

- If the answer to any or all of the above is no, what criteria
  will be used to decide whether subjects are to be included
  in the intelligence file?

There are no pat answers to these questions. Some units may decide to make
all subjects of investigations a part of the intelligence file, but to exclude
subjects of complaints that do not lead to investigations. Others may require
that a series of complaints be received against an offender or group before

---

[56]See pp. 71-81.

inclusion in the intelligence system. Still others may make a qualitative decision to include subjects on the basis of the scheme alleged and harm done to victims regardless of official disposition of a case. Once again, the major point to be made is that this decision-making process must be thought through and anticipated and clear guidelines established. Agency legal counsel should be consulted with respect to these issues, since they are currently the subject of substantial legislative and judicial attention.

3. How Comprehensive Will the Intelligence File Be?

Closely related to who will be the subject of an intelligence file is the nature and comprehensiveness of materials contained in that file. Beyond policy and utilization questions noted above, office space may affect the number and size of files that are possible for the unit. Lack of space may require that a central filing system include as much information as possible, regardless of qualitative differences existing between file entries.

Where space is not a particular problem an important design question arises concerning the comprehensiveness of a central intelligence file versus reliance on supplementary files for additional information. Usually supplementary files are specialized and contain only one type of information, a mugshot file or an alias file, for example. The burden introduced by the use of supplementary files is that they must be cross-referenced with the relevant central files. The advantages of supplemental files are that many "dead" entries (in the sense of mere cross-references) can be eliminated from a central file; that they are relatively easy to update and maintain; and that they permit specific information searches to be done in specialized files rather than requiring entry to a large and more general central file.

Some units prefer to maintain a separate alias file, for example, where a name can be quickly searched and reference to a central file discovered. Others feel that the several steps involved in such a process discourages file use. Once again, the decision on central file comprehensiveness is best made by those who will use the system. There is no right answer, and unit preference should prevail.

4. A Simple Intelligence System Design

Once the above decisions have been made, it should be stressed that they need not be cast in stone. Indeed a unit will certainly want to modify its system once it has had some experience with it. Flexibility should be built into the system.

The intelligence system described in this chapter is a simple one. It is one designed to be well within the capacity of even the smallest of units and does not envision implementation within any specific agency structure. It is based on the assumption that a unit will need at least three sets of files: investigations files (past, closed and on-going); a complaint file (past, closed

and on-going); and a central intelligence file.[57] It does, however, also
allow for the situation in which supplementary alias, business name, mugshot
or other files may also be used as part of an integrated intelligence system.
Since it is expected that both investigations and complaint files will have
a predetermined format, the discussion following focuses on the intelligence
file itself and the intersection of this file with these other files. The
design presented here uses a mastercard as the cover sheet(s) for the central
intelligence file and therefore calls this file a mastercard file. The idea
behind the mastercard is that it provides summary offender information to a
user of the system without requiring him or her to wade through an entire
file. It also allows, as will be discussed, for several arrangement options of
the central file. Although most of the discussion following concerns information necessary to the mastercard itself, the kinds of information indicated
also reflect the major content of its accompanying file.

C. INFORMATIONAL INPUTS OF A WHITE-COLLAR INTELLIGENCE SYSTEM

White-collar offenders present great potential as intelligence subjects
but that does not make development of an intelligence system regarding them
and their activities an easy task. This is because although the white-collar
thief has a well-developed and defined manner of operating, his basic scheme
is subject to innumerable variations. This makes his activities far more
challenging to probe than those of the average thief. There may, for example,
be only a limited number of ways to gain entry to a premises, or to open a
safe, but the ways in which an advance fee scheme may be perpetrated are
limited only by the imagination of the perpetrator. Because white-collar
offenders are capable of a large number of "variations on a theme," the com-
pilation and analysis of information regarding them can be complex indeed.

At the same time, however, there is a simplicity to the activities of
the white-collar thief that derives primarily from the fact that the offender
himself is an important component of his modus operandi. Whether it be the
studied glibness of the swindler, the unrelenting persuasiveness of the con-
man, or the manipulative influence peddling of the corrupt public official,
the personal characteristics of the white-collar offender play an important
role in advancing his activities. As such, they become distinct and unmistakable hallmarks of his activities regardless of how many variations on a theme
he perpetrates. They are the composite of what might be called his "style."

Because style is something of an indefinable quality, it is easy to com-
plicate it. But to do so is to miss the realization that the white-collar
thief's style is his least changing feature and the one quality easiest to
learn about him. The simplicity of style for many such offenders is often
their most marked characteristic and the one by which their handiwork is best
recognized.

---

[57]It should be noted that the mastercard file described below can con-
solidate and perform some of the same functions as the files described in
Chapter II, Section G, Information Process Flow, at pp. 71-81.

But how does one communicate "style," particularly for intelligence purposes? The first step is to understand what style really is, for it is nothing more than the personal application of available tools to effect a particular fraud or deception. Knowing the tools of the white-collar offender, then, when combined with a knowledge of how and to or against whom they are used, constitutes a good, substantive definition of his style.

Even a relatively simple intelligence system relevant to the white-collar offender must take into account both the complexity of his activities and the simplicity of style. The mastercard file system suggested here is designed to do this. It includes a front sheet with a summary profile of the offender or offenders in question (the Mastercard) and indicates other files in which more detailed information is available. The specific items discussed below should be included in summary form on the mastercard and can be treated more extensively in the master file itself. At minimum, the mastercard and its accompanying file should contain the following kinds of inputs: 1) information bearing on usual or primary fraudulent activity; 2) information bearing on personal background and characteristics; and 3) information beraing on style of operating. Each of these is discussed below.

1.   Fraudulent Activity of the Offender or Offender Group

A key item in a mastercard intelligence system is an indication of the dominant fraudulent scheme or activity in which a white-collar offender or offender group engages. Generally, this item will consist of a broad categorization of the type of crime preferred by the white-collar thief. It might, for example, consist of a notation such as advance fee schemes, land fraud, bait advertising, repair fraud, etc. Under this heading, additional information relating to known variations of a general scheme used by the offender should be included together with a notation indicating the source of the information and/or where additional information may be available. Thus, for a land fraud operator, an entry covering dominant scheme or activity might be prepared as follows:

DOMINANT SCHEME: Land Fraud

KNOWN VARIATIONS	SOURCE OF INFO	ADDITIONAL INFO AVAILABLE
Investment Opportunities (Maine seacoast properties)	Prior investigation - J. Cronin, Investigator	I - file #2967
"Retirement paradises" (southwest desert sites)	John Rodgers, N.Y. Atty. Gen. Office	Correspondence file under "Rodgers"

In this example, the offender's variations of land fraud schemes are characterized by the manner in which he presents them to potential victims, i.e., as an investment opportunity. Similarly, the bait used to lure victims is indicated, here "Maine seacoast properties." In the second item, the language used by the offender to describe his bait, i.e., "retirement paradises" is used in the file since it best characterizes the scheme and may be used again in the future.

The first line item above is identified as having been the subject of a prior investigation of the unit generating the file. The user of the file is told not only who the previous investigator was but is also directed to an investigations file (I-file) for additional information. The second line item consists of information received from another agency and directs the user to a correspondence file for additional information. In both cases, the mastercard entry attempts to communicate <u>basic</u> information clearly and concisely while at the same time assisting the user in acquiring additional information. This is the function of the mastercard system since it avoids having an investigator read through voluminous notations on a subject in whom he is not interested; rapid access to the major activity of the offender and known variations used should enable the investigator to easily determine whether or not the subject noted is one in which he has an interest.

2. Personal Characteristics and Background of the Offender

A second item integral to a white-collar offender mastercard file relates to the personal characteristics and background of the offender. Because the white-collar thief often confronts his victim directly or is well-known to the investigator, personal appearance data is usually available and can be given in some detail. Minor changes in personal appearance can and should also be noted, such as the addition of a mustache or glasses, for example. Generally, the white-collar offender does not attempt to disguise himself, so that while his activities may change his basic appearance can be expected to remain constant. Thus, it is often on the basis of victim descriptions of the offender that new entries to the above category, i.e., "dominant scheme or activity," can be made.

The background of the white-collar offender can also provide useful information to the investigator. Depending upon the nature of the offender (an ad hoc or abuse of trust violator, for example), he is likely to have roots in the community and be employed. Where his scheme relates to his employment or business, information relating to his business affiliations will be helpful. In the first instance (where the white-collar thief is an employee), such information may identify individuals who may be usefully interviewed in an investigation. Where he owns a business, the nature of the offender's business may suggest additional remedies as against an offender, such as the seeking of an injunction against his pursuit of specific business practices.

But even if the white-collar offender is not rooted in one place, he may have a background of employment which contributes to his skill as an offender. Prior experience as an insurance salesman, for example, may equip to advantage a white-collar thief engaged in investment swindling.

Knowing the specific skills of the offender (which he may have legitimately acquired) may explain not only the schemes in which he is likely to engage but also the tactics to which he may revert in perpetrating them. Legitimately acquired skills, then, may constitute an important element of the white-collar thief's "style" providing him with the language and mien of a reputable profession or occupation.

Master file card information relating to the personal characteristics and background of the white-collar offender should include such entries as the following:

PERSONAL CHARACTERISTICS & BACKGROUND:

DOB:

RACE/SEX:

HEIGHT: WEIGHT: EYES: HAIR:

VOICE TONE:

MANNER:

CHANGES IN APPEARANCE:

[Include mugshot or refer to mugshot file #.]

PLACE OF BIRTH:

LKA: PERMANENT ADDRESS:

BUSINESS ADDRESS:

BUSINESS OR OCCUPATION:

PRIOR EMPLOYMENT HISTORY:

KNOWN SKILLS OR PROFESSIONAL COMPETENCE:

KNOWN ASSOCIATES: [Should include financial associations, if member of gang should indicate position within gang.]

---

3. The Offender's Style

A final component important for inclusion in a mastercard file for a white-collar intelligence system concerns the "style" of the offender. We said earlier that style is really nothing more than the personalized application of a particular scheme or fraud. Style can still, however, be a difficult offender characteristic for an intelligence system to verbalize and communicate. In characterizing the white-collar offender's style, then, it is helpful to describe those modus operandi components contributing to it. We will describe four here as illustrative of the style of white-collar criminal activities. There are undoubtedly others that the experienced investigator may add or find useful and revealing. The four style elements described below are: (a) the legitimate tools used by the offender to initiate and consumate his scheme; (b) the illegitimate tools used by the offender; (c) the characteristics of the victims against whom he acts; and (d) the approach he uses to identify and contact said victims.

(a) Legitimate Tools. White-collar offenders are often quite astute in the use of legitimate devices and tools to advance their schemes. Such a tactic produces two broad effects. First, the legitimacy of the tool or device itself often contributes to a false perception that the offender himself is reputable. Second, the use of tools which by themselves are not illegal often complicates the investigation of and case-building against the white-collar thief. The "stuff" of his crimes may be "legal," though the totality of his acts may be totally illegitimate. The summing up of individual, technically legal acts into an illegal whole is far more difficult for an investigator than is the documentation of individual, illegal acts in support of overt criminal activity.

The legitimate tools used by the white-collar offender will vary widely with his access to specific devices. A public official, for example, may have the capacity to utilize many of the trappings of his position (stationery, office space, etc.) to excude a facade of legitimacy to the activities he proposes. His use of such tools may even create the impression that his acts are "authorized" in some manner by those with greater position and power. Other white-collar offenders may use the good reputation of various trade journals, newspapers or other publications to advertise themselves, in this way banking on the potential victim's perception that the publication "vouches" for the advertisement's reputability.[58] Dishonest franchise peddlers may hold conferences in the best hotels in an attempt to create similar impressions. The rental of office space replete with all the "right" furniture, for example, implies a legitimacy to a business that may

---

[58]The _Wall St. Journal_ of October 19, 1976, for example, reported that the newspaper refused an advertisement touting business opportunities that had been submitted by Miller Pork Packers, Inc. The _Journal_ refused when it was learned that Miller's president was the sister of Tino De Angelis (mastermind of the Great Salad Oil Swindle 13 years ago) and that ad responses were to be sent to De Angelis' brother. _Wall St. Journal_, October 19, 1976, p. 1.

not in fact exist. The selection of an office suite itself may create an unassailable image of the operation located there. Having a prestigious or well-known business address can evoke an impression of reputability; as can location adjacent to a well-respected law firm, at such an address.

It should be noted that none of the above acts, i.e., the rental of office space, the leasing of a hotel for a conference, or advertising in a publication, is itself unlawful. And yet each may be a preparatory step in a white-collar thief's scheme, much like the casing of a premises (which can be a crime) is for the burglar. Many of these acts, however, signal the initiation of a scheme by the white-collar thief, reflecting a reapplication of his personal style of criminal behavior. And, because his style is well-studied and developed, such acts are likely to be characteristic indicators that he is on the move again.

(b) Illegitimate Tools. Not all white-collar offenders confine their activities to the use of legitimate tools. Often the white-collar thief will employ tactics that are themselves unlawful but may not be understood as such by the victim. For example, in a consumer fraud, customers seeking advertised bargains are conned into accepting a more costly substitute or the explanation that they were "too late" for the bargain --- though this device is now actionable as a fraudulent and deceitful sales tactic. Many con games rely on a naivete of the victim or a specific lack of such information on his or her part to successfully execute an illegal scheme.

Other white-collar offenders may illegally use the mails or offer investment opportunities in direct violation of state and federal law. In such cases, they may rely on the already-secured investment (i.e., monetary commitment) of the victim to avoid detection for the use of such tactics. Some victims may continue to hope against hope that their "investment" will eventually pay off and assist the offender in concealing his illegal acts. A style characteristic of many white-collar thieves is to draft victims into becoming their "tools." Similar to this situation is the one in which the original victim becomes a co-conspirator with the offender --- as in many public corruption cases.

Itemizing the many tools --- both lawful and unlawful --- employed by the white-collar offender is essential to building a complete picture of his operating style. It can also help in anticipating how he will proceed in the perpetration of future schemes. Similarly, where an offender's characteristic preparatory step is observed and recognized as such, his next move(s) can often be predicted. Knowing that the offender's unmistakable style is often merely a patterned invocation of a finite set of legal and illegal tools robs from the white-collar thief some of the "mystery" in which he likes to shroud his activites. It also tells the investigator that tedious and time-consuming though it may be, a careful cataloguing of the thief's tools and tactics will stand him in good stead vis-a-vis the white-collar offender.

(c) <u>The victim profile</u>. The white-collar thief is a predator and as
such, an important component of his style of operating is the nature of the
victim on which he preys. Building a profile of the characteristic victim of
an offender becomes, then, an important element in any intelligence system
seeking to control him. Often the white-collar thief's victims consist of a
definable class based upon their business or occupation rather than their
personal attributes. For example, many investment frauds are aimed at physicians and other professional men seeking income tax shelters. Other white-
collar crime schemes may aim their activities at groups of victims who share
a common attribute or station in life. Retirees or those near retirement age
may be prime targets for fraudulent land investment operators. The examples
are numerous. The point is, however, that choosing certain particular kinds
of victims is a part of the white-collar thief's style, and essential to
development of an intelligence profile which will be of practical use to the
investigator.

(d) <u>Approach to the victim</u>. Closely related to the choice of victim
in determining the white-collar offender's operating style is the offender's
manner of making an approach to the victim. Often the initial overture is
impersonally made by employing some of the legal or illegal tools noted
above. Such an overture may generate victim self-selection by requiring the
victim to perform an act that insures further contact (sending back a request
for information, for example) or resulting in a direct seeking of the offender
by the victim. In other instances, the offender may make a direct, personal
overture to the victim utilizing various tools in a sales pitch-type of
technique. He may show the victim impressive looking brochures and phony
endorsements by prominent individuals. He may show copies of trade journal
ads and construe his visit as a follow-up contact that he believes the victim
to have requested. Often, then, the style of the offender is a combination
not only of the tools he uses but also of the order in which he invokes
their use in his approach to the victim.

In some cases a victim's anonymous participation in a public event can
be the basis for future contact. Nominal admission fees to a large gathering, for example, can provide the offender with names of individuals who can
be "followed-up" in some manner. They may be told that they were "specially
selected" to participate in a rare opportunity. The opportunity presented to
them may be distant in time and nature from the substance of the gathering in
which their names were acquired, making the approach to the victim a tortuous
route to probe. The more complex the route, however, the more distinctive it
will be as a stylistic trademark of the offender's mode of operating.

4. <u>The Mastercard File--A Summary</u>

Intelligence mastercards containing summary information relating to an
offender's dominant scheme (and variations), personal characteristics, and
operating style should be attached as cover sheets to intelligence files and
arranged alphabetically according to subject name. Where the subject of
intelligence is a group rather than an individual, the common group name should
be used as the mastercard heading. Prominent individuals in the group can also
be listed separately but should be cross-indexed with the group's mastercard
file.

Although the subject's name represents the file card heading, information concerning dominant scheme or activity should appear on master cards before personal information. This will allow arrangement of files by types of fraud if that is preferred, with alphabetical filing within each type. For example, a file might contain a section labeled "Advance Fee Operators" followed by an alpha card file of appropriate subjects. A later section of the file might be labeled "Land Fraud" and be followed by a similar alpha listing. Some units prefer to handle types of frauds or crimes by a supplementary file and leave the mastercard file intact with one alpha arrangement of all subjects.

A mastercard file can include cross-reference sheets noting all aliases or business names used by white-collar subjects. Alternatively, a unit can limit such additional references by using supplemental alias and business name files to deal with the issue separately and avoid overburdening the mastercard system. In the first instance, the mastercard file might contain an entry for the subject under his true name followed by AKA "_____" indicating all known aliases. Separate entries would cross reference each alias followed by: TRUE NAME "_____" and refer the reader to that mastercard. In the second situation, the mastercard would be filed under the true name and refer to the alias file in which all other known or suspected aliases would be listed. Business names should be treated in a manner consistent with that used for aliases.

As discussed above, the sources of information on the subject's scheme or variations should be noted. This is particularly true where such sources are previous investigations. Where the subject has been a suspect because of prior activities but an investigation was not initiated, it will be helpful to include such information. Often this can be done by referring to a complaints file in which the suspect is noted.

Personal data are rather straightforward items for the mastercard file. In addition to those noted earlier, units might want to include summary arrest history information although that is usually more appropriately included in the file rather than on the mastercard.

Style characteristics related to legal and illegal tools used by the offender can be handled several ways. Pre-printed cards might list examples of tools to be checked off appropriately, with an open ended "other" listing. What is likely to be more useful, however, is to allow ample space in which tools and tactics can be listed. This will allow for additions to be made and supplemental notes to be included when appropriate. Victim profiles and approaches should be similarly handled.

Below are reproduced sample mastercard file entries. All names and information are fictitious as this is merely an illustration. The entries shown reflect the most complex entry situation for such a file, one in which a group and individuals with aliases associated with that group are noted. Four cards are presented. Items on each card that are starred indicate where supplemental files may be used. Sample cards for several such additional files are found in Figures 9 and 10.

FIGURE 5. MASTER CARD FOR OFFENDER GROUP

MASTER CARD #007

SUBJECT: Anderson Enterprises   AKA "Enterprise Associates," etc. OR (See Bus.
name File #316)**
    SEE ALSO: Anderson, Edward (MC #004), Martinson, Andrew (MC #142)

DOMINANT SCHEME: Advance Fee

KNOWN VARIATIONS	INFO SOURCE	ADDITIONAL INFO

SUSPECT VIA COMPLAINTS:

# COMPLAINTS	TYPE OF COMPLAINT	DISPOSITION

BACKGROUND & CHARACTERISTICS:

    MUG SHOT: Include mugshots or reference to mugshot file #s** for group members

    BUSINESS ADDRESS: List all business names and addresses or reference to
business name file.**

STYLE:

    LEGAL TOOLS: Read local business directories; Ads placed in business publications looking for financing.

    ILLEGAL TOOLS: False references. Brochures misrepresenting accomplishments in securing financing. Sequences of form letters to lull victims or delay complaints.

    VICTIM PROFILE: Businessmen seeking financing for expansion of inventory or facilities; or to tide over business crisis period.

    VICTIM APPROACH: Representation that fee is contingent on achievement of desired financing; demand for partial advance on ultimate fee (with or without guaranty of advance in event of non-performance).

FIGURE 6. MASTER CARD FOR OFFENDER IN GROUP

MASTER CARD #004

SUBJECT: Anderson, Edward   AKA   "Kansas City Ted" or alias file #2075**
                                          (MC #007)
        SEE ALSO: Anderson Enterprises
DOMINANT SCHEME: Advance Fee

KNOWN VARIATIONS	INFO SOURCE	ADDITIONAL INFO

SUSPECT VIA COMPLAINTS:

# COMPLAINTS	TYPE OF COMPLAINT	DISPOSITION

BACKGROUND & CHARACTERISTICS:

DOB: 11/4/19   PLACE OF BIRTH: Wilton, Missouri

RACE/SEX: White/Male   HAIR: Grey   EYES: Blue/Grey

MUG SHOT: (Or ref. to file #)**   APPEARANCE CHANGES: None

VOICE/MANNER: Polite/Professional   PERMANENT ADDRESS: Unknown

LKA: 1600 Oak Street, Collegeville, IL   BUSINESS ADDRESS: Ace Enterprises, Box 707,
                                             Collegeville, IL (See also bus. name
                                             file #)**

EMPLOYMENT BACKGROUND: Former sales rep., National Insurance, Co., St. Louis, MO;
                       sold directory advertising

SKILLS: Basic accounting; salesmanship

KNOWN ASSOCIATES: Associated with Martinson, Andrew (MC #142); Marie Kenan,
James Anderson (brother), Carl Wilson; all play minor roles in schemes. Wilson
and Anderson, James, often act as phony references for subject.

STYLE:

LEGAL TOOLS: Read local business   ILLEGAL TOOLS: False references. Brochures
directories; Ads placed in business   misrepresenting accomplishments in securing
publications looking for financing   financing. Sequences of form letters to lull
                                        victims or delay complaints.
VICTIM PROFILE: Businessmen seeking financing for expansion of inventory or facilities;
or to tide over business crisis period.

VICTIM APPROACH: Representation that fee is contingent on achievement of desired
financing; demand for partial advance on ultimate fee (with or without guaranty of
advance in event of non-performance).

FIGURE 7. MASTER CARD OFFENDER ALIAS

MASTER CARD #121

SUBJECT: Kansas City Ted   SEE: Anderson, Edward MC #009
                                        Anderson Enterprises MC #007

DOMINANT SCHEME:

KNOWN VARIATIONS	INFO SOURCE	ADDITIONAL INFO

SUSPECT VIA COMPLAINTS:

# COMPLAINTS	TYPE OF COMPLAINT	DISPOSITION

BACKGROUND & CHARACTERISTICS:

DOB: PLACE OF BIRTH:

RACE/SEX: HAIR: EYES:

MUG SHOT: APPEARANCE CHANGES:

VOICE/MANNER: PERMANENT ADDRESS:

LKA: BUSINESS ADDRESS:

EMPLOYMENT BACKGROUND:

SKILLS:

KNOWN ASSOCIATES:

STYLE:

LEGAL TOOLS: ILLEGAL TOOLS:

VICTIM PROFILE:

VICTIM APPROACH:

115

FIGURF 8. MASTER CARD - BUSINESS NAME OF GROUP

MASTER CARD #214

SUBJECT: Enterprise Associates

SEE: Anderson Enterprises (MC #007)
Anderson, Edward (MC #004)
**Business Name File (#316)

DOMINANT SCHEME: Advance Fee

KNOWN VARIATIONS	INFO SOURCE	ADDITIONAL INFO

SUSPECT VIA COMPLAINTS:

# COMPLAINTS	TYPE OF COMPLAINT	DISPOSITION

BACKGROUND & CHARACTERISTICS:

MUG SHOT:

BUSINESS ADDRESS:

STYLE:

LEGAL TOOLS: ILLEGAL TOOLS:

VICTIM PROFILE:

VICTIM APPROACH:

FIGURE 9. SAMPLE CARDS, SUPPLEMENTARY ALIAS FILE

#2075

ANDERSON, EDWARD (MC FILE #007)

DOB: 11/4/19

RACE: White   SEX: Male

BACKGROUND:

ALIASES:

Kansas City Ted (best known)

Ted Anderson

Stewart Anders

#3016

"KANSAS CITY TED"

Alias of Anderson, Edward (MC #004)

OTHER ALIASES:

Ted Anderson

Stewart Anders

FIGURE 10. SAMPLE CARDS, SUPPLEMENTARY BUSINESS NAME FILE

#316

ENTERPRISE ASSOCIATES
Box 707, Collegeville, Illinois

Front for Anderson, Edward (MC File #004)

OTHER NAMES USED:

Anderson & Associates

Martinson, Wilson & Sons

Ace Investment Corp.

#402

ANDERSON ENTERPRISES
Box 707, Collegeville, Illinois

Front for Anderson, Edward (MC File #004)

OTHER NAMES USED:

Enterprise Associates (best known)

Ace Investment Corp.

Martinson, Wilson & Sons

D. SOURCES OF INTELLIGENCE INFORMATION

Victims of white-collar offenders are, as in most crimes, a major source of information both for intelligence and investigative purposes. Most personal and style characteristics for a mastercard, for example, can be determined by careful victim interviewing. Other typical sources of information such as records checks in local and state systems are also helpful. Similarly, once a sound intelligence system has been established, methods for obtaining inputs from other parts of the agency or other law enforcement agencies can be facilitated. Thus, a white-collar crime unit in a police agency may decide to develop special forms on which patrol officers can report field information. This will assure the flow of information and that officers are given due credit for their contributions.

Depending upon the nature of the white-collar subject in question, inter-agency communication may be of great assistance. Traveling cons, for example, are likely to have records in many jurisdictions. If specific information on the travels of such groups are not known, a knowledge of scheme perpetrated and/or the victims selected by the group may help investigators to narrow down those agencies likely to have relevant information. For example, if the dominant scheme involves use of the mails, inquiry placed with the Postal Inspection Service is likely to pay off. Similarly, if victims are selected on the basis of attendance at a public event, materials distributed at the event may indicate the location of prior events or individuals at the site of the event may have information about the groups' travels. Agencies in these former locales can then be contacted. Regular intelligence meetings such as those discussed in Chapter II, Organization,[59] are extremely valuable mechanisms for insuring the value and utility of a unit's intelligence system.

The white-collar offender with roots in the community is likely to be easier to track. If the individual is a member of a professional occupational group or some particular business such as direct mail advertising, surprising amounts of information are available in national directories (the AMA directory of physicians, for example, provides age, medical school, specialty, address, etc.). Employers, employees, and business associates are also good sources of general information on subjects. The offender may volunteer information about himself that has no apparent culpability dimensions, but which will give clues as to his modus operandi and style.

Once an offender has been the subject of an investigation, much of the information required by the mastercard is likely to be available. Initial contacts made in the course of an investigation can remain valuable information sources for on-going intelligence. The major value of the mastercard is that it isolates specific information considered to be important. This provides a focus to inquiries made not only to the victim but also to other agencies. In this sense, the mastercard can serve as something of a checklist of basic information needed, helping to structure both initial and on-going intelligence efforts.

[59]See pp. 54-55.

E. INITIATION, MAINTENANCE AND UPKEEP OF THE INTELLIGENCE SYSTEM

It should be clear that even a simple intelligence system like the one described here, using a mastercard file can be a significant and time consuming task. While much actual file production, including cross-indexing and referencing, is a clerical function, basic mastercard file information requires experienced investigative decisions and input. Getting such input can represent an important management undertaking. In new units, mastercard file development can be used as an organizational and orientation project in which relevant information within the agency can be tracked down, reviewed and digested into proper format. Units that have some prior history of fraud investigation but are newly constituted, might use the mastercard file development process as a general updating and housecleaning task, getting old files in some order for the new effort. Often information known to the unit, but not appropriate for investigative files can find a "home" in the mastercard index. This gives the intelligence process an opportunity to provide some information benefit from the very beginning, setting a tone that can affect the level of use and upkeep to which the intelligence system will be subjected. Finally, working on mastercard development can also help to train and orient new unit investigators.

Despite the frequently tedious tasks associated with the initial file development, the process is an extremely important one. Effective and appropriate managerial stress on its importance, combined with the marshalling of adequate clerical resources, can remove the more arduous elements and insure that the process is well-initiated and completed. While the unit supervisor should have overall responsibility for management of the system, the intelligence process is important enough that day-to-day responsibility for maintenance and upkeep should be specifically delegated. The ideal situation (if the unit has sufficient resources) would be one in which the staff of the unit includes an intelligence analyst, expert in the design and upkeep of files and in the assessment of information provided for file inclusion. Under such an arrangement, data provided by patrol officers (if it is a police unit), investigators, outside agencies, etc. would be routed to the analyst who would maintain records of such communications and make decisions on how and to what extent new information would modify existing files.

Keeping records of communications is important even if information from a source is not used, for two reasons. First, it can permit the analyst to assess the reliability of various sources; and second, even if information is redundant, the source can and should be encouraged to continue to provide input. Thus, contributions to the intelligence system of the unit by a particular investigator not in the unit can be provided to those making personnel decisions about that individual. Members of the unit, of course, should be expected to actively engage in seeking intelligence information and should be frequently utilizing the files.

Major decisions concerning such an intelligence system should remain a unit-wide responsibility and not be left in the province of the analyst. The decision to initiate a file, for example, should begin with an investigator's request to the unit supervisor. The supervisor should review the investigator's rationale and consult with others in the unit knowledgeable about the subject(s). If a positive decision is made, the analyst should then be directed to gather the relevant materials from the investigator, briefly review the subject's significance and determine the best formatting of the file, in consultation with the lead investigator. It is then the analyst who prepares the mastercard and organizes the file. In a particular case, of course, an analyst might identify a crime and trigger the opening of a file in consultation with the unit supervisor or an investigator.

The decision to purge a file, on the other hand, may be initiated in the opposite manner. It is the intelligence analyst who is in the best position to identify the files which go virtually unused. Periodic assessments by the analyst may result in the pulling of unattended files for unit review. A staff meeting to review the continued necessity of maintaining the file(s) would then be in order. While the final decision will rest with the unit supervisor, the entire staff should be involved. Where uncertainty about the value of a particular file exists, the decision may be deferred until specific sources can be checked. Thus, for example, the subjects of some files may be discussed at multi-agency intelligence meetings and information derived from that contact may determine whether continued maintenance is required.

If a unit cannot afford to have an intelligence analyst attached to it, it would be wise to consider designating one investigator to take major responsibility for the intelligence system. While an intelligence officer cannot be expected to be as expert in the design of files as would be an analyst, there may be some advantages to this model. First, an investigator/intelligence officer may be more credible to outside contacts than would be an analyst and so could serve as the focal point for inter-agency communication with the unit. Such an individual could represent the unit at intelligence meetings and take responsibility for handling much of the unit's correspondence. Similarly, an intelligence officer, while less expert in the techniques of file maintenance, would be more likely to be attuned to the needs of investigators and therefore may be better able to make decisions relating to organization of files to best suit the investigative efforts being undertaken.

It makes no sense to establish an intelligence system without delegating specific responsibility for its upkeep. The usefulness of a white-collar intelligence system is inextricably tied to the quality of maintenance it receives. Initial development and on-going maintenance cannot be divorced. If no commitment is made to maintenance, there is little reason to initiate the system in the first place. A similar error, and one often as fatal, made with regard to intelligence systems, is the failure to provide adequate clerical assistance for the maintenance function. Even the best analyst or intelligence officer can quickly get bogged down

without sufficient clerical assistance. This situation will detract
significantly from the quality of the system and the use made of it.

Earlier it was noted that the system suggested here is one of simple
design. Agencies having access to computer services can obviously handle
much more information in more complex ways than others. It should be
remembered, however, that added complexity requires adequate staffing for
optimum benefit. Computers do not confer automatic benefits; you can be
snowed under by computer printouts. In addition, some basic points
remain. First, the simpler the overall design of such a system, the
easier upkeep becomes and the more useful the system will be. Because of
this the ultimate system users must be intimately involved in initial
design and policy decisions.

Second, no matter how carefully designed and how ideal the staffing
for an intelligence effort is, it should be subjected to a semi-annual
review. At this time, a thorough housecleaning can occur and the overall
policies concerning the system can be re-evaluated. Shortcomings of the
system should be addressed and decisions for future improvement made at
this time. While such decisions do not have to wait for a 6-month review
time, scheduling such a review will insure that needed system assessment
occurs.[60]

Finally, resources in any white-collar enforcement effort must be
judiciously expended. Therefore, it is necessary to most carefully weigh
the justifications for such expenditures. Constraints on the use of
resources for specific purposes must also be considered. Intelligence
efforts undertaken in the white-collar crime area hold great potential for
providing useful information obtained and organized in an optimal fashion.
Legal restraints bearing on the permissibility of the form of intelligence
activity adopted, however, may severely dilute its potential. Half-
hearted attempts at an intelligence system will produce the same result.
A unit facing either of these situations, then, might better place its
resources elsewhere in the fight against white-collar crime. For, like
so many other things, what one gets out of an intelligence system is
directly related to the investment and continued commitment put into it.

_____

[60]See Latham, op. cit., Note 46, at p. 54.

IV. CONDUCTING INVESTIGATIONS OF WHITE-COLLAR CRIME

Investigation of white-collar crime calls for imagination, patience, and clear understanding and appreciation of the range of possible approaches which can be employed in the investigative process. All of the skills required in more conventional investigations will be called for, plus other skills, but even conventional techniques will have to be employed with different emphases.

It will not always be easy to focus directly on a specific criminal act and to gather evidence bearing upon it. The investigator is far more likely to observe a pattern of general criminal activity which will be subject to attack in a number of its aspects. For example, a merchandising scheme could give rise to federal mail or wire fraud charges, to the use of state statutes dealing with larceny or false pretenses, local laws involving licenses to solicit, or federal or state income tax or revenue collection laws. In addition, even where a criminal investigatory focus is possible in the early stages of an investigation, the investigator must realize that for a variety of reasons the prosecutor may decline to criminally prosecute. This is not to suggest that an investigator's time was mispent, for his investigation may bear fruit through (1) governmental civil or administrative litigation to stop the wrongful, fraudulent activity, (2) governmental, civil action to achieve restitution for white-collar crime victims, (3) laying the groundwork for private action by victims, and (4) educating the public to the frauds being investigated, i.e., contributing to crime prevention and deterrence.

The approach of the investigator, whether he or she is in a police department, a prosecutor's office, a state attorney general's office, a local consumer protection office, or a private agency --- must therefore be geared to gathering of information which will be useful in achieving remedies in addition to that which is the primary goal of the investigating agency. The "additional" remedy may be more or less severe than the primary remedy. Some examples:

- an investment fraud investigation is facing difficulties under a local larceny statute. However, such a case might be moved forward under a local false pretenses statute, or under mail fraud or securities fraud statutes.

- a police investigation of an auto repair fraud may not yield evidence which convinces the prosecutor that he can show guilt beyond a reasonable doubt. But the prosecutor may have enough evidence to meet a civil burden of proof and thus commence civil action or may refer the case to the state attorney general's office or a municipal consumer protection office for civil action to protect victims or for appropriate injunctive action.

• a local municipal consumer protection office which is primarily
engaged in mediating complaints by consumers against merchants
may, in the course of gathering facts to support its mediation/
restitution efforts, develop evidence which indicates a potential
for criminal prosecution and refer its evidence and findings to
an investigating or prosecuting agency which has criminal
jurisdiction.

Beyond all this, the white-collar crime investigator must realize that
the "crime" being investigated will not have a clear beginning and end,
in the same way that there is a clear beginning and end to a specific
assault, or burglary. White-collar crimes are usually schemes which operate
over periods of time. Thus the evidence which is gathered may well be the
missing piece of the investigative jig-saw puzzle that the same or some
other investigator confronts in the future --- so the investigation may
be a success even if no remedy is invoked, just so long as it is done
thoroughly, expertly, and with proper regard for the presentation and later
retrievability of the evidence which has been gathered.

The techniques of investigation discussed here cannot, therefore,
be viewed as a group of tools to be rigidly applied to parts of the job
of investigating white-collar crime, but rather as an inventory of perspectives which will (1) help to identify what evidence should be gathered,
(2) show the different ways in which investigators can better accomplish
conventional investigatory tasks when working in this field, and (3) be a
roadmap and guide for the analysis and organization of evidence for maximum
attractiveness and utility to prosecutors or other litigators. How such
techniques are employed will vary, of course, depending on the nature of
the case, the manner in which the case is brought to the attention of the
investigating agency, and the character/mission/resources of the investigating agency.

The special distinguishing features of white-collar crime investigation
stem from the fact that white-collar crimes are usually hidden or disguised
within the framework of apparently legitimate undertakings (the crimes are
not obvious to the victims as would be the case in robbery, burglary,
homicide, etc.). Investigators of white-collar crime are required from
the outset to direct their efforts toward determining whether a crime has
in fact been committed and whether there might be legal evidence to support
a prosecution. They must therefore not only become adept at the application
of general investigation techniques such as handling victim complaints,
interviewing, interrogation, finding documents and public records, finding
expert assistance for specialized technical areas, and preparing a package
for the district attorney; they must also develop the special techniques
which will enable them to identify and develop the evidence which proves that
a violation has been committed rather than that certain specific acts were
committed.

This chapter first discusses the special relevance and importance of
shaping the investigation to bring together proof of the elements of
white-collar crime. It then goes on to outline the ways in which general
techniques of investigation can best be employed in white-collar crime

cases to develop proof related to these elements. The principles underlying these approaches should be generally valid regardless of the particular jurisdiction or its specific statutes.

It is important to note, however, that the total proficiency of
the investigator, i.e., the investigator's ability to avoid wasting time
and effort on a hopeless case, to avoid fruitless investigative steps,
to innovate, and to build a sense of professional confidence, demands
continual supplementing of these fundamentals by self examination of
what succeeds and what fails.

First, then, we turn to examination of the elements of white-collar
crime.

A.   THE ELEMENTS OF WHITE-COLLAR CRIME

One of the characteristics which most distinguishes investigation
of white-collar crime from that of common crimes is the necessity for
the investigator to establish the intent and underlying motives of the
subject by placing together jig-saw puzzle pieces of apparently legitimate
activities to add up to a picture of illegitimacy --- rather than by a
simple showing of one event which by itself flatly demonstrates wrongful
intent. For the most part, within the broad frame of references associated
with legitimate undertakings in private and government organizations,
the intent and motivation of the subjects of investigation tend to be
obscure and confusing.

It would be helpful, of course, for the investigator to have a
thorough knowledge of every kind of white-collar crime, and the ways in
which they have been investigated and prosecuted. The field of white-
collar crime is, however, too large and too varied for investigators,
or prosecutors, to fully possess and utilize all such experience. Furthermore, the investigator will not always find an obvious and definitive
legal theory to rely upon when he starts on a case. Definitions of
specific white-collar crimes will also vary from one jurisdiction to
another.

The absence of such legal certainty need not be an excuse for
inaction. Thorough knowledge of all technical points of law affecting
white-collar crime is not an essential prerequisite for successful
white-collar crime investigation. What is essential is a clear understanding of the basic elements which can tell us whether or not a white-
collar crime has occurred. Once there is such understanding of the
elements, the investigator will focus on what wrongs were done, and how
they were done --- rather than on statutory definitions of crimes.

Investigators should not be locked into any rigid legal framework
of definitions with respect to white-collar crime violations. They must,
however, understand and maintain an awareness of the almost universal
existence of a set of elements common to all white-collar crime, which were
discussed in Chapter I of this manual.[61]   They are:

---

[61]See pp. 21-26.

(1) *Intent* - to commit a wrongful act or to achieve a purpose inconsistent with law or public policy;

(2) *Disguise of purpose* - falsities and misrepresentations employed to accomplish the scheme;

(3) *Reliance* by the offender on the ignorance or carelessness of the victim;

(4) *Voluntary Victim Action* to assist the offender; and

(5) *Concealment* of the crime.

If the right mix of these elements is present, there is a high probability that there is a white-collar criminal violation and a parallel civil remedy. However, though these elements will amost always be present in a white-collar crime scheme, it is not necessary that there be evidence on every one of them to support a criminal or civil case. Each element should, however, be considered in deciding on the scope and nature of the investigation.

It does not matter what type of white-collar crime, what level of sophistication or what type of victim the case involves. It may be an investor who is induced to purchase shares in a fraudulent oil-drilling venture; a businessman who pays a fee to a promoter to obtain a loan which is never forthcoming; a retired person who is induced to buy worthless desert land; a consumer who responds to false advertising; the public who unknowingly are paying excessive fees because of the establishment of a monopoly in a public service industry such as garbage collection; or persons seeking to improve their income who are induced to invest savings to become distributors of products when in actuality the only way to make money is to induce others to become distributors. The crimes can be as different as antitrust violations and bank embezzlement, or tax fraud and ordering merchandise with no intention to pay. When a set of circumstances can be reconstructed by the investigator which strongly supports the conclusion that certain combinations of the above elements exist, there is a high likelihood that a prosecutable violation exists. We therefore now turn to these individual elements and discuss them in turn.

1. Criminal Intent

For an investigation to result in a prosecutable case there must be adequate evidence that the subject of the investigation intended to commit the wrongful acts with which he is charged. This is customarily shown by gathering evidence from witnesses and documents which prove that the subject knew he was involved in wrongful activity, or that the circumstances are such that any contrary conclusion lacks credibility.

There are a number of ways of doing this, the most common of which are to show that the subject:

(a) could have had no legitimate motive for the activities in which he was engaged;

(b) repeatedly engaged in the same or similar activity, of an apparently wrongful nature;

(c) made conflicting statements;

(d) systematically organized the dissemination of misleading information;

(e) made admissions;

(f) acted to impede investigation of the offense; or

(g) made statements he clearly knew to be false.

The last, (g), will be discussed at length in a following section entitled MISREPRESENTATION AND DISGUISE; (a) through (f) are considered here.

(a) Activity Inconsistent with Legitimate Intent. Subjects of investigation will often aruge that they are respectable, legitimate businessmen, professionals, or citizens who acted in good faith and never intended to violate any laws. The investigator should consider every possibility which may show the subject's activity may have had some legitimate purpose. If there is sufficiently persuasive evidence that there was such a legitimate purpose, the subjects will have a defense which may make prosecution and conviction impossible, or unjust. Conversely, if their activities can be shown to have been performed in bad faith, i.e., with intent to defraud, a court or jury will seriously question any other defenses, and the subjects will be less likely to risk cross examination by taking the witness stand in their own defense.

Recognizing that white-collar crime suspects will often be prepared to defend their activities by seizing on every possible argument which could show they were operating in good faith (although foolishly, unwisely, sloppily, or incompetently) the investigator must continually consider in detail wnat explanations the subjects of the investigation will offer in defense of their specifically questionable activities. Such an analysis will be a guide to the search for evidence which will cut off avenues of escape in much the same way that an alibi is handled when it is checked out in investigation of a common crime. Eliminating the possibility of a legitimate explanation of the subject's activity will thus increase the probability of ultimate conviction and heighten the prosecutor's willingness to accept and actively prosecute the case which has been prepared by the investigator.

In white-collar crime cases legitimacy or illegitimacy of a subject's activity can often be determined simply by comparing the suspected activities to regular business practices. In many cases, the investigator will be dealing with normal and understandable business and personal transactions, or at least with transactions that can be analyzed by experts (who can usually be consulted by the investigator) to determine whether the suspect's explanations are consistent with legitimate ends. Let us consider a number of specific examples:

- A lawyer uses money entrusted to him by a client. He had placed the money in his own personal bank account, and in his defense now claims he spent it accidentally because he was confused as to what was his and what was the client's. This argument will clearly lack credibility. Attorneys' state canons of ethics clearly provide that lawyers who hold moneys for their clients should not mix clients' moneys with their own, but should deposit such funds in special and separate bank accounts. There could have been no legitimate reason for mixing these funds in the first place.

- A used car dealer rolls back the odometer in a car offered for sale. There is no explanation for such activity which can possibly be consistent with honest dealing.[62]

- A manufacturer wishes to sell merchandise to a department store. At the same time that he sells a large order to the store's purchasing agent, he draws cash out of his business bank account, charging it to "miscellaneous cash expenses." He then goes to an automobile dealership with the purchasing agent who selects a car. The manufacturer makes the $1,000 down payment for him. No loan security in the car is retained by the manufacturer, nor does he take a promissory note. When charged with commercial bribery the manufacturer is hardly in any position to legitimize the transaction. He might say that he was "making a personal loan to a friend," but such a story is suspicious based on comparison to normal business and loan transactions.[63]

- A store owner buys merchandise on credit at a cost of $50,000. Shortly after delivery, he sells the merchandise for $20,000 in cash, and a promissory note for $35,000. The buyer picks up the merchandise and is never heard from again. The store owner goes bankrupt. When charged with bankruptcy fraud, he claims

---

[62]In this instance, as in other examples discussed here, the activity which is not explainable in legitimate terms is related to the subject of MISREPRESENTATIONS, which is discussed later. The distinction to be kept in mind is that the rolling back of the odometer is the unexplainable activity which shows the criminal intention of the subject, while the offer for sale of a car with an altered odometer reading is the misrepresentation

[63]Many cases are matters of degree. Thus, if the manufacturer bought the buyer an expensive lunch, or sent him a bottle of whiskey at Christmas, it would be explainable as being in line with some common perceptions of normal business. Standards will differ, based on time and place, customs of the industry, etc.

he cannot locate the purchaser, and that he lost the
$20,000 at a gambling casino. This strange transaction,
i.e., the acceptance of a $35,000 note from a stranger who
can neither be identified nor located is relatively unexplainable in normal business terms and may, with other
evidence, contribute to a successful prosecution.

- A welfare recipient applies for and receives duplicate
benefits under a real name and also under a false name.
There can be no legitimate reason for one person receiving
duplicate benefits.

The above examples are straightforward and may be read to imply
that the techniques for determining legitimacy are relatively simple.
They are not. The investigator must understand that actual cases are
not always so clearcut. Techniques to be followed may range from the
very simple to those which could be quite time consuming and complex.
For example:

- If, in the bankruptcy fraud example above, the store owner
is a food wholesaler who bought the merchandise at a
cost of $50,000 on credit, payable at the rate of $10,000
per month, and then sold it for $55,000 payable to him at
the rate of $11,000 per month, this would indicate that
at the end of 5 months he would make $5,000 profit. But
for 3 or 4 months the wholesaler receives no payment but
does receive letters purporting to be from the buyer indicating that the merchandise received was damaged or in
some way not in accord with what was expected. Letters are
exchanged, and over that 5 months period the wholesaler
receives a total of $20,000 in payment, does not pay anything
to his creditors, or at most makes a token payment, seems
lethargic in taking any action, and then goes bankrupt.
These transactions raise questions. But in order to demonstrate that they are not explainable in normal business
terms the investigator must probe below the surface. He
should certainly be suspicious and should follow up, for
example, if the allegedly damaged merchandise consisted of
canned goods, guaranteed by the canner, and the wholesaler
made no claim against the canner when he was denied payment
for merchandise shipped.

An investigator may have to consult with experts depending upon the
particular kind of business activity under investigation. In cases involving
intricate financial transactions, for example, an accountant could help an
investigator to determine whether a particular transaction made sense in
legitimate business terms. Similarly, a state bank examiner could help an
investigator understand intricate banking transactions. Investigators
should not dismiss out-of-hand the possibility that businessmen may sometimes
act incompetently or irrationally --- rather than with wrongful intent.
Experts can help in this area, but here as in any other criminal investigations motives should be considered in trying to determine what the subject
was actually doing.

128

Consideration whether or not there are possible legitimate explanations
for questionable activities on the parts of subjects of investigation is
also important because it is common in a white-collar crime investigation
to defer interrogation of the subject until close to the conclusion of the
investigator's work, and often to totally refrain from such interrogation.[64]

In summary, the investigator in a white-collar crime case should carefully analyze possible motives for the transactions which are at the core
of the alleged violations (as in any other criminal investigation) as well
as other transactions in which the subject may have participated. In
addition to countering potential defenses (white-collar crime alibis), such
consideration and related investigation will prevent misallocation of
investigative and prosecutive resources and/or a highly publicized but
later embarrassing indictment because of the failure of an investigator
to understand the legitimate reason for an activity which on its face
appeared to be suspicious.

(b) Repetitious Wrongful Activity. As emphasized in the previous
sub-section, the white-collar crime investigator must continually consider
what explanations the subject of an investigation will offer in defense of
specific questionable activities. A common defense or explanation to an
accusation of wrongdoing is for the suspect to claim that a false representation was a "mistake," an unintentional slip of the tongue or the pen.
Although the commission of a single wrongful act is sufficient in theory to
bring a violator within the jurisdiction of a criminal statute, as a practical
matter, a single instance of wrongful behavior will in many white-collar
crime cases not be sufficient to support a finding of the necessary criminal
intent. To counter such a claim by the suspect, the investigator must try
to develop evidence that the suspect made the same, or similar, "mistakes"
repeatedly. One of the principal means of establishing the required element
of intent (and often to prove that a fraud was in fact committed) is to
demonstrate that misrepresentations, use of false pretenses, and promises
made by the suspects were not limited to a single instance.

The investigator, through either victim/witness statements, witness/
non-victim statements or through undercover operations should seek evidence
of similar misrepresentations repetitively made to the same victim, to other
victims, and to non-victims. The investigator should also seek evidence
concerning the previous history of the suspect. Such evidence may be used
to support the conclusion that the same misrepresentations were made in other
situations and that fraudulent activities were not limited to this one
instance. By expanding the number of instances, it may be possible to
charge a broader scheme.

Before a jury may infer fraudulent intent from the commission of an
act, it must be proved that the act was committed. The investigator must
therefore anticipate that the subject will very readily seek to deny the
testimony of a single complainant, or a small number, who quote him or
describe what he did. For example, an individual complainant's statement
that a salesperson made certain representations about a product may catch
the attention of an investigator but it will not prove to a jury that the
representation was in fact made. Statements from several persons that the

_____

[64]The subjects of Interviewing and Interrogation are discussed in detail
below, see pp. 153-172.

salesperson made the same representation to them will tend to give credibility to the testimony of each that the representation was in fact made. If dozens of complaints are received, the investigator may need no further evidence to prove that the statement in question was made. If the investigator has only a few complaints with which to begin his investigation, additional corroborating evidence may be required. The investigator's objective is to acquire more and more corroboration that wrongful acts of the suspect are not unique or limited to a single incident.

Some specific guidelines for acquiring evidence of repetitious fraudulent activity are the following:

● The investigator should maintain contact with the complainant, locate other victims and witnesses and interview all of them to determine:

1) whether false or misleading statements were made repeatedly or only once during the course of a presentation - a single misrepresentation made during some course of questionable conduct may prove nothing more than that the misstatement was made. In contrast, misstatements made repeatedly to the same audience is evidence which will better support a prosecution because repetition is inconsistent with accidental misstatement.

2) whether the statements were made repeatedly to different individuals, audiences, or gatherings - this is even stronger evidence of fraud than 1) above. When an investigator receives several complaints, to verify the repetitiousness of the misrepresentations he can verify that the various complainants heard the false statements at different times, and repeated episodes will support the conclusion that misrepresentations were made pursuant to a plan.

3) whether they know of any others who might have been victimized.

4) whether they know of any others who attended the same or similar gatherings.

5) whether they know how the suspect got their name - if the answer to this question is no, the investigator might obtain leads by following up with detailed questions regarding the interviewee's employment, memberships, education, military background, hobbies, etc. From these questions he may deduce common characteristics among certain of the complainants which will help him find more victims and others who were solicited but did not become victims who can verify that the false statements were made. Some of the major possibilities are that the

suspect used mailing lists, club rosters, school enrollment lists, or similar sources to obtain the
names of potential victims.

● Another method of corroborating the statements of a small number of
initial victim/witnesses is to seek statements from persons who were
witnesses to the suspect's acts but were not victimized. Statements
from non-victims can be particularly useful in the following ways:

1) they add to the number of witness accounts of a suspected
fraudulent transaction;

2) their evidence might be weighed more heavily by a jury
because they have no apparent selfish motivations;

3) individual non-victims may have been frustrating targets
for subjects being investigated. Under such circumstances it is not unknown for fraud artists to redouble
their efforts to persuade, by recourse to additional and
perhaps more readily disprovable false statements, or
statements inconsistent with those made to others; and

4) the investigator can improve his understanding of the
scheme if he knows the reason that these witnesses
were not victimized. For example, the non-victim may
have known at the time that some of the suspect's
representations were false, or at least suspect. The
non-victim may have asked some specific questions
which elicited answers that made him suspicious. How
the non-victim came to the conclusions which prevented
his becoming a victim may help the investigator to discover new aspects of the fraud. Similarly, the non-
victim may not have known at the time the suspect made
his representations that they were false, but may have
discovered this during the course of an investigation
which he, his attorney, financial manager, broker, or
banker conducted. The fruits of financial or other investigations made by others can be very useful to an investigator. Such a prior investigation may include evidence
of the falsity of some of the suspect's statements, useful
information about the suspect himself, and also information
about variations in modi operandi at different times in
the course of execution of the criminal scene.

● Complaints may also be obtained from other agencies, public and private,
which have some relationship to the activities under investigation.
This would be an additional way of finding other victims, benefitting
from prior investigations, etc.

● Corroborative evidence of a suspect's repeated wrongful acts may
be acquired through the use of undercover operatives. Undercover
operatives posing as potential victims can record, or, where pro-
hibited by law, simply take note of the various circumstances under
which the suspect repeats the crucial misrepresentation. The use of
undercover operatives enables law enforcement agencies to produce
corroborating witnesses in cases where complainants are few and non-
victims cannot be located. To avoid legal problems, such as exposure
to the entrapment defense, the investigative agency's legal adviser
should be consulted where possible.[65]

● Evidence that the suspect had in the past participated in similar
frauds or made other misrepresentations similar to those involved
in the case under investigation, may be used to show that:

1) the suspect was in fact in the habit of committing the
acts he is presently accused of making; and

2) that the misrepresentations were made with knowledge
of their falsity and with the intent to deceive.

The use of evidence showing past participation in similar fraudulent
activities has its difficulties. Where such similar fraudulent activities
resulted in a conviction, these earlier events will be useful evidence as
part of the prosecution case in most instances. More commonly, this kind of
information is most useful in challenging the credibility of a defendant
who has taken the witness stand to argue, for example, that he had no
way of knowing that a statement which he had inadvertently made, would
mislead victims. Under such circumstances he can usually be cross-examined
to show that he had been called on the carpet earlier (in other investigations
or by consumer protection offices) with respect to the misleading effect
of the same kinds of misrepresentations --- even if criminal action had not
been taken or a conviction obtained.

As a practical matter, an investigator cannot search every corner for
evidence that his suspect participated in a fraud similar to the one under
investigation. Nevertheless, the investigator should be alert to gather
evidence of similar frauds. Routine search into the background and activities
of his suspect is fundamental, including systematic checking of a unit's own
intelligence file. Standard sources where an investigator may very likely
uncover evidence of earlier frauds are the public and private agencies
which have responsibilities for or interests in the activity under investigation. In a real estate fraud, for example, the Department of Housing and
Urban Development, the Federal Trade Commission, Securities and Exchange
Commission, State Division of Real Estate, real estate brokerage associations, etc., often maintain files pertaining to various land frauds and the
persons involved. Better Business Bureaus will have files on merchandising

_____

[65]See the discussion of Covert Operations, below at pp. 173-178.

frauds, home repair frauds, etc. Similarly, in a medical fraud involving quack cures for diseases or ailments such as cancer or arthritis, such agencies as state and local health departments, the American Cancer Society, the Arthritis Foundation, etc. will often have information about medical frauds and medical fraud artists. In nearly every area of fraud there are public and private agencies with responsibilities for or interests in the activity under investigation.[66]

Identifying non-complaining victims or persons who successfully resisted blandishments or other pressure to become victims is sometimes beyond the capability of even the most experienced investigator, since most investigators lack the power to compel the subject of the investigation to answer questions or to produce books or records. Such power does exist in many regulatory agencies, for example, where the right to be in a regulated business depends on licensing and agency access to books and records. When the prosecutor interests himself in the case, however, the investigator should ask him to consider whether a grant jury or inquiry judge subpoena should not be issued to obtain records pertaining to such items as mailing lists used, telephone records, salesmen's compensation claims showing names of those solicited and expense claims in connection therewith. This information will not only serve to identify other victims and those who were solicited but avoided victimization, but also will help to be sure that the prosecutor (and ultimately the court and jury) has the full scope and magnitude of the scheme in proper perspective.

(c) <u>Conflicting Statements</u>. Evidence that the subject of the investigation made conflicting statements to different audiences will usually be helpful in proving his fraudulent intent. The investigator's objective is to gather facts which will ultimately help the prosecutor to convince a court or jury of a consistent disregard for truth on the part of the suspect. A legitimate business person will generally make consistent statements of fact to different audiences. In contrast, a dishonest promoter will say whatever is necessary to consummate the fraudulent scheme.

Representations made by the subject of investigation, whether verbal or written, may be obviously inconsistent. For example:

- A sales force for an underwriter selling stock to investors makes repeated oral representations that the company whose securities are being sold averaged $150,000 per year in profits during the previous three years, while certified financial statements filed with the state agency regulating securities sales showed an average net loss for the same period.

- A promoter of distributorships for a particular product will, in response to one prospective client-victim's concern about his lack of sales experience, tell the prospective victim that lack of experience is unimportant and unnecessary to success in the

---

[66]See the sections entitled "Finding Documents/Public Records and Finding Experts/Resources, below, at pp. 179-183 and pp. 192-195.

venture. Under similar circumstances with another client who has previous sales experience, the promoter will tell the experienced client that this particular business opportunity is "tailor-made only for experienced personnel."

Conflicting representations may also be in written or verbal forms which are not so obvious, i.e., they appear to be mere exaggeration for promotional purposes. For example:

- A store advertises a sale of merchandise valued at $100. A short time later the store advertises a sale of the same merchandise but now valued at $150.

- A merchant tells one customer that the stereo on sale for $200 is really worth $300. The same merchant tells another customer that the same stereo equipment is valued at $350. The merchant tells a third customer the stereo's worth is $250. The true value may be none of these.

Where conflicting statements involve highly subjective judgment questions, such as matters of value, it is very difficult to make a fraud case without much more evidence of other kinds.

The investigator should be continually alert to eliminating the possibility that the suspect will be able to explain away his conflicting statements when a case comes to trial. The suspect's first line of defense regarding such statements might be to deny having made inconsistent representations. A second line of defense might be to claim mistake or, as in the case of not so obvious conflicting degrees of misrepresentation, to claim that the inconsistent statements were mere "sales puffing" or expressions of opinion. Each of these defense claims may be overcome by evidence that the suspect's acts were part of a deliberately executed pattern of activity. In order to develop a showing of a pattern of conflicting statements from which fraudulent intent can be inferred, the investigator needs evidence of repeated inconsistent statements. The method for establishing the repetitiousness of inconsistent statements are the same as those discussed in the preceding sub-section with regard to complainants, victims, witnesses, and other agencies.[67] Proof of repeated inconsistencies establishes the fact of their occurrence and also refutes the claim that the misstatements were innocently made.

Of added significance to the investigator is the fact that although conflicting statements may not in themselves be sufficient as proof of fraudulent intent, they do indicate a deliberate disregard for truth on the part of the suspect and thus provide support for determining fraudulent intent. This consideration is important in persuading a court or jury that so-called "inconsistent puffing" was really part of a fraudulent scheme.

_____

[67]See the discussion above concerning "Repetitious Wrongful Activity" at pp. 129-131. ·

(d) <u>Systematically organized dissemination of misleading information</u>. Large scale fraudulent sales schemes do not rely solely upon the sales skills of individual sales persons. Most, if not all, large scale consumer frauds, land frauds, investment frauds, pyramid schemes, and other white-collar crime schemes, base their operations on carefully planned training sessions for sales personnel. At these sessions sales personnel are instructed on various techniques for successful sales, usually including either the careful dissemination of misleading information or methods to avoid providing victims with relevant information which, if they had it would cause victims to reject the deal offered to them. The systematic dissemination of misleading information is most likely to be made orally, since oral statements are more difficult to prove. However, misinformation will often be systematically disseminated by white-collar criminals in written form through brochures, prospectuses, charts, graphs, and pictures accompanying oral presentations. An investigator should therefore take particular care to collect copies of all brochures, prospectuses, and other such written information provided potential customers (victims) by suspects. Similarly, investigators should, during their interviews of victims and witnesses, always inquire about the use of any brochures, prospectuses, graphs, photographs and illustrations which may have accompanied an oral presentation, or were passed out during the presentation and later collected. Such written material may include misleading information, which explains why it was collected at the conclusion of a presentation. Some victims, or non-victims who were present, may have deliberately or accidentally retained copies. In addition, just knowing that such material was in existence at one time will provide the investigator with an opportunity to try to get hold of it.

Let us consider a specific scheme which exemplifies the personnel training requirements of a white-collar crime scheme and a systematic approach to committing a fraud.

The promoters of a land development scheme plan to use a standard sales approach --- inviting a group of people to attend a dinner where a sales presentation will be made. The promoter plans several such dinners. The scenario might be as follows:

(1) The promoters hold a training session for twelve salespersons, and instruct on how to make their sales pitches, including ways to avoid giving information on lack of water, utilities, and other facilities. Plans for the use of confederates in the audience will be discussed, including ways to ensure that questions will be asked in a way which will make it possible to provide answers which mislead others in the audience.

(2) At the sales presentation dinner a professionally produced film is shown. The film includes views of developed real estate, intermingled with illustrations of the land for sale. The film and narration strongly implies that the land being offered for sale is a part of the developed real estate shown, and that the facilities, utilities, and amenities shown in the developed real estate are already

being constructed in the area where the lots are being sold.

(3) The lights go on and the prospective client sees a large professionally prepared chart on the wall that shows how an investment of $1,000 multiplied enormously. (The chart contains no information regarding the who, what, when, where or why of the $1,000 investment.)

(4) A salesman approaches and relieves the prospective client's doubts by assuring him that the land for sale is registered with the Office of Interstate Land Sales in Washington, D.C. and offers to show verified audited statements of the actual expenditures that the developers have poured into developing the land.

(5) Another distinguished looking member of the audience (a confederate) then volunteers that he is a senior partner in a well known accounting firm. He is attending this meeting only out of curiousity and he would certainly insist on examining these figures if he wanted to buy property. He volunteers to examine these figures and the salesman passes him an impressive file folder containing the figures.

(6) The salesman spends a half-hour "explaining" the chart with $1,000 and how it grew.

(7) All specific questions are answered with official sounding responses such as "I can show you a letter verifying . . ." or "we have already signed a contract for . . ." or "you get a full title insurance policy. . ." or "ground has already been broken. You can see it for yourself if you visit the land . . ." and so on.

(8) The doors open, food and drink are wheeled in.

(9) The prospective client observes at least 3 or 4 people (confederates perhaps) opening checkbooks and signing contracts. The audience is told that this is their chance to "buy land," whereas the actual contract may only give them the legal right to take title to the land after the promoters have collected enough money to buy it; or the land may already be mortgaged.

(10) One friendly salesman says he took a liking to the victim and will personally tear up the contract if the victim changes his mind. This is pre-arranged, as are arrangements for transfer of these contracts to financing businesses and institutions.

(11) Prospective victim with just a little more urging
says "What have I got to lose?"

Such techniques and other similar ones perhaps less professionally prepared, tend to prove an intent to deceive and mislead. When taken together
with other circumstances described in this section, a fair inference of
intent to defraud is raised.

There are basically two techniques for gathering evidence on such
systematic dissemination of misleading information The first technique is
the development and use of informants. This involves identifying and
"turning" one of the perpetrators, usually a salesperson associated with
the scheme, and recruiting him to cooperate with law enforcement. In one
instance, where salesmen were trained with the use of taped recordings to
instruct them, a salesman who "turned," was able to provide a set of tapes.[68]
Such material, as well as the informant's own testimony will make it
possible or help to prove that misleading information was being systematically
disseminated.

There is little or no experience to indicate that there is any value
to planting undercover operatives to obtain evidence of this kind. There are
far better uses for investigative resources.

The second technique is the gathering of physical evidence. As
stated above, the charts, graphs, photographs, illustrations, or other
apparatus employed as part of a scheme should be vigorously sought; where
compulsory process is available, as through an inquiry judge or grand
jury, they should be subpoenaed --- but the more the investigator knows
about them the more likely it is that all these documents will in fact be
produced. All such physical evidence provide excellent visual examples with
which to explain to a jury how the suspects operated. Since such evidence
is easily destroyed or hidden, the investigator's timing of a seizure and
obtaining search warrants must be carefully planned as in any criminal
investigation.

(e) Admissions. As part of every investigation, the investigator
should be alert to any acts or statements made by the suspect which clearly
demonstrate that he knows that he has lied and has been perpetrating a
fraud. These acts or statements may have been made to his associates or
even to victims. The investigative techniques of handling complaints,
interviewing, interrogation and using undercover informant operatives
(discussed in later sections) provide the procedural details for discovering
such evidence.

Particular emphasis should be placed on trying to get a statement from
the suspect immediately at the time of arrest. Even though a confession is
not forthcoming, the white-collar criminal will generally tie himself down
to some story, particularly if his bail is high and he has no local assistance
readily available. White-collar criminals are usually confident of their

---

[68]The subject of informant motivation and development is discussed below
at pp. 173-174.

ability to convince others of the truth of their statements or the image they present. After all, deception is their stock in trade. Nevertheless, statements will often contain inconsistencies when compared with other evidence obtained from victims, which may be tantamount to admitting that they lied to victims. It should be recognized, however, that most white-collar criminals will have had the opportunity to anticipate arrest (they frequently surrender by pre-arrangement between their own counsel and the prosecutor, in lieu of normal apprehension and arrest), and will not be likely to waive their rights and make helpful statements.

At this point it is helpful to consider the importance of "turning" lower level functionaries in a white-collar crime scheme. These schemes, particularly in consumer fraud or investment fraud areas, customarily involve numbers of salespersons who drift from one scheme to another. These salespersons are not themselves attractive targets for criminal prosecution, and generally lack assets which make them attractive defendants in civil actions. They are, however, in a position to provide a wealth of detail as to how the scheme being investigated was implemented, and to supply evidence bearing on the guilty knowledge of the higher-ups who conceived and managed the scheme --- but who may never have been seen by a victim. Intense attention to the "turning" of lower-level white-collar crime subjects is frequently the only avenue for making a case against sophisticated fraud artists who systematically insulate themselves from the activities of agents who act at their direction. Also --- the early turning of such a subject may open floodgates of additional evidence from others.

(f) Acts which impede an investigation. Evidence that a suspect attempted to hinder or sidetrack an investigation may also bear on the issue of his criminal intent. It is perfectly reasonable for the guilty as well as the innocent to attempt to prove their innocence. But when the overall scheme includes such things as fabricated evidence, destroyed evidence, pre-contrived defenses, pre-planned payoffs to complaining victims to preclude their complaining to law enforcement officials or acting as witnesses while making no similar payments to non-complaining victims, intimidation of witnesses or investigators, and similar impediments, the investigator can use these as evidence to show that the suspect acted with fraudulent intent. Evidence of commission of such acts should be gathered and submitted to the prosecutor for possible use as corroborative evidence of criminal intent or as the basis for a separate prosecution, e.g., for attempted bribery, obstruction of justice, and similar offenses.

2. Misrepresentation and Disguise[69]

It is characteristic of white-collar crime that the subjects of investigation will have misrepresented facts and disguised their true purpose in

---

[69]Since the element of RELIANCE BY OFFENDER ON IGNORANCE OR CARELESSNESS OF VICTIM (see pp. 23 - 24 , above) is closely related to element of MISREPRESENTATION AND DISGUISE, and to VOLUNTARY VICTIM ACTION TO ASSIST THE OFFENDER (next section, p. 145 ff) its investigative implications are addressed in this and the following sections rather than in a separate section in this chapter

order to deceive their victims. This can most readily be seen in the case
of frauds which involve land sales, securities sales, advance fees, home
improvements, medical quackery, false advertising, personal improvement,
investment and business opportunities, pyramid sales, and chain referrals.

In these and other fraudulent schemes the subject attempts to induce the
victim to part with money or property by deliverate deception such as:

- Making an intentional misrepresentation of facts or omission of
  key facts relating to the quantity, quality, value, nature, utility,
  status, or other characteristic of an article, service, or proposed
  transaction - for example, a promoter represents that certain land
  offered for sale can be used as a retirement home while omitting to
  state that the land is under six inches of water year-round or
  that the land is on the side of a mountain on a 70 degree slope;
  or an applicant for a bank loan fails to indicate significant
  liabilities.

- Making representations which are true but create an impression which
  is false - for example, in a work-at-home scheme, a promoter suggests
  that the victim may earn supplemental income through some minor
  part-time effort at home; or in a business opportunity scheme a
  promoter purports to help the victim go into business for himself.
  The representations in these cases are at least literally true ---
  the work-at-home victim can, for example, buy a sewing machine and
  materials at the prices stated; or the would-be businessman can
  invest in a vending machine route. At the same time, however, the
  promoter creates a false image of the actual amount of work
  involved and/or potential earnings in the victim's mind when, in fact,
  there is no market for the products to be made at home or dispensed
  through the vending machines. In some instances the promoter will often
  talk in terms of "guaranteeing" purchases of materials produced at home,
  or cite phony figures purporting to be the earnings of others who operated
  the vending machines being pushed by the same man.

As another example, a promoter mails solicitations to subscribers
appearing in the yellow pages section of telephone directories.
The solicitation actually asks that they purchase space in the promoter's
directory. But the solicitation is purposely contrived to resemble
the normal payment request used by the telephone company for the
already existing yellow page listing. The victim-companies make
payments because they are deceived by the image of the invoice while they
do not pay much attention to the specific words in the invoice; they are
asked to make checks payable to a payee company wich resembles the
name of the telephone company.

The detailed methods and specific types of misrepresentations will vary
from case to case. Nevertheless, the investigator need not know the specific
profile of every possible scheme so long as he maintains an awareness of
the general characteriatics of misrepresentation. *Misrepresentations may
be more than direct false statements made to a victim.* Creating an appearance
which is false and deceptive by misstatement or omissions is also a

misrepresentation. This can occur in a number of ways, for example, through a careful arrangement of words, through the manner in which they are displayed, the circumstances in which they are used. Any of the innumerable deceptive practices used by a suspect to con his victim into "signing on the dotted line" may be admissible and persuasive as proofs of fraud.

For example, a representation that land is ideal for a retirement homesite, "with everything you can desire for gracious living" will be misleading if in fact the land in question is (1) not connected to a water supply, and (2) it would cost $50,000 to sink a well --- even if nothing was said to represent availability of water.

The investigator's task is therefore to gather evidence which will tend to prove that:

(a)   the representation in question was made;

(b)   the representation was false, by commission or omission.

How the investigator should go about performing this task is discussed in detail immediately below. It should be noted that the requirements discussed in the previous sub-section are, of course, still applicable. The investigator must not only gather evidence of the misrepresentations but must be able to prove that the misrepresentation was made knowingly and with the intention of deceiving the victim. In many cases, where the falsity of the representation is obvious, proving that the representation was actually made will also tend to prove criminal intent.

(a)   Proof that Misrepresentation was Made

(1)   Suspect's written material--The variety of written material used to induce fraud victims to part with their money or property is boundless. The following list, which is at best a partial list, is intended to provide an investigator with a guide to gathering evidence:

- correspondence, received by victims, or others solicited

- sales brochures

- newspaper or magazine ads

- prospectuses

- securities

- financial statements

- purchased or rented lists of prospective victims, e.g., from companies which supply mailing lists

- lists of other investors or endorsers of the scheme

- contracts

- receipts

- warranties

- guarantees

These types of data and documentation should be routinely collected and analyzed by the investigator. Such written material may serve as corroborative evidence of representations already alleged by victim. They may also be a source of additional false representations not noted by victims.

(2) Records--In certain types of fraud, a set of government or private records will exist which may help prove that misrepresentations were made. It is frequently difficult to determine just who is involved in a white-collar scheme. Many business enterprises cannot operate without filing with some public agency; even though "front men" may be used, these individuals can often be contacted and induced to disclose the identity of those for whom they are fronting. Such filings would include articles of incorporation, certificates to do business under a trade name, applications for licenses to solicit for charities or door-to-door sales, information filings to legalize sales of securities or real estate, etc. Careful searches for such material may not only make it possible to identify and reach the principal perpetrators of schemes, who wish to discourage pursuit of civil or criminal liability, but may also make it possible to invoke criminal statutes which penalize false statements made in such filings, or which provide penalties for failure to file.

The key element to be looked for, in addition to leads for further sources of evidence --- whether one is looking to public or private records --- is information which shows that the filings or applications, or other records, disclose information originating with the subject which is at variance with that provided to the victims. For example:

- A fly-by-night home repair operator may tell a prospective victim that he has been in the home repair business for 30 years, but his contractor's license shows otherwise;

- An alleged medical doctor practicing quack cures, which in themselves cannot be easily proven as quackery, may have no license to practice medicine or may have lied on a license application; and

- As an example of records in the private sector, consider a nationwide computerized credit verification system which has been programmed with false credit information. A business loan applicant provides information to a banker on a loan application. The banker requests verification of the applicant's credit through the above credit verification company. The company verifies the applicant's credit. The discrepancy between the computer records and original data records not properly entered are a principal way to show that there has been tampering with the computer system.

As we have noted above, for almost every type of business there is a government agency responsible for issuing licenses, permits, and charters, or responsible for collecting taxes, license fees, unemployment insurance and workmen's compensation, or which has jurisdiction over some technical aspect of the business. *Both the presence or absence of such documentation and records may serve an investigator in gathering evidence of false representations made by a promoter to a victim.*

For example, in schemes designed to extract payment from the government or avoid payment to the government, in the form of unemployment compensation, welfare payments, loans, padded payrolls, false travel and expense claims, overpayment on a contract, underpayment of taxes, etc., false representations can be found in the applications, invoices, contracts, reports and other forms which are submitted to the government agency. Similar considerations apply in connection with frauds against private enterprise. Private institutions or companies dispense their money and property usually on the basis of financial statements, letters of credit, and types of written endorsements which verify the promoter's assets, liabilities, need, character of business, etc.[70]

    (3) <u>Suspect's Oral Representations</u>--Investigative techniques for proving oral misrepresentations were considered earlier in the discussion of Repetitious Wrongful Activity, in the previous sub-section on proving criminal intent.[71]

When a misrepresentation is made orally to a single victim, the investigator might attempt to get the promoter to repeat the misrepresentation. The investigator should consider the use of a hidden tape recorder, or insure that there will be witnesses to the misrepresentation.[72] Without such corroboration the promoter can easily deny having made the statements attributed to him. Another alternative is to develop proof that a suspect committed similar acts. The cumulative effect of several witnesses attesting to the fact that the suspect made the representation in question is very persuasive in court.

Investigative techniques applicable to handling complaints, finding other victims, interviewing, interrogation, and undercover operations are all applicable to gathering evidence of misrepresentations. These techniques are discussed in detail in other sections of this manual.

---

[70]This topic is discussed in greater detail in the section entitled "Finding Information/Documents/Public Records," at pp. 179-183.

[71]See pp. 128-137.

[72]Legal issues relating to the use of electronic devices in investigations are continuously being examined by federal and state courts. Prosecutors, or the investigative agency's legal adviser, should always be consulted before using these investigative techniques.

(b) <u>Proof of Falsity</u>

False representations, false pretenses, and false promises can take an infinite variety of specific forms depending upon the type of fraudulent scheme. They can be in the form of false statements, omissions of key facts, or creation of false impressions about an article or a service which is part of a transaction between the suspect and victim. The misrepresentation may concern the quantity, quality, value, nature, utility, status, or other characteristic of an article, service, or proposed transaction.

(1) <u>Investigative requirements</u>--The investigator's approach to collecting evidence as to the falsity of a representation may entail:

- gathering evidence from victims which indicate that the product or service was not as represented;

- testing the validity of the suspected misrepresentation; for example, actually trying out a product or service to an extent which will convincingly indicate the falsity of the representation;

- accumulating documentation which disputes the suspected misrepresentation; and

- obtaining expert testimony which is counter to the suspected misrepresentations.

(2) <u>Examples and applications of investigative techniques</u>--The following are examples which serve to illustrate the varieties of investigative approaches used to achieve the above requirements.

Example: A group of victims of a land sale scheme do not know that their property is not worth what they paid for it. They are sought out through advertising by a corporation, whose representatives make the following oral statements in order to get money from them.

a) the corporation will publish a magazine, in which they will advertise the landowner's property for sale;

b) the corporation already has a list of investors, mostly foreign, who have contacted them for help in investing in United States land because the dollar has depreciated;

c) the corporation does not have to be licensed in the victim's state because it is already licensed in another state;

d) the corporation has been in business for six years;

e) there will be no charge for the advertising unless there is a sale, in which case the charge will be 6% of the sale price, but there is a $100 "registration fee" which will be applied to the 6% charge.

In truth and in fact, while it may be difficult to prove, this is simply a scheme to con more money out of persons who have already demonstrated their vulnerability to white-collar schemes.

Representation a) is a future representation which is almost impossible to prove to be a false representation unless there is documentary or oral testimony (from the schemers themselves) that they had no intention of publishing the magazine at the time they said they intended to publish it. After all, the promoters might easily be able to publish a magazine. But, the promise to publish would not have been sufficient to induce potential victims to part with their money. The promoter, therefore, spiced up his pitch with statement b) which shows the reasonableness of the idea; statement c) which relieves a certain doubt in the mind of a prospective victim; and statement d) which gives the promoter's company an aura of respectability. Note that b), c), and d), unlike a) are representations of facts, and are either true or false --- thus good target areas for investigation.

This is the kind of case which will generally call for help from the prosecutor, who should be persuaded that it bears all the outward indications of a traditional advance fee scheme. Subpoenas of the books and records of a corporation, for example, should disclose the existence or non-existence of a foreign buyers list, which can be checked for authenticity.[73] Telephone and cable records can similarly be checked to determine whether there was wire contact with alleged prospective foreign buyers. The 6% charge would very likely be construed as the equivalent of a real estate brokerage commission under the laws of some states, making it important to check other states to determine whether any such license had been obtained; if yes, there might be helpful information in the application; if no, there would be one additional misrepresentation. In any event there might be a violation in the investigator's own state for failure to get a license.

> Example: A salesman represents that a carburetor attachment will increase gas mileage. In such cases which involve technology, investigators should seek out expert testimony. Another alternative is to have the device tested at a testing laboratory or university with appropriate facilities to determine the truth or falsity of the representation.

> Example: A scientific laboratory advertises countrywide with the representation that it will analyze urine samples and provide its customers with prescriptions for vitamins based on this analysis. The ads placed in medical journals falsely imply that recent research at a major hospital has demonstrated the value of "hormone urinalysis in anticipating nutritional deficiencies." The promoter's names are *added with the appropriate titles of "M.D." or "Ph.D." The victims,* many referred by medical doctors who read the ads, pay for the urinalysis and subsequently receive high sounding reports with recommendations regarding purchase of vitamins.

---

[73]Foreign investigations of issues such as this can be done with the help of Interpol. See pp. 194-195.

In an actual case of this nature, the investigator checked the urin-
analysis reports and found that every report contained a recommendation
for vitamins. Consulting faculty members at a medical school, the
investigator learned that less than one percent of all Americans suffered
from the kinds of vitamin deficiencies discovered in the urinalysis reports.
The investigator also tested the representation by submitting many samples
of his own and others' urine as well as some synthetic samples under different
names. The only consistency in the urinalysis reports was the prescription
for vitamins, which was being sold by the same promoters at inflated prices.

This case examplifies the value of seeking expert assistance such as that
found in health and drug regulatory agencies and medical schools. In addition,
the investigator can in such cases patiently test the product or service
offered until the data statistically support a conclusion concerning the
truth or falsity of the representation. The investigator should, however,
make sure that experts test both the samples of urine (or whatever item is the
subject matter of a fraud) and the providers of the samples (if such is
relevant) before they are sent in, to be sure that the experts' testimony
will be relevant and admissible at trial.

> Example: A fraudulent land company sells land it purports
> to own to unsuspecting victims. The land company offers
> the land on a contract with a comparatively low down payment
> and relatively low monthly installments. In truth, it is only
> the down payment that interests the company. Upon receiving
> the initial payment, and prior to any effective title search,
> the company closes its office and leaves the victims with
> worthless land contracts.

Similarly a renter leaves a payment of one month's rent with the purported owner of a house for rent with the intention of moving in two
weeks later. He arrives two weeks later to move in only to find that
there are twenty other renters all with receipts for the down payment
of one month's rent in advance.

In such cases (aside from the problem of locating the suspects
who will usually have long since vanished), the investigator will have
to develop the falsity in the misrepresentation of true ownership or
title. In real estate cases the county recorder and assessor will usually
have records appropriate to such proof. In cases of other types of
property, the investigator must develop proof of falsity through documentation such as receipts, sales slips, cancelled checks and the like.
When such documentation is not available, the investigator should try to
develop circumstantial evidence from interviewing others who may have
factual knowledge which disputes the representation in question.

> Example: In a scheme involving the sale of silver
> certificates, a promoter operating out of a very im-
> pressive office represents that the silver is pur-
> chased through a well-known "X" silver brokerage house
> in another state; that the actual silver is stored
> in "Y" bonded warehouse, also out-of-state; and that
> delivery of silver will be made within 30 days upon
> presentation of the certificate. The scheme is basically
> one in which the promoter encourages the victim to trade

in silver certificates through the promoter, rather
than calling for actual silver at any time. An investigative check with the "X" brokerage house and the "Y"
warehouse regarding the accuracy of the representations
is the first step, and it is found that the suspect has
had no business transactions with "X" or "Y". From the
fact that the promoter's local offices contain no silver
storage facility such as a safe and no silver is ever found
on hand, one might conclude that no delivery of silver was
ever intended.

Example: A promoter induces his victims to purchase
distributorships in a referral selling scheme. The promoter fails to inform the purchasers that among the many
papers they are signing are real estate mortgages on their
homes, though he has made clear that they are signing
promissory notes for the cost of the distributorship. Although this is misrepresentation by omission, the investigator can develop evidence by acquiring testimony from one
or more victims that the purchase would not have been made
if they had known the truth, i.e., that they were also
acquiring mortgages on their homes as well as distributorships.

3.   Voluntary Victim Action to Assist the Offender

As discussed earlier in this Manual, two essential elements of white-
collar crimes are *reliance of the white-collar criminal on the carelessness
or ignorance of the victim* and *voluntary victim action to assist the offender,*
i.e., some affirmative action by the victim to cooperate with the per-
petrator(s) of the crime.

Proof of *voluntary victim action* is relatively easy to obtain. The
victim is quite capable of supplying it if he or she is at all cooperative ---
testifying to signing a contract, sending a letter with a check, etc.
Even where the victim is an institution it can usually provide evidence
through its officers or employees that it accepted as valid a false loan
application, or a deceptive claim for goods or services allegedly delivered.
Government itself may supply the testimony that its officials provided the
affirmative action essential to execution of the fraud (as victim, or
indirectly) by accepting as valid and truthful a claim for goods or services,
or by accepting and filing what were purported to be truthful and complete
disclosure statements required before securities or certain real estate
subdivisions of land can be offered for sale.

Information (evidence) on the steps taken by the white-collar criminal
to make him confident that the victim would respond in the way he wishes,
will generally involve proof of more subtle misrepresentations made by the
suspect to increase victim confidence. It is therefore most important that
the investigator carefully question victims to determine what caused them to
more easily accept written or oral misrepresentations. What was there in
the setting in which their signatures were obtained which made them act without
doing much checking? This is not to suggest that the victim ever has an
official duty to check up on everything --- but rather that where the offender
can be shown to have deprived or conned the victim into not checking, it

will be a stronger case. The answers to such questions may well produce
information which gives deeper meaning to vague sales pitches, transforming
them into clear and obvious misrepresentations. Examples of the kinds of
evidence which will contribute to showing the anatomy of the fraud to a
court or jury (or to a prosecutor who is considering either civil or
criminal action) would be the following:

- False statements made to a regulatory agency which must
  clear securities or land sales, will often be accepted and
  the resulting prospectuses will carry the legend that the
  facts contained therein were filed with the state, or
  federal agency as required by law. The same legend will usually
  include a statement that acceptance for filing or registration
  does not constitute any form of government approval. Nevertheless, the very fact that there has been some governmental
  surveillance of the transaction tends to increase victim confidence in the bonafides of the opportunity.

- The investigator in such cases should therefore concentrate
  on showing that misrepresentations were made to the government regulatory agency (which is usually a violation in and of
  itself), with the aim of getting the state agency to accept
  the suspect's filing, as part of the scheme to defraud the
  ultimate victim. Possible lies by the white-collar criminal
  operator to the accountant who prepared a financial statement
  for filing should be targets of inquiry. In a land fraud case
  every attempt should be made to question surveyors and water
  experts who produced data for filing to gain testimony which might
  indicate that their findings were distorted to induce the regulatory agencies to take the affirmative step of accepting
  the filing.

- Careful attention should be given to obtaining details as to the
  setting in which fraudulent deals are closed, to see how
  voluntary victim action was procured. Misrepresentations, or
  even vague statements become more deceptive if shills are present
  to stampede victims into signing on the dotted line. The deceptive
  pitch of a personal improvement scheme, promising a great
  theatrical career for a victim, can be perceived to be even
  more deceptive if there is evidence that the perpetrators gave
  victims talent tests as a prerequisite for admission to a talent
  school, but that it was part of the scheme that no one was ever
  allowed to fail such a test.

- Evidence should be sought as to the manner in which relatively
  innocent third parties, or parties with lesser degrees of
  culpability, are used to help procure *voluntary victim action*.
  It is not uncommon, particularly in investment schemes, for fraud
  operators to enhance their own credibility by using otherwise
  legitimate investment advisers, accountants, and attorneys, to
  persuade clients to invest. Often these intermediaries will be

lured into conflict of interest situations by special
sales commissions or free or cut rate participations in
the same investments. Their position is equivocal, since
they helped to perpetrate the fraud but are not particularly
important subjects for prosecution. Under these circumstances they will frequently "turn" and provide evidence
as to how they were used to lull their clients into
acquiescence, and particularly if they are apprehensive
about being prosecuted. They should generally not be
treated as innocent victims if they received special
compensation; if so treated they will be apprehensive
about being sued by their clients, and will be lost as a
source of evidence. Furthermore, in some cases these
intermediaries will have operated so closely with the principal
scheme operators that they can be charged as co-conspirators,
and their own misrepresentations can be introduced in evidence
against the principal scheme operators as co-conspirators.

- In chain referral or pyramid schemes, perpetrators generally
persuade victims to bring other victims (often their own
friends) into the net, by making it financially rewarding
to do so. Statements made by first-tier victims to second-
tier victims, etc., should be carefully collected to determine
how they were inspired. Victims, including those who start
to lose faith and bother the fraud operator, will receive
special encouragement and advice as to what to say to persuade
a friend or acquaintance to buy into the same fraud; careful
questioning of the first-tier victim as to where he obtained
the information for his "pitch" may well produce evidence
laying responsibility for clear misrepresentations at the
doorstep of the principal fraud operators.

- One form of fraud against government is bid-rigging, i.e.,
collusion among bidders to present a facade of competitive
bidding while ensuring that the colluding bidders determine
the winner and the price of the goods or services. In addition
to seeking evidence that there was an illegal agreement to act
in concert among the bidders, the investigator should go further
to get information on steps taken to enhance appearances of
competition, i.e., half-hearted appeals following bid awards,
carefully contrived random-appearing bid disparities, and
agreed-upon winners, etc. --- all undertaken to procure the
voluntary victim action by the agency awarding the sought-for
contract by creating a facade of bona fide'competition.

Evidence of activities designed to procure *voluntary victim action*, such
as those described above, can be extraordinarily important to the success
of a case, and to the prosecutor agreeing to take a case. If the investigator simply procures evidence that misrepresentations were made, that the

148

victim acted in reliance on these misrepresentations, and lost his money
thereby, it may be sufficient for a technical legal case. But the
extra dimension provided by evidence of the many activities employed to
break down the victim's resistance can spell the difference between a
prosecutor taking or not taking a case, between a case being appropriate
for criminal prosecution rather than civil or administrative action, and
between winning and losing.

4. Concealment

The *concealment* element of white-collar crime generates the most
significant distinctions between the investigation of white-collar and
other crimes. In white-collar crimes there are rarely any simple indicators or events which trigger law enforcement reactions, as would be
the case in common crimes such as homicide, robbery, burglary, or vice
crimes such as gambling, narcotics, or prostitution. In common crimes,
though there may be a problem in obtaining evidence, it is relatively clear
victims almost never know they have been victimized until well after the executed transactions or occurrences, and, in fact, may never know they have
been victimized. The element of *concealment* addresses those aspects of
execution of a white-collar scheme which are undertaken to keep the victim
in perpetual ignorance of his victimization, or delay the victim's
realization, and the importance of those aspects to the investigator.

This discussion differs from those in which Misrepresentations were
considered at length[74] in that the earlier discussions basically concerned
evidence on the use of guile and deception to gain victim acquiescence,
i.e., to get the victim's signature or money --- while here we are concerned
with what evidence the investigator should seek to show what the white-collar
criminal does, or relies on, to cover up the fact that a crime or wrongful
act has taken place.

Acts in furtherance of *concealment* may simply be another aspect of,
or implicit in, the steps taken to obtain victim acquiescence. Or they may
be an entirely separate and distinct series of deceptive acts, a continued
cover-up of what has taken place. In either situation it is important that
the white-collar crime investigator ask, in every case he investigates,
what the perpetrator did to conceal or cover-up; both while "taking" the
victim and after obtaining the proceeds of the fraud. The Supreme Court
of the United States has specifically held, for example, that lulling
letters, to keep the fraud victim quiet after the victim has fully parted
with his money, can still be part of a scheme to defraud.

[74]See pp. 137-145.

Regardless of the type of scheme or method of concealment, the investigator should use the same basic sources of leads to aid in detection and gathering evidence of white-collar crime concealment, as in proving other elements of the crime, i.e., victim complaints, intelligence concerning individuals, intelligence concerning possible criminal activities, financial investigations, and affirmative searches for violations. The investigation process which stems from victim complaints is discussed in detail in the sections entitled Locating Other Victims,[75] and Interviewing.[76] As an added consideration, the white-collar crime investigator must be continually alert to the hidden nature of most sophisticated white-collar crime. The investigator should, therefore, consider the following in gathering and organizing evidence of white-collar crime concealment:

(a) <u>Crimes Too Small to be Recognized as Crimes by the Victim</u>

The ideal white-collar crime, from a perpetrator's point of view, is one which will never be recognized as a crime. A classic example is the charity fraud. A charity fraud may involve a large amount of money which is ordinarily an accumulation of small amounts taken from large numbers of people. Accordingly, no victim will have a sufficient personal interest to attempt to follow up on what is done with his money. The health fraud example given earlier[77] in which the scientific laboratory did "hormonal urinalyses" and always recommended vitamins, is another example where the individual amounts taken from each victim are small enough to practically guarantee concealment of the fraud. The specific tactics used by the investigator to collect evidence in the hormonal urinalysis fraud involved the investigator's becoming a victim and obtaining statistical evidence of fraud, by submitting many samples of his own and friends' urine under many different names and also getting experts to refute the claims of the perpetrators. In a case of charity fraud, the investigator could collect evidence such as 1) data on the applications for permits (fraudulent charities will often fail to get permits), and 2) financial trail of the collected funds, i.e., how they were used or failed to be used.

(b) <u>Lulling the Victim</u>

There is another type of concealment which is prevalent in frauds that have to be continuous in nature in order to succeed. For example, bankruptcy frauds and "bustouts" require that over a period of time the criminal promoter establish sufficient credit with suppliers to be able to purchase

---

[75]See pp. 185-187.

[76]See pp. 154-167.

[77]See p. 143.

large quantities of materials without payment. To conceal such frauds
during the weeks or months of their perpetration, the criminal subject may
lull the victim with a series of official sounding letters or telephone
calls reassuring the victim and explaining why the particular payment
in question cannot be made "at this time." The letters and telephone calls
will often be made by people who have previously established a relationship
of trust with the suppliers, may be fronts for organized crime which have
hooks into ostensible owners of business, and will frequently result in
granting of additional credit. Token payments to the victim, comprising only
a small percentage of the amount due, may also be used to lull him. Finally,
the perpetrator goes bankrupt, or just closes the doors of his company and
disappears.

In an advance fee loan scheme, a businessman seeking a loan will agree
to pay $2,000 to a loan broker for securing a $75,000 loan. The loan
broker will ask for $500 or $750 initially, graciously offering to waive the
balance until he has delivered the promised financing. The loan broker
has no intention of ever earning the balance. His objective is to obtain
the initial retainer. A series of lulling letters is then used to keep the
victim quiet while others are being victimized, and to tire the victim out.
Finally, the loan brokerage firm collapses. A year may elapse while pre-
programmed lulling letters continue until finally the victim learns that
the loan brokerage company is no longer in existence.

In all such cases it is essential that the investigator carefully
check representations made for the purpose of lulling victims; the falsity
of such representations will be strong evidence of fraud.

(c) Creating a Complex Organizational Structure to Discourage Victims

Concealment may also be achieved by design of a complex organizational structure which discourages complaints or pursuit by victims. For
example, a victim may refuse to continue payments for his purchase of a
faulty product or service because it was misrepresented to him. He finds
out that his installment payment agreement has been sold to a bank or
collection agency which refuses to be held responsible for the performance
of the supplier.[78] The victim's complaints result in legal-sounding
responses which are confusing. The victim's ignorance of the law and the
spectre of huge legal expenses might easily discourage him from pursuit
of an elusive adversary, and may even cause him to continue to make payments
for the faulty product or service.

In such cases the investigator should seek to detail the exact steps
taken by the suspect, carefully considering whether each step had some
business purpose other than to discourage the victim from pursuit. Where
an installment payment agreement has been sold to a bank, finance company, or
collection agency, the investigator should search for information which might
show collusion between the suspect and the institution purchasing the agreement --- such as 1) a heavily discounted price, which might indicate the
finance company was aware of some problem in the deal, or 2) proof that the
finance company was well aware of the way the suspect did business by reason

[78]U.S. Federal Trade Commission rules now make this particular tactic more
difficult to implement, but there is little doubt that it will continue to be
used as a fraud tactic on the theory that many victims will not be aware of
their rights.

of numerous complaints arising out of prior transactions, or 3) the finance company purchases were executed without standards of care usually employed by legitimate purchasers of such contracts. None of these might, in themselves, be conclusive, but could lead to cumulative evidence of intent to frustrate victim follow-up action.

(d) Creating Satisfied Victims for a Period of Time

Certain white-collar crimes, by their very nature, can only be concealed for short periods of time. In such cases the perpetrators will stop the scheme prior to its reaching the point of discovery, and then either disappear or try to make an outward showing that the losses resulted from a mere business failure. In a classic Ponzi scheme, for example, the perpetrator will use money from new investors to make the expected dividend or interest payments promised to earlier investors. Investors are thus kept satisfied for a short period of time, as would be the case if a $1,000 investment resulted in three monthly payments of $50 each, an annual return of 60 percent in contrast to bank interest of approximately 5 percent. By the end of the third month, early investors have told their friends and relatives about this "good deal" and investments pour into the subject's cashbox. The end is inevitable, though in some instances Ponzi schemes have been prolonged for several years.

In cases involving large numbers of investors, who are scattered geographically, the investigator should consider the possibility of using the media to encourage victims to come forth. Victims of schemes which employ such concealment devices can usually provide substantial, detailed evidence of oral misrepresentations used to discourage complaints, frequently backed up by letters, etc. If a list of investors is available the investigator should consider the use of questionnaires,[79] where the list is a long one.

(e) Crimes which are Detectable and Provable only through Audit Procedures

White-collar crimes such as embezzlement, tax fraud, bankruptcy fraud, unemployment insurance fraud, and the like, require some form of audit procedures, i.e., a physical examination and analysis of financial accounts, transaction records and documentation, inventories, etc., as a prerequisite to finding out and proving that a crime has been committed. In today's world the use of cash to conduct major transactions is practically non-existent. Almost all businesses, financial institutions and government agencies use some form of computerized system to conduct all or part of their business making the problem of auditing particularly difficult, and compounding the difficulties in detection.

---

[79]See later section entitled "Questionnaires and Form Letters at pp. 187-192.

Example: A computer programmer in a bank adjusts the program for detecting overdrafts to ignore overdrafts of his personal account.

Example: A con-artist sets up a fictitious business with six fictitious employees, pays the minimum amount of unemployment taxes for the minimum period required. The con-artist then assumes identifications as the fictitious employees and then applies for and collects unemployment insurance. The investigator seeking to detect such a fraud must examine the forms submitted to the state agency that handles unemployment insurance and the records of applications and payments to the employees to see if there are any patterns which indicate that a fraud is underway. For example, a group of firms with similar lists of employees who all make applications for insurance as soon as the minimum time for qualifying has passed; or the use of a recent series of social security numbers which might indicate false social security cards being obtained by a single person.

Example: An insurance company creates fake life insurance policies and sells them to reinsurers (i.e., other insurance companies who assume the long term risk) for an immediate income, hoping that they will be able to make the annual payments to the reinsurers either through investments or other business or by selling more fake policies. The accountants who are responsible for the audit report their suspicions to their superiors but are repeatedly put off when they request to see original paperwork to back up the computer printouts. The delays are for the white-collar scheme operators to gain time to prepare forgeries of "original" documents.

Example: A computer is programmed to show that an oil company's barge is receiving 2,000 barrels of oil each trip, when in actuality the barge is receiving 4,000 barrels. It is evident that some form of double-check upon the computer data, e.g., a spot audit of any individual transaction records which indicate amount of oil delivered or an audit of inventory would be the only way to detect such a crime, other than informants or accidental detection. Incidentally, one such theft continued intermittently for seven years.

Investigators should possess, or have ready access to auditing and accounting skills, since tracking of a white-collar scheme along an audit trail is frequently the most efficient way to develop evidence which will effectively preclude the spinning of fictitious explanations by suspects; it is very, very difficult to change the records of past transactions which are perpetuated in the documents and books of third parties such as banks, telephone companies, landlords or innocent suppliers of goods and services to the white-collar scheme operators. Detailed discussion of how to do all this is beyond the scope of this manual, but the reader is referred to Richard A. Nossen's The Seventh Basic Investigative Technique: Analyzing Financial Transactions in the Investigation of Organized Crime and White-Collar Crime Targets, represented as Appendix D in this manual.

(f) Crimes of Overwhelming Size and Complexity

Extremely large scale white-collar crime operations may be so complex and have absolutely no outward appearance other than that of a legitimate, competitive, normal business, that the sheer size and the character of the sponsorship makes a crime seem an incredulous possibility. A single complex scheme of this kind may involve many different categories of white-collar crime and peripherally may also involve many common crimes. The connection between the perpetrators of the common crimes and white-collar criminals will rarely be evident to any outside observer and the entire process may include a variety of transactions into which an investigator must dig. Take, for example, the establishment of a monopoly by an organized criminal enterprise in an industry such as garbage collection. The process by which this occurred may take a variety of forms such as the gradual takeover of competitors through first undercutting prices then buying out the failed companies; or perhaps bombing of competitors' trucks or other types of violence which insure that competitors will not resist takeover; and perhaps bribery of public officials responsible for regulating the industry or collection routes.

To develop proofs in such situations will require imaginative searches for evidence on such issues as: the true identity of company owners; the sources of finance (i.e., the possibilities of criminal funds being laundered through investment in this business); the associations between company owners and political figures who might influence the selection of contractors and establishment of collection routes; the pattern of bids by alleged competitors; and relationships between the suspects and relevant labor unions.

5. Elements: A Summary

The elements discussed here cannot be separated one from the other, with each provable by a showing of entirely different sets of facts or occurrences arising in the course of commission of a white-collar scheme. Neither must there be evidence as to each of these elements in every case. They should be viewed, rather, as different lenses through which the white-collar scheme can be seen. Examination from the different perspectives disclosed through each of these lenses will help the investigator to be sure that he can identify the kinds of evidence he needs to be certain that a court or jury will understand what occurred, the criminal design which made it occur, how the victim was manipulated, and what was done to the victim.

By establishing such a solid basis for identifying the kinds of evidence needed to make a case, and by making such identifications, the investigator will be in a good position to employ the investigative techniques to which this manual now directs its attention.

B. INTERVIEWING AND INTERROGATION

Few skills are so important to the effectiveness of the white-collar crime investigator as having firm command of interviewing and interrogation techniques. For purposes of this manual the distinction between the two situations is determined by differences in the prime objectives and the types of persons involved in the meeting. Thus *interviewing* involves the systematic questioning of persons who have knowledge of events, persons involved, or circumstances surrounding the case under investigation, including the obtaining of documentary or physical evidence; *interrogation*, on the other hand, involves questioning of suspects and/or uncooperative witnesses for the purpose of obtaining evidence or proof of significant omissions --- or to give the subject of the investigation an opportunity to volunteer facts which might have the exculpatory effect of putting the transactions being investigated in a different light.

The line between *interviewing* and *interrogation* is often quite fluid. For example, an uncooperative witness being *interrogated* may decide to cooperate, or one of the subjects of the investigation may be "turned" and agree to provide evidence against others. In such a situation the *interrogation* will necessarily take on the attributes of the *interviewing* process and call for the employment of many of the *interviewing* techniques discussed below --- though with careful regard for sensitive legal issues and apprehension about whether the apparently cooperating subject or formerly recalcitrant witness is truly cooperating. In these situations, where *interrogation* is shading or edging into *interviewing*, tactics and techniques must be carefully employed or modified to take into account the interviewee's special motivations and objectives.

It should also be recognized that the opposite may occur. In the course of questioning a witness thought to be an innocent and incidental party to a transaction, the investigator may sense that the person being interviewed (even in some instances where such person was a victim at some stage) may also be culpable. In such a situation the investigator will wish to modify his tactics or techniques in the opposite direction, or to cease his questioning entirely, either because the proffered cooperation is untrustworthy, because the investigator may disclose more about his case than he wishes to do because of his line of questioning, or because serious legal issues may arise (or may already have arisen) because of failure to warn this subject as to his or her rights.

1. Interviewing Victims and Witnesses

    (a) Purpose and Objectives

        At the outset of an inquiry into a crime the investigator usually possesses very limited information concerning the occurrence. In some instances the information may be more complete, such as where a trade association has investigators who previously undertook a substantial investigative effort.

In the more usual situation, this is what will face the investigator:

- A crime may have been committed but the fact of its commission must yet be established.

•There may be a complainant or a victim, perhaps an individual,
a corporation, or a government entity.

•There may be some physical evidence of the crime.

•There may be some intelligence regarding a crime and
there may be a suspect.

In white-collar crime one of the major investigative tools required to
close the gap between these items of information, and evidence to support a
prosecution, is the interview. It is fundamentally from interviews that the
investigator achieves the following significant objectives:

•obtains information which establishes the essential
elements of the crime;

•obtains most of his leads for developing the case and
gathering other evidence;

•obtains the cooperation of victims and witnesses in
recounting their experiences in court; and

•obtains information concerning personal background and
personal and economic motives of those to be considered
for witnesses at the trial.

Although there can be little standardization of technique in the
actual approach to and conduct of an interview --- a process strongly dependent
on the personalities of the investigator and interviewees --- every investigator should follow a set of guidelines which will insure maximum probability
of achieving the above objectives.

(b) Planning for the Interview

(1) Why plan? Proper planning enhances the probability of the
investigator's success and effectiveness in the interview situation. The
investigator should ascertain as many facts as are reasonably available to
him prior to conducting any interview, including careful review of
relevant documents to refresh his memory. Rarely will the investigator
be able to follow a format which is routine, that he can commit to memory.
It is, therefore, advisable to prepare questions in advance. This is
particularly important when investigations may involve new schemes with
which the investigator is unfamiliar. Without proper planning the investigator will find himself in over his head, he will not understand the
responses being given, nor will he know what further information to seek in
order to conduct an intelligent investigation.

(2) Time and place. There are very real advantages (principally
to the efficiency of the investigation) in conducting the interview at the
investigator's own office. In many cases, however, it may be far more

advisable to visit the witness at his home or office --- a method which has
several advantages:

a)   The interviewee is more likely to have papers,
     appointment books, etc. available for production if
     they become relevant to the interview. The interviewee
     may also be in a position to immediately call on
     members of his family, or co-workers for additional
     information and corroborative evidence.

b)   It may be more convenient for the interviewee, thus
     making it more likely that he will agree to the meeting
     for the interview in the first place.

c)   The investigator will have a more difficult time
     eliminating distractions, such as from inquiries
     from his supervisors or colleagues who need help if the
     meeting is at the investigator's own office, than will
     interviewees on their own turf --- for whom the process
     will be a unique and impressive experience.

d)   It may also be advantageous to catch the potential
     interviewee off guard, before he can have second thoughts,
     talk to someone else, develop fear, or be contacted by the
     subjects of the investigation.

When the interview is to be held away from his own office, the investigator should make a specific appointment for optimum convenience of both
parties, unless there is some special reason not to do so, such as indicated
in d) above.

Interviews should always be arranged so that there is enough time to
conduct a full interview. It is always better to have extra time than to
create additional irritations by terminating an interview early or making
excuses for breaking or delaying appointments which are scheduled to
follow. When you know you are going to be late, telephone, apologize, and
inform the person to be interviewed when you will arrive, or schedule another
appointment immediately.

If interviews are attempted without prior appointment, the investigator
risks not finding the person or finding that the person is completely unprepared. This problem is particularly important when the investigator
desires to obtain documents such as cancelled checks of a victim, sales
literature from a witness, or advice and supporting documents from an expert.
Be sure to tell the interviewee what you would like him to have at the
interview, or to assemble and have on hand. When calling on a person without
an appointment, it is important to select a time that would be least likely
to irritate the interviewee --- this seems like an elementary point but enough
witnesses have been turned off by failure to follow this obvious precaution
that it is well worth stating again.

The investigator should take the special characteristics of interviewees into account. When dealing with witnesses/victims whose native language is not English (and where the investigator does not speak the foreign language), appointments should be made by some secretary or other office personnel familiar with the foreign language --- if at all possible. The investigator should take special pains to be certain there is no misunderstanding as to time and place and should, if possible, arrange for someone fluent in the foreign language to accompany him.

It is highly desirable to schedule appointments as quickly as possible after the first contact with an interviewee --- within 24 hours if at all possible --- and to take the time to telephone to confirm the appointment a few hours before it is to take place. Misunderstandings and faulty memories can cause investigators more trouble than recalcitrant witnesses in such situations --- since confusion easily triggers loss of confidence on the part of the victim/witness.

The investigator will find that the process of making the appointment will itself be a source of valuable information, both to the effectiveness and efficiency of the investigation. The response of a witness or victim to the request for the interview should alert the investigator to special problems he might encounter (such as language problems, fear, lack of awareness on the part of the witness that he was a victim) which will help the investigator to properly plan the forthcoming interview.

(3) <u>Setting</u>. When under control of the investigator, the setting for an interview should be selected to provide a minimum number of roadblocks to <u>talking</u> and, more importantly, <u>listening</u>. Distractions such as telephones, other voices, other conversations, other persons can have a disastrous affect on the recall capabilities of a victim or witness. Interruptions, unrelated to the problem at hand, will often convey to the interviewee that the investigator is not really interested in what is being said. When the interview is conducted at the investigator's agency, he should use an interviewing room designed for pleasant but serious conversation, without too many decorative distractions, and which insures privacy.

The investigator should also consider other possibilities for creating an environment which will be helpful in obtaining information --- all directed toward putting the witness at ease and heightening the witness' trust in the investigator. For example, the witness should be encouraged to tell his story in his own way, even if it rambles; the investigator should interrupt only for clarifications and refrain from pointed questions until the witness, particularly the victim-witness, has unburdened himself.

(4) <u>Information to be obtained</u>. Investigators must be prepared with knowledge of the types of information they are trying to collect. Figure 11 is a chart which illustrates the types of information generally important to white-collar crime investigation. It lists and categorizes the types of information that might be collected from victims, potential witnesses, or third parties who may have peripheral information or expertise relating to the case under investigation.

This list is intended as a guide only, and should be modified as the particular occasion demands. For example, although all of the items listed

FIGURE 11

GUIDELINES FOR INFORMATION TO BE COLLECTED IN INTERVIEWS

ABOUT THE INTERVIEW

    Location, date and time
    Names of investigators

ABOUT THE SUBJECTS BEING INVESTIGATED

    Names of promoters, their representatives, agents, etc.
    (individuals and company names)

    Addresses of individuals and companies

    Legal status of companies (corporations, partnerships, state of
    incorporation, etc.)

    Telephone numbers of individuals and companies

    Physical descriptions

    Title, salary, tenure, duties and responsibilities of
    suspect (particularly important in embezzlement cases)

ABOUT CONTACT BETWEEN SUBJECTS AND WITNESSES

    How was initial contact made? -- e.g.,

        Advertisement in newspaper, radio, or television

            Get name of paper, station and dates

        Sales letter

            Get copies of letter, envelopes, other material included

        Personal contact

            Telephone or in person --- get dates, names, locations
            and content of conversation

        Reference through third party (attorney, friend, etc.)

    Were there any previous relationships between promoter and victim?

    How did the promoters or their representatives get the victim's name?
    or learn about the victim?

FIGURE 11 (continued)

ABOUT THE SITUATION AND CONTENT OF MEETINGS, CONVERSATIONS, TRANSACTIONS, ETC.

Date, location and time of occurrence

Names, addresses, titles, etc., of all who were present

Full details of all representations (promises)

    Method of representation
    What was said?
    What was shown? What was handed out (letters, brochures,
        prospectuses, sales literature, warranties, guarantees,
        contracts)?, etc.

Which person made each representation?

Victim's degree of reliance on representation

    Did victim have reservations?
    Did he express them?
    Did he ask any questions?
    What were the answers? Who made them?
    How were his reservations overcome? By whom?
    Was anything done to discourage victim from a detailed
        reading of papers, consulting friends or attorneys,
        accountant, banker, etc.?

Representations which victim believes were false

Representations which victim believes were omitted but should have been
told

Was victim put under any time or other severe pressure to enter into
transaction? How?

Full details of transaction

    Amount of dollars
    Method of payment --- check, cash, agreements or contracts
        to pay in future, etc.
    Date and circumstance of payment --- in person, by mail, to whom, etc

ABOUT THE VICTIM

Name, address, telephone numbers (home and business)

Motivation behind the complaint:

    To recover losses
    Anger or outrage
    To protect others from same scheme

If information as to victim motivation not based on victim statement,
what is basis for above information?

FIGURE 11 (continued)

Circumstances will dictate when the investigator should advise victim that criminal action does not guarantee restitution nor does it insure success in a civil action, but it is proper to point out that one possible outcome of action is restitution following criminal or government civil action.

Victim's background (may assist in finding out how promoter got victim's name and thus help in locating other victims)

How and when victim discovered representations were false

Has victim complainted to promoter?

What did victim do or say?
Did victim complain himself, or through a friend or attorney?
Has victim complained to any other private or public agency? With what results?

Financial losses suffered

Victim's source of funds lost

Psychological suffering

Has victim withheld information from members of his family or business associates?

Victim's willingness to assist in investigation and testify in court (circumstances will dictate appropriate timing for addressing these issues --- e.g., this may not be suitable in the early stages of interviewing non-complaining witnesses)

Will victim sign statement, or affidavit swearing to truth of what was said?

ABOUT PHYSICAL EVIDENCE

Borrow or copy all physical evidence --- cancelled checks, receipts, brochures, sales literature, prospectuses, warranties, guarantees, letters, envelopes, contracts, etc.

Give receipt for all items borrowed

Have interviewee initial and date each page of each item

on the chart would be applicable to a complaining victim, not all of them would be applicable to a witness who was not victimized. The specific requirements of interviewing the principals or suspects in a scheme is covered in the next section, which deals with interrogation of suspects.[81]

(c) <u>Conducting the Interview</u>

(1) <u>Investigator's demeanor</u>. An investigator when dealing with any member of the public, whether in person or via the telephone, must always be efficient, courteous, polite and careful with regard to language. The investigator represents his agency and the impression he leaves is the impression the public will have of the agency. Acceptance of even the smallest gratuity, including offers of refreshment, can lead to problems for the agency's image as well as the development of the case.

The following are some suggestions regarding an investigator's conduct during an interview.

- Never talk down to the person you are interviewing. Never assume that the subject is less intelligent than you. Any hint of disrespect or condescension can quickly turn a cooperative subject into an un-cooperative one.

- Never use language which disparages the intelligence or competence of the interviewee, even if you may think he acted foolishly in being victimized, in not preventing victimization of a friend or associate, or in failing to notify law enforcement officers when it would have been common sense to do so.

- Be sensitive to the personal concerns of the victim or witness, especially when these involve perceptions of how interviewee may be treated because of sex, race, religion, or ethnic background.

- Be businesslike. Conduct the interview in a professional manner. The investigator should be friendly, but not familiar. Certain pleasantries are sometimes necessary but the interview should not become a social occasion.

- Do not become authoritarian or attempt to dominate the interview.

- Make it clear that anyone, no matter how smart or well-trained can be victimized --- that there are others who are and and have been in the same boat.[82] If possible, cite examples of well known people or professional groups who have been similarly victimized.

---

[81]See pp.

[82]See Chapter I, pp.

- Always be sympathetic and respectful to victims and complainants. Never suggest that a victim is a victim because of something he did. You must be extremely careful not to injure his pride in his own judgment, not to belittle his loss, and not to build up any false hopes as to the possibilities of his recouping all or part of his loss.

- Give careful thought to the language to be employed during the interview to make sure that it is consistent with the approach and understandable to the interviewee. Avoid law enforcement or other bureaucratic jargon.

- Compliment the victim or complaining witness for taking the trouble to complain and cooperate --- that not to complain and cooperate would be playing into the hands of the subject of the investigation.

- End every cooperative interview with thankful sincere appreciation. Perhaps this will encourage the subject to maintain contact if he acquires or remembers more information.

(2) Note-taking. The method of taking notes permits little standardization. Whatever the form, notes should reflect accurately the data obtained during the interview. Names, places and dates should be written out with correct spellings, otherwise subsequent identification will be very difficult and may be impossible. To insure minimal dependence on memory, immediately after the interview the investigator should review the notes, then clarify and elaborate on all areas which could not be fully written out during the interview. A follow-up telephone call to the interviewee should be made as soon as possible to clear up any confusing areas.

If a tape recorder is permitted by the interviewee it should be used as a backup to note-taking --- and not as a substitute for note-taking. Otherwise the investigator will find himself consuming a great deal of time just listening to tape recordings and preparing memoranda from that information, much of which may have no value. Always make sure that the first thing on tape is the investigator's request for permission to tape the interview, and that the oral consent is absolutely clear and loud enough to record.

For interviews that may be complex, technical, or of singular importance to the investigator, the interview should be conducted by two investigators if possible. One can take the lead in questioning and the other can take notes.

Remember that interview notes may eventually result in a memorandum or signed affidavit which will be used as evidence in a trial, that there is a very real possibility that if there is criminal or civil litigation the defendant may have the right to inspect these notes or memoranda --- and that the investigator may be called upon to explain them. It is therefore vital that the words put down be clear, not fuzzy, even if the investigator knows what the words mean. Few things are worse, personally and for a case, than for an investigator to try to explain on cross-examination why words mean something other than what they may seem to mean.

(3) Other considerations

- The investigator must consider the emotional state of victims or witnesses being interviewed. The loss of all or part of their money has been a shock if they are victims; if non-victims they may have great apprehensions about being involved. Victims will often have unsupported opinions regarding the circumstances connected with the crime. These should not be disparaged, but should be pursued to a logical conclusion. Apparently unsupported opinions may ultimately prove justified; people's feelings often have some logical basis even though they may not be able to clearly articulate that basis.

- The victim may feel that if the governmental agencies conducting the investigation had stayed out of it, everything would have been all right. He may want and expect that the investigator's agency will help him recover his losses. Agency policy in this regard should be carefully explained with attendant suggestions regarding assistance which can be acquired from private attorneys, and other public or private agencies which can offer assistance or which may have specialized enforcement or remedial jurisdiction.

- Concentrate deeply on what the interviewee is saying. Think about one topic at a time and not about your next question. Follow up each topic to its logical conclusion. If the interviewee wanders from the question do not stop him --- the response may lead to other topics which have exceptional possibilities. Always bring the interviewee back to the original topic with a specific question.

- Remember that when you interview a victim or a witness you necessarily give some information about what you know, and what you suspect. If you don't want a piece of information to surface, be careful and think about how you use it. Such information may be inadvertently disclosed to the subject of the investigation.

- The determination of whether the interviewee is telling the truth is always a consideration. If untruthfulness is suspected, the investigator must judge whether or not to confront the interviewee. If the decision is affirmative, the investigator must be prepared with facts to refute the untruthfulness. It is better to terminate an interview than to lose control of the interview by a confrontation without sufficient evidence. Remember, an untruthful interview can still be very useful at a later time, after more evidence has been developed. People confronted with evidence of their untruthfulness might be more readily convinced to assist in the investigation and prosecution of a case.

- If the investigator suspects that the interviewee is untruthful, or may be culpable, he should consider these options:

  (i) stop the interview immediately and make a written record of the reason. This will be especially important if the investigator suspects the interviewee may become the subject of a criminal prosecution;

  (ii) allow the interviewee to continue to talk, on the theory that by confronting the interviewee with his own falsities, he may push the interviewee into giving valuable information or evidence. The investigator (especially if he is in an agency which has criminal investigative jurisdiction) should be sensitive to the possibility that the interviewee must be informed of his legal rights before proceeding further.

- Observe carefully the demeanor of those being interviewed. They should be put at ease from the first and this ease should be maintained throughout. The discussions should continually and systematically go more into depth. When it appears that the pressures on the interviewee have become intense and will result in destroying possibilities of continued cooperation, the investigator should remove the pressures immediately, e.g., by temporarily bringing the interview around to other subjects; or sincerely confirming the importance of the information by explaining the investigator's role and goals of the investigation before getting back to the subject; or by having a higher level official do this.

(d) <u>Obstacles to Successful Interviewing of Victims</u>

The white-collar crime investigator often faces problems and obstacles which relate to certain characteristics of victims/witnesses, or to the situations in which they find themselves. There may also be differences, in this regard, between interviewees who are only victims, or only witnesses.

(1) <u>Personal Embarrassment of Victims</u>. Jonathan Kwitny has pointed out that ". . . Somewhere in the human psyche lies an element that induces many people to hand over their savings rather than risk the possibility that some total stranger might think them stupid. If this element did not exist, neither would the fine art of swindling. . . ."[83] This same element provides the greatest obstacle to the investigator, first in locating victims and second in getting victims to participate in a situation, such as an interview or on a witness stand, in which they must make "admission[s] of having been duped . . . [or that] their victimization stemmed from such things as personal greed, stupidity in not listening closer to disclaimers or in not reading all the terms of a contract, or failure to fulfill their part of the bargain, etc."[84]

(2) <u>Institutional Embarrassment</u>. Both privately-owned and government enterprises operate on the basis of public trust and confidence. Banks, savings and loan associations, business organizations in general, brokerage houses, fiduciary organizations, and government agencies rely, in large part, on public confidence for their success. The commission of a white-collar crime may not only cause an immediate financial loss, but the attendant publicity may also cause a loss in public confidence and a corresponding drop in business prestige or public trust. The enterprise may prefer to conceal the occurrence and forego a prosecution rather than risk a loss of public confidence.

(3) <u>Previous Denials and Inconsistent Stories</u>. The victim, whether individual, private enterprise, or government agency, may have already related a false or erroneous account of the situation or question to family, friends, news media or others. The victim may, therefore, have a stake in an erroneous or false story and attempt to stick with it --- or may even have come to partially believe it.

(4) <u>Nothing to Gain</u>. Most victims do not welcome appearances in court, particularly when they know there is little chance that it will help to restore their loss.

(e) <u>Obstacles to Successful Interviewing of Witnesses Who Are Not Victims</u>

A witness who is not a victim may be uncooperative for a variety of reasons such as fear of reprisal, dislike of law enforcement, and fear of self-incrimination. Even totally innocent witnesses may just consider it too much trouble to spend their time assisting law enforcement.

---

[83]Jonathan Kwitny, <u>The Fountain Pen Conspiracy</u> (New York: Alfred A. Knopf, 1973), p. 12.

[84]Charles A. Miller, <u>Economic Crime: A Prosecutor's Hornbook</u>, publication of the NDAA Economic Crime Project, July 1974, at p. 70.

Technical experts may be reluctant to participate at the outset of an investigation for fear of eventually inviting a civil liability suit. For example, an honest certified public accountant who prepared the financial statements for a business which was defrauded might be concerned about being sued for negligence because he did not uncover the fraud in the course of his professional work.

(f) Suggested Methods for Overcoming Obstacles

The following suggestions should be considered only as potential tools for use by the investigator. The specific approach must be determined by the demands of each individual situation. As stated in the introduction to this section it is not possible to provide a set of standard techniques which would be applicable to the personality and capability of each investigator and to each situation.

(1) With particular regard to situations involving previous denials and inconsistent stories, the investigator must develop the following approaches:

- Persist in following up every question or topic under discussion to a logical conclusion;

- Pursue the same topic from a variety of perspectives, any one of which might generate additional responsiveness, e.g., a discussion from a technical perspective of how the fraud under consideration is generally perpetrated might trigger responses that would otherwise remain dormant if the interviewer just repeated the who, what, when, where, how and why questions; and

- Be ready to use all information obtained earlier, whether from file documents or memory, to refute denials and inconsistencies and to impart varying degrees of damaging information about the scheme and its promoters in order to cultivate cooperation.

(2) In all cases, but especially those involving private and government agencies, particular care should be taken to indicate to victims what steps will be taken to insure that their embarrassment will be minimized. When applicable, the investigator should also indicate that credit will be given for assistance in the investigation.

(3) Since, in actuality, the investigator is usually working for the public, of which the victim/witness is part, the investigator should always attempt to encourage both victims and witnesses to cooperate because it is their duty to assist law enforcement.

(4) The investigator may find it desirable to encourage cooperation on the basis that such cooperation will protect other potential victims from similar victimization. This will be particularly important where the interviewee obviously distrusts the "establishment", whether business or government or both. In such cases the investigator can point out that this is

witness' chance to "fight back"; that someone wants his story about
how he, or those he knows, were mistreated and that this is something the
witness can do for those with whom he identifies himself.

(5) In attempting to gain cooperation, it is always advisable at
the initial stages of interviews to be sympathetic to the victims' or
witness' attitudes even though they impede swift resolution of the obstacles.
The investigator should also consider the advisability of expressing thanks
and making the interviewee feel that he is part of the law enforcement team
--- which he really is when he cooperates.

(6) Since most victims are primarily concerned with the losses they
have sustained, the investigator may encourage cooperation by pointing out the
possibilities of restitution resulting from the agency's criminal or civil
action; the steps which might be undertaken by the interviewee to initiate
action (concentrate on referrals, not legal advice); and (where it is true)
the fact that the agency would consider it an obligation to assist a
citizen that had provided assistance to the agency. The investigator
must, of course, be certain that the interviewee understands that criminal
action does not guarantee restitution nor does it insure success in a civil
action. In most instances the investigator's agency will not provide counsel
or representation to victims, and therefore victims should not be even
indirectly led to infer that this kind of assistance will be provided.

2.   Interrogating Suspects

(a) Purpose and Objectives

The investigator's obvious purpose in talking to a suspect is
to get him to provide information (evidence) about the problem being investigated or to obtain admissions which will be useful and persuasive at trial.
Such an interaction with a suspect may arise from either a request of the
suspect or his attorney, or from the desire of the investigator to get the
other side of the story or an admission of guilt.

In the first situation the suspect, his attorney, or both, may request
or even clamor for an interview because word of an actual or possible
investigation has reached them and (they claim) it is important to the
suspect that his business and personal reputation are not injured by false
accusations. (The investigator must consider the possibility that this may
be true.) In such a situation the sole objective of the investigator is to get
the suspect to talk extensively about his business. The investigator must
always be aware that the suspect and his attorney may attempt to get information about the status of any investigation. The investigator must be extremely
cautious about inadvertently providing information to the suspect which could
create problems in the investigation or eventual prosecution. He should out-
wardly assume that since the interview came about at the suspect's request
that the suspect also has the same objective, i.e., that they are both professionals attempting to ascertain the status of the situation and to obtain
a fix on what the other knows.

In the second situation, in a meeting with a suspect which is initiated by the investigator, the objectives may be any of the following depending on the actual case:

- to fill in any missing pieces of the investigation;

- to elicit incriminating statements from the suspect --- while these incriminating statements will rarely take the form of admissions of guilt, the suspect may make false or inconsistent statements, especially if the investigation takes him by surprise and the facts confronting the subject dramatically and conclusively point to guilt;

- to anticipate the suspect's possible defenses --- during the suspect's responses to questions regarding the nature, characteristics and specific methods used in the venture under investigation, the investigator may learn about contrived defenses which will help to develop tactics and further investigative steps to refute them; and

- to confront the suspect with the evidence and provide an opportunity for exculpatory explanations or admissions.

The possibility of achieving the purposes or objectives stated above in an interrogation situation is subject to debate. A great many experienced investigators express serious doubts about the worthwhileness of interrogation --- though all reocgnize its usefulness in specific situations. Investigators must take into consideration the unique aspects of each case prior to making a judgment regarding the value of interviewing or interrogating the suspect. They must consider:

- the type of white-collar crime being investigated --- e.g., consumer frauds using false business fronts, frauds using real business fronts but involving misrepresentations about products and services, confidence games, etc.;

- the type of suspect --- e.g., age, experience, past history, etc.; and

- the scheme itself --- e.g., fly-by-night or some degree of permanence, etc.

Each of these factors presents the investigator with different criteria for making judgments regarding whether or not to interview or interrogate a suspect, and when and how to do it.

In considering the arguments pro and con, the investigator should know that he treads on dangerous legal grounds --- which may not only imperil his entire case but also hurt his credibility with the prosecutor --- when he adopts this tactic against a subject he has already clearly identified as a

likely defendant in a criminal prosecution. This is not to say that an
interrogation should not take place under such circumstances, but investigators who do not have a thorough grounding in the legal issues and
prior experience in considering how to deal with them should consult with
a prosecutor or with their agency's own legal adviser.

The investigator should also consider whether it is desirable to
conduct such an interrogation if the suspect wishes to have his or her
attorney present. Under no circumstances should the investigator ever allow
himself to be placed in the position of seeming to deny a suspect the
opportunity to consult with or be accompanied by counsel --- but remember ---
the risks of interrogation to the case go up, and the prospective benefits
go down if the suspect is accompanied by counsel. It is often wise to defer
an interrogation, in such cases, until after the prosecutor or agency legal
adviser gets into the case. It should be noted, however, that many agencies
are specially geared to dealing with this problem, particularly regulatory
agencies which employ attorney-investigators or whose non-attorney investigators are thoroughly oriented to such issues.

We now turn to the arguments for and against interrogations of suspects,
and the techniques to be employed.

(b)   Interrogations - Affirmative Considerations

(1)   Staffs of many white-collar crime investigative units, particularly those with both investigative and prosecutive responsibilities,
believe that confronting a suspect with overwhelming evidence already
accumulated during a thorough investigation, will induce suspects to plead
guilty. These units have used interrogation and disclosure as means of
inducing pleas of guilty in cases where proof of guilt is overwhelming, or
almost so. Since white-collar subjects are likely to be represented by
particularly astute and skilled attorneys, this is no place for the
bluffer, and any slipshod investigative or legal work will cause this tactic
to backfire. Where this tactic is approved as a matter of office policy,
suspects are frequently confronted with a full disclosure of the evidence
against them so that they and their attorneys can intelligently weigh the
risks and benefits of a public trial and the attendant publicity.

A high plea ratio is important to units with joint investigative and
prosecutive functions, since the resources saved when a suspect pleads guilty
can be used to prepare other cases. In one case where this approach was
skillfully employed, early confrontation of the suspect was almost immediately
followed by the charge of a corporate defendant, plea of guilty, and sentence
--- all in the same day.

While the use of confrontation as a means of inducing pleas of guilty has
been employed by units with joint investigative and prosecutive responsibilities, the principle and its benefits would not appear to be limited to
such units. Investigators should be able to reap similar benefits from
confronting a suspect in an interrogating manner with overwhelming evidence
of guilt. This may, especially if the suspect is taken by surprise, have
such psychological impact as to provoke an admission of guilt, or constitute

the first step in a series of steps leading to a plea of guilty. Finally, an interrogating confrontation with a suspect which induces any kind of substantial demoralization will add to the prosecutorial attractiveness of the case. The suspect's demoralization will sometimes heighten the possibility that he will plead guilty.

(2) A meeting with a suspect prior to completion of evidence-gathering will rarely elicit an admission of fraudulent intent, but it may serve as a means for learning about the suspect's activities. Because such meetings frequently will occur at the suspect's request, the investigator is often in a favorable position to expect the suspect to discuss his business fully. By assuming an objective approach, i.e., a professional attempting to determine facts in a situation which has provoked certain complaints, the investigaror may be able to get the suspect to talk, and talk extensively, about the operation of his business. If, however, the investigator is not already fairly well oriented as to the facts and modus operandi of the type of business and activity being investigated, there is always a danger that he will be misled or sent up blind investigative alleys.

(3) One rule of thumb used in deciding whether interrogation would be wise is to evaluate the experience of the suspect in question. Experienced suspects who have taken steps to develop a fraudulent scheme will in all likelihood also develop contingency plans and explanations in case the scheme is investigated. Thus, interrogating such individuals would possibly give them more information than it would the investigator. Inexperienced suspects, on the other hand, may not yet have developed sufficient occupational experience to handle an interview or interrogation. This would lessen the danger that the suspect will learn something from the interrogation, and the lack of a (possibly tested) contingency plan may prevent him from exploiting what he does learn. The shock of discovery and resulting fear may result in the suspect making incriminating admissions or giving up incriminating documents.

(4) Investigators should remember that they have no power to confer immunity nor to bargain on pleas or sentences. They should take great precautions to avoid any speech or other conduct which could be misunderstood in this regard. They should be particularly on guard where the suspect's attorney is present at the interrogation. Immunity can often develop inadvertently. Prosecutors or agency lawyers must be consulted with respect to these dangers; they should be the ones who make decisions relating to plea bargains or grants of immunity.

(c) Arguments Against Interrogation

(1) There are a number of pitfalls which will face the investigator who gets involved in meeting with and questioning a suspect. Such pitfalls are most likely to be present when the evidence of the suspect's guilt is still inconclusive and particularly when the suspect is accompanied by an

attorney. For example:

- The investigation and prosecution may be stymied by disclosing the fact that an investigation is underway or a prosecution is being considered.

- The suspect may learn something during the interview or interrogation from which he can figure out how to obscure evidence or manipulate victim and witness attitudes and willingness to cooperate.

- The suspect might flee the jurisdiction before charges are filed and bail set.

- The investigator may be deceived by the suspect and consequently either waste investigative resources on a false lead or allow the suspect more time to put together a scheme to counter the investigation process.

- The investigator may be intimidated by the suspect's position, image, and demeanor. An investigator who is confronted by a well-educated and respected businessman accompanied by an attorney will sometimes develop inappropriate feelings of deference and respect for the image presented, resulting finally in a loss of confidence and loss of control of the situation.

(2)   The character of a suspect may be a factor which might make interrogation prior to arrest a waste of an investigator's time. The likelihood of many white-collar criminals admitting guilt or providing useful information is extremely remote. White-collar criminals are, in the main, proficient liars. Many of them thrive on the challenge of their ability to deceive people --- and it is their "stock in trade"; investigators are not necessarily immune to these skills. Investigators should be aware that this factor is rarely under their control and thus makes the failure of the interrogation more likely than not, except when such results are expected and desired, e.g., when the anticipated lies are perceived to be useful as evidence against the suspect.

(3)   Interrogation of a suspect prior to arrest may be unnecessary or undesirable in cases where the investigation has developed solid comprehensive evidence for a prosecution. What the suspect has to say prior to arrest may not matter. The fact that law enforcement has found it previously unnecessary to confront the suspect may also have a tremendous psychological impact upon him. It is demoralizing for a suspect to believe that the case against him is so strong that investigators found it unnecessary to even inquire into his explanation --- and this could be a factor in an ultimate plea of guilty.

172

(d) Conducting the Interrogation

Most of the principles and methodology of interviewing discussed
in connection with victims will be applicable to interrogation situations.
Courtesy and consideration are always in order, and can pay off in "turning"
a suspect to cooperate against his confederates. There are, however, a number
of additional factors which the investigator must consider when interviewing
or interrogating a suspect.

(1) When Interrogation is Held at the Request of a Suspect. The
suspect who asks for a meeting may be motivated by a desire to clear up the
situation, or he may wish to influence the investigator, or learn how much
the investigator knows. Regardless of his motivation, the fact that the suspect requests the meeting puts the investigator in a favorable position to
get the suspect to talk about his business. The investigator should assume
that this is the suspect's desire. Following delivery of a warning to the
suspect as to his legal rights, he should adopt the objective attitude of a
professional seeking to understand the suspect's business in the fullest
detail possible. The investigator should avoid denunciatory questioning,
even if untruthful statements are made. Such questioning will inhibit the type
of free discussion desired and may lead to untimely disclosure by the
investigator of what he knows, and does not want the suspect to realize
he knows. Additionally, false statements made by the suspect during such an
interview may prove to be the most significant evidence of criminal intent
developed in the investigation.

(2) When Interview is Held at the Request of the Investigator. When
the investigator elects to initiate an interview with a suspect or non-
cooperative witness, he should be aware that the person being interrogated
is quite likely to lie, but more often will simply prefer to evade the
investigator's questions or give non-responsive or misleading answers. Many
suspects will be skillful in misdirecting the investigator and distracting
him from the salient points which were the purpose of arranging the interview.
The investigator must be ever alert, must maintain his concentration, and
refuse to be sidetracked. This will require listening very carefully but
never forgetting the original question. Frequently, a question will have
to be rephrased again and again to elicit any useful response --- don't
be afraid to look stupid because the original question has to be repeated.
The failure of the investigator to "understand" is more likely to reflect
a non-responsive answer than lack of comprehension on the part of the
investigator.

(e) Interrogation - A Summary

There are no textbook formulas for conducting an interrogation.
Neither is there any dependable and invariable guide to inform an investigator
as to whether or when to agree to or seek to interrogate a suspect or hostile
witness. The infinite variations in personalities and backgrounds of
investigators and suspects, as well as the different character and status
of investigations makes it both hazardous and unwise to act as if there were
such dependable guides.

C. COVERT OPERATIONS

While covert operations are only very rarely called for in investigations of white-collar crime (unless such investigations are directed at organized crime figures), the proficient white-collar crime investigator should know:

- how to recognize when certain persons, who have access to information or personal knowledge which may be valuable in a prosecution by reason of intimate involvement in the criminal operation might be cooperative with law enforcement;

- how a qualified law enforcement officer might penetrate a criminal organization to gain such access;

- how to give a suspect the opportunity to act unlawfully while under surveillance without "entrapping" him;

- how and when covert observation of fraudulent operations might be useful.

These operational tools fall within the general investigative techniques of informant development, undercover operation and surveillance. Although it is beyond the scope of this manual to cover these methods and implementing techniques in detail, some general guidelines and discussion of the strategic utility of these techniques as applied to white-collar crime investigations are discussed below. Sensitive and changing legal, tactical, and other considerations which govern covert operations generally will equally apply to the use of such operations in white-collar crime investigations.

1. Informants

All possible persons who are in a position to know something of value, or who may be able to gain access to valuable information should be considered as potential sources of information. Those who may be receptive to cooperating with law enforcement should be considered as possible witnesses or for undercover work. A potential informant may be one who was formerly involved in the criminal scheme, but who is frightened about what he got into, or who for some reason has fallen out with those with whom he is or was involved. In many instances these people themselves believe they have been cheated in some way by the scheme's managers.

One investigator, with more than a generation of experience in the field, has put it this way:

> "He may be an advertising agent, printer, or supplier, or perhaps a competitor close enough to the scene to have gained a substantial insight into the operation. He may be a salesman who fears his own involvement has been

sufficiently established as to make it prudent for him
to join the other side. Whatever his capacity or
personal involvement an "insider", if properly cultivated,
can save an enormous amount of investigative time. He
may unfold the scheme, identify the players and the
parts played, expose the "wheels within the wheels", and
most importantly, supply evidence of fraudulent intent on
the part of all participants or leads to such evidence . . .
[He may provide] testimony as to the use of aliases, forged
signatures on contracts or other documents, unguarded in-
house comments suggesting contempt for customers or normal
business ethics, and other such incidents which can be
immensely valuable in proving intent."[85]

The informant may be the only avenue to evidence on the involvement of
"higher ups" who have otherwise insulated themselves. He may be able to
provide documents, or tapes, taken for his own purposes prior to cooperating
with or being approached by the investigator and --- sometimes most important
of all --- explain the purpose of activities which the investigator does
not understand. He may be able to identify incriminating evidence with
sufficient specificity to support a most productive search pursuant to warrant.

In dealing with well organized criminal frauds, the investigator should
always keep in mind the possibility that some type of consideration may be
traded with a lower level subject for insuring the ability to make a
successful case against higher echelon criminals. He should realize that
he does not have the power to deliver on such promises. Any attempt to provide
such assurances will not only backfire against his case, but also severely
and negatively affect his and his agency's relationships with prosecutive
authorities. The prosecutor should be immediately consulted if any such
arrangement is considered.

In cases where the investigator has already decided to talk to the
subjects under investigation, it should be a general rule to talk also
to all persons in any way innocently connected with the operation, such as
employees, particularly secretaries, bookkeepers, and accountants. Their
cooperation will often be invaluable to an investigation.

In all cases, the investigator must remind himself that people
providing information may eventually be called as witnesses in a trial.
To prevent compromise of a case and detraction from the investigator's professionalism terms like "informer" and "snitch" should always be avoided,
even among investigators themselves. They are considered derogatory and can
be totally misleading. Many of those who cooperate in covert operations may
be innocent themselves, or trying to work their way out of situations into
which they were gradually inveigled by circumstances.

---

[85]Miller, op. cit., Note 84, at pp. 76-77.

2.   Undercover Operations

Under certain circumstances it may be feasible to employ law enforcement personnel or "informants" to penetrate a criminal enterprise as participants, or as victims of the scheme. As a general rule, however, undercover operations which involve penetration as participants are far less valuable in the white-collar crime area than in other areas of criminal investigation, unless the investigator is dealing with white-collar crime related to other criminal activity, i.e., organized crime, fencing, arson, extortion, etc. Such operatives will have their uses in some cases, described below, but use of this technique is likely to be a matter of rising to an occasional and unusual opportunity, rather than a standard and frequently-used part of the investigator's arsenal. To employ undercover operations, the investigator must know:

(a)   How to Penetrate a White-Collar Crime Operation

In white-collar crime the most likely method of penetration is in the guise of an employee. For example, large numbers of such criminal operations require salesmen. An investigator could respond to such an advertisement, receive the necessary instructions in how to perpetrate the scheme such as how to evade answering searching questions, how to get the contract signed, how to get payment, how to use confederates, or similar instructions which are evidence of criminal intent. All of the specific techniques used by investigative units in setting up undercover or decoy operations may be applied as the situation dictates. For example, development of an operational plan; selection of the undercover officer on the basis of his ability to fit the situation, i.e., how to dress, speak, etc.; development of cover including background, status, and activities and all necessary identification and credentials to prevent detection; establishment of security and safety measures; designation of a supervisory control officer; training in operational and legal restrictions; what to do in case of emergency; etc.

(b)   How to Become a Victim

An investigator may obtain valuable evidence by becoming a direct victim of the fraud. For example:

- An investigator can respond to a letter invitation to be a guest at a promotional dinner for sale of real estate. Detailed, first-hand evidence of the sales presentation (perhaps on tape) could be important evidence should the promotion turn out to be fraudulent.

- Undercover agents can join fraudulent religious organizations, respond to medical quackery schemes as potential patients, etc.

- A consumer fraud investigator can respond to advertising, observe or record the sales tactics, purchase the products, etc., thus obtaining similar evidentiary material.

3. Decoy Operations

     Many agencies, in every part of the United States, have undertaken decoy
operations in which appliances, automobiles, etc. which are in good working
order except for some minor and early discovered and repaired fault, are
entrusted to repairmen. There are certain common principles involved in
decoy operations, which are discussed here in the context of automobile repair
frauds.

     In order for decoy operations to be effective, they must be executed with
great care and thoroughness; half-way measures will not work. The example
of a decoy car operation is described below to illustrate the effort that
must be made in all decoy operations to develop cases that will stand up in
court.[86]

     The decoy vehicle should be one that is beyond warranty age, and should
look like a family car, with family objects attached or inside (books, gloves,
decals, baby seats, worn trailer hitches, ski racks, etc.). It should be
made to look dirty from road dirt, perhaps by first driving it over a
newly oiled road and then over a dusty one; it should be wetted down to
cause rusting.

     In the unit's garage, or in a garage where security can be maintained,
the vehicle should first be stripped and the glove compartment and underseats
cleaned out. The shop number and all other identifying numbers should be
recorded. The vehicle should be returned to factory specifications with
factory parts, not with parts that are claimed by the parts maker to be
equivalent to factory parts. All working parts should be brought as near
as possible to perfection, i.e., the front end suspension, brake system,
engine, transmission, and the muffler. Before the car is reassembled,
each part should be marked (e.g., holes in metal; serial numbers on rubber;
a wire on springs) in such a way as to be relatively unnoticeable, yet still
visible when put back on the car, even after being covered by grease and
oil for camouflage purposes. The marked parts should be photographed in the
presence of both the investigator and the mechanic, both before reassembly and
after each step in the reassembly process. All repair and periodic service
work done on the decoy should be recorded, both the investigator and the
mechanic retaining copies of the repair and service orders, including
complete information (date, make, model, shop or license number, mileage).
The car should be periodically inspected and kept in absolutely top condition
with the mileage kept to a mihimum.

---

[86]This section is based upon unpublished instructional outline prepared
by the Bunco-Forgery Division of the Los Angeles Police Department for
the guidance of its auto repair decoy operations.

The driver of the decoy vehicle should be both mechanically, investigatively, and legally sophisticated; should be able to fit into any neighborhood; have an appearance and manner consistent with the car's characteristics; should know how to extract statements, yet avoid causing entrapment, etc. Before starting out on an operation the car should be certifiable as being in perfect condition, with the exception of one obvious and minor defect. The engine or any other rleevant part should be photographed from the mechanic's eye level just before it leaves the unit's garage, with the deliberately inflicted defect showing clearly. The operator can select his target garage on the basis of complaints, suspicious ads, or just random sampling. He should drive to it in the most direct way. He should check the adjacent area so that he can develop a good cover story for his being in the neighborhood (e.g., visiting a brother on such and such a street). He should check the garage for number of stalls, amount of work, presence of owner, number of employees on duty, the exterior signs, etc. (In states in which use of a tape recording is legally permissible, all relevant tape recording procedures should be used.)

After the decoy vehicle driver takes the car into the garage and reports the symptoms of difficulty, he should make an excuse and leave in order to give the mechanic time and privacy to prepare a repair order. After the driver returns and receives a statement of repairs allegedly needed and an estimate, he should again excuse himself and leave with the car so that the unit's own mechanic can re-check the car. (In states in which it is legal to tape record telephone conversations, the operator should then call the mechanic to re-confirm his suggested repairs.)

Where a fraudulently inflated or suspicious repair order or estimate is received, the investigator/driver should return to the garage. Upon returning to the target garage with the car, the decoy car driver should ask the mechanic to point out the defect and the consequences of not correcting it; to indicate whether other mechanics, the service manager, or owner have also checked the car. The decoy car driver should appear convinced, then sign the work order, inquire about and get details as to any work guarantee, and retain a copy of the order (but not give a phone number).

Upon picking up the car, the decoy car driver should ask again what work was done, request the parts removed, and ask to see what was wrong. At this point, the operator can either confront the mechanic or take the car back to his garage for checking again. In either case, the car needs to be secured as evidence. The unit's own mechanic needs to have the critical parts photographed again from mechanic's eye level. He also needs to remove, inspect, and photograph the parts as they are removed --- in the presence of the investigator/decoy car driver. The mechanic should then make a statement and a complete record of the findings and of the date, time, mileage and location.

If target garage operators lie about needed repairs, and/or charges for repairs not done or for parts not supplied, these investigative techniques have been found to be effective in making both criminal and civil cases. These procedures, it should be kept in mind, apply to other repair areas as well as to automotive repairs.

4. Surveillance

Other than standard uses of investigative surveillance for the purpose
of identifying criminal associates, there are relatively few circumstances
in white-collar crime which lend themselves to surveillance techniques. One
example might be a bankruptcy fraud operation where all products in a
suspect's store are received, never uncrated, and then removed; combined with
non-payment of the suspect's suppliers, the suspect's disappearance or
declaration of bankruptcy, or report of burglary. In such cases, surveillance
and photographing the receipt and removal of the products, learning of
their destination, making records of people, merchandise, autos and trucks,
may provide both useful evidence as well as investigative leads. Crimes
such as insurance frauds involving fake accidents, transfer and sale of
stolen vehicles, and public corruption will usually necessitate surveillance
for evidence and leads.

When an investigator is faced with problems in finding other victims,
associates of the suspects, or other organizations with which the suspect may
be involved, he should consider the possibility of establishing a surveillance
of the mail delivered to the suspect or his business. To do this he will need
the help of the Postal Inspection Service. The procedure has been outlined
as follows.

> "A law enforcement agency may ask the Postal Inspection
> Service to institute a mail cover for a 30-day period on all
> mail addressed to a firm or individual. [The period may be
> extended under certain circumstances.] The postmark and name
> and return address of the sender, if any, is recorded from the
> cover of the mail and furnished the agent or agency making the
> request. Mail covers may only be placed with respect to
> investigations relating to: (a) the protection of national
> security; (b) efforts to locate a fugitive; and (c) efforts
> to secure evidence of the commission or attempted commission
> of a crime. This process can reveal an enormous amount of
> information about a fraudulent promoter, i.e., identity of
> banks, suppliers, advertising agents, customers and potential
> customers, and numerous other leads to additional sources of
> information. There are certain restrictions on its application,
> however, and it should not be requested routinely but reserved
> for investigations in which other sources have proved fruitless
> or impracticable. The local Postal Inspector is the point
> of contact for mail cover requests."[87]

White-collar crime investigators should look to general law enforcement
expertise with respect to use of surveillance equipment such as audio and
video tape recorders, binoculars, radios, motion and still cameras, and to
agency legal advisers with respect to legal issues relevant to such
operations.

---

[87]Miller, op. cit., Note 84, at pp. 76-77.

D.   FINDING INFORMATION/DOCUMENTS/PUBLIC RECORDS

The variety of types of documents, public records and sources for
obtaining specific information is so vast that development of a complete
source reference manual for every type of information which might be required or useful to a white-collar crime investigator would be impractical
for this manual and would require continual modification.

This section is therefore designed to provide:

   • general guidelines for seeking information; and

   • recommendations for developing an information guide.

In using this section, it must be kept in mind that involuntary production of private or business records is not required and will not be
available, except pursuant to warrant or subpoena. Public records or
private records voluntarily produced may well provide information which
can contribute to the legal basis for compulsory access to other records.
This discussion therefore deals with what records there may be, and where
they may be, and how they may be used.

Rapidly developing laws and court decisions dealing with privacy
inhibit many kinds of voluntary cooperation on the part of third parties
who have records, i.e., telephone companies, banks, etc. This eliminates
many "short-cuts", and will compel the investigator to more carefully
organize his case and use his imagination --- on balance such challenges
to the investigator's skill and imagination may more than compensate for
the loss of "short-cuts".

1.   General Guidelines for Seeking Information

   (a) Investigators' Own Files

        When seeking information contained in documents and public records,
the investigator's own files and those of his agency should be checked first.
Examination of this material may provide important leads.

   (b) Other Agencies' Files

        The second step is to seek out other enforcement and regulatory
agencies that may have an interest in the case under consideration.[88] The
investigator must through his own research learn what is available in each
type of public agency. For example, if a company involved in land fraud

_____

[88]See Chapter II, pp. 53-58.

operations raised money from investors in order to launch its effort, filings in the records of the U.S. Securities and Exchange Commission or equivalent state agencies may provide a wealth of information, which may provide leads --- such as disclosures of litigation which raises doubt as to the capacity of the seller to convey good title. As another example, most investigators will be aware that the National Crime Information Center (NCIC) contains information about persons who are wanted for crimes. They should also be aware the NCIC also maintains information on stolen securities. Numerous municipal, state and federal agencies all have files, some with computerized indexes, which can be used for obtaining leads, past histories, and a myriad of other pertinent information.

(c) General Information Sources

The investigator must at times search through the files of publications, such as newspapers, periodicals, reports, etc. and seek out public or private organizations which might provide significant information. In numerous instances, licenses are needed to conduct certain businesses --- requiring initial and often continuous periodic submission of information. Because the potential sources of information are so numerous, the investigator must become adept at using the many indexes available in public and private libraries, and in obtaining information from official agencies, from trade associations, etc. In most public and trade libraries, librarians on duty are most helpful in showing how to use card catalogs and other indexing material. From these indexes the investigator can locate information which identifies corporations, unincorporated businesses, articles in newspapers and periodicals, and almost every variety of reference material an investigator might find useful.

(d) Suspect Company Records

Investigation of white-collar crimes very often requires the examination of company books and records. As pointed out above, access to such records will frequently require legal process which few investigators can command. Where access can be obtained, e.g., by appropriate subpoena or other lawful means, these are the considerations to be kept in mind.

Company records will vary in size, character, and complexity, and may not even exist in small companies. In some fraud operations checks are written without even filling in the stub to indicate the purpose of the payment. Large companies will have a corporate charter and by-laws, corporate minute books of director's and shareholders meetings, lists of shareholders, correspondence and memorandum files, formal books of accounts, financial statements, advertising materials, brochures, advertisements, etc. In smaller operations and in fly-by-night schemes, the above types of documents will be either fragmented or non-existent. Of particular interest to the investigator, regardless of the size of the enterprise under investigation, are transactional documents such as contracts, purchase agreements, sales slips, escrow agreements, deeds of trust, leases, orders, production records and the like.

Investigators must be alert to the possibility that records can be destroyed, lost and altered. Sometimes a subpoena for such records can be served before the suspect company is aware that there is a problem, or before its operators realize that proceedings have developed to the point where legal process is warranted. Even if a complete examination cannot be made at that time, process such as issuance of a subpoena might deter destruction of or tampering with the records. It is important for an investigator to know what kinds of records a company is likely to keep so that he will know what to look for. Investigators who lack such knowledge should consult with some expert in the particular business area regarding the type of records which are normally maintained by the particular type of company which he is investigating.

When company records are not readily available, e.g., in companies which do not keep formal books of accounts, the investigator should look for bank statements, deposit slips, checks or other money storage and transfer methods which might have been used by the suspect in a fraud scheme.[89]

(e) Third Party Records

The investigator should keep in mind that subjects being investigated do business with others, such as suppliers, printers, etc., whose records will reflect what should be in the books of the subjects. Many such third parties are not in sensitive relationships with their customers, as are banks, telephone companies, etc. and are free to disclose their own operations and records. Thus the printer of a sales brochure can show his production and sample files without being in the sensitive position of a telephone company voluntarily disclosing with whom a customer was talking.

In seeking records from third parties that require a subpoena, as may be the case with respect to banks, utility companies, telephone companies and others, it is advisable to make contact in advance with an officer of the institution whose records are being subpoenaed. Since the investigator may have to make more than one visit, it is important to develop good relations from the outset. Advance notification may prevent the possible alarming effects which a surprise visit could have.

Investigators who fail to develop a rapport with these institutions will find a negative attitude in response to their requests for records. Even with a subpoena, without this rapport, the investigator will find himself searching through vast complicated files of records without assistance.

2. Developing a Unit Guide to Sources of Information

Every white-collar crime investigative unit should develop its own Guide to Sources of Information. The guide should be designed to provide an easy reference for investigators seeking information. Three key points

---

[89]See Appendix D, p. 325 ff.

should be kept in mind in preparing such a guide:

- The guide should be indexed by type of information rather than by source, i.e., all pertinent sources should be listed under each type of information which may be required.

- The guide should be dynamic. Since no single guide can ever be perfectly complete, provisions should be made to continually add new types of information and new sources as experience is gained.

- The guide should outline the form in which information will be found, and any special legal or other problems which may be encountered in obtaining information.

- Investigators should prepare forms containing a checklist of the information which probably will be required in each specific type of investigation; e.g., home improvement fraud, investment fraud, etc. Then when an examination is made or a subpoena is requested, the investigator can go through his list and thus insure a high probability of comprehensiveness in finding documents and public records. In addition, each time he has a similar case he can start with the appropriate list and also add to the list each time a new document is discovered.

(a) Sample Guide to Sources of Information

At Appendix B in this manual is a "Sample Guide to Sources of Information," based upon one which was prepared by the Orange County, California, District Attorney's office for its use. It is indexed by the type of information desired. The investigator considering development of such a Guide can use this sample guide as a starting point or model to build upon, taking into account parallel sources in his or her own jurisdiction and special considerations related to the subject matter in which his or her own unit specializes or is most frequently involved. For example:

- The guide could be expanded to include a number of major industry and trade associations which are of particular importance to the fraud investigator. Organizations such as the Insurance Crime Prevention Institute; National Association of Credit Management; American Medical Association; Recording Industry Association of America; are directly involved in fraud detection and investigation, maintain complaint and offender files, and work closely with law enforcement.

• The guide could also be expanded to include every
  licensing, fee collecting, and regulatory agency in the
  state. Most states have one or more agencies which
  formally issue booklets listing every such agency.

(b) Developing Unit Legal Guides

Many federal, state and private white-collar crime investigation
agencies have prepared documents summarizing fraud laws, such as California's
"Summary of Consumer Fraud Law," and "State Laws Against Piracy of Sound
Recordings: A Handbook for Enforcement and Prosecution," produced by the
Recording Industry Association of America. Documents such as these can be
useful in guiding an investigator to a variety of prosecution alternatives
and other documentation.

E. HANDLING EVIDENCE

A major responsibility of the investigator is to maintain the evidence
he collects in such a form that it will not lose its value as evidence or
as a source of additional leads for follow-up investigation by himself or
others. For example, if an investigator is unable to identify and
substantiate from whom an evidentiary document was received or when it was
received, the document is worthless as evidence. Similarly, if oral
evidence, i.e., statements made in an interview, is not properly preserved,
potentially important information may be lost, lowering the effectiveness
of follow-up investigation.

The following are suggested guidelines for handling both oral evidence,
such as witness statements, and physical evidence, such as documents,
business records, financial records, letters, memoranda, products of a
sales or service scheme, and similar items.

1. The Memorandum of Interview

If an interview provides information which might be useful either as
evidence or as an investigative lead, the investigator should preserve
such information. This can be done by obtaining an affidavit or signed
statement from the interviewee, or by preparing a detailed memorandum. Good
notes, or a tape recording of the interview are essential to the preparation
of a good memorandum.

All information of any significance should be made part of a checklist
to insure that it is part of the material submitted to the prosecuting
attorney, or to other investigators to whom the information might be
useful. This will be important not only to effective presentation of the
case, but also to the prosecutor's duty to make full disclosures of information which a defendant or his counsel may have the right to see.

Considering the problem of discovery applicable to the jurisdiction, the
investigator must make a judgment as to whether or not to include his own
personal opinions about the interviewee's answers, e.g., truthfulness,
competence, etc. If discovery is no problem, such opinions may be stated

at the end of the memorandum along with any recommendations for additional investigative steps. It is not uncommon for an investigator's opinion to (very legitimately) change as an investigation unfolds; he should be prepared to explain these changes if he volunteers such opinions in his memorandum.

2. Physical Evidence

As soon as potential demonstrative or documentary evidence is obtained, the investigator should note information on the item itself, or by a tag attached to the item. At a minimum this information should include:

- name or description of the item;

- from whom it was obtained;

- when it was obtained;

- whether it is an original or a copy of an original; and

- initials of the investigator receiving the document.

When confronted with minor items, large quantities of items, or voluminous documents, the investigator may have to weigh his priorities and decide whether preparing a list for future reference will suffice.

When a sworn affidavit or signed statement is obtained from a witness, the investigator should attach copies of any documentary evidence obtained from the witness as exhibits to the affidavit or statement. When the physical evidence is to be kept in the investigator's or his agency's custody, an official log of custody must be maintained, as in any police or other law enforcement operation.

During the course of an investigation it is often necessary to handle physical evidence for the purpose of study or to develop new leads. As a precaution against loss or deterioration, it is advisable to make copies of documents rather than work with originals. When large numbers of documents are involved, microfilming should also be considered.

There are situations where the original documents will be required in court, but the witness wishes to retain the original. In such cases, in addition to obtaining a copy, the investigator should explain the importance of the evidence to the witness, and take all possible steps to be sure that the evidence is preserved. This should, in the first instance, be done through discussion, in which the witness is queried about how he proposes to protect the evidence. This should be followed by specific suggestions, if appropriate, to improve protection of the evidence. Where there is special concern, the investigator should request the prosecutor or his agency's legal adviser to write a letter to the witness regarding the need for care of the evidence and --- in some cases --- pointing out that there may be legal consequences if the evidence is destroyed, e.g., the possibility of an obstruction of justice violation. As soon as the investigation has progressed to the point where grand jury or inquiry judge subpoenas are available --- or if the administrative or regulatory agency has subpoena power, compulsory process should issue to obtain the evidence.

3. Tape Recordings

In addition to tape-recorded interviews or interrogations, the investigator may wish to use as evidence a tape recording made during an undercover operation, e.g., a recording made of the misrepresentations made at a business opportunity meeting. The following guidelines are suggested:

- Use good equipment, in good working and operating condition. Check batteries carefully. The investigator should be able to testify as to his past experience with the equipment and that the equipment was in good operating condition.

- On the recording itself, after the recording has been made, identify the individuals engaged in the conversation, any other persons present, the time, date and location.

- Immediately after the original has been made, make a copy for use in transcribing the conversation or follow-up investigation, then seal and store the original.

- Keep a record of the custodians and storage from the time it was originally recorded to the time it was submitted as evidence.

- When tape recordings are going to be used in taking a confession, advise the suspect of his rights and have the subject state at the start of the tape recording that he is aware that the recording is being made.

F. LOCATING ADDITIONAL VICTIMS/WITNESSES

In the types of frauds which involve false pretenses, representations, and promises, the investigator will at times find that the only possible way of proving the case is to obtain evidence of repetitious wrongful activity As discussed earlier, one of the principal means and also one of the most effective ways in a courtroom for establishing such proof will be the statements of additional victims and of witnesses who were solicited but avoided becoming victims. A parade of such witnesses is a most persuasive way to demonstrate that the false pretenses, representations, and promises were not accidental.

This sub-section discusses a number of alternatives available to the investigator for finding additional victims. In using the repetitious wrongful activity method of proving bad faith on the part of the subject, investigators must continually be aware of the possibility that the promoter of the scheme might be able to demonstrate good faith by producing satisfied customers, but investigators should also recognize that satisfaction may be irrelevant, as in the case of bait and switch victims. Satisfied customers, by their testimony, may create a level of uncertainty regarding whether a fraud has been committed. The investigation must therefore include a determination of good as well as bad transactions made by the promoter, i.e., not overlook the possibility that there may be satisfied customers, as well as unhappy victims.

1. Sources for Identifying Additional Victims

In all the methods discussed below for finding additional victims, the techniques and precautions discussed in the sections on interviewing and interrogation are applicable. In particular, the investigator must recognize when victims may be reluctant to cooperate because law enforcement is interfering with an undertaking in which they have a monetary interest.

(a) Complainants

In interviewing the initial complainant, victims, or third parties, the investigator should always ask those being interviewed whether they know of any other persons victimized by the suspect. If not, the investigator may obtain leads to other victims by inquiring whether the complainants know how the subject got their names. If the answer to this question is no, the investigator can obtain leads by following up with detailed questions regarding the interviewee's employment, memberships, education, military background, hobbies, etc. From these questions he may deduce common characteristics among certain of the complainants which will help him find more victims and others who were solicited but did not become victims. Some of the major possibilities are that the suspect used mailing lists, club rosters, school enrollment lists, or the like to obtain the names of potential victims.

(b) Suspects

(PRECAUTION: A PREMATURE DIRECT APPROACH TO A PROMOTER COULD HAMPER THE PROCESS OF GATHERING EVIDENCE AND PRECLUDE EFFECTIVE RECONSTRUCTION OF THE FACT SITUATION.) The investigator must be ready with all legal tools for use when available, i.e., subpoenas, search warrants, for obtaining immediate access to books and records. (NOTE: The investigator should be aware that businesses today store much information regarding customers in computers; computer printouts should also be considered as a business record.)

(c) Other Agencies

The number of municipal, state, and federal agencies combined with the many private agencies that handle public complaints is too large for inclusion in this manual. When there is a complaint against a business enterprise, other agencies should be checked to find if they have received similar complaints against the same subjects. Many such agencies will have

computerized files and thus be able to provide rapid response. Once good
liaison is established, the investigator should consider a search of official
records in other agencies to be a preferred first step for identifying
additional victims and witnesses. In addition to the possibility of identifying other victims, such searches may produce information regarding
previous investigation of the same suspect firms or individuals which can
be integrated into a new investigation.

Most states and municipalities have pamphlets or other documentation
which identify agencies which receive public complaints. Many of these
agencies are listed in the "Sample Guide to Sources of Information," in
this manual.[90]

Another productive source of complaint information is the local Better
Business Bureau. Such organizations vary considerably in the degree to which
they monitor the business community or cooperate with law enforcement.
Nevertheless, they can often be helpful, not only as a source of complaint
information, but also as a source of background facts and data on member
firms and others doing business in their locality.

The mail cover provided to law enforcement agencies by the Postal
Inspection Service, described in the sub-section on Covert Operations, can
be used to provide leads to victims.[91] Questionnaires and form letters,
discussed in the following section, may also be used to find other victims
and witnesses.

G.   QUESTIONNAIRES/FORM LETTERS

The fundamental reason for use of questionnaires and form letters as
an investigatory tool is to gather large amounts of information more
quickly, efficiently and at lower cost in manpower than would be possible
through direct interviews. In investigations which may have numerous widely-
scattered non-complaining victims or "satisfied customers" (e.g., suspected
charity solicitations, securities sales, medical and health cures, contests,
land sales, etc.), a quick and useful method of gathering initial facts or
finding other victims is to send a questionnaire to all known contributors
and purchasers.

Use of questionnaires and form letters should be confined to routine
and low priority situations when it doesn't make any difference if the
suspect knows about the investigation. An exception would be a situation
where there is substantial reason to believe that fraud has occurred and
other means of gathering initial facts and finding other victims has proved
fruitless; e.g., a case where the promoter or his records have disappeared
or in other respects he has refused to cooperate. Questionnaires can also
be useful during an investigation when there are a large number of possible
victims and additional leads are desired for the purpose of strengthening
the case. Where the number of possible victims is overwhelming, investigators
should consider the use of sampling techniques to reduce the magnitude of the

---

[90]See Appendix B, at pp. 267-275.

[91]See p. 178.

the task.

1. Design and Use of Questionnaires and Accompanying Form Letter

There is no standard questionnaire or form letter design. Questionnaires should always be structured to fit the situation at hand. The sample form letter and questionnaire in Figures 12 and 13 are presented as a guide to demonstrate certain features which apply to their use in white-collar crime investigation, as follows:

- The letter should include no prejudgments or derrogatory information regarding the firm or individuals under investigation.

- An attempt should be made to reduce to a minimum the possible harmful effects that the inquiry itself might have. For example, a sentence is included in the form to the effect that the inquiry should not be regarded as a reflection on the integrity or reputation of the individual or firm in question.

- The questionnaire should be designed to elicit answers to all of the routine who, what, when, where, why, and how questions needed to make a decision as to whether or not a violation has occurred.

- A request for possible evidentiary materials should be included.

- A request for cooperation, a statement of the importance of the response and the fact that it will be given careful attention should be included.

- A self-addressed, stamped, return envelope should be included.

Remember that the following samples are only samples. While such a standard form could be used as a guide, suitable modifications and additions should be made for each specific case being investigated. All questionnaires should be preserved; they can serve as a starting point for design of other questionnaires in the same or other similar cases.

2. Other Form Letters

Specialized form letters may be used for a variety of reasons, such as:

(a) to advise a suspect or suspect company that complaints have been received which indicate that the activity or transaction in question may constitute a violation of a particular statute.

(b) to request the recipient to appear at the investigator's office at a certain date and time to discuss complaints.

FIGURE 12

SAMPLE FORM LETTER AND QUESTIONNAIRE

Dear _____:

   The *(name of agency)* is conducting an investigation to
determine whether there have been any violations of the _____
statutes, in the *(describe the promotion - e.g., sale of "X" stock,
solicitation of charitable contributions by "X" Foundation)*. In
the course of the investigation, your name appears as a possible
(investor, purchaser, contributor, etc.) with this organization.

   The fact that such investigations are in progress should not
in itself cast any reflection upon the integrity or reputation of
the firm or individuals involved. This letter and the attached
questionnaire are sent to you for the sole purpose of ascertaining
the facts which led you to become an *(investor, purchaser, contributor, etc.)* and in particular, what reliances you placed on
oral or written representations made by these firms through their
sales representatives or other agents.

   The attached questionnaire is self-explanatory. Please answer
each question as completely as possible. If it would be easier to
use one or more additional sheets of paper for your answers, please
feel free to do so.

   Your cooperation is earnestly solicited and your responses will
be given careful attention. A self-addressed envelope, requiring no
postage, is enclosed for your convenience in replying.

   Please furnish the originals, or copies, of all related items,
such as any advertising, envelopes, correspondence, cancelled checks
(front and back), memorandums of any telephone conversations (noting
with whom, the date, circumstances, and what was said), and any
additional related exhibits. Should additional postage be required,
you will be reimbursed.

                          Sincerely yours,

FIGURE 13

SAMPLE QUESTIONNAIRE

1. Did you *(invest in, purchase from, contribute to, etc.) (name of organization "X")*?

2. How did you first become aware of "X"? *(how, when, where, through whom, etc.)*

3. What are the names of the particular people you dealt with? *(owners, salesmen, agents, brokers, etc.)*

4. What were you told, either orally or in writing concerning "X"; type of businesses engaged in, the profits to be realized, and the reliability of *(investing, purchasing, contributing, etc.)* to "X"? *(by whom, how, when and where)*

5. Did you receive any letters or literature in the mails?

6. What literature were you supplied regarding "X", its products or services?

7. Please summarize your transactions with "X".

   (a) Dates of transactions:

   (b) Dollar amounts:

   (c) Item *(invested or purchased)*:

FIGURE 13 (continued)

8. Are you satisfied with the purchase?

9. If you were not satisfied, what action have you taken to rectify the situation?

10. If not mentioned previously, please list names of all persons with whom you've had contact regarding the above (*investment, purchase, contribution, etc.*). Describe circumstances and conversations.

IMPORTANT: Please furnish your complete name, address and telephone numbers at home and at work, in the spaces provided below.

NAME:

ADDRESS:

HOME PHONE:

BUSINESS PHONE:

(c) to request the production of certain documents relative to
the complaints.

Any one or combination of the above might be developed as a form
letter for situations where the investigation calls for gathering facts from
individuals or firms that may be unintentionally violating the law, or in
routine cases involving established businesses within the community.

Such letters should advise the recipient that his appearance and production of documentation is voluntary. The letters should also request
notification of the recipient's intention to appear or not to appear
several days prior to the requested appearance date. This will allow time
for arranging for a court reporter or tape recorder if it is deemed necessary
to make a permanent record.

H.   FINDING EXPERTS/RESOURCES

The variety of types of legitimate undertakings is so large that it
would be totally impracticable to expect investigators to have detailed
knowledge of every type of business they come across. The intricacies of
modern businesses, professions, and technologies will frequently require that
white-collar crime investigators and prosecutors seek help from experts.
The need for expert assistance is usually self evident when a case is
finally being prepared for presentation in court. But there are many circumstances where expert assistance is essential to the efficiency and success
of the investigation itself.

Experts are not necessarily needed to participate directly in an
investigation but they can often be valuable in providing either answers
to specific questions or crash training and advice regarding the peculiar
aspects, special terms, systems and practices used in the business operation
or transactions being investigated. For example, an investigator will have
great difficulty in investigating medical quackery fraud without some
familiarity with the consensus of informed medical opinion as to the nature
and treatment of the disease involved; an alleged computer fraud without some
elementary knowledge of how a computer is used in a business; an advance fee
scheme of the loan variety without some knowledge of loan financing; an
alleged securities fraud without some basic knowledge of securities trading
and factors which affect securities valuations; or insurance fraud without
at least a rudimentary understanding of the relevant features of the
insurance business.

Some basic knowledge about a business area may be needed at the very
outset of an investigation, e.g., at the receipt of a complaint, for the
investigator to understand the complaint and collect the maximum information possible from the complainant. The same holds true when an investigation is initiated by other sources such as an intelligence unit, informants, or by referral from some other agency. If the unit is conducting its
own affirmative search for violations, such knowledge is needed prior to
starting the investigation, for example, in using decoy vehicles to detect
auto repair fraud.

The development of basic skills for investigating business and financial transactions is well within the capabilities of any competent investigator. However, when complex and extensive auditing is required the investigator will wish to supplement his own knowledge with direct assistance from an expert accountant. Auditing books and records for possible fraudulent practices is a professional and technical task.

1.   Where to Go to Get Assistance

The following discusses some general guidelines and approaches to obtaining expert assistance and education as well as other resources not available to the investigative unit within its own agency.

  (a)   Expert Assistance

Where the services of accountants are not readily available to white-collar crime investigation units, help should be sought from other government bureaus or departments which employ accountants on a regular basis. If the accountant so recruited does not have investigative accounting experience, the investigator should keep in mind that the accounting investigation will require a combination of the investigator's knowledge of the criminal elements of fraud and the accountant's knowledge of record-keeping and the meaning of individual transactions.

Investigative accounting can be quite specialized, but most accountants can be helpful if the investigator tells them what is suspected, what kinds of information will be helpful, and the suspect's probable modus operandi.

Private sources can be extraordinarily helpful in ad-hoc training during the course of an investigation. One's own bank officer, family doctor, real estate agent acquaintance, securities broker, or insurance agent can be of great help. Even without personal acquaintances in a particular field, it should not be difficult to obtain assistance, given voluntarily and with pride, from members of the local business community --- e.g., a reasonable request by an investigator for a guided tour of a brokerage house and a crash course in securities would rarely be refused by a brokerage firm, a good auto mechanic can help to identify a transmission expert who in turn can advise on investigation of a transmission repair fraud.

The investigator should be prepared to help the prosecutor find witnesses who will be accepted by a court as "experts," and who can provide admissible expert opinions because they are qualified by professional, scientific, or technical training, or by practical experience, to testify as experts in the particular field under investigation. As a first source, the investigator should explore the possibility of getting expert assistance from within his own or another government agency, or from a university faculty. There are a number of reasons for seeking experts from these sources prior to private or commercial sources. First, expert witnesses will usually be questioned regarding their motives for testifying. Those from schools and government might generally be less suspect with respect to their motives. Second, as a matter of professionalism and civic responsibility, highly qualified academics and government personnel in highly technical fields such as computers, medicine, engineering, sales and marketing, economics, geology, etc. will often provide their time and expert advice at minimum cost, even to the extent of testifying in court. Finally, there is a possibility that jurors and judges will be more familiar with and respect their local university or government agencies, making expert testimony from these entities more acceptable and persuasive.

Local "experts" will frequently be reluctant to testify against one in his field, e.g., an auto mechanic against a local garage. In such cases, expert help can be sought from other communities.

In selecting experts, care should be taken to recruit those who can personally relate to the real world of jurors and who can explain their interpretations and opinions in simple, lay language.

There are numerous government agencies at the municipal, state and federal levels which will cooperate with an investigator. Personnel with expertise in many fields and disciplines can be found in these agencies. The investigator who operates under the premise that the required expertise must be available in his own agency will surely stunt his own development as a white-collar crime investigator and limit the overall success of his agency.

(b)   Other Resources

The white-collar crime investigator will find extensive opportunitie for employing the standard resources normally used in investigations other than white-collar crime, such as the crime laboratory in analysis of fingerprints, questioned documents, chemicals, and handwriting; the identification bureau in searching for previous criminal history; or the intelligence unit in searching for associated persons or organizations.

2.   International Investigations

White-collar crime activities frequently flow across national boundaries, and information and evidence will have to be sought abroad --- using the facilities of foreign police agencies. When the trail leads abroad, the unit can call on the services of INTERPOL, an international criminal police organization which has experience in helping with white-collar crime investigations.

INTERPOL will help the unit by arranging for voluntary cooperation in more than 120 countries abroad. Such assistance covers a broad range, including but not limited to criminal history checks, locating suspects, fugitives, and witnesses, and even full investigations which could lead to arrests and extraditions. Where such help is needed, the unit should contact INTERPOL by letter addressed to the agency at:

> Room 1116
> Main Treasury
> Washington, D.C.   20220

The letter of request should briefly state the nature of the investigation
or assistance required, and from whom assistance is sought. No special form
is needed. If the unit is not certain as to who should be contacted abroad,
INTERPOL will advise. If the matter is of great urgency, and delay would
render assistance meaningless, or less valuable, INTERPOL should be telephoned
at the U.S. Main Treasury Building in Washington, D.C.

There is no charge for INTERPOL assistance. The United States office
is located within the U.S. Department of the Treasury and is staffed by
personnel from federal law enforcement agencies (Customs, Secret Service,
Drug Enforcement Administration, Bureau of Alcohol, Tobacco and Firearms).

3. General Support

In setting up a white-collar crime investigative unit, or in expanding
the scope or magnitude of its operatons, there are two basic approaches.
The first is to seek support through normal, local channels such as internal
agency authorizations of manpower, space, and money. The second is to
seek grant support through L.E.A.A. discretionary or block grant sources
(which require actual contributions out of local resources), or the advice
of expert consultants who can sometimes be provided through L.E.A.A. programs.
Advice as to these sources should be sought through state criminal justice
planning agencies, or L.E.A.A. regional offices.

With respect to either of these two basic approaches, it will be
essential to seriously organize the agency and unit's position with respect
to unit goals and objectives, the manner in which the proposed new or
expanded effort will be organized and implemented, the community or public
interests or people who will be benefitted, and the evaluative steps which
will be undertaken to guide implementation and to assess performance. Each
of these factors have been addressed elsewhere in this manual.[92]

I. PREPARING A PACKAGE FOR THE PROSECUTING ATTORNEY

The organizational relationships between investigator and prosecuting
attorney[93] may take many forms. The most common investigative arrangement is
one in which the investigator consults intermittently with the prosecuting
attorney during the course of an investigation, but primarily acts on his
own in gathering the evidence. When the investigator believes the investigation
is complete, or has gone as far as it can go without compulsory process, he will
submit the investigation file to the prosecuting attorney with a recommendation

---

[92]See Chapter VI, Evaluation of a White-Collar Crime Effort, pp. 214-225.

[93]It should always be kept in mind that there may be civil or administrative, as well as criminal prosecution outcomes from investigations, and that
many investigators work in agencies which do not have criminal jurisdiction.
For purposes of brevity, however, terms "prosecution" and related terms are used
in this section to include other than criminal prosecutive litigation.

for criminal, civil, administrative, or further investigatory action.
Arrangements may range from situations in which investigators, prosecuting
attorneys and perhaps other investigators with specialized skills work as
a team, to situations in which investigators do not consult with anyone at
all until they believe their investigation is complete.

Despite all the possible varieties of investigator-prosecutor relationships and the resulting differences in requirements placed upon investigators
for preparation of evidence for prosecution or other litigation, the
proficient investigator must be able to present his work product in written
form and organized in a way that permits efficient access to all information
and evidence important to the case. Even the best case is likely to be
declined by the prosecutor if it is poorly organized and presented (whether in
writing or orally). The prosecutor should not be blamed for this. It is
the investigator's responsibility to organize the material to enable the
prosecutor to make his decision; it is not the prosecutor's responsibility
to exhaustively examine papers and question the investigator to determine
what should have been clearly presented to him in the first place. The
prosecutor is taking on a big job; he needs selling and every bit of help
he can get.[94]

Figure 14 provides an outline guide for the preparation of a comprehensive report for presentation to a prosecuting attorney. In each investigation, depending upon case complexity and the particular organizational
arrangement with the prosecuting attorney, the investigator should be able
to select those elements of the outline which are applicable to the
particular case. In preparing reports the investigator should carefully
and explicitly distinguish between his suppositions and the facts he has
established by investigation.

---

[94]For discussion of the organizational dynamics of presenting the case
to the prosecutor or litigating attorney by the investigator, see Chapter II,
pp. 67-69.

FIGURE 14

GUIDELINES FOR PREPARING A COMPREHENSIVE PACKAGE
FOR THE PROSECUTING ATTORNEY

1. Introductory Summary -- A brief narrative which explains:

    a. The type of scheme
    b. How it came to the attention of law enforcement
    c. Period of operation
    d. Names, fictitious names, company names, etc. used by perpetrators
    e. Evidence of prior criminal activity
    f. Whether warnings were given
    g. Type and total amount of loss
    h. Number and type of victims
    i. Possible statutes (criminal, civil, administrative) which were
        violated

2. Description of Proposed Defendants -- A standard identification record
    may be used, which contains at least the following:

    a. Name
    b. Alias
    c. Addresses (home and business)
    d. Physical description
    e. Place and date of birth
    f. Criminal identification number (FBI or State)
    g. Occupation/employers
    h. Associates/accomplices
    i. Prior record
    j. Identification of those who have cooperated or might cooperate
        with the prosecution

3. Description of Offenses -- A detailed exposition of all pertinent data
    concerning the who, what, when, where, why and how of the scheme from
    its conception through its perpetration. For example, for each occurrence,
    to the extent possible describe:

    a. How was the scheme conceived?
    b. Who executed it? Who played what parts?
    c. Where was it put into operation?
    d. How long was it in operation?
    e. What was the nature of the scheme, the types of merchandise,
        service, or concealed trickery involved?
    f. Whether the victims can be classified as to economic, social,
        educational, or other background.
    g. What was the specific loss to each victim? Total losses to all
        victims?
    h. Any information which will provide the prosecuting attorney
        with a firm comprehension of the magnitude, nature and
        characteristics of the scheme.

FIGURE 14 (continued)

4. <u>Results of Investigation</u> -- A narrative description containing the evidence which may possibly be used for development of proof of misrepresentations, fraudulent intent, or other essential element of the statutes violated.

    a. Any occurrences which might lead to a conclusion of criminal intent. To this should be attached any diagrammatic outlines of the white-collar crime operation which may have been prepared.[95]

    b. When applicable, each major misrepresentation, false pretense, or false promise which the defendants used in obtaining money or property from the victims.

5. <u>Possible Evidence</u>

    a. List of witnesses (including cooperating subjects of investigation and law enforcement) addresses, telephone numbers.

    b. Oral, documentary, and physical evidence associated with each witness.

    c. How obtained -- interview, surveillance, survey questionnaire, etc.

6. <u>Other Agencies Involved</u> -- A brief description of the involvement or interest of other government, law enforcement or private agencies.

---

[95]See the earlier discussion, Link Network and Time Flow Diagrams, Chapter II, pp. 82-88.

V. COMPUTERS: TOOL OF CRIME AND
INVESTIGATIVE RESOURCE

The constant growth in computer use throughout the world of business and government is steadily adding new horizons to the problem of white-collar crime. Procedures for transferring, exchanging, and keeping records of money, securities, titles, and money substitutes such as checking accounts, credit cards, letters of credit, and money orders, are continuously being converted to the use of computer and data communications technology. Negotiable securities, bank accounts, accounts payable, credit ratings, etc. are now stored magnetically and electronically as data within a computer system and transferred from one place to another by radio, telephone, and other communications systems. All but the smallest business and government organizations employ computers. Most banks are automated and would probably be unable to function without computers. Computers are thus rapidly taking over the processes and environment of white-collar crime.

In practically all white-collar crime some form of "paper" is used as a means of deception or as a tool for concealing the true purpose of a transaction. The ability to conceal transactions is enhanced by the computer, in that data is stored by magnetic and electronic symbols. In a matter of seconds a computer can be instructed to transfer large amounts of money and the instruction can be just as easily removed leaving no trace of the fact that a temporary change was made inside the computer. A computer can deal with large volumes of data at very low cost, increasing the posibility of creating large groups of victims in a single act, such as creating large numbers of "personalized" letters, paychecks, or as in the Equity Funding case discussed below, insurance policies.

Computers now dominate processes for control of inventories, so that large-scale thefts of goods can be executed and cover-ups manipulated through computerized systems. Padded payrolls or fictitious payees can be invented and paid, and false verifying documentation can be entered into these systems.

Through the use of computers, individuals and groups who perpetrate frauds and embezzlements have been able to enhance their M.O.'s, add new M.O.'s, and steal larger amounts of money while at the same time lessening the chance of detection. For example, an early case of embezzlement by computer occurred over a period of three years, garnered the perpetrator over $1.5 million and was detected by accident. In this case the chief teller of a New York savings bank received a customer's deposits, pocketed the money, and typed into the computer the information and instructions necessary to transfer money into the customer's account from one of hundreds of other accounts which had shown little or no activity for several years. Every three months the chief teller temporarily transferred the "electronic money" back to the appropriate account for the purpose of calculating quarterly interest. Whereas this elementary bookkeeping manipulation could easily have been detected by a computer audit (i.e., auditing the computer transactions as well as the final printouts),

this did not happen. The embezzlement was detected when the New York Police
raided a bookie, found that one of the bookie's best customers had at times
bet $30,000 in a day. A background check of the bettor revealed that he was
the chief teller of the savings bank who earned only $11,000 per year.

A study completed in 1973 showed that the average losses resulting from
bank embezzlement by computer were ten times higher than general bank embezzlement losses.[95]

The Equity Funding Insurance fraud is an example of a case in which a
computer served as an essential tool for accomplishing a major fraud which
clearly will ultimately result in well over $100,000,000 in losses to
stockholders, customers and reinsurers, and involved manipulation of over
$2 billion in money and assets.[96] This fraud involved mass conspiracy and
continued for many years; it never could have reached such vast proportions
or lasted so long without the aid of computers. To sustain its image as a
successful company and satisfy its need for cash during a recession period
in which sales of its special mutual fund/insurance package dropped alarm-
ingly, the Equity Company produced fake insurance policies. The fake
policies which were recorded in the computer were sold for cash to other
insurance companies in the business of reinsurance. The company was thus
able to report steadily increasing earnings during a recession which caused
the price of its stock to rise considerably. When, after viewing the computer
printouts, the auditors for the reinsurers asked to see the actual original
paperwork, such as policy applications and policies, they were stalled until
forgeries of these documents could be produced by a division of the company
set aside solely for the purpose of producing such forgeries. The executives
from whom the auditors requested the spot check of original documents were able
to tell which of the requested documents had to be specially forged by noting
a secret code number on the computer printout. The computer also was programmed with a special code which caused the system to skip the billing
procedure on fake policies.

More recently, in 1976, a criminal group simply used a file clerk in the
office of a nationwide credit reporting company to alter the credit rating
data entered into the computer. Individuals with poor credit ratings were
solicited and were willing to pay as much as $1,500 to have their ratings
altered. These altered credit ratings made it possible to victimize
nationally known credit card companies, banks, department stores, and other
businesses.

At this stage of discussion, the investigator can see the increased
potential for fraud and embezzlement crimes afforded by the computer. The

[95]Donn B. Parker, "Computer Abuse", Report prepared by Stanford Research
Institute, Menlo Park, California (1973).

[96]Donn B. Parker, Crime By Computer, (New York: Charles Scribner's Sons,
1976), pp 118-174. This book presents a comprehensive picture of the
methodology and challenge of the criminal who exploits the vulnerability
of computer technology.

varieties of modus operandi increase. There are new types of people who might otherwise never commit a crime; e.g., people who write the instructions (program the computer), people who provide original data to the computer or who convert data from the English language into language or symbols which the computer deals with; and people who operate and maintain computers. But the computer, even though only a tool to manipulate data, is often felt to be a mysterious monster beyond understanding as related to the needs of the average law enforcement investigator. Understanding computers is no more of a problem to the white-collar crime investigator than understanding financial investigation, banking procedures, accounting, sale and transfer of securities, and similar specialized areas. ' Just as the white-collar crime investigator should learn how to recognize a problem in these areas and when to seek expert assistance, he should do so when confronted with computer-related investigation issues.

The purpose of this chapter is to cut through the mystery and technical confusions which frequently inhibit investigators who should deal with computer issues. It is not intended to make the reader an expert on computers, or to address the very considerable technical issues which computers present. Rather, it is to give the investigator a basis for dealing with these computer issues as they arise, to develop some sense as to when and where he will need expert assistance in this field, and to help him communicate with these experts.

In addition, the investigator should also consider the utility of the computer, not only as a tool for fraud, but also as a tool to assist law enforcement in fraud investigation. The computer's ability to handle and analyze large amounts of information in an organized manner may be of great assistance in analysis of situations, to help detect patterns of possible fraudulent activity, and even to determine the modus operandi of a crime. Examples of such use will be discussed later in this chapter.

A. COMPUTERS IN BUSINESS DATA PROCESSING

1. What is Business Data Processing?

Business data processing deals with a flow of information needed to run a business. In manufacturing and selling types of businesses, such information might be divided into many separately processed elements such as payroll, accounts receivable, accounts payable, inventory control, production scheduling, sales scheduling, production monitoring, sales monitoring, cost analysis, general ledger accounting, etc. Many of these sale elements also would be pertinent to banking insurance securities, publishing and other businesses which also have need for other specialized types of information such as loan payment accounting, demand deposit accounting, premium payment accounting, policy files, pension payments, customer securities accounts, direct mail addressing, subscription lists, etc. Government agencies use computers to process information elements such as payroll, tax registers, purchasing control, traffic violations, and licensed vehicle numbers.

2. <u>What is a Computer?</u>

(a) <u>Definition</u>--A computer is an electronic machine capable of accepting data, performing mathematical and logical operations on the data and supplying the results of these operations--all without human aid and with:

- extremely rapid processing speed

- extreme processing accuracy and consistency

- the ability to interrelate data from multiple files flexibly and efficiently

When a computer is designed to serve a wide variety of applications such as those listed above, it is called a general purpose computer. A computer which is dedicated to a fixed, unvarying application; e.g., a computer used to control the navigation of an aircraft or spaceship, the flow of water in an aqueduct system, or a drill press in a manufacturing facility--and does nothing else--is called a special purpose computer. In this discussion our interest lies primarily with the general purpose computer.

(b) <u>Computer Structure</u>--The physical structure of the electronic devices or hardware consists of:

- <u>A central processing unit</u>--the major hardware unit of a computer system. This unit contains the electronics that control the sequence of operations, much as a person who controls a desk calculator by pushing buttons (program control). It also performs calculations: it can add, subtract, multiply, or divide, and can perform logical operations such as comparing two numbers for equality or determining which is larger (arithmetic and logic). It contains electronic devices which store the instructions, or program, which direct the computer's operations and the data on which the program is operating at any given time (memory/working storage). When very large amounts of data are involved (e.g., all of the vehicle license numbers in the state) or when the computer is to be used for many different applications, peripheral equipment outside the central processor is used to store data (memory/ user files).

- <u>Input-output devices</u>--data are stored on devices such as punched cards, magnetic cards, magnetic tapes, magnetic discs, magnetic drums, and punched paper tape. A familiar data storage medium which should be readily recognizable is the magnetic ink used to print characters appearing at the bottom of personal and business bank checks. Computers are equipped with hardware devices for reading the data from these storage devices.

Persons can communicate directly with computers, i.e., enter information or take it out, through other devices such as the typewriter terminal or cathode ray tube. High-speed printers are a commonly used output device. A computer can process very rapidly a large number of similar input items, taking one item at a time. For example, after a payroll processing program is loaded into its working storage, the computer can take one employee's time card and the master file information for the same employee into memory and perform all the processing for that transaction, including gross pay, deductions, net pay, etc., as well as update the master file regarding the total year's record. The computer may also develop figures on over-time by department and by job, or the labor cost by job and issue the results of these accumulations and others after all time cards have been processed. Once the processing for a particular time card is completed, the computer processes output records (e.g., a paycheck and an updated master file record for that employee) and moves this information out of the memory to one or more input/output devices. The computer then brings in the next time card and master file record for another employee and repeats its processing for this transaction, until all timecards have been processed. The entire process for a single employee may take much less than a second. The computer may then be loaded with a different program and different input and master files for some other processing operation.

3. What is a Computer System?

A computer system consists of the computer hardware discussed above, together with the necessary additions that will make the inanimate computer hardware element perform in accordance with some predetermined specifications to achieve some predetermined results. These additions are the operational entities which:

- Collect all data on which the computer is required to operate and convert this data to electronic or magnetic form.

- Write out the instructions (programs, also called software) which the computer must follow in order to achieve the results required for such application.

- Control and administer all the processes relating to computer operation.

The investigator should note at this time that each of these operational requirements involves people who, because of specialized skills, have access to various elements of data, programs, and operational processes associated with the computer. Each of the above areas are briefly described below.

(a) Input data collection and conversion. Original data are usually in the form of some recognizable letters, numbers or symbols written on a piece of paper. These data (which, for example of a payroll, would consist of a person's name, pay rate, number of regular hours worked during the pay period, number of overtime hours worked, federal, state and city taxes, social security taxes, etc.) must be collected and then converted into an electronic or magnetic form which the computer can operate on.

One common example of a device used for conversion is the punched card. To create a punched card, a key-punch machine which looks something like a typewriter is used to convert letters and numbers into holes on a card. Prior to feeding the data on a punched card into the computer, a verifier machine may be used to electronically read the punched card and convert it back into understandable language for the purpose of verifying that the card was punched correctly. Other common means for collection and conversion of data include magnetic tape, perforated tape, and typewriter terminals.

(b) Computer programming. This is the activity of writing the specific instructions--the procedural manual which the computer will follow in carrying out each assigned computing task. The person who writes these instructions is called a programmer. A programmer starts out by writing a set of logical, orderly statements in a special language. These statements are based on an analysis of the specific needs of the application (assigned computing task) for which the program is being written. The person who performs this analysis is called a systems analyst. This language is called Programming Language, and the program is called the Source Program. This Source Program, which uses the letters of the alphabet and numbers, is then converted into the language of the computer, sets of 0's and 1's (bits) which is the system by which electronics are used to represent the letters of the alphabet and numbers. This language is called Machine Language, and the program in this form is called the Object Program.

In modern computers a variety of object programs are stored permanently in the working storage of the central processing unit. These are usually the programs which are common to applications, including such things as calculations, logic operations, control of computer operations, input/output devices, etc. This set of object programs is called the operating system. The computer runs itself by executing these programs, transferring from one to the other as necessary.

The operating system and the computer form a computer system which can then execute automatically other predetermined programs for individual applications (e.g., payroll, inventory, etc.) fed to it by humans. These applications programs are most usually fed to the computer in the form of punched cards or magnetic tape. A single applications program could have as many as several hundred thousands of instructions. The development of such programs (software) is a major business in the United States running into billions of dollars annually. A single software package could be worth millions of dollars.

(c) <u>Computer Administration</u>. This includes all the activities such as schedules, controlling and administering the system elements, i.e., the computer and its operating and maintenance staff, the input data collection and conversion personnel, and the systems analysts and programmers. The specific organizational characteristics for administering a data processing operation will vary depending on a number of factors. With a fully staffed data processing operation on the premises, all three elements may be employed by the using organization. There also are computer systems in which many users share the same computer (time-sharing system). In such cases the user may use his own staff to collect and convert input data, an outside company to run these data on its own computer hardware, and even a third company to provide analysis and programming services. Almost any combination is possible.

The major point to consider for investigation purposes is that the personnel associated with the demands of a large data processing system may be employees of a single organization or may be scattered through a number of organizations. For example, when a computerized data processing system uses an off-premises computer, the personnel requirements on the user will be determined by the data conversion requirements. Computer operations and maintenance personnel are provided by a computer rental center and system analysts and programmers may be provided by the computer rental center or by another supplier entirely. Companies who have idle time on their own computers will often rent time to reduce their own expenses.

(d) <u>Operation of Time-Sharing Systems</u>. As stated above, there are computer systems in which many users share the same computer. One version of this approach requires the users to bring all their data to the computer facility. The data and program for the particular user, which may be stored at the computer facility on a magnetic tape or set of punched cards, are then loaded into the computer, and the computer operates on the entire batch of data provided by the user at that time (Batch Processing). A more familiar way in which one computer is shared by many users is the time-sharing system. In time-sharing systems users may have their own input-output terminals or may gain access to the computer through telephone lines. Access to the computer is controlled by programming the computer with secret code numbers or passwords. This is designed to prevent one user from accessing another user's programs or data. Time-sharing systems provide such rapid services that it might appear that the computer is operating simultaneously for many users while in actuality it operates on one at a time.

B. COMPUTER-RELATED CRIME AND INVESTIGATION

The computer has created revolutionary changes in the record keeping and bookkeeping systems used in businesses and government. The operational procedures which businesses and government use depend less and less on visual reviews of individual transactions. For example, in non-computerized business data processing, there are a number of checkpoints where the flow of paperwork would stop completely if certain actions were not taken. It might be that a Mr. Jones in the accounting department will not approve a request for payment until he has physical possession of documents from both the purchasing department and the receiving department, indicating with appropriate signatures that the item had in fact been ordered and received. In automated systems there is less reliance on the usual check by Mr. Jones, and more reliance on checks generated by the automated system itself. As another example, on a payroll system it may be a clerk who makes changes in an employee's master file, i.e., pay rates, deductions, etc. Between the clerk and the magnetic tape which stores these data, there may be no visual review, enabling a crooked clerk to change the master file with ease. Operational procedures have advanced to a point where business and government now employ automated means for producing all their records; e.g., payroll accounting can be mechanically handled, including the presigning, printing and mailing of checks.

These new procedures, of which the above are only a small sample, combined with rapid growth of new types of specialized personnel (e.g., computer programmers), who are often untested by time and service in their employment, make the computer highly vulnerable to misuse and abuse. The computer has created new opportunities for accomplishing embezzlement and fraud or theft of property or valuable information. By virtue of its entry into every phase of living, the computer's importance has grown to a point where it has become an object for attack or sabotage.

The problem of investigating cases which involve computers are little different from cases which involve other white-collar crime weapons such as false financial statements, false invoices, worthless securities, false entries in accounting ledgers, and the like. In the case of computers, the specific weapon might be a false entry in an output document or a false computer program, with the following complication:

- large transactions can be accomplished in a matter of seconds.

- system complexity makes it difficult to detect errors--and even harder to detect a program change which has been changed back again.

The investigator must use all the investigative techniques discussed elsewhere in this manual in approaching a computer-aided crime. As would be the case in obtaining expert technical assistance from an accountant in examining a complex set of books, so too should the investigator obtain expert assistance when necessary to examine and deal with the contents of a computer system.

The following examples are presented for the purpose of indicating the variety of crimes in which computers served as an essential tool, to help with recognition of those factors which determine the investigator's role when confronted with the computer-related crime.

EXAMPLE: In 1976 a management consultant providing doctors with services such as obtaining payment for back medical billings (for which he received a 25% fee) learned through acquaintances in Blue Shield and through examination of Blue Shield's computer manuals, that the computer system was programmed to examine the dates, as well as the other specifics on requests for payment. If the date on the request for payment was less than a year old, the computer was programmed to recognize it as a possible duplicate, on the presumption that monthly bills are sent out and that the most recent could have been sent while payment was in the mail. However, if the date was over a year old, even though all other information was the same, the computer was not programmed to consider the possibility that the request was a duplicate. The consultant arranged to meet and eventually conspired with the claims supervisor to submit duplicate claims from his various clients dated over one year old. The conspirators ran a test claim, found that it worked, and started to file duplicate claims.

The Blue Shield computer fraud was discovered as an ancillary result of hearings being held by a commission investigating fiscal management in the state's Department of Health. The investigation involved all standard investigative procedures such as:

- interviews with the doctors and their office personnel

- interviews with Blue Shield personnel

- identification of the suspect, criminal history check, and identification of associates

- interrogation of suspect who at first denied knowledge and subsequently confessed and agreed to cooperate

- submittal of "marked" claims to the claims supervisor to further test the system and gather evidence of the insider's operations.

- obtaining search warrants on suspect's house, Blue Shield, and all banks used by conspirators.

An added feature of this case was the employment of a state government computer consultant, interviews with Blue Shield computer personnel, and interviews with the defendants for the purpose of making recommendations for changes in the Blue Shield claims processing system.

The investigator's attention is particularly directed to the following facts:

- no computer program changes were required to commit the fraud

- collusion by an insider was required

- the investigation was performed by investigators with no special qualifications in computers

EXAMPLE: One of the most famous cases of fraud occurred in 1973 when a graduate student with expertise in computers found a set of a telephone company's computer system instructions in a garbage can. These documents gave him the entry code into the telephone company's computer and also the quarterly loss figures allowed by the company on its various materials and repair parts distributed to its personnel in the field. Using a touch-tone telephone, the schemer entered orders for items from the company's systems manual, which he had obtained by befriending some telephone company personnel. To prevent detection by establishing a pattern, he varied the parts orders by quantity and location. He also kept the orders within the loss allowance so as not to exceed the tolerance programmed into the computer.

The fraud continued for two years and involved over one million dollars. It was discovered only through the report of an informant. The defendant at his trial rationalized that he wasn't really stealing because there was no loss.

The investigator should note from this case:

- the difficulty in detecting certain computer crimes

- the involvement of persons not normally involved in criminal activity

There are numerous individual variations of computer-related criminal approaches which have surfaced, such as the following:

- A payroll programmer chopped a few cents off each paycheck and added them to his own. Note that the company's accounts balanced.

- Two clerks in a bank worked in the section that handled mutilated checks. Mutilated checks could not be handled by the computer equipment which reads the magnetic ink character record at the bottom of all checks. The clerks deliberately mutilated their checks so the computer would reject them. When the checks were delivered to their section, they just threw them away so that their own accounts would not be charged with the checks they had written. Note the new procedures and new opportunities provided by computer technology.

- A bank programmer whose program calculated savings account interest, instead of dropping off fractions of pennies, had them added to his own account.

- A computer consultant found a blank form used for adding a new employee to the company payroll. He added his own name to the payroll list and picked up his check as it came off the automatic check-writing equipment. Note the ease with which a visiting outsider gained access.

- Two systems analysts set up their own company while working for another company that sold metal ores. Their own company bought ore from their employer and sold the same ore back to their employer at a profit. The entire transactions were accomplished by a computer which they controlled.

- A computer expert working for a bank typed his own bank account number on hundreds of blank bank deposit slips. He took actual deposits from various firms, replaced their deposit slips with his own, writing in the firm's account number and handling the deposit slips and money to the tellers. Because the computer thief used a magnetic typewriter and because he knew that the computer was programmed to read the magnetic tape before any other notations, all the money went into his own account. He collected $50,000 in one day.

The above examples and those discussed earlier in this chapter by no means exhaust the possibilities of computer crimes. They have been discussed here primarily to show that while the investigator will often require the assistance and advice of those who are familiar with computer applications and technology, the crimes themselves differ only in mechanics, but not in substance from other white-collar crimes. The investigator's own role is central and essentially unchanged merely because computers are involved.

C. POTENTIAL COMPUTER WHITE-COLLAR CRIME PERPETRATORS

The following provides a general idea of the possible perpetrators of white-collar computer-related crimes, and their modi operandi:

1. Systems Programmers

   - deliberate installation of errors or logical oversights into the computer program, providing a weak point which can be exploited over again and again.

   - disclosure of protective measures to outsiders.

   - disabling or neutralizing the protective features of programs.

2. Computer Operators

   - deliberate substitution of programs which have been tampered with.

   - disclosure of organizational and procedural safeguards.

   - copying of files for sale to competitors or other buyers.

3. Maintenance Personnel

   - use of test programs to examine or copy files or alter system programs.

   - disabling protective hardware.

210

4. <u>Users</u>

   • impersonation of other users

   • falsifying own files to deceive third parties

   • penetration of operating system and alteration of object programs.

5. <u>Others</u>

   • data processors who provide or handle input data.

   • supervising personnel.

D. <u>COMPUTERS AS AN INVESTIGATIVE TOOL</u>

All investigators are concerned with the storage and retrieval of information ranging from investigative leads to evidence. Investigators store
such information in their heads, on scraps of paper, in narrative reports,
and in indexed manual filing systems. In recent years law enforcement agencies have begun to use computers for storage and retrieval of many varieties
of information. This section describes some possible uses of computers for
analytical aid in investigation of white-collar crime.

The investigator should visualize the computer as an immense filing cabinet in which almost unlimited amounts of information can be stored, and from
which the information can be retrieved in a form designed specifically for
his needs. This would be a cabinet in which it would hardly matter in what
particular drawer a particular bit of information is located, or how long
it has been in there since the computer provides almost instantaneous
examination of the cabinet's total contents. This imagined system is practically attainable <u>if</u> the investigator is able to effectively categorize or
index the desired information. Even when an investigator cannot put all
desired information from a report into the computer, he can have the computer
direct him to the location of the original document which contains the
information.

The computer's ability to store and organize vast amounts of information,
and to be programmed for easy retrieval of this information in any order or
form desired by the user, makes it's use an excellent way for an investigator
to store information on complex cases which cover long periods of time. Many
cases involve large amounts of details which are difficult to keep track of
manually. The computer can also be used to monitor any data for the purpose
of identifying significant patterns which might be of interest to the
investigator, such as who communicated with whom, and how often, over
what period of time, etc.

The following are some actual examples of computer use as an analytical
aid for investigation. Examples 1 and 2 are actual examples; example 3 is
hypothetical at the time of this writing.

1. <u>Complaint Handling</u>. The San Diego County (California) District Attorney uses a computer-based complaint file to identify patterns related to fraudulent activities. The following data on all complaints are stored in the computer:

- names and aliases of suspects.

- names and aliases of victims.

- nature of alleged crime.

- complaint disposition and date.

- current status of the case.

- cross references to other related complaints.

As cases are developed and new data are acquired, additional entries are made to the computer file. A print-out of the data organized by the above headings enables rapid detection of patterns of victims and suspects and thus allows a relatively accurate judgment to be made as to whether the case involves an isolated incident or an extensive and repeated pattern of abuse, and enables rapid identification of chronic complainers.

The print-out is updated weekly and distributed to other agencies which ensures that overlap of effort is minimal and provides general intelligence to other interested agencies.

The computer file is purged of dead cases periodically. A separate dead file is maintained in the event that new complaints are received which might require reopening of an investigation.

It should be noted that the above pattern analysis steps which are performed by manual, concentrated inspection of the print-out can also be programmed into the computer and performed automatically. The criteria which are used by the person examining the print-out can be developed into program statements which will provide for automatic pattern analysis of all data.

2. <u>Fraud Detection--Using Existing Computer Files</u>. Many businesses and government agencies record and store vast amounts of data concerning their customers, clients and transactions in general. For example, insurance systems, whether private such as a life or automobile insurance company, or government such as medicare, medicaid, unemployment or welfare--all maintain computer filing systems. Pertinent data from their files often can be analyzed for patterns to detect fraud against these agencies.

Consider the example of a fictitious company unemployment insurance fraud. A fraud operator might set up six fictitious companies, each with two fictitious employees, anticipating that he and his confederate eventually will apply for unemployment insurance, posing as the laid-off employees. The phony businessman registers with the state's unemployment insurance department, and pays unemployment insurance taxes for the minimum period allowed by law. The two conspirators then assume the identities of the fictitious employees, using phony social security and other identification to collect unemployment insurance.

To execute such a fraud requires that the phony companies and employees be registered with the appropriate state agency. The registration data, employee data, taxes paid, etc., are usually stored in computer files. The state's computer could be programmed to analyze all the computer file data and identify first all companies who have had employees applying for unemployment insurance where the company had paid taxes for only the minimum period. Then from these companies the computer could analyze the employees requesting unemployment insurance for similarities; e.g., the computer could show that six companies all had two employees who applied for insurance in a short period of time. The social security numbers could be analyzed by the computer to determine if they were issued during a certain time period. Similarly, where any frauds are discovered with a particular modus operandi, these can then be treated as indicators, and file data can be scanned for similar patterns of activity because there would be some higher likelihood of fraud. In effect the computer search becomes one pro-active form of white-collar crime detection.

3. _Fraud Detection--Creating New Computer Files_. At this stage the reader should realize that a computer can store and organize vast amounts of data and be programmed to retrieve isolated items of data based on any criteria, including many sophisticated mathematical and statistical analysis techniques. Investigators should recognize the possibilities for using the computer as an analytical aid in cases where there are large amounts of data, many categories of data, or where data must be gathered and periodically analyzed for trends or patterns.

For example, assume that only three major companies in a state are qualified to bid for certain construction contracts. Further, assume that these companies have conspired to rig their bids so that each will get a one-third share of the contracts at prices much higher than would be normal for competitive bidding. The ability to recognize the possibilities that such a bid-rigging fraud is in operation requires a detailed analysis of bid data including technical work proposed, estimated costs of materials, estimated costs of labor, total price, etc. All the bids of each individual company would have to be analyzed in sequence to detect changes in their patterns of estimating costs. All bid details would have to be analyzed against each other to show patterns of winning and losing bids. It is conceivable that the data to be analyzed would cover a period of many years. To accomplish such tasks using manual techniques simply is not practical for an investigator whose time cannot be spent in extremely lengthy and tedious research and analysis.

The entire analytical process, of which only a smattering is mentioned above, can readily be accomplished with the assistance of a computer. Presuming an appropriate computer system is available, the investigator need only lay out his interests to a qualified systems analyst. The process of programming for a particular data processing application, such as analysis of the possible bid-rigging scheme described above, is a relatively straightforward task. Once the programming is accomplished, historical data can be fed into the machine, new data can be added as received, and periodic analyses can be run until a judgment can be made. Such a computer analysis would, of course, be quite costly, and would not be undertaken without substantial indication that the investigative effort would ultimately be successful.

VI. EVALUATION OF A WHITE-COLLAR CRIME EFFORT

A. INTRODUCTION

Having looked at the tactics and techniques of white-collar crime enforcement and at the organization required to accompany such efforts, it is important
to review and discuss another task essential to efficient management and continuity of existence of a white-collar crime effort. This task is evaluation.
Too often when "evaluation" is spoken of, it is seen as a troublesome
requirement imposed upon activities, but of little intrinsic value to them.
To share this view is to totally misunderstand evaluation.

Whenever choices are made between competing uses for scarce resources,
there is a need for a comparative assessment of the relative merits of the
competing uses. This comparative assessment (or evaluation) occurs both before
choices are made as well as once they have been made. In the first instance,
evaluation serves as a decision-making tool; in the latter case, as a validation mechanism, confirming or rejecting the soundness of the original decision.

Many of the decisions made with regard to law enforcement resources are
so automatic that they are not thought of as constituting evaluative choices.
Thus, nearly every police agency of relevant size employs both uniformed and
plainclothes divisions in order to accomplish its overall goals, implying
relative values attached to a visible uniform presence and an ununiformed
investigative capacity. Some choices do not involve evaluative assessments,
but rather reflect larger moral and social choices pursued independent of
evaluative findings. In this area we might place the maintenance of specialized homicide units. Homicide is not a frequently-occurring event in
every jurisdiction, and yet no one would seriously argue that law enforcement
agencies should not create and have available specialized resources to
respond to so serious--though rare--a crime event. The point is that the
organization of law enforcement agencies implies a series of evaluative
decisions about their mission and short- and long-term goals. Because many
of these decisions were made long ago they are taken now as "givens" and
not subjected--rightly or wrongly--to close scrutiny and assessment.

In many agencies, however, white-collar crime enforcement does not have
such an established and accepted status, and will be subjected to critical
evaluation, both of a decision-making and validation nature.

B. EVALUATION AS A MANAGEMENT TOOL

Recognition that a white-collar crime effort necessarily will use resources
that otherwise might be deployed elsewhere and therefore that it will attract
intensive scrutiny does not mean that those engaged in such a unit or in making the decision to create such a unit should adopt a defensive posture. On
the contrary, the pressure for evaluation should be viewed as a management
asset, producing positive benefits for the unit staff in their relationship
with the agency administrator and with external funding sources. In addition,
such a posture will prove beneficial to the unit supervisor and unit members
as they go about their work.

1. <u>Evaluation Needs of the Agency Administrator.</u>

An agency administrator for whom white-collar crime enforcement is a new
venture must be armed with considerable information in order to decide to
embark on such an effort. But his needs will not stop there. Once having
decided to go the white-collar crime route, he will continue to need
information--evaluative in nature--which provides him with feedback concerning his decision. The unit which pursues self-evaluation carefully and
seriously will be at some advantage in relating to the needs of the chief
administrator of its parent agency.

2. <u>Evaluation Needs of External Funding Sources.</u>

Many white-collar crime efforts will be undertaken with the support of
external grants-in-aid. Such grants carry with them evaluative requirements
that too often are viewed as troublesome meddling. This is not a healthy
interpretation of such requirements. Funding sources, like operating agencies,
have hard choices to make concerning where they will expend their limited
resources. Like all decision-makers, they need both prior information and
on-going feedback concerning their funding choices. A sound self-evaluation
plan can assist a white-collar unit both in meeting the evaluative needs of
an external funding source and in fulfilling its own information needs.

3. <u>Evaluation Needs of the White-Collar Crime Unit.</u>

Because efforts in the area of white-collar crime enforcement are sometimes novel ventures for an agency, the roles and expected performance
criteria for those participating in them can be somewhat ambiguous. Therefore
it often will be unclear to unit members what expectations their agency has
of them--not to mention what specific expectations they should have of
themselves. This can easily cause the white-collar effort to bog down.

Avoidance of such situations by supplying both the unit supervisor and
unit members with adequate and continuous feedback concerning their efforts
should be the goal of a sound self-evaluation plan. What follows is a design
for self-evaluation of a white-collar crime enforcement effort. Its purpose
is to provide general guidelines applicable to many kinds of white-collar
crime enforcement efforts, to highlight general information needs related
to self-evaluation; and to describe the process of evaluative efforts.

C. <u>DESIGN FOR SELF-EVALUATION</u>

A sound self-evaluation involves consideration of four fundamental
steps:

1. determination of unit goals and objectives;

2. clear statement of criteria bearing on achievement of goals and
objectives;

3. development of plan for collection and analysis of information
related to performance; and

4. statement of expectations concerning goal attainment.

Both the timing and necessary participants involved with each of these evaluative steps will vary and will be included in the discussions below.

1. Determination of Goals

To be most useful, self-evaluation of a white-collar enforcement effort should begin at the planning and pre-implementation stage. This is because it is at this point that careful enunciation of reasonable goals and accompanying objectives capable of being measured or otherwise assessed, can occur. Unless specification of goals and objectives is undertaken, there is little basis on which an evaluation can proceed. Clarification of the unit's mission, in other words, must occur in order to assess its performance in relation to that mission.

Goal determination is not ordinarily an evaluative step that can be undertaken in a vacuum. Participants in such a determination should include relevant agency and administrative staff, the designated unit supervisor, representatives of the agency's planning section, and (if feasible) members of the unit staff. Unfortunately, there is no recipe for selection of "proper" goals by agencies. Situations vary greatly among jurisdictions, as do the powers of enforcement bodies and resources available to them.

In addition, white-collar crime enforcement has some unique dimensions that make the determination of goals and objectives a particularly difficult undertaking. To begin with, the term "white-collar crime" represents a complex and extremely varied range of conduct. One cannot, then, merely set the goal of an effort as that of "reducing white-collar crime" because that would be meaningless. Instead, it is necessary for evaluative purposes to settle on what white-collar crime activities, or specific types of conduct does the unit seek to reduce? Second, white-collar crimes in general are believed to go substantially unreported. Add to this the number of agencies and levels of government which have a responsibility of some kind to deal with various white-collar abuses, and it is highly unlikely that any one agency could possibly be the repository of even the events that are reported in a given jurisdiction. Instead, the reported events are likely to surface in many different agencies. To approach white-collar crime generally as an enforcement problem with a view to reducing it is to set a goal, performance toward which is impossible to measure or adequately assess. Finally, because of the variety of acts and actors embraced within the concept of white-collar crime, it is unlikely that even the most talented, well-staffed and organized enforcement unit could successfully respond to more than a few segments of the activity.

Setting goals and related objectives in the white-collar crime area, then, is largely a process of specifying and limiting the focus of an enforcement effort to some manageable portion of this crime area. Recognizing that the enforcement effort cannot do everything, there must be some determination of what best can be done and what can be done well with the staff, resources, and time available and the jurisdictional powers possessed.

What can be done well is largely a function of staff characteristics and resources. What can best be done, on the other hand, must relate primarily to an assessment of what is occurring in the agency's environment. Such an assessment should seek to answer the following questions: What abuses are taking place and with what frequency? How are these being responded to? An agency interested in whtie-collar crime enforcement should review carefully the major abuses affecting its jurisdiction as against the current responses to these abuses. Where a major abuse is not met with a response, or is inadequately met, the agency should then determine if it can appropriately and effectively provide the response needed. A good assessment, then, should produce a matrix similar to that shown in Figure 15.

Below, three examples of the kinds of goals and accompanying objectives that might be chosen for a white-collar crime effort are described. It should be stressed that these are merely examples. Their appropriateness to a given agency must be carefully weighed.

(a) <u>Setting goals with reference to victim groups</u>. In some jurisdictions, assessment of white-collar crime problems will reveal that some segments of the population are especially victimized by specific kinds of fraud abuses. In such situations, one method of setting goals for a white-collar crime enforcement effort is to relate that effort to identified groups who are specially victimized with the hope of favorably impacting on that victimization by deterring or preventing it and/or by seeking "justice" for such groups should they be victimized.

Setting unit goals with respect to identified victim groups has several advantages. First, it gives the effort a clear focus. Second, because the group selected to benefit from the effort is believed to experience a high level of victimization, the prospect for showing impact is also high. This serves not only to motivate unit investigators but also to provide them with satisfaction in their accomplishments. Finally, by focusing specifically on the victimization of a particular group in the population, the effort is likely to limit the range and kind of cases it deals with. This is particularly advantageous for a new and inexperienced white-collar crime unit, since it will allow unit members to develop a depth of expertise in a limited number of areas that can give them the confidence to go forward into less familiar investigative territory.

This method carries with it some affirmative requirements that may prove troublesome for some agencies. First, a focus on victim groups is likely to obligate the commitment of resources and time to a substantial public education effort, both to inform targeted groups of the unit and to encourage complaint reporting. While some degree of public education will be a part of any white-collar crime effort, the obligations of the victim-oriented enforcement effort are likely to be greater than usual. White-collar crime units located in agencies for which public education is not a major activity, i.e., police departments, may not, then, be prepared for the kind of educative tasks required, or to meet demands for attention flowing from rising expectations on the part of the identified victim group.

FIGURE 15

MATRIX FOR DETERMINING AGENCY GOALS IN WHITE-COLLAR CRIME ENFORCEMENT				
MAJOR AND/OR FREQUENT ABUSES	RESPONSES TO ABUSES			
	QUALITY OF RESPONSE			MAJOR AGENCY(IES) RESPONDING
	POOR	ADEQUATE	GOOD	

Consumer affairs offices, on the other hand, may find the public education
requirements of a victim-oriented effort more consonant with overall agency
functions and more consistent with their view of their mission.

The targeting of victim groups, then, provides a method of setting goals
that can contribute a specific focus and agenda to a white-collar crime
effort. While providing these, however, the method also demands a commitment to a range of activities and roles that can contribute greatly to the
investigative role but which lie outside it. Agencies unprepared to
recognize, plan for and reward these additional functions might better use
another method for setting goals.

Having weighed the advantages and disadvantages and chosen a victim-
oriented focus for the white-collar crime effort, the agency must then
formally enunciate its goals and define objectives it believes will assist
in attainment of those goals. An example of a victim-oriented goal and
accompanying objectives would be the following:

> Goal: To reduce and prevent the victimization of elderly
> persons residing in this jurisdiction resulting from
> white-collar criminals engaged in home repair fraud,
> medical quackery and medicare abuses, BY

> Objectives: • informing elderly citizens on how to avoid being
> victimized by such frauds;

> • increasing the reporting rates of elderly citizens
> victimized by such crimes;

> • assisting elderly victims in filing complaints
> and pursuing official redress in their behalf;

> • securing appropriate remedial action (i.e.,
> restitution and mediation outcomes) for elderly
> citizens who have been victimized.

(b) Selecting goals with reference to specific abuses. Another
method of setting the goals or focus for a white-collar crime effort is to
target particular abuses, or groups of abuses for special attention. Once
again the singling out of specific abuses should be based on some assessment
of the offenses being committed in the agency's jurisdiction and implies
that such an assessment has been undertaken. It would be foolish, for
example, for a white-collar crime unit to select land fraud as a focus of
attention, where there is little evidence that such frauds are occurring there
or that its public is experiencing victimization from such acts. Similarly,
the selection of abuses for enforcement attention should reasonably reflect
the resources available to the unit and the jurisdictional constraints under
which it will operate. Thus, for example, even where land fraud victimization appears staggering in an agency's jurisdiction, if the agency has neither
the resources nor the statutory authority to intervene appropriately, the
singling out of land frauds for attention will be ill-advised.

It should be underscored that setting goals on the basis of selected offenses relies heavily on two factors: (1) the presence of adequate information from which intelligent selections can be made; and (2) the planning of the subsequent effort to provide the resources necessary to adequately address the offenses selected. Lacking either of these factors, use of this method for goal determination is reduced to a hollow exercise that will provide little guidance or sense of mission for a subsequent white-collar crime unit.

An example of abuse-related goals and attendant objectives would be the following:

Goal: To reduce the incidence of land fraud within this jurisdiction, BY

Objectives: • thoroughly investigating real estate and land transfer practices in this region;

• alerting the public to tactics of the land fraud specialist;

• increasing the reporting of questionable practices concerning sale of land by public;

• enlisting the aid of real estate professionals to report abuses in their industry;

• seeking criminal prosecution and maximum criminal penalties in land fraud cases developed by the unit;

• assisting other jurisdictions in prosecuting land fraud operators that come to the unit's attention but are not within its jurisdiction.

(c) Setting goals with respect to the development of expertise. One final method for goal selection may be used by a white-collar crime unit, and this concerns the setting of objectives related to the development of expanded expertise in the unit to respond to a range of white-collar crime activities. Often this goal is combined with other more specific goals such as those described above. Clear statement of expertise development as a goal can be particularly important for a newly constituted white-collar crime unit, since it logically constitutes a first-phase goal designed to enhance the achievement later of more specific offense-related goals-- while at the same time facilitating on-going enforcement efforts.

One advantage of making skill development an object of unit achievement is that it will encourage the white-collar crime effort to undertake cases of greater significance and impact on the public--which frequently will be cases of greater complexity and difficulty, more time-consuming and demanding of investigative resources. Enhanced skills and related willingness to take

on new challenges in familiar areas is also likely to encourage unit personnel to exercise these skills in the challenge presented by new forms of
white-collar crime which emerge in their jurisdictions. In addition the
capacity to deal with particular white-collar crimes often will facilitate
their recognition as prosecutable offenses.

The disadvantage of such a goal--especially when used in isolation-- is
that no clear focus is provided the unit. This raises the danger that such
a unit may too easily drift from one investigative area to another with
little sense of a coherent set of priorities. Unless, then, such a goal
is carefully guided by more substantive concerns, the record of a white-
collar crime effort easily could lead to a situation in which the unit
brushes by many white-collar crime abuses, victims, and offenders, but
fails to do very much at all in any one area.

An example of an expertise-development goal and accompanying objectives
is provided below.

Goal: To substantially improve the capacity of this agency to
respond successfully to problems of white-collar crime
BY

Objectives: • taking advantage of special training programs designed to
enhance or impart white-collar crime investigative skills;

• improving the quality of investigative and case preparation
materials for official processing;

• undertaking investigations in novel and complex cases
and bringing them to satisfactory conclusions;

• completing complex investigative tasks in cooperation
with other agencies;

• improving the satisfactory delivery of services to
victims of white-collar crime.

(d) Setting goals - a summary. The first step in any self-evaluation
should be the setting of unit goals (at the pre-implementation stage if
possible). Without clearly enunciated goals and objectives and a sense of
overall mission, a white-collar crime effort will be hard pressed to evaluate
its performance. Lacking evaluative capacity, the unit will fail to benefit
from the guidance provided by self-assessment and may flounder--knowing
neither where it has been nor where it is going.

2. Establishment of Performance Criteria

Once goals and objectives have been selected for a white-collar crime
effort, the next step is to establish acceptable criteria by which performance

222

can be evaluated in relation to those goals. The term "acceptable criteria" is not meant to imply that some standards are better than others, but rather to suggest the process by which they should become established. Performance criteria must be agreed to, accepted and understood by all concerned in order for the evaluative effort to be useful and valid. Thus, performance criteria, like goals and objectives, should be established (before implementation of a new unit) and should involve maximum participation of the unit staff as well as agency supervisory and planning personnel.

It is obvious that "acceptable criteria" must reasonably relate to the goals and objectives to which they will be applied. Thus, if the major objective of a unit is to secure criminal penalties for particular abuses, then an acceptable criterion of performance should relate to cases accepted by a prosecutor, rather than those to which civil or mediation outcomes were applied. Similarly, where a unit has stated one objective to be the seeking of maximum criminal sanctions, an acceptable criterion would not be calculation of the actual penalties but rather would more appropriately be documentation of the steps taken to assure strong sanctioning, such as comprehensive preparation of information for inclusion in pre-sentence reports which fully document the gravity of the violation and its impact on victims. Sound performance criteria should seek to measure not only outcomes, but also the consistency and rigor of the processes by which particular outcomes were achieved. This is why the mere counting of numbers of investigations, convictions or cases and/or the tallying of the dollar total of restitutive settlements do not serve as sound evaluative measures. Instead such measures must be combined with other criteria in order to be interpreted properly. Thus, the raw number of investigations must be grounded in some framework which adjusts for quality and significance of investigations so that the supervisor can distinguish quality, time-consuming investigative efforts from the mere spinning of investigative wheels to drive up the tally. Sound performance criteria, then, can provide managerial guidance to supervisors as well as contributing to unit evaluation.

It should be noted that performance criteria are related specifically to objectives rather than to goals. This is because while goals generally constitute hoped-for results of an effort, objectives represent statements of concrete and controllable steps the agency proposes to take in order to reach a particular result. It is more practical to attempt to gauge success in meeting objectives which are more concrete than to measure ultimate consequences to a community. This is not to suggest that performance criteria do not contribute to an evaluation of the extent to which goals are achieved. To the extent that stated objectives are logically, positively, and determinatively related to achievement of goals, it is clear that successful performance with regard to a unit's objectives will result in satisfactory progress toward goals.

3. Development of Data Collection and Analysis Plan

The third step that must be taken in a sound self-evaluation is to decide what kinds of information will be needed to determine if performance criteria have been met, who will gather that information, when it will be gathered, and who will be responsible for organizing and presenting it. This may sound like a massive and arduous task, but if the evaluation plan has been sound to this point, it will not be. Instead what a unit and an agency will see is that the information needed for the evaluative effort is largely the same as that required for management of a well-organized and supervised unit. In fact, the files and record-keeping mechanisms described earlier when the flow of information in a unit was discussed[97] are likely to be the major sources of information for self-evaluation. Thus, good supervision of a white-collar crime unit dictates that investigators keep individual records of their activities for review by the supervisor. Good evaluation requires the same documentation of staff activity. Similarly, maintenance of a complaints-received file which can permit the unit supervisor to observe changes in the pattern of complaints and make decisions concerning the allocation of resources also serves as a valuable source of evaluative data. In this instance, the evaluative and the supervisory purposes are precisely the same.

What a sound self-evaluation plan does in effect is to provide the supervisor with a framework in which to interpret the information he receives--not in the sense of its being good or bad, but rather in the sense of its being "where we should reasonably expect to be." Having this framework allows the supervisor to provide feedback to the unit staff; to congratulate where appropriate and to make suggestions or redirect activities that appear unproductive.

A data collection plan for evaluation should provide the unit supervisor with information needed to manage his unit, since his management needs for information will parallel evaluative requirements. The unit supervisor should have available a clerk or analyst to whom can be delegated the preparation of monthly summaries of evaluative data, which regardless of the objectives and criteria involved, will amount to a synopsis of unit activities during the reporting period. This summary should be made available to unit staff and agency administrative personnel. On a less frequent basis (quarterly, for example) cumulative summaries should be prepared and a formal presentation by the supervisor of the unit's milestones and progress should be considered.

The kinds of information specifically needed to satisfy a particular evaluation-management plan will depend, of course, on the stated goals, objectives and criteria adopted by the unit and its parent agency. Using illustrative materials previously introduced, some examples are presented in Figure 16.

---

[97]See Chapter II, at pp. 71-81.

Figure 16

MATRIX FOR DATA-GATHERING PLAN

CRITERIA	INFORMATION NEEDED	SOURCE OF INFORMATION
what changes occurred in patterns of reporting questionable land sales?	initial number of land sale complaints. changes in number of reports and complaints changes in kind of complaints received	complaints received file
what proportion of land fraud cases were presented for criminal prosecution	number of land fraud cases developed, compared with all cases outcomes of all cases number criminally prosecuted	investigations files past & completed closed on-going
what proportion of target population received information?	size of target population how many persons in population received information	Census statistics. local office on aged. Investigator activity files Public Service groups dealing with elderly

4. Statement of Expectations

The final step necessary for a sound evaluation design is the formal statement of expectations with respect to both the short and long term. This step often is overlooked, producing much consternation and/or confusion. What this step essentially requires is that both the parent agency and those involved in the white-collar crime effort carefully think through and formally state what they see as the course the effort will take. What do they expect will occur in the first three months as opposed to the last six? What activities are likely to be most prominent at one stage and not at another? And why?

The statement of expectations is particularly important for top agency administrators who probably will not be closely apprised of the unit's day to day operations, may only see monthly or quarterly activity summaries, and may hold unreasonable expectations for the unit. Such a statement can

225

prepare the agency head not to expect, for example, an immediate round-up
of large numbers of white-collar offenders--an event quite unlikely to occur.
Similarly, it can prepare a new unit for the kinds of painstaking drudgery
or growing pains it is likely to encounter. For an already existing unit,
it can document what it knows from experience to be the course of things in
the white-collar crime enforcement area. Finally, the statement of expectations, by stressing the relationships and differences between the short
pull and the long haul, helps the unit and its agency to avoid the situations in which an effort is unjustifiably condemned or lauded prematurely.
By setting a steady, defined course, it prevents the kind of recrimination
or self-adulation that can prove fatal to overall success.

One example of the kind of information that should be included in a
statement of expectations will serve to illustrate its purpose and value.
Suppose 1) that a white-collar crime effort chooses as its goal the reduction
of the victimization experienced by a particular target population; 2) that
it proposes to attain that goal through a public education effort and by
increasing the crime reporting by this group. At the end of a particular
period it may be found that by fulfilling its objectives, the number of
abuses reported has substantially increased--a result somewhat in conflict
with the ultimate goal. What the statement of expectations can and should
do in this situation is explain that increases in the number of reported
abuses is a fully intended outcome of a strong public education and
reporting drive among members of the target population. Rather than con-
founding the ultimate goal, the unit, by successfully meeting its objectives,
will have brought to light many abuses that would have gone unreported and
received no official attention. To the extent that the unit can show a
stable, new, and higher reporting level for the targeted population, then,
it can expect that its ability to reach the ultimate goal will be enhanced
since it will be aware of and able to deal directly with a greater proportion
of the actual abuses occurring.

5. Self-Evaluation--A Summary

Evaluation can be made to seem an onerous and unproductive activity.
It is hoped that the design for self-evaluation presented here has provided
a different perspective on it. What should be clear is that the steps that
make up a sound evaluation, i.e., setting of goals and objectives, establishing performance criteria, developing a data collection plan, and stating one's
expectations, are precisely the steps needed for a sound organization and
management plan. No mystery need attach to the evaluation process. Most of
it is just common sense. After all, the best way to get somewhere is:
first, to know where you want to go; second to decide how you plan to get
there; and finally, to honestly state how far you expect to get over a given
period of time. A good evaluation will assist a white-collar crime effort
not only in attaining its goals, but also in clarifying the process and
documenting the milestones that are the substance and tokens of that
achievement.

APPENDICES

APPENDIX A - TRAINING FOR WHITE-COLLAR CRIME ENFORCEMENT

TABLE OF CONTENTS

APPENDIX A - TRAINING FOR WHITE-COLLAR CRIME ENFORCEMENT

TABLE OF CONTENTS (continued)

APPENDIX A

TRAINING FOR WHITE-COLLAR CRIME ENFORCEMENT

A. <u>INTRODUCTION</u>

The recruitment and selection of investigators has been discussed in
this Manual, and guidelines suggested for these tasks. Proper selection
is very important, yet it is only a beginning of the process of developing
first-rate investigators. Candidates for the position of investigator
require further training to develop a high level of professional skill,
even if they have prior investigative experience. A detective who has
worked only in homicide or even in street bunco may have to be oriented
toward new types of investigative techniques, such as more subtle ways of
talking with witnesses and interrogating suspects, more care in planning
of arrests, more familiarity with the paper trail. Some investigators may
have had experience only with certain limited types of white-collar crimes,
such as embezzlement, and may not be oriented to other types of criminals
and crimes, such as land fraud which is perpetrated more openly.

Resources or other factors will often prevent having a recruiting
procedure that capitalizes on the personal motives of candidates, e.g.,
personal motivations and qualifications to deal with white-collar crime.
Therefore recruits often will need to be educated to the importance of
white-collar crime, as well as to the skills involved in investigating
such crime. In many situations, white-collar crime units may have to
cooperate with agencies which have different priorities. In such cases
there is a danger that personnel in these other agencies will have to learn
the importance of white-collar crime, since they may tend to relegate it
to a low priority.

Even officers who are experienced white-collar crime investigators within
an agency may need to learn about new crimes, and new techniques of
investigation. A consumer fraud specialist in an agency may need to learn
about stock fraud if there is a sudden increase in the latter in the
agency's jurisdiction; or about computer fraud which relies on a newly
developing technology.

In the sections below, a number of different approaches to training
are described. Not all of these approaches are especially useful for all
types of agencies and units. Some agencies may be so big that they can do
their own training; others may be so small that they can only send recruits
to training schools held on a regional or even national basis. Some agencies
may be highly experienced in white-collar crime investigation and can capital
ize on this experience to help train new investigators; other agencies are
entirely new, and will have to depend on the investigators' own talents and
backgrounds and on outside resources for training. In larger agencies, the
investigators are more likely to specialize and would need to secure training

in other specialties, either inside or outside the agency. In small agencies each investigator is more likely to need to be a generalist, taking on all types of white-collar crime investigations within its geographic, legal, and subject matter jurisdiction.

In describing the possible training approaches below, the appropriateness of particular training techniques for particular agency sections will be pointed out. It should be recognized, however, that where appropriate training approaches are limited by resources, the pooling of resources among agencies and across jurisdictional lines can help solve the problem, for example by the use of regional schools when formal training is most appropriate.

In the following sections guidelines for training white-collar investigators are suggested. These emphasize active, participating learning in which the trainee practices various techniques, discusses various issues, critiques performances, etc. This approach stands somewhat in contrast to much of what is now done in white-collar crime enforcement training courses, in which more time is given to straightforward lecturing, often describing what should be done in various types of cases. Obviously, such lecturing has an important role to play in training investigators; the invited expert lecturer can present very valuable and useful material which in many instances can be presented in no other way. In smaller units with very limited resources it may be the only way possible. On the other hand, the guidelines below attempt to achieve a better balance between the listening and learning approach and the active (participatory) learning approach. In order to achieve this, much of the discussion below is oriented to the participating learning approach, on the assumption that its lessons can more easily be transferred to the lecture format than the other way around.

In line with this approach, there are at least three ways in which investigators can be trained: informal on-the-job training (OJT); informal cross-agency training; and formal training. We will consider each in turn.

B. INFORMAL TRAINING FOR WHITE-COLLAR CRIME ENFORCEMENT

1. On-The-Job Training For Individual Investigators

This training is especially effective if the agency has already established itself in the area of white-collar crime investigations. Also, larger agencies may be better able to allocate their own resources for these purposes than smaller ones. Nevertheless, small agencies with limited resources may be able to use OJT only, since they do not have the funds for formal training.

OJT would be most effective in an agency with a very low level of competitiveness and secretiveness among its staff. Unless the more experienced investigators or prosecutors within an agency are willing to share knowledge, on-the-job training will be slow and uncertain. In traditional detective agencies the tendency is for each detective to develop his own net of informants, investigative techniques, etc., and not to share these with his fellow investigators. Partly this tradition stems from an evaluative emphasis on the number of cases cleared or good arrests made. If a white-collar crime unit has developed out of a traditional detective unit, it is important to actively try to reduce this secretiveness, not only for the organizational reasons mentioned elsewhere in this manual, but also because such secretiveness prevents effective on-the-job training. Nevertheless, experience has shown that personnel in white-collar crime agencies are cooperative in spirit, so that on-the-job training can be conducted effectively.

OJT would also be especially useful for agencies which recruit their trainees from other investigative ranks, such as detective bureaus, federal agencies, etc. In such cases the trainee is already a professional in investigations, but may not have the particular expertise needed for his new work. Some of the skills and ways of relating to victims, witnesses and suspects that he brings from another agency may be inappropriate or even counterproductive in the area of white-collar crime. He needs to learn how to meet a corporate executive vice president eyeball-to-eyeball and how to talk to him in an appropriate manner, in contrast to talking to an addict informer or a burglarized family. Even if he has been a white-collar crime investigator with another agency, he needs to learn about local problems, crimes, businesses, victims, agencies, etc., which may be quite different. If he has a background in federal agencies, he may find it hard to adjust to and understand the limitations of local investigative units.

To facilitate OJT, it is very valuable to have regular staff conferences in which on-going cases are discussed. This not only helps the trainee, but should also add to the cooperativeness and openness among the regular staff. Where the trainee comes from another agency, or another background, he can make his own unique contribution to the training of others. In such conferences both the trainees and the experienced investigators should present cases. If at all possible a prosecutor, either from within or from outside the agency, should participate in these meetings. Such cross-discussion is more valuable than relying solely on manuals or other written training materials. In some agencies such training meetings have been considered too costly in time, especially if the whole staff participates. A solution to this problem might be simply to replace the total staff meeting with a series of smaller meetings of sub-groups of the staff.

Some of the benefits of regular staff conferences can be achieved by other techniques: hour-long brown-bag lunches in the agency in a common area; having a physical arrangement which enables people to meet and chat in hallways, work-spaces, etc; making all public relations material, including press releases, talks, radio shows, etc. available to the on-the-job trainees.

On-the-job training is frequently implemented by starting the new investigator off on simple cases, working at a desk next to an experienced investigator. The trainee might sit in on some of the interviews, interrogations and meetings of the experienced investigator. Or the experienced investigator can team up with the trainee so that they can work complex cases together. The trainee's background and the needs of the agency should determine which is the most appropriate.

Some experienced investigators may be particularly effective as trainers and should be given recognition for their efforts. The progress of the trainees should be evaluated in periodic three-way conferences among the trainee, the experienced investigator, and the supervisor of investigation. Involving the supervisor will tend to minimize any tendency for the investigator to "hoard" the trainee's effectiveness by keeping him as an assistant longer than necessary for his training.

2. On-The-Job Training for Entire White-Collar Crime Units

In new and small units, one form of training is to train the unit as a whole on the job; i.e., the new investigative staff can be assigned cases more on the basis of their value in training than for their value in other respects. The staff as a whole, as individuals or as teams, might be assigned relatively simple cases at the beginning of their training, in which they have a good chance of being successful. Furthermore, if such cases are likely to generate much public interest, then a successful prosecution can encourage the young agency to acquire even more skill.[98]

3. Informal Cross-Agency Training

One variation of on-the-job training is to temporarily assign investigators to work in agencies which are either similar to, or functionally closely allied to the trainee's own agency. For example, prosecutors' offices have had police detectives work as investigators in their offices for a period of time, after which the police have returned to their own departments, where they become a reservoir of white-collar crime investigative skills. In some instances, when the trainee returns to his home agency he is replaced by another trainee from the same agency or from another. The trainees most likely to benefit would be those who have at least some experience in investigative work, such as that involving street bunco, homicide, etc., but who need to learn some of the special skills involved in white-collar crime investigation. Cross-agency training would be most useful for small or large agencies in metropolitan areas where there are more likely to be a host of agencies which are difficult to learn about from the outside. Obviously, only a large agency can itself afford to give up an investigator for a while, although the cost can be reduced by having exchange relationships among agencies.

The advantages of cross-agency OJT are several. First, they have all the strengths of OJT mentioned above. Second, close personal ties can be

---

[98]See Chapter VI, Evaluation of a White-Collar Crime Effort, pp. 220-221.

established between agencies which otherwise might hold each other at a distance, thereby facilitating communication and cooperation. Third, personnel in each agency will have a better understanding of the other and therefore be better able to work together. Fourth, the trainee might feel less pressure, since the mistakes which he inevitably would make would probably be known only by personnel in the training agency and less likely to be known by his peers and supervisors in his home agency. Fifth, the trainee does actual productive work during his training.

All personnel in the host agency need to be fully apprised of the values to them of cross-agency training. Otherwise, the trainee would have to use up too much of his short stay just gaining support and acceptance. The value would be enhanced if there actually were an exchange of trainees between agencies.

The model for all cross-agency training might be the executive training model used in some corporations, in which an employee marked for executive level position is systematically moved through several parts of the organization. However, it is important that the employees he works with know in advance of his coming and why he is there; otherwise the suspiciousness of the "spy" would make his experience much less valuable.

A home agency might develop a long-range plan for rotating its investigators through a variety of organizations. As mentioned in this manual's section on the selection of investigators, [99] it is very valuable to have investigators with experience in a variety of businesses. Since it is likely that unit investigators might be totally unfamiliar with some important types of organizations, the agency might send its investigators to work in them or to spend some time in them to become familiar with their mission and operations.

Regional conferences or even national conferences dealing with white-collar crime can also contribute to effective cross-agency training, especially if the participants in the conference are from different types of agencies and represent different kinds of skills. Presentations at such conferences and the formal and informal exchanges of ideas and information which take place can serve as a form of cross-agency training.

It should be noted that many federal agencies provide specific training in the field of white-collar investigation. For example, the U.S. Securities and Exchange Commission hosts regional conferences at which expertise and experiences are exchanged with state officials concerned with securities and investment enforcement. The F.B.I. recently initiated special training courses dealing with white-collar crime investigations. In addition, there are for example investigative units in regional offices of the U.S. Department of Housing and Urban Development which can provide know-how with respect to cases involving housing construction and financing; and it

---

[99] See Chapter II, at pp. 89-97.

can reasonably be anticipated that the resources currently being mobilized by the U.S. Department of Health, Education and Welfare to combat Medicaid frauds will ultimately develop into a similar repository of expertise in the medical fraud area.

C. FORMAL TRAINING FOR WHITE-COLLAR CRIME ENFORCEMENT

This section offers some suggested guidelines for the development and operation of programs to train white-collar crime investigators, together with illustrative training materials to show how such guidelines can be applied. It is, however, beyond the scope of this manual to present a complete training package. Common elements of such a package are outlined, always with the recognition that different agencies will find only particular portions useful to them, or will elect to apply them in ways different from that suggested here. The sections are therefore described so that they can be used somewhat independently of each other.

In the discussion below, it is assumed that most agencies are not large enough to afford their own, internal formal training programs. Thus the training is most likely to occur on a regional or even national basis. However, if the agency is a large one, such as a metropolitan police department or a statewide law enforcement agency, then it might conduct its own formal training; such instances are assumed to be rare. Or in many instances, some of the independent parts of the training programs described below can be used in-house as part of staff meetings or at other times set aside for training purposes. Some of the procedures outlined below were deliberately structured for use by agencies with severely limited funds and resources.

Much of the program described below involves a heavy emphasis on simulation of actual investigations, role-playing, discussions, practice exercises, etc., in contrast to the more traditional lecturing approach. This approach reflects recent trends in training in police academies, executive training programs, intelligence agency training, and in other types of programs. However, the salient points of the content of the material communicated through this approach can also be made through lectures, so that a trainer who prefers to lecture can view the material presented below as points to be covered in lectures. Most of the material discussed below is quite readily adaptable to the lecturing format.

Since the content of a training program depends in large part on the cooperation of the student body, it is first necessary to discuss whom to train in special programs. The concern here is as to the numbers and types of agencies from which the students should be recruited, the rank of the student body, their relative degrees of experience, etc. Furthermore, the question of training for associated professionals and staff, such as prosecutors, patrolmen, receptionists, etc., needs to be dealt with. After these issues are discussed, then the guidelines for the control of the training will be discussed. It should never be lost sight of, however, that the selection of the type of content will depend in large measure on the composition of the student body. There is no one way to do formal training.

1. How Many Agencies and How Many Trainees from Each?

Sometimes a trainer may not be in a position to influence the selection of agencies from which trainees are drawn and the number of investigator-trainees from each. But, at other times, the trainer may be in a position to influence the selection. In that case, he is faced with a number of questions: Should you limit training in any one course to but one investigator from each of several units or agencies? Should you train more than one from more limited numbers of agencies? Should you seek to simultaneously train the entire investigative staff or staff-to-be of an agency? If the formal training is done within a large agency, which units within that agency should be tapped for trainees?

In answering these questions, one should bear in mind that training in white-collar crime investigation is often not like training a newcomer of a unit to get up to the speed of the oldtimers; that is, to learn the same sorts of skills that the oldtimers already have. Instead, the training is likely to involve bringing some new ideas, new approaches, even new goals to a unit. For example, the graduate of the training program may be bringing back some ideas about investigating land fraud to an agency or unit which never thought of coping with this type of fraud. If the graduate is the only one interested in land fraud he is likely to get caught up in the pressures of other assignments. If, however, he has been trained with another investigator from the same unit, together they may be better able to get the cooperation of the unit to give recognition and higher priority to white-collar crime in general, as against other agency enforcement efforts--as well as to launch efforts against land fraud. It is probably more effective to have a larger number of trainees from a fewer number of units than to spread the training thin.

Since white-collar crime investigative units in law enforcement agencies are frequently new agency efforts, it may sometimes be necessary to train a whole new squad. There are a number of advantages to training them together as a unit, either separately or in a training program with other trainees. The squad can get to know and trust one another in a situation in which the pressure to work on cases is absent. They can learn to cooperate, to share information and ideas as they help each other through the training, so that the traditional detectives' tendency to hoard information may be minimized. They all start at the same level, with no established hierarchy of oldtimers and novices. When they return to their parent agencies, they return as a unit and can start functioning as a unit; there is no need to face the lonely task of re-entry. As mentioned above in the discussion of on-the-job training, such new units may then be given cases to work specially selected for their value as training exercises.

Although there are advantages to having more than one trainee from each agency in a training program, there also are advantages to having trainees from a variety of different agencies at the same program. If the training is done within one large agency, there are similar advantages to selecting trainees from several units within the agency. It is most important, from both a training and operational viewpoint, to develop personal contacts across agency and unit lines. After returning to their agencies or units, the graduates can gain valuable information through the contacts; extradition may be facilitated; additional victims of a scheme may be found information about modi operandi and about the movements of bad actors can be shared. In short, the training program can serve as the basis of a regional or cross-jurisdictional information exchange, as well as within an agency.

Training programs should be organized to facilitate the development of such information and cooperation networks. Time for socializing should be provided. Joint homework assignments may be given to teams of people from different agencies. A list of members, agencies, and telephone numbers should be prepared and distributed to all trainees during the sessions-- these may later be invaluable for the participants. In fact, it may sometimes be possible to recruit trainees from several agencies which would have a high likelihood of benefiting from such a network of personal contacts. These trainees might be recruited from agencies in the same geographical area, but with different types of responsibility; for example, investigators from a police department and from the office of a prosecuting attorney in the same area, or from an attorney general's office in the same area, or from an attorney general's office and a state regulatory agency.

If the trainees have already had some experience in white-collar crime investigation and come from a number of different agencies, their knowledge can be shared as part of the training program. Similarly, a trainee who has had some kind of experience in a particular trade, such as auto repair, or construction, can make a special contribution. When the trainees arrive at the beginning of the program, or even before they come, a questionnaire regarding their particular skills could be administered. Some of them may be asked to make presentations to the others; some may conduct seminars in certain types of investigations. For example, one who knows about decoy operations could be given the assignment of working one up for the others to learn from and critique.

Such sharing of expertise of either an investigative or trade nature may be especially useful if certain types of white-collar crime schemes are currently spreading. A pyramid, or other type of scheme will frequently operate across jurisdictional lines, or a gang of home repair con men may be moving across state lines. The training session could be used as a good setting for sharing expertise in how to investigate such schemes, or even particular criminals under such circumstances. Concrete investigating information, such as AKA's, MO's, VIN's, may be exchanged. An information network can start right in the training sessions, and this provides excellent training in the value and method of sharing information. This not only would be practice, but also a real law enforcement effort. This is practice right on the spot.

2. <u>Who Should be Recruited from the Agency--Indians or Chief?</u>

If the area of white-collar crime enforcement is a new one for an agency, its higher echelon persons are probably not as expert as they are in the more commonly recognized areas such as street crime. If some of their subordinates become expert in an area in which agency heads do not even have a minimal working knowledge, such subordinates obviously would be placed in a difficult position. In short, Chiefs need to be oriented before the Indians. Of course, if the chief is already an expert, this is not a problem.

However, there are other, very important reasons for orienting police or agency chiefs, and their higher-level assistants, before other subordinates. If agencies are to be effective in this area, white-collar crime investigation has to have a high priority in the allocation of resources, and in the setting of agency policy. There is always pressure against moving into new areas and devoting new resources to them, especially in a political and media-sensitive area such as white-collar crime. Thus, agency heads need to learn about the impacts and significance of white-collar crime, of its relationships to organized and street crime, etc.

Not only is such orientation valuable for agency chiefs in its own right; but the investigative staff who work on white-collar crime need to know that their chiefs have received this orientation. If they know that the chief is on their side, they can take more pride in their work; can feel secure that they will have a reasonably fair shake with respect to promotions and other benefits, that they will get their fair share of the department's resources. Policy statements by agency heads, even directives, will be less important than consciousness in the white-collar unit that the agency head understands the nature and importance of its work. One good way for agency heads or their deputies both to acquire this knowledge, and to convey their understanding, is to attend white-collar enforcement orientation conferences which are more and more frequently held for the special benefit of criminal justice executives.

There are real advantages in having agency chiefs involved in separate programs or workshops from their subordinates, who should attend subsequent programs designed for them. Furthermore, these agency heads need to be more concerned with certain matters and less concerned with others, as compared to investigators. They need to learn more about the impact of white-collar crime and less about how to trace a check from bank to clearinghouse to bank. They need to know about how to organize a white-collar crime unit rather than how to develop a fraudulent merchandising case.

3. <u>Should Trainees with Varying Amounts and Kinds of Investigative Experience be Trained Together?</u>

As was mentioned in the section on personnel selection, there are great advantages to staffing a white-collar crime unit with people having a variety of backgrounds, skills, and experience. However, this raises the question of whether people of different degrees of experience in investigative work, even outside the white-collar crime area, should be trained together. For example, in a police department should the classes consist of all detectives, all patrolmen straight off the street, all newcomers to law enforcement, or should these groups be mixed together for white-collar crime enforcement training? This question needs to be answered separately for beginning classes and programs for more advanced classes.

With respect to beginning classes, groups with no law enforcement experience obviously would need to learn some about the structure and organization of the criminal justice system, its administrative processes and procedures, etc. The law enforcement group with minimal experience with business would need to learn some facts about business which may be elementary to people with a business background. On the other hand, people with some street crime investigative experience might have to learn what the differences are between the investigation of street crime and white-collar crime. Among the areas of indifference are the difficult challenge of determining whether certain events constitute a crime; the longer period of investigation before a case is developed, the difference between interviewing and interrogating crime suspects, witnesses, victims, etc., as between white-collar crime and street crime. This is not just a matter of learning what is new in white-collar investigation, but in learning not to do some of the things that one does in street crime investigations, such as the usual practice of interrogating suspects early in the investigative process. In short, there are many reasons for keeping the beginning introductory classes homogeneous.

If the classes consist of both experienced investigators and novices, some trainees would become bored with the material and some trainees might begin to feel suspicious of the others, or relatively inadequate because of the differences in knowledge and experience. Some might not appreciate the significance of some of the unlearnings that need to occur.

On the other hand, once some of the introductory material has been covered for each of the groups, then it would be well to combine them into one class or into a series of mixed classes. Then all of the groups might be acquiring more knowledge, such as what sorts of information can be gained from certain federal agencies, what the legal restrictions are on the release of information, how to trace money through a series of companies, the legal subtleties of fraudulent consumer practices, etc. The value of mixing the groups is not just a matter of economizing on the costs of training. It is also a matter of an exchange of knowledge, trainee to trainee, as each of the specialized groups make special contributions from their special areas of knowledge. A person with a background in real estate might, for example, himself provide valuable and essential background on some of the ways in which advertising is handled, or paper is processed, in a real estate firm. Some detectives may have more practical and subtle knowledge about how prosecutors' offices function. The instructors cannot possibly have information about the whole complex mass of business and criminal justice transactions, and these students' input would be most valuable.

4. What about Joint Training with Prosecutors?

The logic of having investigator-trainees from a variety of agencies and backgrounds training together immediately points to the need for training with and for prosecutors. As was mentioned earlier,[100] one of the most crucial relationships in the law enforcement community's work against white-collar crime is that between prosecutor and the investigator. If these two professions are to relate in the most constructive fashion, it is vital that they understand each other's ways of doing things, needs, goals, etc.

Most new white-collar crime investigators have at least some prior training in the rudiments of the criminal process. In the white-collar crime area, however, it is most important that they acquire some basic knowledge of statutes dealing with white-collar crime and related abuses, civil, regulatory and administrative remedies, etc. Formal training they receive in a white-collar crime training program should augment this knowledge. On the other hand, most lawyers do not receive training in the techniques of investigation in general, let alone training in the techniques of white-collar crime investigation. This lack of training no doubt contributes to some of the problems in the relationship between the two. It would therefore be very valuable if training programs for investigators not only were open to prosecutors, but prosecutors were actively encouraged to attend, especially those who were just beginning to get into the prosecution of white-collar crimes. Prosecutors who are new to this area appear to learn much from experienced investigators and come to have a deeper and more knowledgeable appreciation of the complexities of investigation; investigators can likewise learn from prosecutors both what is legally required to make a case and what, as a practical matter, might be needed to persuade a jury.

In practice exercises the lawyers could take the role of lawyers interacting with investigators, and also reverse roles to act as investigators relating to investigators, to suspects, to witnesses, and to lawyers.

In small agencies with limited resources, such investigator-prosecutor training can be conducted with just the local prosecutorial agency, or with the prosecutors if they are part of the same unit. Some of the practice sessions described below can be set up easily without the use of outside resources and can be made part of a regular in-service program.

5. What about Training Patrolmen?

As was mentioned earlier in this manual,[101] there are many ways in which the officer on the beat can help in fighting white-collar crime. In their training in the police academy, patrolmen in general are rarely made aware of these possibilities. In fact, most officers are convinced that many of

---

[100]See Chapter II, pp. 64-71 and Chapter IV, pp. 195-198.

[101]See Chapter II, pp. 48-53.

the instances of white-collar crime they have contact with are really private civil disputes. It is very important, therefore, that patrolmen learn to recognize the criminal character of white-collar crime early in their careers, in the academies. Furthermore, even if academy trainees learn to recognize white-collar crime, they are likely to need to be educated with respect to all of the arguments they have, or will later encounter, about why not to do anything about such crime. As will be indicated below, these issues need to be faced in any training program, but the issues are even more serious with respect to patrolmen since they have so many other responsibilities which can easily dominate all of their time. Minimally, the trainees need to learn what white-collar crime is, that their department has responsibilities with respect to detection and investigation of these crimes, and that there are ways in which their department can deal with it.

Because of the pressure to deal with street crime and because of the strength of tradition among officers of treating white-collar crime as a civil matter, it is important that any white-collar crime investigative unit develop in-service training procedures for patrolmen. Minimally, this can be done by means of special flyers, written directly for patrolmen; by brief video-tape presentations at roll call; by direct, in-person oral presentations by investigators or by all these in combination. Examples of flyers used in the Los Angeles Police Department are shown in Figures 17 and 18. These presentations should be official police department activities, pursuant to department directives. It is not wise simply to wait for requests from patrol for presentations regarding white-collar crime.

The presentations should focus on those instances in which an officer can respond to possible white-collar crimes, be it only to turn in a report. Even better would be orienting the officers with respect to an on-going unit program, such as a coordinated effort against door-to-door peddler frauds,[102] in which the patrol officer can directly participate. If the program involves giving patrolmen full credit for arrests which were made jointly with investigators, even more cooperation will be forthcoming.

Patrol officers should also be made aware that fighting white-collar crime has a relationship to enforcement against street crime,[103] and that better relationships with (services to) fraud victims in patrol areas will make these victims more likely to cooperate with police, to report street crime, etc. Furthermore, it is important to explain to the patrolmen that white-collar crime information which does not lead to arrests immediately may feed into an on-going investigation of a scheme.

6. Training Receptionists and Complaint Handlers

In consumer fraud agencies or any other agencies dealing with the public directly, it is very important that the first person the citizen contacts be someone who can react effectively and appropriately to him or her. An

---

[102] See Chapter II at pp. 51-53.

[103] See Chapter I at pp. 7-8, and Chapter II, at p. 37.

TRAINING BULLETIN

LOS ANGELES POLICE DEPARTMENT   EDWARD M. DAVIS, CHIEF OF POLICE

VOLUME VII, ISSUE 2   *JANUARY 26, 1973*

CONSUMER FRAUD VIOLATIONS
AUTO REPAIR
PART II

Officers need to have a basic understanding of the Business and Professions Code laws regulating auto repair, which were summarized in Part I of this bulletin. Essentially, the information that officers need is that automotive repair businesses must register with the State Department of Consumer Affairs; must provide a detailed invoice of work done and parts supplied; must provide written estimates for repair work; and must return replaced parts. With this knowledge, the following information is prepared to assist officers in their handling and investigation of auto repair fraud complaints.

TRAINING BULLETIN

LOS ANGELES POLICE DEPARTMENT   EDWARD M. DAVIS, CHIEF OF POLICE

VOLUME VII, ISSUE 1   *JANUARY 26, 1975*

CONSUMER FRAUD VIOLATIONS
AUTO REPAIR
PART I

All officers have heard complaints from friends or relatives regarding the "quality" of repair work performed by some of the automotive repair shops in Los Angeles. However, few officers are aware of the extent of the problem. Auto repair fraud is the number one *consumer* complaint in Los Angeles and California. Nationwide, motorists are bilked out of nearly TEN BILLION DOLLARS annually by either incompetent, unnecessary, or fraudulent auto repairs.

Auto repair fraud encompasses automobile repairs *completed but not needed, and repairs paid for but not received*. Some of the most commonly heard complaints include cases of repair shops rebuilding transmissions that only need additional fluid, rebuilding carburetors and replacing fuel pumps when an adjustment of the idle is all that is necessary, or performing a major brake system overhaul when minor adjustments will suffice.

The Investigation of Auto Repair Fraud

The Department instituted the Auto Repair Fraud Unit within Bunco-Forgery Division to investigate the numerous auto repair complaints and violations. The personnel assigned to the unit are experienced in automobile construction and mechanics, and are specialists in auto repair consumer fraud laws.

Past experience has indicated that the successful prosecution of many auto repair frauds is dependent upon the field officer's initial contact with the victim and suspect, his knowledge of the auto repair laws, and his knowledge of the Department's policies concerning the handling of auto repair complaints. The succeeding section of this bulletin will explain the recent auto repair legislation, and define the officer's responsibility in the field when confronted with a possible auto repair fraud situation.

The Auto Repair Act

Enactment. The California State Legislature passed the Auto Repair Act in March 1972. This act added laws regulating auto repair to the Business and Professions Code. As a State law, its enactment preempted the City of Los Angeles Board of Police Commissioners' responsibility for issuing permits and regulating auto repair businesses. The California Bureau of Automotive Repair now has this responsibility, and reviews complaints and conducts investigations, but has very limited resources. Therefore, this Department continues to investigate and prosecute auto repair fraud schemes.

Jurisdiction. The Auto Repair Act established procedures and regulations for all businesses performing auto repair in the State of California. However, *excluded* from the jurisdiction of the Auto Repair Act are businesses, such as gasoline service stations, that perform the following minor services:

* Repairing or changing tires,
* Lubricating vehicles,
* Installing light bulbs, batteries, windshield wiper blades and minor accessories,
* Cleaning and adjusting spark plugs, and

investigator may be the best possible person, since he or she can usually
follow through sufficiently on complaints to determine whether any criminal
matter is involved. However, if budgetary or organizational problems
preclude the arrangement, then it is important that the non-investigator who
is the citizen's first contact with the agency be quite knowledgeable about
the purposes and functioning of the organization. Otherwise, many criminal
matters may go unnoticed or "referred out" to inappropriate agencies; or
the citizen simply may become embittered.

In some instances on-the-job training may be sufficient to make the
contact person sensitive to such criminal matters -- but, when possible, he
or she can be given enough special training to become competent for this
purpose. This training could consist in participating in appropriate
parts of an investigator training program, especially in the section on
complaint handling. In addition the contact person should be fully involved
in programs done "in-house" by the agency, so that the contact person is kept
abreast of any changes in policy, changes in law, etc. In small agencies
with limited resources, the contact people can be trained in-house by
setting up proactive sessions under supervision, as described below.

7. <u>Guidelines for Training White-Collar Crime Investigators</u>

Following are guidelines for one type of model training program for
white-collar crime investigators. Needless to say, the ideal cannot be
expected to be immediately attainable; nor is it always necessary that it
be fully attained. However, the guidelines indicate the goals and style
of such a program. It is described so that parts of it can be compressed
or expanded, like an accordian. Obviously, situational differences in
available resources and needs can indicate which parts should be expanded,
and which parts compressed.

In much of the material presented below, there is an emphasis on simulation, practice, role-playing, etc. As mentioned earlier, this emphasis is
consistent with much of recent developments in training in police academies,
military training, etc. However, many of the points that are listed below
to be made through such training can also be made by means of lectures.
Thus, in programs which cannot use the simulation approach for reasons of
lack of resources, consideration should be given to presenting these lessons
in a lecture format. The amount of resources needed is often minimal.

The trainees should be given an agenda at the beginning of the program,
but the purpose of each section of the training should be presented to them
at the outset. It should be pointed out to them that the training will
deal with cases in a manner which reflects actual investigating practice,
and that they will have ample opportunity to discuss the issues raised in
the training.

(a) <u>Emphasizing White-Collar Crime as an Enforcement Goal</u>. Regardless
of who the trainees are, it is a gross oversimplification to assume that
because a trainee is present at the training program, he automatically
shares the goals of the training program. He may have been sent to the

program for a variety of reasons, such as enhancement of the effectiveness of the agency or upgrading the performance of the least competent person. The area of white-collar crime investigation is so relatively new for traditional, non-specialized law enforcement agencies that there is not a strong tradition to support vigorous law enforcement efforts directed at white-collar criminals. Thus, it is necessary to frontally face the issue of why there should be such an effort, and why the trainees should want to participate in it.

In this manual's introductory material, the issues involved are set forth: the economic, moral, political, and personal impacts of white-collar crime and its very serious and pervasive indirect effects. On the other hand, many of the reasons that law enforcement personnel, along with many other people, have for not fighting white-collar crime were also set forth in that chapter and dealt with. Training programs should start by following the same format. Not only should the reasons for law enforcement's involvement in white-collar crime be discussed in depth, but the counter-arguments should be discussed directly and forthrightly from the outset. Even some of the investigators who have had experience may be motiva ted with respect to one type of crime, and be relatively indifferent to another. One investigator may care greatly about automobile repair fraud, but care little about stock fraud. Another might care greatly about crimes directed at retirees, but not those with young people as victims. Some experienced investigators may have been overly impressed by the "greed" of some of the victims and how this made them vulnerable; such investigators may over-generalize and start to consider victims primarily or equally at fault with white-collar offenders. Even experienced hands may have to get their ideas on the table so they can be dealt with.

If the reservations that some of the trainees have are not faced squarely in the beginning of the training, their lack of full commitment may interfere with learning, cause them to be less attentive, to spend less out-of-class time working on readings and exercises, and --- most important - to be less likely to function well when they return to their agencies. What they do learn may be applied by them in a mechanical, unimaginative way.

Since white-collar crime is constantly taking new forms, new twists and "angles," investigators need to be at least as imaginative as the criminals. If a trainee is highly motivated, he will come to think about some of the problems and possibilities and go beyond the books, lectures, and exercises. But if he is not motivated, he may learn by rote, and become a routine investigator, with a set, comfortable way of handling the problems dropped in his lap. As soon as he and others like him become routine and predictable in their behavior, the white-collar criminal will no doubt develop ways of exploiting this.

Another reason for facing up to the issue of the goals of white-collar crime investigation and prosecution is that white-collar crime investigators will encounter resistance from the people in their agencies, in other agencies, and from members of the public. They are very likely to be confronted with all the arguments for avoiding white-collar crime law enforcement,[104] and some of these arguments might be somewhat new to them. If they are not prepared to counter them, they will be embarrassed by their inadequacy; they will lose confidence in the ability of the total criminal justice system to cope with white-collar crime; and may come to question the worth of their mission and goals in fighting white-collar crime. On the other hand, if they have dealt with these arguments during their training and have resolved their own doubts, confrontation with indifferent or hostile attitudes toward white-collar enforcement efforts can become very positive and productive. The trainees' ability to cope with the opposition is especially important if they are or would be expected to become administrators of investigative agencies, since they would have to deal with policy and procedure in other, related agencies, to fight budgetary battles, to counter indifference, etc.

Still another reason for dealing with the arguments for and against fighting white-collar crime at the outset is that the trainees will no doubt have to investigate situations in which some of these arguments may appear to have some justification. The investigator may well encounter a victim whose excessive greed made him vulnerable; a victim with enough business experience to have known better than to believe the con man; a victim who chose not to read the fine print; etc. He may find criminals whose behavior he can appreciate, for example the small businessman who attempts some desperate step to delay some business catastrophe, hoping to make it all right later. The investigator might be concerned about the economic impact of his efforts, since vigorous enforcement might result in closing down a business which employs many honest people; he may cut off sources of credit to the poor; he might force the price of some goods up by requiring that the goods be of higher quality; he may discourage potential investors in legitimate business by making them overly suspicious of all investments. Each one of these possibilities has to be faced at the beginning, as well as during the whole training program, so that when the investigator encounters them, he will be well armed to deal with them.

(b) How to Face the Issue of Why Combat White-Collar Crime. This issue needs to be faced in a completely candid and open fashion. Since the trainer will probably have to face unexpected objections and arguments from the trainees, he should be a person who is comfortable facing challenges--on his feet. Obviously, he would need a very broad and deep knowledge of the area of white-collar crime, and possess a fund of detailed information about all types of schemes and their impacts.

If a unit is small and therefore cannot afford to send an investigator to a formal training program, it might still be able to afford to bring a trainer into the agency for a day or two to conduct a training session. If this is not possible, a senior investigator or prosecutor in the agency might do a fine job in larger units by a formal presentation, and in smaller

---

[104]These arguments were noted in Chapter I, at pp. 8-10.

ones by informal discussion. Some written material, such as the bibliographic references provided in Appendix C, may be useful.[105]

As much time as possible should be devoted to this issue, even relative
to some of the more "how-to-do-it" materials, since highly motivated trainees ultimately will learn much "how-to-do-it" on their own.

(1) Definition of white-collar crime. Presenting the definition
in terms of the elements of fraud is important for several reasons. First,
presenting a definition in terms of fraud, deception, etc., places the
behavior clearly in the criminal area rather than the civil, and drives
home the fact that the subject matter is wrongful activity. Secondly, the
definition should make it clear that the concern is not restricted to such
"white-collar crime" as embezzlement, forgery, employee theft, etc., but
also covers every kind of fraud, deceit, and related abuses together with
civil remedies appropriate thereto. Such terms as "consumer protection"
need to be avoided; "consumer fraud" is both more accurate and more meaning-
ful.

(2) Examples and typologies. The person presenting the material
should give a description of the general categories of white-collar crime,
following the outline given in Chapter I.[106] This will give the trainees an
idea of the scope of the problem. The examples cited should have a number
of characteristics.

First, victims cited should be people who are not especially greedy, who
are not morally culpable victims themselves. These might be retirees
buying retirement property; people being taken in by charity fraud schemes;
ordinary people being cheated by an auto repair shop, etc.

Second, the victims should be people rather than large institutions.
If examples are used of large institutions such as insurance companies,
local government, etc., then the consequences for individuals need to be
made obvious; for example, taxpayers, rather than the municipal treasury;
premium payers, rather than the insurance company profit account, etc.

Third, the examples need to be of victims who could not really have been
alert or aware of the scheme, even given average or even above-average
intelligence. Such victims might be old people living alone who are not
as alert or knowledgeable as they once were; new immigrants to the U.S. or
to the particular region; hospital or nursing home patients who are essentially at the mercy of the hospital or home; etc. In many cases, the scheme
described should be one in which even an alert person can be taken. These
could be automobile repair frauds, TV repair frauds, frauds depending on
the holder-in-due-course doctrine, consumer frauds in which the product will
not last as long as the payment obligation, etc.

---

[105]See Appendix C, pp. 314-324.

[106]See "Classifications of White-Collar Crime," Chapter I, at pp. 26-31.

Fourth, among the examples should be those in which the trainees or people personally known to them are highly likely to have been victimized. These might include charity frauds, home improvement frauds, pyramid schemes, land frauds, etc. Law enforcement personnel, including police, are just as vulnerable to white-collar crime as are others. The auto repair fraud area may interest most officers, since probably they have all been victimized and their jobs involve the use of automobiles.

(3) <u>Impact</u>. The comparison between the economic losses through street crime and white-collar crime should be emphasized. Furthermore, the ways in which white-collar crime may contribute to a general breakdown in the respect for legal and ethical principals, and therefore facilitate or provide a rationale for street crime need to be pointed out. Cynicism about the even-handedness of law enforcement because of its concentration of efforts against street crimes is an impact that may be directly material to the trainees and their agencies. Any information about local, city or regional impact will be especially helpful. As in many other aspects of the training, the trainees will be able to provide many examples from their own backgrounds and experience.

(4) <u>Rebuttal to the reasons for not fighting white-collar crime.</u> In this section, the trainer needs to be especially alert, secure and knowledgeable. Each argument against involvement needs to be articulated fairly and completely. Any effort to make what even appears to be a biased presentation will tend to undermine the credibility of the total training program. After each negative argument is presented, there needs to be a thorough and complete rebuttal. None of the negative arguments should be treated lightly or contemptuously. The negative argument can be made in completely good faith and should be treated as such, especially since many of the trainees no doubt agree with some of them. No attempt should be made to gloss over the fact that white-collar crime investigations can be time-consuming and frustrating--but this should be put in the context of both the benefits of white-collar enforcement and the impacts of these crimes. It should be kept continually in mind that when one squarely faces such difficulties in training, <u>it is, at the same time, an opportunity to instruct trainees as to how they can best deal with obstacles they will encounter in actual enforcement operations</u>.

Before the presentation of the negative arguments and the rebuttal (or exploration) of each in turn, the presenter should tell the trainees that there will be a full discussion of these arguments when he is through. At the end of his presentation, there should be about two hours left free for a full discussion of the issues presented, with as much encouragement as possible for the trainees to express their reservations. If necessary, it may be helpful to have someone other than the presenter direct the discussion, with the presenter contributing to the discussion as appropriate. About 15 minutes before the end of the allotted time, the presenter should give a critique of the issues raised, then summarize the points he made earlier.

(c) First principles in How to Fight White-Collar Crime.
After the basic issues described above about combatting economic crime have
been faced and dealt with, the trainees are ready to get down to principles
and to cases. Such principle and case presentations can also be done in-
house in small agencies by having a senior investigator conduct a training
session. Since much of the training consists of a presentation of actual
cases, the senior investigator does not have to spend a great deal of time
preparing lectures, but should use cases that he has worked on.

The basic format of the training is the presentation of principles of
investigation which are illustrated by cases tied to the principles. The
trainer should present each principle first in general terms, then he should
describe a case which exemplifies the application of the principle; and
then re-articulate and discuss the principle in the light of the case.
He should repeat this for each of the principles. One principle might be
to use preliminary investigations as a first reaction to a complaint or a
report. Another might be the value of getting information from other
agencies.

The presentation of the cases should be detailed descriptions of the actual sequence of events in law enforcement agencies dealing with actual
cases, from the receipt of the initial information or complaint, through the
investigation, to the presecution.[107]   All of the false leads and difficulties should be described in detail, and mistakes as well as successful tactics
In other words, what is laid out should not be merely a logical description
or analysis of the scheme, crime, etc., which could be constructed after
the fact but should be in the style of a good detective story, but with
ordinary fallable human beings as the detectives, and not super-sleuths.
The purpose of such presentations is to provide a first brush, concrete
example of a principle or technique. After presenting each case, the trainer
should return to a discussion of the general principles of investigation of
white-collar crime, illustrated by the case. The cases should be selected
and presented with a number of actions and guidelines in mind, as follows:

- None of the investigative techniques illustrated should
  require technical knowledge beyond what the ordinary person would be expected to know. Technical knowledge should
  be developed later in the training course. At this point
  in the training, the objective is to communicate some broad
  principles, not to get the trainees to know how to trace a
  check, read a balance sheet, etc. The trainer should tell
  the trainees that they will be given time to delve into the
  technical details later.

- Materials from the cases should be presented either concretely and, if possible, audio-visually. Documents,
  reports, mug sheets, photographs, etc., can be presented
  by an overhead projector. Any tape recording legally

---

[107]In all the places below in which the use of case material is recommended,
it is assumed that these will be actual cases and that the trainees will
know this.

obtained might be played, though legal advice should
generally be sought before doing so. If concrete evidence
is relevant, like a phony security, useless therapeutic
device, a rolled-back odometer, etc., these should be
presented. Such audio-visual and concrete presentations
will make the case very real, maintain the trainees' attention, and begin to familiarize the trainees with the type
of documents, evidence, and procedures they are to use.
The use of such props and projection devices need not be
expensive, since most of the materials are readily available
to most agencies.

- Charts and diagrams illustrating the organization of white-
collar schemes should be used; e.g., who controlled whom;
what parallel series of events occurred; how multiple similar
events were fitted together to make a showing of deliberate
wrongful behavior. Such chart presentations will not only
facilitate communication and add interest, but will also
illustrate how the trainees can themselves prepare charts
and diagrams for the management of complex investigations
and for presentation to prosecutors, judges, and juries.
If charts are not available, blackboards should be used.[108]

- If at all possible, the cases should be those with which the
trainer is directly and personally familiar, preferably
from having been the investigator on the case. Such personal
involvement will make the cases more alive and vivid; the
trainees will give it more credibility; the trainer will
be more able to answer probing questions; the trainer will
be more motivated and secure in his presentation.

- The trainees should be encouraged to ask questions and make
comments throughout the presentation of the cases, following
on and reinforcing the pattern of open discussion developed
in the previous training sessions.

- In case presentations which involve issues such as why
certain lines of investigation are followed, or the use of
certain techniques, it will be important to discuss not only
why particular decisions are correct or incorrect, but also
the process through which these decisions are arrived at.

- After the principles and cases have been presented, the
trainer can give the trainees a list of the principles
illustrated and discussed.

---

[108]See pages 82 to 88, illustrating use of Link Network Analysis and Time
Flow Charts.

D. SPECIAL ISSUES AND PRINCIPLES IN WHITE-COLLAR CRIME ENFORCEMENT

1. Legally Speaking, What is a White-Collar Crime?

The first concern should be orientation as to what wrongful activities constitute white-collar crime and related abuses--against the backdrop of the elements discussed in this Manual,[109] and the statutory and case law applicable to the subject matter of concern to the agency or unit, e.g., securities law enforcement, consumer protection, etc. If the agency cannot afford to send its investigators to a formal training school, a local prosecutor, especially one with whom the unit works regularly, can make a presentation. There are some advantages to such presentations by local prosecutors, since local laws and the subtleties of the particular prose-cuting style can be communicated. The challenge of preparation for such a presentation will provide the prosecutor with motivation to develop or reinforce his own legal skills in a way directly relevant to white-collar crime enforcement efforts, as well as receptivity to such cases--and his participation should create valuable personal relationships with the train-ees which could pay off when they come to him with their cases. Copies of the outline of the presentation should be given to each trainee, preceded by a list of the major points to be covered.

While investigators should not allow themselves to be hamstrung by highly legalistic concerns as to what is or is not a crime when they see serious wrongful activity, it will be important that they know about different types of statutes which provide prosecutive options; they should not get into a rut with respect to a narrow group of statutory violations, or get discouraged because they cannot easily see a statutory violation where they instinctively know there is criminal activity. The presentation should therefore cover general laws against fraud, and their relationship to the elements of white-collar crime as well as particular laws for particular types of fraud and general theft statutes which might be applicable. They should know about bribery and conspiracy statutes, as well as those which proscribe tax evasions and obstruction of justice. Furthermore, the trainees should learn about civil laws and administrative law, so that they can work with either type of approach, or relate to agencies which can handle non-criminal approaches if their own unit deals only with criminal matters. Since the involvement with civil matters may be a new factor for many of the trainees, it is especially important that they learn about the potency of civil rem-edies, so that they can help to develop alternatives when criminal remedies are either not possible or when a public good might be better accomplished by a civil action. It is very important that the investigator become fully aware of the fact that civil remedies are not restricted to suits between private parties but are also remedies which government can invoke on its own behalf, and on behalf of white-collar crime victims.

Trainees should not be given the impression that they are locked into legal technicalities of a limited set of statutes. They should learn that however

[109]See Chapter I, pp. 21-26 and Chapter IV, pp. 121-153.

important it is to know certain statutes, they or the prosecutor may be able to find some additional statutes to apply in cases which do not appear to fit the statutes they are most familiar with.

Sensitivity to the legal aspects of matters under investigation can also assist the investigator in knowing what other agencies can help in the investigation and prosecution. For example, if a case involves invest- ment in some joint venture, the SEC may have jurisdiction even if no stocks or bolds are sold. Many cases illustrating these points should be presented, using as wide a variety of statutes as possible. Since the trainees may have to become trainers of other law enforcement personnel when they return to their agencies, they need to have these points very strongly developed. This presentation should be of the lecture-discussion type, again with ample time for discussion, since it is important that the presenter gear his level of instruction to the level of legal sophistication of the trainees.

2. How Does One Deal with Complaints and Other Sources of Information?

Trainees should be encouraged to trust their judgment as to whether or not a complainant has been victimized by some white-collar crime scheme, and whether to start to gather information where they believe there has been such victimization. They should be encouraged to assume that where there is a wrong there is quite possibly some remedy if enough of the facts are assembled. There are a number of ways of training with respect to this starting point. Most common is the lecture approach, which calls for no special discussion here. Another training alternative involves simulation or role playing, some techniques for which are considered below.

The starting point of an investigation is most typically a telephone call from a citizen, a lawyer, or a person in another public agency, such as a complaint handler. The trainer could lecture on the salient points about responding to such calls, but a more effective way would be to use a simulation approach. Accordingly, the training should consist of actual demonstration of, and practice with, such calls. Such simulations can be done in large training programs or in small agency in-house training, since the cost is minimal, although some time may need to be spent preparing the simulation. One way of proceeding is for the trainer first to discuss fully some point or principle. Then he can proceed with a demonstration in which he acts as an investigator (or complaint handler) taking a call. The role of the person making the call can be played by an assistant trainer or by one of the trainees. The latter should be a volunteer from the class. He should be told in advance that his involvement is not a test of his ability, but purely a learning experience for him and the others. The whole group of trainees who will be observing the demonstration should be told what the investigator's and agency's roles are supposed to be, but not be told any- thing about the complainant. He should be given a one-page description of his complaint or information, and an indication of why he is calling the particular agency. The situation should be carefully designed to illustrate the basic issue the trainer discussed briefly before the demonstration, such as choice between the civil vs. criminal remedies. After the trainee has and digested the material, he should go to the front of the class, and sit down at one of two dummy telephones (or any reasonable facsimiles) placed in front of the class, with his back to the other phone. The latter phone is manned by the trainer, who also turns his back to the trainee. By not looking at each other, visual cues are minimized. The trainee then places his call to the trainer, and they enact the actual call.

When the call is over, the trainer, trainee and the other trainees should have a full and free discussion of the issues raised by the demonstration. Obviously, the issues that the situation is designed to illustrate should be most prominent in the discussion, but others that emerge either in the actual enactment or during the discussion should also be dealt with.

After two or three such demonstrations, using different types of calls with different trainees enacting the role of complainant or informant, the trainees can take on both roles in a series of demonstrations. The trainee who enacts the role of investigator should be given a short description of his role and agency. This description should be read aloud by the role-taker, so that the other trainees will understand his side of the conversation Once again, it should be made clear that these demonstrations are not tests, but are being done for training purposes only. Hopefully, each trainee will get a chance to play each of the two roles. The situation should be designed to raise a whole series of issues, such as those cited above. If some issues have not been brought out sufficiently because of the way that the complainants make their calls, then the trainer should repeat the situation, playing the role of the complainant himself.

This training method offers several benefits. First, the trainees will see the concrete relevance of the legal and investigative principles that have been presented up to that point in the training. Second, the trainees can learn of the problems involved in application of the principles. Third, they can learn some of the factors to keep in mind in deciding how to react. Fourth, practicing the role of the complainant or informant will enable them to handle such calls by having a better basis on which to predict the behavior of the callers and thus deal with them better. Fifth, having a full and free discussion minimizes the possibility of the trainees simply learning a routine way of handling calls; they will be more likely to understand the full ramifications of a call. Sixth, by observing others, they can learn of the many possible ways in which problems can be dealt with, so that they can have a large repertoire of possible reactions. Seventh, the interest level and involvement of the trainee can be kept at a high level. Eighth, the trainees can make their mistakes in a situation in which the mistakes can be pointed out and corrected with no damage to their standing in their agency or damage to the agency and public. Ninth, when the trainees begin to take calls themselves, on returning to their agencies, they will feel more secure because the experience is not unfamiliar to them.

The following are examples of descriptions that could be given to the role players:

Citizen-
Complainant   You have just returned from a visit to your aged
                   father in a nursing home. When you stopped in the
                   office to pay your bill, you happened to notice on
                   the nursing home copy of your accounts--but not on
                   your copy--that they were charging you for a hearing
                   aid for your father, when, in fact, he does not use
                   one. When you protested, the cashier claimed to know
                   nothing about it. This is the first time you had
                   noticed the charge, but were not sure whether it had
                   occurred before. Nevertheless, you did not want to
                   jeopardize your father's treatment, and paid the
                   bill with a check. You thought about this on the way
                   home, and considered whether this was some sort of
                   fraud. You decided that you had better call the con-
                   sumer fraud division of the district attorney's office.
                   You now make this call. (You may fill in details of
                   your situation as you wish.)

Investigator: You are an investigator for the fraud division of the
                   local district attorney. The policy in your office
                   is for investigators to take telephone calls from
                   citizens. Up to this point, you do not know of any
                   frauds in the medical or health area.

Since some complaints might come in writing from other agencies, parallel exercises can be developed in securing written complaints from citizens or from other agencies. The trainees would then practice how to answer such letters. Before the sessions are over, the trainees should be given lists of the principles which the training was designed to point up. This list should be discussed at the end as a summary review, and as a way of assuring that all the principles are covered. The role playing, practice sessions just described do not have to be conducted in a formal training program, but can also be conducted in-house by some member of the staff or the supervisor in either large or quite small agencies Some preparation of the training material is needed, but again, the content of these materials can be developed from the actual work of the agency, and therefore should not be time consuming or difficult to prepare.

3. What Sort of Information to Look for and Where to Look.

A most important investigative skill is to recognize what information to look for, and where to look. The trainer should present to the trainee a series of talks which contain the following in general terms: a) What sorts of information are needed to determine whether a crime has been committed; b) where such information might be found; c) the form in which it might be found; and d) problems of gaining access to it.

Throughout the talks, there should be identification of points in the investigative process at which it would be especially valuable to consult a prosecutor or agency legal adviser, and the particular legal issues which might be raised at these points. The trainer should especially emphasize the distinction between a preliminary investigation on the one hand, in which the purpose is to determine whether a complete investigation is worth pursuing, and a complete investigation on the other. The trainer should distribute copies of investigative questions, preferably in tabular form, and a list of agencies which might have the information to answer each question, an indication of the form in which the information might be found, and some comments about special problems in gaining access to such information.

After passing out copies of such investigative questions, the trainer should lead a discussion regarding each of the items. The trainer should invite the trainees to interrupt at any point. The concentration should be on the problems of where to look, not on the detailed format of the records in which the information is kept. Also, the trainer should give as many tips as possible about how to gain access to sources of information, for example in public records, how to deal with custodians of records who could be helpful, etc.

After the discussion of the tables is complete, the trainer should present an information-seeking problem for the group to work out as a total group project. The problem should be one in which some difficulties on an investigation have begun to develop and the problem is where next to look. This too can best be developed from the trainer's own experience, both because it will have the ring of truth to it and will require less preparation time for the trainer.

After the example has been discussed, the trainees should be divided into groups of three each to work on a series of such problems. The answers should indicate where to look or, with the possibility of a rank-ordered series of sources in terms of either the ease of obtaining information or its utility, the forms in which the information might be found and ways to gain access to this information. Each group should be given the same set of problems, and a fixed time, such as 20 minutes, to complete work on all the problems. Then each group should designate one person to report its answers back to the total group, with the trainer leading a discussion. This process might be repeated several times in one session, with the problems ranging from those in preliminary investigation to complete investigations and gradually becoming increasingly difficult.

This procedure can be used both in large, formal programs, and in smaller, in-house ones, since there is minimal cost involved and because experienced investigators in the agency can do the training.

4. Learning About Various Business Organizations.

Up to this point, the proposed training program has not gone into detail on the functioning of the business organizations with which white-collar crime investigators frequently come in contact, either because they are possible vehicles for fraud, or sources of evidence. The reason for delaying a presentation on this point is that the trainees first need to see the legal relevance of gathering certain types of information so that they can appreciate the meaning and significance of all sorts of records. Once this has been done, the trainer is ready to turn to description of different types of business organizations. Among those that should be dealt with are the following: retail businesses, wholesale businesses, home and appliance repair businesses, manufacturing and contracting businesses, real estate, medical facilities, securities agencies, banks. Of course, training programs for specialized agencies will want to focus on those business areas with which they regularly deal in their work. If possible, the presenter should be an investigator with experience with the types of business discussed, rather than a representative of the business world. If the training program is being conducted in-house in a small agency, such an investigator may be recruited for a few hours from another agency, if none is available in-house.

In each case, the following information should be presented: 1) the various parts and functions of the business, including a glossary of business terms; 2) the records which are kept; 3) the laws governing the business, both criminal and civil; 4) the governmental organizations at the local, state and federal levels having particular legal and regulatory jurisdiction over them; 5) outline of the types of schemes characteristic of each type of business; 6) some special indicators of crimes in that type of business; 7) outlines of special investigating issues; 8) subpoena and other powers for securing information from these businesses. The trainees should be given outlines of the presentation, following these guidelines, and giving some of the salient information in concrete detail. In the presentation, examples of the forms used by businesses should be shown and discussed.

After each type of business is discussed, a concrete investigative problem relating to that business could be presented to the trainees. The problem should involve one in which it is not necessary to develop information from some agency outside the business organization itself, but which should present some problems within it, such as determining if the same real property was sold more than once, finding records of use of a prescribed therapy, etc. The trainee group should be divided into three-person groups to work on the problem no more than 15 minutes, and then report back to the total group. Again, preparation time for such an exercise should be minimal, since the best source of problems is the investigator-presenter's own experience.

5. Government Agencies

It is obviously necessary for the investigators to learn about federal state, and local agencies which are either directly involved in or can help in the fight against white-collar crime. Among the groups which should be described in detail are:

Federal

FBI, SEC, Postal Inspection Service, FTC, IRS, FDA, investigative branches of HUD, HEW, Department of Labor, Agriculture, etc., U.S. Attorneys.

State

AG, Consumer Protection in AG's office, Department of Licenses, State Police, Anti-Crime Commissions, State Securities (Blue-Sky) Agencies, Agencies where corporations must file to do business, where charitable organizations must file and disclose financial data, and where business names must be registered, etc.

Local

Consumer Protection agencies, license departments dealing with weights and measures, etc.

For each agency an investigator from that agency should give a presentation, explicitly providing the types of information indicated below. The list of types of information needed should be given to agency representatives well in advance, so that they can come fully prepared. They should be told which other agencies will have already made their presentations, and generally what they are expected to present. They should also have a general knowledge of who the trainees are, what has been imparted to them up to that point in the program, and how the sessions have been conducted. The agency representatives should understand that the more realistic and practical their presentations, the more likely they are to gain the cooperation of the investigators in future interactions. They should understand that any one of the trainees might later be the very investigator who will call on him for help, and vice versa. It is very helpful, though not absolutely essential, that these representatives of the agencies make the presentations. Every effort should be made to avoid standardized, public relations descriptions.

The information which is to be provided is as follows:

a) Goals of the agency.

b) Criminal and civil jurisdiction of the agency and geographical jurisdiction.

c) Organization of the agency, especially the role of their own investigators (if any).

d) Types of information which they possess.

e) Special investigative techniques employed by the agency.

f) Information systems of the agency.

g) Legal processes involved in transfer of information to and from the agencies.

h) Issues of overlapping jurisdictions, including task forces or strike forces.

i) Organizational relationships to the branches of the same level of agency (e.g., FBI to other federal agencies).

j) Problems that these agencies have had in dealing with other branches of government, at any level.

k) When federal prosecutors make presentations, they should give local and state investigators some information about relevant federal laws, the jurisdiction of federal courts, and the overlap of laws and jurisdictions between federal, state, and local levels. State agency representatives should give parallel information in presentations to local law enforcement training efforts.

l) Lists of names and places to contact in each geographical area, and what their specific competencies are within the total agency.

m) Ability to supply expert witnesses.

n) Ability to develop contacts in other agencies.

The supervisor of the training program should check the agencies' proposed presentation to eliminate duplication and to make certain that these guidelines have been followed. An outline of each presentation should be given to the trainees in advance, following the above guidelines, presenting detailed concrete information.

The regular trainer should be present during the invited presentation, while the invited trainer should remain present as a resource person for the rest of the time his agency is discussed. After each of these agencies has been described and discussed, a concrete investigative problem concerning that agency should be presented as discussed above. However, in this case, the trainee groups should be organized to provide the maximal variety of agencies and professions in each of them. For example, local, state and federal trainees should join together; or a lawyer and two investigators should work together.

The representatives of these other agencies should be solicited for sample problems from their own experience, from which the concrete investigative problems for the attention of the trainee group can be selected.

6. _Private Anti-White-Collar Crime Agencies and Sources of Information_

Many industry-supported or public interest groups can be of great assistance to the investigator both as sources of complaints and as sources

of information. Examples of the kinds of private organizations which could
be helpful are: Insurance Crime Prevention Institute, Better Business
Bureau, Credit Card Investigators, Consumer Union, "Calls for Action,"
telephone company investigative units, etc. The trainers should be
investigators who have had experience with these groups. In in-house
training programs in small agencies, such investigators may have to be
recruited from other agencies. Again, costs for such presentations are
minimal. Representatives of these groups should be brought in only after
the experienced investigators have made orienting presentations to the
trainees, since the former may tend to present a rather glowing view of
the organization and may not present the material necessary for investigators.

For each private group, the following information should be presented:

a) purposes of the group, both official and unofficial.

b) funding and governing of the group.

c) legal status of the group.

d) its relationship to government.

e) its relationship to business.

f) organization of the group.

g) materials for public distribution.

h) types of information they can generate.

i) forms in which the information is available.

j) difficulties in getting cooperation from the group.

k) subpoena and other powers in getting information from these
agencies.

l) what the private agency can do for local law enforcement and
what local law enforcement can ethically and legally do for the
agency, as well as policy considerations involved in such mutual
helpfulness.

m) ability to provide expert witnesses.

n) ability to develop contacts in other organizations.

The trainees should be given outlines of the presentations, following these
guidelines and providing detailed, concrete information where appropriate.

A concrete investigatorial problem should be presented to the trainees with respect to the potential benefits and problems of working with specific agencies, as was done with respect to internal business problems in the earlier sessions. It would be advisable to alter the composition of the small trainee groups from prior sessions, in order to open the trainees up to new ideas and insights from interacting with different people.

7. Relationships between Investigators and Prosecutors

The most crucial relationships that an investigator has are those with the prosecutor or litigating attorney who will take his case to court, or before a regulatory or administrative tribunal--because the best investigation is of little value if not used, or if not used properly. Since these relationships are complex and often difficult, it is important that they be given special attention in training. An effective approach would be to have two prosecutors or litigating attorneys make presentations. One would be a prosecutor or attorney who has worked with investigators in his own agency as part of a team, and the other would be one who has worked with investigators from other agencies. The reason for this split is that the problems may be quite different in each case. For in-house training programs, the prosecutor with whom the investigators are most likely to have to work should make the presentations.

The prosecutor (the term, as used below, should be read to include the litigating attorney) should be told in advance what has been covered in the training course, so that he does not cover the same material and thereby tend to appear to talk down to the trainees, and should be asked to cover his perceptions of the following:

a) The stage in an investigation where consultation with a prosecutor would be valuable.

b) The stage in the development of a case where a prosecutor should consult with an investigator.

c) The types of issues or problems about which it is most important for an investigator and prosecutor to work together.

d) The types of problems which investigators are likely to have with prosecutors. (For this topic, the trainer may have to "coach" the prosecutor or make a supplemental presentation himself.) The prosecutor should suggest some possible remedies.

e) The types of problems which prosecutors are likely to have with investigators, with some possible remedies.

f) Prosecutors' point of view on prosecuting borderline cases, plea bargaining, sentencing, etc.

g) Legal issues, such as search and seizure, motions of discovery, disclosure of confidential sources, etc.

Ample time should be allowed for discussion of these issues, with the main trainer present to contribute to and monitor the discussion. He needs to actually participate so that he has a chance to express and to discuss some of the problems that investigators have with prosecutors. Trainees may be reluctant to do this.

After there has been ample time for discussion, the trainees should again be broken up into small groups. This time the groups should be organized so that if there are any lawyers among the trainees, no more than one is assigned to any group. The guest trainer (prosecutor) might join in one of the groups. The groups should be given a problem involving face-to-face interaction between a prosecutor and an investigator. One of the group members should be assigned the role of prosecutor, another the investigator. If there are any lawyers in the group, they should be assigned the role of investigator so that they can learn the subtleties of the viewpoint and work of the investigators and thereby learn to communicate and cooperate better with them. The other group members would be observers who will later re-port back to the total group on the interaction which took place. Then the participants would receive written descriptions of their roles, the problem, the issues, etc. These descriptions might even include something about anticipated situations, such as investigators' perception of the reluctance of the prosecutors' office to work on marginal cases, the lack of knowledge of white-collar crime among new, young prosecutors, flaws in the quality of evidence gathered by some investigators, etc. Again, prep-aration of these descriptions should not be difficult, since they should arise from the prosecutor's own experience. The trainees would then enact the roles, the observer noting some of the issues involved and possible solutions. The observer would then report back to the total group. If time permits, several such exercises might be enacted with different situations, and with the trainees shifting roles.

E. SPECIAL INVESTIGATIVE TECHNIQUES

In this section we will discuss specific types of investigative techniques, rather than specific organizations to involve in investigations. Some of these techniques will apply more to some organizations than to others, but are sufficiently general in application to be treated separately in training. Many of the training procedures described below can be used in-house by either bringing in experts or by using agency personnel. Obviously, agencies with limited resources may very well use such in-house programs. In presenting each technique, a list of types of information and leads which can be garnered from that type of investigation should be presented.

1. Investigative Accounting

The depth of training in accounting that is necessary for investigators will vary with their agencies, the availability of professional investiga-tive accountants, the types of cases their agencies investigate, etc.

Nevertheless, all investigators should have enough knowledge of accounting to know when to recognize that accounting help is needed, to know what sorts of questions can and should be put to accountants, and to know how to evaluate what accountants give to them. This knowledge is essential because most accountants can best help the investigator when they are oriented in what to look for. This training should be done in two parts:

The first part should be conducted by an investigator-trainer who has used accounting help, and can give his perspective on where and how to call on it. Then bring in the investigative accountant. The second part should be conducted by an investigative accountant, or an auditor who has worked with law enforcement rather than an accountant or even an auditor who has only general experience. He should illustrate his lecture with specific cases.

The trainees should be given a crash course in double-entry bookkeeping. The courses should contain not only many examples of ledgers, balance sheets, etc., but the students should have individual practice cases of simple double-entry accounting that they can work on and then compare to the correct way. This work should be done individually and they should score their own exercises.

2. Tracing of Money

The trainees should receive a detailed description of the ways in which money and checks are processed through and among banks and other businesses, with a glossary and guidelines. The trainees can be given individual exercises of bank records, credit card records, etc., to trace money. Copies of such material used in actual cases can be readily made, thus keeping costs down. Materials such as The Seventh Basic Investigative Technique[110] should be used here.

3. Use of Newspapers

The use of media, principally newspapers, can be very helpful. Hardly a day goes by, in the Washington Post, the Wall Street Journal, New York Times, Los Angeles Times, etc., when there are not a number of stories and advertisements which have rather substantial white-collar crime implications. If, during a training program, there could be assignments, challenging the students to find all of the stories with such implications, and hold them for close to the end of the course, for discussion, analysis, etc., it would be quite exciting; it would keep the courses from getting into a rut; and, it would be a very real challenge for the instructors. Students and teachers could argue about what potential violations were posed by particular stories or ads, what techniques might be used if they

---

[110]See Appendix D, in the Manual, at p. 325 ff.

were to go out on a pro-active investigation, etc. Consider having a two-week subscription to three such newspapers for each group of three students who could share and compare views. In addition, this technique could be used for on-the-job training in small departments or even in large ones.

4. Computer Fraud.

Since so much of modern society depends on computers and since computer fraud is on the rise, it is important that investigators become at least familiar with the functioning and issues involved in them, without becoming computer experts. They should know enough to recognize when they need to enlist a computer expert and what questions to ask him. Unlike other training topics, this area is one in which a simple straightforward lecture may be the most appropriate method, along with visual presentations.

The lecture should include a presentation of the importance of computers, definition of computers, and knowledge of different systems, knowledge of computer terminology, use of computers in business and accounting, and the types of fraud. The problems of detectives and prosecutors should be mentioned. The students should receive a glossary of computer terminology.[111]

5. Shopping and Decoys.

The material here can be presented in lecture form, but it might be preferable that the trainees be given practice in shopping or inviting a solicitation by a fraud operator by a variety of role-playing techniques--shopping with respect to investment frauds, consumer frauds, land frauds, etc. One of the aspects of the situation that needs to be emphasized should be how to make the "shopping" as believable as possible to the suspect, such as by the shopper's dress, type of person doing the shopping, background knowledge that a real shopper would have, plausibility of the reason for being in the shopping situation, etc. Another aspect is making the investigator as effective as possible in gaining information from observation and from conversations, to gain the most from possibly fraudulent statements by suspects. The trainees also need to be made aware of the possibility of eliciting such statements from as many people in the "business establishment" as possible, from both underlings and supervisors, by means of appropriate questioning and probing. In addition the trainees should be made fully aware of the dangers of inadvertently crossing the line between giving white-collar offenders the opportunity to "do their thing," and engaging in entrapment. In states in which recordings can legally be made of such conversations, techniques for the proper use of the equipment should be practiced.

The use of decoys themselves is much more complex. If training in the use of decoys is to be done properly, it should be done completely, since half

---

[111]See Chapter V, Computers: Tool of Crime and Investigative Resources, pp. 199 ff.

measures in the use of decoys are worthless. Thus, the training should be done in a police garage, electronic shop, etc., rather than in the usual classroom setting. The whole process of setting up a decoy car needs to be examined and observed from both a legal and technical point of view, including the use of experts.[112]

Another form of shopping is the reading of mail advertisements, newspaper ads, and other printed advertisements. The alert investigator can catch many frauds by such pro-active measures. Examples of fraudulent advertising, investment invitations, etc., can be examined by the trainees, with descriptions of the cases that were developed on the basis of the spotting suspicious advertisements. The trainees could individually work on sets of models of fraudulent and honest advertising, mixed together, with the task of trying to pick out those likely to be fraudulent. Their opinions could be checked against the actual cases and the indicators of fraud could be discussed.

6. Interviewing Victims and the Informants and Witnesses.

In this manual's section on handling complaints,[113] issues in interviewing victims when they first complain were considered. Trainees need to develop skills in interviewing beyond the initial contact. This section in the training should be introduced with a discussion of the differences between interviewing victims, informants and witnesses on the one hand and interrogating suspects on the other. The trainees should know that interrogation of suspects will be treated separately.

The trainer should present some general guidelines for interviewing[114] witnesses, as indicated in Chapter IV of this manual, but should not spend more than a half hour on these general guidelines. After the general discussion the trainees should again break up into small, three-person groups, to work on exercises in interviewing. Two members of the group should be given short descriptions of the roles, with the third acting as the observer-commentator. Such descriptions would not be very difficult to prepare since they emerge from experience. Each of the participants can be given paragraph descriptions of the situation from their points of view. The practice situations should be as difficult as possible, such as a victim who is very reluctant to admit having been hoodwinked, a witness who also was partially involved in a scheme, an informant whose motives are highly questionable, a potential witness who may have been bought off, a witness who may not stand up in court, a victim who might be using law enforcement as a collection agency, etc. It would be well to have a series of such problems, with the trainees rotating their positions, and the observer-trainee commenting on the performance after each problem. Among the criteria for the trainer's comments on trainee performance should be the following:

---

[112] See the earlier discussions in this Manual of the use of Decoy Vehicles, at pp. 176-177 and the use of Expert Witnesses, at pp. 192-195.

[113] See Chapter II, at pp. 72-78.

[114] See Chapter IV, at pp. 155-167.

a) Did the interviewer secure detailed, explicit information?

b) Did the interviewer secure or learn about all relevant documents?

c) Did the interviewer determine something about the motives of the witnesses?

d) Did the interviewer establish enough rapport to assure continued cooperation with the investigation?

e) Did the interviewer develop any further leads?

After the small groups have worked through a number of such exercises, then one member of each group should report back to the entire trainee group, but unlike the previous sessions, the group's reporter should emphasize what effective techniques have emerged from the exercises, such as techniques to sooth a ruffled ego, to cut through a facade, to test for reliability, to trigger recollections as to possession or location of documents or physical evidence, etc.

The same sorts of exercises can be done with interviews with government officials, other investigators, businessmen, with special concerns for the issues involved with interviewing these people, such as their vulnerability to pressures, their concern for their own organizational needs, political problems they may have, etc.

At the end of the session, each trainee should receive a list of principles involved, and the trainer should discuss them, referring back to the role playing experience as a review-summary and as a way of making sure all the points have been covered.

7. Interrogation of Suspects.

The trainees should first be made fully familiar with the problems discussed in Chapter IV about whether and when to approach a white-collar crime suspect, [115] especially since the stage of the investigation at which an approach is made may be quite different from what would be the case in non white-collar crime investigations. Furthermore, the trainer should empha- size that the suspects here are generally brighter, more verbal, more knowledgeable, and more personable than non-white-collar criminals. The importance of approaching the suspect from a position of maximum strength in advance should be emphasized. Although these points can be made in a lecture, the same type practice exercises as were used in the interviewing could also be used here.

There are, however, some special problems in using such situational exercises which should be carefully considered before setting them up. The main difficulty arises from the fact that white-collar suspects often have

---

[115]See Chapter IV, at pp. 167-172.

higher community status than ordinary suspects, and are surrounded by many
props to support their facades of legitimacy--all of which will tend to
place the investigator in a very difficult position unless his case is
already well developed and he has a very strong sense of personal security
which will sustain him in such situations.

Any situational exercises should, therefore, be preceded by a lecture
and discussion period in which these issues are gone into in detail, with
stress on the point that white-collar criminals are criminals, that the key
to successful interrogation is intensive preparation and such command of the
facts of the case as will strengthen the role of the investigator and
undercut the confidence of the suspect being interrogated.[116]

In the event that training films can be developed to deal with the
challenge of suspect white-collar crime interrogation, as has been done in
police training situations where effective simulation is difficult to
achieve, [117] this would be a most useful training device. It is to be hoped
that such a training film or video-tape could be prepared for use in the
future to cover settings such as richly furnished lawyers' offices,
impressive suspect homes, and dealing with such types as the glib talker, the
bombastic intimidating type, and the cultured and cultivated operator who
allows his surroundings and carefully dramatized activities to misleadingly
undercut an investigative examination or interrogation.

However the training in interrogation methods is conducted, stress
should be placed on actual case examples of "impressive" suspects, on
how they attempted to spin investigators, what tactics were used to cope
with these attempts, and what types of preparation and countering methods
were involved in both successful and unsuccessful investigator action to
obtain information in the face of the suspect's evasive and misleading
maneuvers.

At the end of the training session dealing with this subject, the
instructor should pass out a list of the principles involved in interrogation, the list being discussed by the trainer as a review-summary and as a
check on coverage.

8. Organizing Investigative Information.

It is obviously possible for an investigation to produce so much information that it would be very difficult for one person to keep track. The use
of computers and other techniques to store information has been discussed
in Chapter II. [118] But there are ways in which information which is either

---

[116]See Chapter IV, at pp. 167-172.

[117]This has been done, for example, in the New York City Police Department,
in its "Shoot-Don't Shoot" training film.

[118]See p. 81.

stored in a computer or in an investigator's notes can be organized so that the organization of a complex scheme can be visually displayed and thus more readily apparent to the investigator. He can thus see patterns, see gaps in the investigative process, etc. This problem of keeping track of all the information is a vital one, not only when schemes are complex, crossing between and among businesses and people, but when a number of different investigator agencies become involved in the investigation. Very useful devices for keeping track of both the scheme and the information about the scheme are Link Network Diagrams and Time Flow Diagrams.[119] Trainees should be instructed as to the preparation and use of such diagrams.

9. Decision-Making in the Course of an Investigation.

One of the basic problems in any investigation is the decision as to whether to continue to investigate, how to continue to do so, and whether to join with other agencies, etc. These problems were discussed earlier. The purpose of training investigators in these matters is not to advocate particular ways of solving these problems. The purpose is simply to get the trainee to be aware of possible alternatives and considerations, and to give him some practice at making such decisions. In this way, he is more likely as an investigator to give some thought to his decisions, to stop more frequently to think through next steps. The trainer should review the material by presenting the trainees with lists of alternative actions, and lists of considerations for making such decisions. This should be done in a discussion rather than a lecture format, if at all possible.

After these issues have been discussed, each trainee should be given a series of practice exercises of cases at various stages of development. Charts might be used in some of the more complex cases. The trainee's job is to make decisions, and to write out his rationale for doing so. All the trainees should receive the same set of exercises. After all of the trainees have completed their exercises, the trainer should conduct a discussion of the decisions and the rationales, case by case.

F. FINAL EXERCISE

In the course of a training program, the trainees will have dealt with parts or aspects of the total investigative process, though hopefully many case examples will have spanned much of the process. If the time and resources are available as part of the training program it would be very desirable to put all the parts together in a simulation of a single investigation so that they can deal with the parts in conjunction with one another. In this way, they can learn better how to integrate the various

---

[119] See the earlier discussion of these diagrams in Chapter II, pp. 82-88.

phases of an investigation. They can learn when to approach other governmental agencies, when to approach witnesses, when to collect different types of documents, when to approach the suspect or suspects; they can learn how to use information gathered at one point in the process to make decisions about how to go farther; they can learn how to integrate the information; and they can learn how to integrate it to make the best prosecutorial case. Working through a total investigation would also give the trainers and the trainees a chance to learn about any inadequacies in the former's performance and to discuss ways of correcting these inadequacies for future training sessions. Furthermore, informing the trainees at the beginning that there will be a final exercise of this sort would give the total program a goal from the start, and a sense of completion and closure at the end of the program.

One way of performing this exercise is to take an actual case which is quite complex in the sense that it involved many discreet steps in the investigation; one where many different investigative tools were actually used, and where many interim investigative decisions had to be made. The trainer should be thoroughly familiar with the case. He should then present the trainees as a group with the first report as it came into the unit. He should then ask the trainees as a group what the next investigative step should be: a check of files, an interview, a check with another agency, etc.? Then after they have discussed the matter thoroughly, they should reach a consensus on what the next step should be. The trainer should enter into the discussion only if a major factor is being overlooked by the trainees. After they have made their decision about next steps, the trainer should present them with the information, if any, they would have obtained from that step. He should be able to do this from his knowledge of the case. This process is then repeated as often as warranted. The trainees can decide that the next step can be consultation with a prosecutor, expert, etc., and can develop Link Network Diagrams or Time Flow diagrams. The case ends when the trainees decide to present the case to a prosecutor.

This exercise can obviously be repeated a number of times.

G. TRAINING - SUMMARY

The key principles to be kept in mind in the training of white-collar crime investigators are:

- Develop in the trainees a sense of the importance and worth-whileness of their mission.

- Ground all training exercises in actual cases, to the maximum possible extent.

- The trainees should have the opportunity to discuss issues with the trainer as much as possible.

- The trainees should participate in practice exercises as much as possible.

- Consciously promote trainee interactions which will continue after the course is completed.

- Emphasize interaction between the investigative agency and other public and private agencies.

- Stress the needs of the prosecutor or litigating attorney, who must "buy" and be able to rely on the investigators' work.

By adherence to these principles, and careful selection of trainees and those who will train them, successful training outcomes can be expected.

H. ONGOING FORMAL TRAINING PROGRAMS FOR INVESTIGATORS

There are a number of valuable training programs to which investigators could be sent. Among them are:

California Department of Justice
Advanced Training Center
1771 Tribute Road
Sacramento, California 95813
Phone: (916) 445-9846

Ohio Organized Crime Prevention Council
State Office Tower
P.O. Box 1001
Columbus, Ohio 43216
Phone: (614) 466-7652

Federal Bureau of Investigation
White-Collar Crime Training Program

New Jersey State Division of Criminal Justice
Prosecutor's Supervisory Section: "Investigation of Criminal
    Financial Transactions."

APPENDIX B

SAMPLE GUIDE TO SOURCES OF INFORMATION

This Guide is similar to one
prepared by and used by the
Office of the Orange County,
California, District Attorney

Part I contains types of information sought,
followed by a number or numbers. The number
directs the investigator to sources listed
in Part II.

This Guide does not purport to be a complete source reference,
as many of the sources are well known, and many other sources
can be added from your own experience. Similarly, the Guide
indicates merely where information can be found and does not
imply that information will be automatically given the investi
gator. In many instances, collection of information is only
possible by use of legal process, i.e., subpoena, etc.

PART I

TYPES OF INFORMATION DESIRED

Type of Information   Refer to:

1. Full Name................................... Part II of Index
                                                  1,2,4,5,6,10,11,16,17,
                                                  24,31,34,35, 36,56

2. Address.................................... 1,2,4,5,6,10,11,16,17,
                                                  24,31,34,35,36,56,62

3. Date of Birth.............................. 2,3,8,13,24,34,35

4. Description................................ 2,3,13,56

5. Photograph................................. 2,3,13,22,62

6. Occupation................................. 6,13,31,34,35,37,55,62

7. Marital Status............................. 12,23,34,55,56

8. Prior addresses of a subject; names
    of persons previously living at the
    same address.............................. 35,36,62

9. Addresses, present and former, whether
    renting or buying; credit references;
    personal and business associates;
    names of relatives, locations of banks
    and finance companies...................... 34

10. Telephone numbers and addresses; how
    long has the suspect had service;
    record of long distance phone calls;
    number of extensions in residence.......... 5

11. Sources of income; expenditures; personal
    and business references; net worth of
    subject; handwriting exemplars............. 31

12. Information as to credit charges which
    have been made; what hotels are being
    used; where has your suspect been buying
    gasoline; employment and credit
    references................................. 15

PART I (continued)

Type of Information   Refer to:

13. Registered owners of vehicles; legal
     owners of vehicles; description of
     vehicles; previous owners of vehicles;
     operators' license numbers, signatures;
     photographs; thumbprints; abstracts of
     traffic citations........................... 56

14. Application for bonds which give
     personal and business references;
     former addresses; former places of
     employment.................................. 32

15. Records of stocks bought or sold,
     profits and losses.......................... 33

16. Recorded deeds, grants, mortgages,
     wills admitted to probate, notices
     of mechanics' liens, powers of
     attorney.................................... 61

17. Record of registration for securities
     offered for public sale; record of
     individuals and firms who have
     violated State or Federal regulations
     in securities traffic....................... 50

18. Information concerning reputation of
     a business; back issues of city
     directories................................. 51,52,62

19. Businesses' worth, associates, family,
     holdings and ratings........................ 34,55

20. Information on persons involved in a
     medical or dental practice, pharmacists,
     barbers, funeral directors.................. 47

21. Names of post office box holders;
     return addresses on mail received at
     post office; mail covers.................... 4

22. To find a forwarding address............... 4,38

23. Marriage license applications;
     addresses, dates of birth; signatures....... 12

PART I (continued)

Type of Information   Refer to:

24. Names of the bride and groom; maiden
    name of bride; ages......................... 23

25. Information on divorces, i.e., place
    and date of marriage; date of separation;
    ages of children; community property;
    signatures; income; places of employment..... 9,62

26. Information on parents of a child,
    i.e., occupations, ages, mother's
    maiden name, name of physician.............. 20,24

27. Disposition of monies from an estate;
    value of estate; inventory of all
    assets of deceased.......................... 30

28. Name and description of the deceased;
    property found on deceased and its
    distribution; cause of death................ 25,29,30

29. Where death occurred; birth place;
    how long deceased lived in the County,
    State or United States; names of
    relatives; whether or not deceased
    was a veteran............................... 25,62

30. Civil suits -- changes of name; liens;
    description of property involved; name
    of court reporter, if any, who recorded
    the testimony............................... 10

31. Political party; physical disabilities
    which would prevent marking a ballot;
    name of spouse; when and where married;
    last place of registration to vote.......... 6,62

32. Ship, Boat & Yacht Registrations............. 41,42

33. Names and addresses of owners of ships,
    boats or yachts............................. 41,42,59

34. Ownership of aircraft....................... 60,65

35. Background on horse owners, jockeys,
    trainers, and people employed at
    race tracks................................. 7,62

Type of Information   Refer to:

36. Case histories of persons on welfare
     (usually good background information)........ 21

37. Student records, past and present
     teachers' records, past and present......... 22

38. List of all county employees;
     occupations and rate of pay; records
     of all financial business for the
     county...................................... 26

39. Presidents and Secretaries of all County
     Medical Associations; names of hospitals
     and sanitariums, number of rooms and
     beds; doctors' names by street and city;
     doctor's year of birth, medical school
     and year of graduation, office address....... 39

40. Bar owners' fingerprints, marital
     status, home addresses, employees,
     associates.................................. 48

41. Information relative to Articles of
     Incorporation, giving businesses,
     associations, records of election
     returns; descriptions of seals used by
     various state officers; papers filed
     by candidates for election to State
     offices..................................... 43

42. Names of associates of a person involved
     in organized crime and which law
     enforcement agencies have information........ 27,62

43. Transcripts of preliminary hearings;
     probation officer's reports;
     subpoenas issued in the case; names of
     attorneys concerned......................... 11

44. Parole reports; inmate contacts;
     visitors; correspondence; work and
     training assignments........................ 53

45. Copies of telegrams and money order
     information; possibly handwriting
     exemplars................................... 37

46. Record of all warrants drawn on the State
     Treasury; accounts of all persons
     indebted to the State....................... 44

272

PART I (continued)

Type of Information   Refer to:

47.   Legal description of property; amount of
      taxes paid on real and personal property;
      former owners of property...................   17

48.   Amount of cost of construction; blueprints
      of construction; information regarding
      location of plumbing and wiring.............   19

49.   Dimensions of property and taxable income of
      real property, and what improvements,
      if any, on the property.....................   16

50.   Maps of streets; locations of drains;
      location of utility conduits; rights
      of way; old names of streets................   18

51.   Maps having elevations, base lines;
      landmarks; important sites..................   28

52.   Sources of information in foreign
      countries...................................   57,58

53.   Information as to anticipated travel
      of a person in a foreign country and
      vital statistics............................   13,62

54.   Addresses of aliens.........................   14,49

55.   Alien information; date of entry; manner
      of arrival; addresses; occupation; age;
      physical description; marital status;
      children; signature; photograph.............   14,49

56.   A guide to newspapers and periodicals
      printed in the U.S. and its
      possessions; thumbnail description of
      every city, including population,
      county, and location with respect
      to the nearest large city...................   40

57.   Information on cattle and dairies...........   45

58.   Mining information, petroleum and
      gasoline, fish and game.....................   46

59.   Arson information and thefts of
      valuable insured items......................   54,63,64

PART II

1. Telephone directories

2. State of California, Department of Justice, Bureau of Identification (CII)

3. F.B.I.

4. Post Office

5. Telephone company

6. Registrar of Voters

7. California Horse Racing Board

8. County Clerk's Office, Vital Statistics

9. County Clerk's Office, Divorce Records

10. County Clerk's Office, Civil Files

11. County Clerk's Office, Criminal Files

12. County Clerk's Office, Marriage Licence Applications

13. State Department, Passports Division

14. County Department of Naturalization

15. Credit card companies

16. County Assessor's Office

17. County Tax Collector's Office

18. Highway Department

19. Building Department

20. Health Department

21. Welfare Department

22. School Department

23. County Recorder's Office, Marriage License Section

24. County Recorder's Office, Birth Certificate Section

25. County Recorder's Office, Death Certificate Section

26. County Auditor's Office

PART II (continued)

27. Law Enforcement Intelligence Unit (LEUI)
    (If your department is a member)

28. County Surveyor's Office

29. County Coroner's Office

30. Public Administrator's Office

31. Banks and finance companies

32. Bonding companies

33. Stock brokers

34. Credit reporting agencies

35. Gas and electric companies

36. Water companies

37. Telegraph companies

38. Moving companies

39. American Medical Directory

40. Directory of Newspapers and Periodicals,
    N.W. Ayer & Sons, Philadelphia 41

41. Lloyds Register of Shipping

42. Lloyds Register of Yachts

43. Secretary of State, Corporate Division

44. State Controller

45. State Department of Agriculture

46. Department of Natural Resources

47. Consumer Affairs

48. Alcohol Beverage Control

49. Federal Immigration and Naturalization Service

50. Securities and Exchange Commission

275

PART II (continued)

51. Better Business Bureau

52. Chamber of Commerce

53. Department of Corrections

54. American Insurance Company

55. Dun and Bradstreet

56. Department of Motor Vehicles

57. Treasury Department, enforcement agencies

58. INTERPOL - Area Code 202 - 967-5685

59. Harbor Patrol

60. Airport Security

61. County Recorder's Office

62. Newspaper Library or Newspaper "Morgue"

63. Insurance Crime Convention Institute - Area Code 213 - 387-3381

65. Federal Avaiation Administration

APPENDIX C

GLOSSARY OF WHITE-COLLAR CRIMES

And

BIBLIOGRAPHY OF WHITE-COLLAR CRIME REFERENCE SOURCES

APPENDIX C (Part 1)

GLOSSARY OF WHITE-COLLAR CRIMES

There are numerous forms of white-collar crime, and innumerable variations of each of these forms. Some general terms, descriptive of these crimes are frequently used. This glossary lists such terms, defines them generally, and provides some comments on them which hopefully will be of assistance to investigators who must cope with them. The glossary avoids legal definitions, stressing instead the most frequent situations in which particular white-collar crimes occur, the most frequent victims of particular abuses, the modi operandi, and the relationships between offenses and enforcement avenues. Where appropriate, references are made to a list of bibliographic sources which follow this glossary and from which additional information on specific crimes may be obtained. Each bibliographic reference in this list is preceded by a number which is used as the citation form in the glossary.

ABUSE OF TRUST--the misuse of one's position and/or of privileged information gained by virtue of that position in order to acquire for oneself (or for another in whom has an interest) money, property, or some privilege to which one is not entitled. Abuse of trust often involves as well a violation of fiduciary duty.

The victims of such abuses are those who rely to their detriment (i.e., who have placed their trust in) the individual or group which misuses a trusted position.

The abuse of trust can occur in many areas but is a situation which arises most frequently in the following four white-collar crime areas:

- banking--where abuse of trust can involve self-dealing in connection with loans or credit to oneself, one's friends or business associates.

- securities--where insider information may be used for personal benefit at the expense of clients, stockholders and others.

- commercial bribery--where the procurement and competitive bidding processes may be manipulated.

- embezzlement & fiduciary violations--where trustees, attorneys, etc., may misuse property or funds in their custody.

Remedies for abuses of trust include criminal, civil, and regulatory remedies, enforceable under federal and state law.

See also: BANKING VIOLATIONS; COMMERCIAL BRIBERY; COMPETITIVE PROCUREMENT FRAUDS; EMBEZZLEMENT AND FIDUCIARY VIOLATIONS, INSIDER SELF-DEALING, SECURITIES FRAUD.

ADVANCE FEE SCHEMES--schemes in which assurances of some future benefit are made, with full compensation to the promisor/perpetrator to be deferred until final performance--but where the perpetrator has no intention of performing or in obtaining full compensation for performance but rather is interested only in obtaining the partial payment requested as a service fee or an advance good faith deposit (often called a "returnable" deposit).

Typical victims of advance fee schemes are businessmen who cannot obtain customary banking or credit sources to continue their business operations or to expand them. They thus pay "deposits" or "fees"to others to arrange loans or credit for them.

These frauds are customarily prosecuted under the federal mail fraud statute and state larceny and fraud statutes. Check with the U.S. Postal Inspector for further information.

Bibliographic references: 42,52

ANTI-TRUST OFFENSES--combinations in restraint of trade, price fixing or other schemes to unlawfully drive competitors out of business; and/or agreements among competitors to share business according to some agreed formula (such as bid-rigging conspiracies and discriminatory pricing agreements); and/or domination of a business area by one or a few enterprises.

Victims of anti-trust offenses are businessmen who are hurt as competitors and purchasers of goods or services who pay higher prices and/or deprived of the choice of where and how they will buy.

Anti-trust offenses constitute violations of both federal and state criminal and civil laws. Check with local prosecutors, state attorneys-general, U.S. Department of Justice and regional offices of the U.S. Federal Trade Commission.

See also: COMPETITIVE PROCUREMENT FRAUD, PRICE FIXING, RESTRAINT OF TRADE.

Bibliographic references: 28,37,55,60,69

AUTO REPAIR FRAUD--a form of consumer fraud involving maintenance services to automobiles.

Auto repair frauds fall into several categories:

- overcharging for labor or parts or use of shoddy or substandard parts.
- failure to perform promised services or repairs.
- charging for services not performed or parts not used.
- performing services or repairs that are unnecessary or unwanted.

Remedies usually involve state fraud or larceny laws, state and local licensing laws, etc. Many law enforcement agencies have adopted pro-active detection techniques, such as the use of decoy vehicles (see pp. 176-177).

See also: CONSUMER FRAUD, REPAIR FRAUD.

Bibliographic references: 71

BAIT & SWITCH--a form of consumer fraud involving misleading advertising.

The substance of the bait and switch is the situation in which a store's advertised "bargain" is little more (and often nothing more) than an inducement (i.e., "bait") to lure a customer to the store where he is presented with similar but higher priced items (i.e., the "switch"). Thus the advertisement does not constitute a bona fide offer for sale of the merchandise in question. This may be because 1) the advertised item is not available on the premises or is available in unreasonably short supply; or 2) acts are undertaken to prevent the customer from purchasing the advertised item in favor of higher priced merchandise (i.e., by downgrading or "knocking" the advertised goods).

Such sales tactics only sometimes are sufficiently blatant to support criminal fraud prosecutions. More frequently they are dealt with through civil remedies invoked by local consumer protection offices and district attorneys (where they have civil jurisdiction), consumer divisions of state attorneys general offices, and the U.S. Federal Trade Commission.

See also: FALSE AND MISLEADING ADVERTISING.

Bibliographic references: 3,21,24

BANKING VIOLATIONS--violations by insiders or by customers of banks, savings and loan association, or credit unions. Insider violations generally involve embezzlements or self-dealing (where insiders lend money to themselves or to businesses in which they have an interest, or take bribes or special favors to make loans or to refrain from collecting loans). Violations by outsiders would include false financial statements to induce a bank to make a loan, the use of fraudulent collateral, check kiting, etc.

Victims are depositors and shareholders, bank stockholders, creditors, the federal government as the insurer of deposits, and surety companies who bond bank employees and officials.

These violations are prosecuted under federal and state statutes proscribing embezzlement, false entries in books and records of banks (including computerized records), and misapplications. Violations in state-chartered institutions are often federally prosecuted because deposits are federally insured. The F.B. I. should first be contacted with respect to suspected banking violations.

See also: ABUSE OF TRUST, CHECK-KITING, COLLATERAL FRAUDS, COMMERCIAL BRIVERY, INSIDER SELF-DEALING.

Bibliographic references: 13,42,68,78,79

BANKRUPTCY FRAUD--frauds involving financial insolvency.

Victims of bankruptcy frauds are usually creditors and suppliers of the failed or failing business, although "silent partners" and stockholders can also be victimized by managers of the business who operate fraudulently. There are two major types of bankruptcy fraud:

- the scam or planned bankruptcy, in which the assets, credit and via- bility of a business are purposely and systematically milked to obtain cash which is hidden by scam operators.

- fraudulent concealments or diversions of assets in anticipation of insolvency so they cannot be sold for the benefit of creditors (i.e., squirreling away assets when bankruptcy appears imminent).

Planned thefts and fencing activities may be associated with either type of bankruptcy fraud as a means by which assets can be diverted and converted to cash.

Bankruptcy fraud is primarily a federal violation; the F.B.I. should be notified if there are indications of such fraud. Some forms of bankruptcy fraud, such as "scams" would also be violations of state fraud and larceny laws.

Bibliographic references: 15,32,39,40,88

BID RIGGING--see COMPETITIVE PROCUREMENT FRAUD.

BOILER ROOM--a technique used to promote fraudulent sales of securities, charitable solicitations, etc.

The "boiler room" technique involves the use of telephone solicitors, who might operate locally or by use of long distance lines, who call lists of victims, soliciting them to buy stock, contribute to charities, etc. The telephone salespersons work on high commissions using pre-planned sales pitches. Their services, particularly in charitable solicitations, are sometimes sold to otherwise legitimate enterprises--which rarely see very much of the collections. The technique depends upon glib misrepresentations.

The use of this technique exposes the perpetrators to criminal prosecution under federal wire fraud and mail fraud laws and under fraud and non-registration provisions of the Securities Acts administered by the U.S. Securities and Exchange Commission. It also exposes the users to criminal or civil action in state and local levels under state fraud statutes, state "blue-sky laws" regulating securities sales, and local and state laws requiring licensing and filing of information in connection with charitable solicitations.

See also: CHARITY & RELIGIOUS FRAUDS, SECURITIES FRAUD.

Bibliographic References: 17,42,59

BUSINESS OPPORTUNITY SCHEMES--one of the most prevalent and multivaried forms of fraud in which victims are offered the opportunity to make a living, or to supplement their income by going into business for themselves (full or part-time), by purchasing franchises or equipment to manufacture some item, sell merchandise, or perform some service.

Victims are generally individuals with some small pool of money they have saved and to whom the prospect of the promised independence and/or income is attractive.

Such schemes range from being total shams to being "opportunities" whose promised returns are highly illusory.

The operators of these schemes have essentially one goal, which is to acquire the money of subscriber or investor victims. Work-at-home merchandising schemes (knitting machines, raising minks, etc.) or the sale of distributorships (cosmetics, special rugcleaning processes, etc.) are common examples of the kinds of situations involved in the business opportunity fraud. The opportunity presented by the fraud operator often includes the promise of "guaranteed" markets for the goods or services to be produced. Often the schemes induce the victim to enlist other victims, creating a pyramid scheme.

These schemes are generally prosecuted under federal mail fraud laws, and state laws which proscribe larceny, false pretenses, etc. Check with U.S. Postal Inspector, U.S. Federal Trade Commission, state attorneys general offices, and local prosecutors.

See also: FRANCHISING FRAUDS, PYRAMID SCHEMES, SELF-IMPROVEMENT SCHEMES, WORK AT HOME SCHEMES.

282

Bibliographic references: 6,21,52

CHAIN REFERRAL SCHEMES--any scheme in which the victim is induced to part with money or property on the representation that he will make money through inducing others to buy into the same deal.

First-tier victims usually believe that those whom they involve in the scheme (second-tier victims) will themselves make money--but since second-tier victims can only make money by involving third-tier victims, and so on, the scheme must eventually collapse. Generally only the fraud operators who manage the scheme make money on it; few first- or second-tier victims (especially if they are honest) have a sufficient number of victimizable friends and acquaintances to come out whole.

One common type of chain-referral scheme is the chain-letter; more sophisticated is the "pyramid scheme," in which (for example) the victim is sold a franchise to sell both merchandise and other franchises, with the promise of profits on merchandise sold and commissions, or "overrides," on merchandise sold by any second- or later-tier victim who buys a franchise from him. The pfofits appear, therefore, to be in selling franchises rather than in selling merchandise. These schemes ultimately collapse of their own weight.

Chain-referral schemes are criminally prosecuted under federal mail fraud statutes, and state fraud laws. Civil actions have been undertaken by the U.S. Federal Trade Commission, state attorneys general offices, and local prosecutors.

See also: MERCHANDISING FRAUDS, PYRAMID SCHEMES.

Bibliographic references: 5,11,49,52,70

CHARITY AND RELIGIOUS FRAUDS--frauds arising out of the fund-raising activities of charitable and/or religious groups.

Almost anyone can be the victim of such frauds often without even knowing it, but even where the victim may later suspect the fraud, his or her individual loss may be so small that there is little desire to pursue the matter. Three types of fraud situations are observed in this area:

- the bogus charity or religious group--where money is solicited for a non-existent organization or cause, or for a charitable front created for the sole purpose of soliciting funds which will end up in the collectors' pockets.

- misrepresentation of association with a charity or religious group--where money is solicited on behalf of a legitimate organization or cause by those with no ties to such organization or cause, and who have no intention of giving money to the group.

- misrepresentation of the benefits or uses of contributions--situation
  in which those solicited for donations to a legitimate charity or
  religious organization are not aware that most of the money collected
  reverts not to the charitable cause but rather is used to cover the
  cost of professional fund raisers and/or administrative overhead
  expenses. (This is a grey area since professional fund raisers perform
  a legitimate service for which they may properly and legitimately
  be compensated).

In some instances charitable organizations themselves are the victims of
con men who use them as a front, keeping the lion's share of the collections, as in the case of boiler room operations (see "Boiler Rooms," above).
In other instances the solicitation falls into a "grey area" where otherwise "legitimate" charities and causes will cover up the fact that most of
the monies collected go to salaries, fund raisers, etc.

Depending on the blatant nature of the operation, or where in the "grey area
a con falls, there may be federal criminal violations (i.e., mail fraud,
wire fraud, etc.), violations of state fraud statutes, violations of local
licensing laws dealing with charitable solicitations, or of state laws
requiring filing of information with state agencies and full disclosure as
to funds collected, costs of solicitation, monies provided charitable
beneficiaries, etc.

See also: BOILER ROOM.

Bibliographic References: 42,59

CHECK-KITING--any of a variety of frauds against banks which depend for
success upon the time it takes to clear checks.

The most common form of check-kiting involves the opening of two or more
accounts. Balances are built up in each by deposits from the others.
Checks are circulated between accounts, with no money taken out of any
account, until at least one of the banks develops confidence in the depositor. Then the depositor takes money out of that bank, depending on the
circulation of checks between the two or more banks, and the several days
it takes to clear checks (especially between different cities), to prevent
detection.

Banks are the victims of check-kites. When first discovered check-kites
appear far more costly than when all transactions are analysed, since
hundreds of thousands of dollars in checks may be circulated to steal only
a few thousand dollars, though in some instances massive amounts have been
stolen. In many instances, however, business men employ check-kites when
they cannot get loans from banks to tide themselves over a temporary
business situation, and intend to (and often do) put the money back into
the accounts before the check-kite is discovered--in such instances the bank
has been fraudulently induced to unwittingly grant what amounts to an
interest-free loan.

Check-kites are generally prosecuted under federal laws dealing with mail fraud and banking fraud. Local law enforcement investigations should carefully consider signs of check-kites in cases investigated, since they may play a part in other, broader fraud schemes.

See also: BANKING VIOLATIONS.

COLLATERAL FRAUDS--frauds involving the holding, taking or offering of collateral pursuant to a financial transaction.

In many instances these will be banking transactions (see "Banking Violations"), above. Beyond this, however, such frauds may be encountered in connection with any transaction in which security is provided, such as security for private loans, non-existent accounts receivable sold or pledged to factors, etc. In some cases collateral used as security may not belong to the person offering it. It could be stolen, e.g. stolen securities, or borrowed, or already subject to an undisclosed lien or other encumbrance, or there can be some gross misrepresentation as to its value.

Collateral frauds may be violations of federal banking laws, the mail fraud statute, or state fraud laws. They may be elements in bank or corporate violations involving self-dealing, as where a bank officer makes a loan knowing the collateral is bad. Collateral frauds may also be involved in organized crime activities, e.g, obtaining proceeds of stolen securities not by an attempted sale which would precipitate discovery when title was transferred, but by their use as collateral for loans.

See also: BANKING VIOLATIONS.

Bibliographic references: 13,42,68,78,79

COMMERCIAL BRIBERY--a form of insider fraud or abuse of trust in which an employee or officer of a private enterprise in some government entity is given a bribe or some other valuable consideration, to induce the employee or official to make a purchase, or grant a contract or some special privilege (such as a zoning variance, license, etc.)

Commercial bribery is a violation of specific statutes in a large number of states, and falls within the proscriptions of more general criminal statutes in other jurisdictions. It may violate numerous federal statutes, depending on the manner in which it is executed.

This crime is one of the most pervasive crimes committed in the U.S., but relatively little prosecuted. Its impact, in undercutting the integrity of our private and governmental processes is vast, and it adds immeasurably to our taxes and to the cost of goods and services we buy.

COMPETITIVE PROCUREMENT FRAUD--unlawful manipulation of the public or private contracting process.

Victims are competitors not participating in the fraud; the public or private entity soliciting bids (which are believed to be competitive); and customers or constituents of those entities who do not realize benefits that would be derived from a truly competitive procurement process.

Three main forms of competitive procurement frauds are:

- bid rigging--form of illegal anti-competitive conduct in which bidders in a competitive procurement collusively set their bids so as to deprive the bid solicitor of a competitive process. The effect is an administered bidding process in which the winner and the terms and prices of the goods and services involved in the procurement are set by the conspirators rather than by the "competitive" process. Parties to the conspiracy are thus able to divide among themselves a relevant set of procurement contracts and to fix prices for goods and services at the same time.

- bid fixing--a form of illegal manipulation of the procurement process whereby one bidding party is provided with inside information (by the bid solicitor or an agent thereof) which enables said bidder to gain an unfair advantage over other bidders.

- bribery/kickbacks--situation in which procurement contracts are let on the basis of the payment of bribes and kickbacks to procurement officials rather than on the basis of competitive procurement guidelines.

Competitive procurement frauds are prosecuted under federal and state criminal laws proscribing mail fraud, criminal conspiracy, bribery, kickbacks, etc. Proof in these cases involves 1) the most painstaking analysis of bidding patterns, 2) examination of relationships between bids to the entity whose defrauding is being investigated and bids by the same bidders to other entities for possible broader patterns of trade-offs, and 3) close scrutiny of performance on the jobs done pursuant to contracts.

See also: COMMERCIAL BRIBERY, FALSE CLAIMS, KICKBACKS, PUBLIC/OFFICIAL CORRUPTION.

COMPUTER FRAUD--frauds arising out of the increasing use of the computer to maintain business and governmental records, such as those relating to inventories, accounts payable and receivable, customer and payroll records.

Computer frauds are rarely uncovered by internal audits. Often the thief or fraud artist is the computer system operator or one having access to the computer's memory system. For a more detailed discussion of computer fraud, see Chapter V, pp. 192-213 of this manual.

Bibliographic references, 1,16,27,31,43,50,51,62,63,64

CONSUMER FRAUD--frauds of the marketplace involving seller misrepresentations to buyers.

Victims are consumers of all kinds, individual and institutional, public and private.

Common forms of consumer fraud include:

- selling of useless goods or services, represented as beneficial; e.g., "miracle" face creams.
- misrepresentation of product performance, benefits or safety.
- false and misleading advertising.
- failure to service items after sale, including reneging on warranties.
- repair fraud.
- hidden charges with respect to financing, necessary follow-up services, etc.
- weights and measures violations.

See also: BAIT & SWITCH, FALSE & MISLEADING ADVERTISING, MERCHANDISING FRAUDS, REPAIR FRAUD, WEIGHT & MEASURES FRAUDS.

Bibliographic References: 9,29

COUPON REDEMPTION FRAUDS--frauds which involve cheating manufacturers or merchandisers who promote sales of their products by offering coupons which return part of the purchase price when the products are purchased.

Many manufacturers, primarily in the food business, place coupons in newspaper and magazine ads offering, for example, "15¢ OFF" if the product is purchased. The grocery store is supposed to redeem the coupon, and will customarily receive a service charge of about 5¢ for handling the transaction. Frauds are committed against the manufacturers by amassing large numbers of coupons and submitting them to manufacturers without any bona fide purchases of the products. These frauds probably amount to many tens of millions of dollars annually.

The modus operandi of this type of fraud involves two basic steps: 1) collecting coupons, and 2) processing for redemption. Collecting coupons may be done by going through large numbers of old newspapers and magazines; sometimes this is done by trash collection or waste disposal companies as a side venture. Processing for collection requires the collaboration of retail merchants, and is most efficiently done with the cooperation of officials of food retail chains, frequently without the knowledge of their companies.

These frauds have involved organized criminal syndicates. They have usually been federally prosecuted under the mail fraud statute, though they could be prosecuted under numerous state fraud statutes.

CREDIT CARD FRAUDS--frauds arising out of the application for, extension and use of credit cards.

Victims are the issuers of the credit cards.

Common credit card abuses include:

- use of stolen credit cards.
- false statements in application for credit card, including application under a false name.
- buying with no intention to ever pay, by use of a credit card which was originally legitimately obtained.

Credit card cases are usually referred to prosecutive agencies by credit card company investigators, who have completed major portions of the investigation. Prosecution can be undertaken under the federal mail fraud statute, and under state fraud, larceny, and forgery laws. Investigative and prosecutive agencies should be careful to avoid becoming collection agencies in such cases by carefully analysing referrals to be sure that the requisite criminal intent is present, e.g., to avoid cases in which a credit card holder badly overextended himself and fell hopelessly into debt--as opposed to cases where he never intended to pay.

Bibliographic references: 14,57

CREDIT RATING SCHEMES--frauds arising out of the application for, extension and use of credit.

Victims are generally the providers of credit.

Common credit-related schemes include:

- sale of good credit ratings to high risk applicants.
- false statements in application for credit.
- creation of false credit accounts for purpose of theft.

The modi operandi of such schemes vary widely. In recent periods employees of credit rating organizations have altered credit ratings for payment, sometimes using computer techniques; false financial statements are a most common method. On a smaller scale is a fraud which operates like shoplifting --opening a charge account with false information in order to purchase and take away goods simultaneously with opening of the accounts.

Cases involving sales of credit ratings and alteration of computerized ratings are being prosecuted under the federal mail fraud statute, since they have been nationwide in scope. They would also be prosecutable under state laws proscribing fraud, false pretenses, and larceny.

See also: LOAN OR LENDING FRAUDS.

DEBT CONSOLIDATION OR ADJUSTMENT SWINDLES--swindles perpetrated against people who are heavily in debt, and against their creditors, by purporting to provide a service which will systematically organize the marshalling of the debtor's assets and income to repay all creditors over a period of time, with creditors refraining from pressing for immediate payment of all sums due. Some such services are provided by legitimate private agencies, and provision is made for such processes in non-bankruptcy proceedings in federal bankruptcy courts.

The modus operandi of this fraud is to use heavy TV and newspaper advertising to lure debtors into signing up. The fraud operators then take their fee, usually a heavy percentage of the total debt, in advance. Sometimes they talk creditors into waiting for their money; in other instances they falsely tell the debtors they have done so. They then take debtors' assets, and a portion of their weekly or monthly earnings, paying themselves first, and (usually only after they have their entire "fee") doling out the remainder to creditors. Frequently creditors receive little or nothing, and the debtors are left minus their fees and still in debt.

These schemes have been prosecuted under the federal mail fraud law, state general fraud, larceny, and false pretenses statutes.

Bibliographic references: 25,52,56

DIRECTORY ADVERTISING SCHEMES--frauds arising from the selling of printed mass advertising services.

These schemes are of two basic kinds: 1) impersonation schemes, in which con men send bills to business enterprises which look like those customarily received; e.g., from the phone company for "yellow page" advertising, with directions to make checks payable to entities which look like legitimate payees of such bills; and 2) schemes in which it is promised that advertising will appear in a publication distributed to potential customers but where, in truth and in fact, distribution will be limited to the advertisers themselves, if the directory is printed at all.

These cases have been federally prosecuted under the mail fraud statute and can be prosecuted under state general fraud laws, larceny and false pretenses statutes.

EMBEZZLEMENT AND FIDUCIARY FRAUDS--the conversion to one's own use or benefit the money or property of another over which one has custody, to which one is entrusted, or over which one exerts a fiduciary's control.

These crimes are prosecuted under specific statutes, such as those dealing with embezzlement, banking misapplications, etc., the federal mail fraud statute, federal and state laws regulating brokers and investment services, and state general fraud or larceny statutes.

Victims would be financial institutions, businesses in general, pension funds, beneficiaries of estates being managed by fiduciaries, etc.

See also: ABUSE OF TRUST, BANKING VIOLATIONS, INSIDER SELF-DEALING, LOAN OR LENDING FRAUDS.

Bibliographic references: 1,12,51

EMPLOYMENT AGENCY FRAUDS--fraudulent solicitations of money or fees in order to find employment for, to guarantee the employment of, or to improve the employability of another.

Victims are generally individuals seeking jobs or hoping to improve skills in order to obtain better paying employment opportunities.

Variations of employment related frauds include:

- phony job agencies--where agency solicits advance fees in order to find employment for the victim when in fact the service is neither performed nor intended to be provided.

- job training frauds--where money is received from victims to train them for specific employment and 1) the training is not supplied; 2) guaranteed job opportunities on completion of training are not supplied; or 3) the training is misrepresented as being "certified" or "recognized" by employers when it is not and does not qualify victim for anticipated employment.

These frauds are prosecutable under the federal mail fraud statute and state general fraud statutes. Substantial recoveries have been made for victims of such frauds by the U.S. Federal Trade Commission.

See also: ADVANCE FEE SCHEMES, SELF-IMPROVEMENT SCHEMES

ENERGY CRISIS FRAUDS--frauds arising out of the sale of goods or services related to energy or fuel use, saving, and production.

Victims are generally individual consumers interested in stretching their dollars spent on energy sources and/or saving energy.

Energy schemes include the following types of frauds:

- merchandising schemes--sale of worthless or bogus items which do not deliver the specific benefits promised or the degree of benefit promised, e.g., carburetor gadgets to save gasoline or phony solar heating systems. Often these frauds occur because of the novelty of the items involved combined with the naivete of the victims.

- weights & measures violations--short weighing or measuring of fuels to customers, e.g., manipulation of gas pump measuring devices, or misrepresentation of fuel, e.g., changing of octane ratings on fuel pumps.

- discriminatory allocation of fuel by distributors to sub-distributors and retailers, in consideration of commercial bribes to distributors' executives or special payments to companies with the power to make distribution in the form of under-the-table payments or required purchases of other items--useful or not needed--in violation of anti-trust or other laws.

These cases can be prosecuted under special state statutes, e.g., those dealing with weights and measures, or violations of specific administrative regulations promulgated to deal with energy crises, and (in appropriate situations) as commercial bribery or anti-trust violations.

See also: ANTI-TRUST OFFENSES, COMMERCIAL BRIBERY, MERCHANDISING SCHEMES, WEIGHTS & MEASURES VIOLATIONS.

Bibliographic references: 52

FALSE AND MISLEADING ADVERTISING--use of untrue or deceptive promotional techniques resulting in consumer fraud.

Victims are consumers relying to their detriment on the false or misrepresented advertising or promotion.

The following kinds of practices are prominent among those which fall under the heading of false and misleading advertising:

- advertising as a "sale" item, an item at the regular or higher price.

- misrepresentations concerning the size, weight, volume or utility of an item.

- falsely claiming an attribute which a good or service does not in fact possess.

- misstatement of the true costs of a good or service through the use of confusing payment provisions or otherwise.

These violations are prosecutable under the federal mail fraud statute, state general fraud statutes, and specific statutes dealing with false advertising.

Administrative and other civil remedies are frequently invoked against these offenses, and local consumer protection offices provide mediation remedies since these offenses frequently fall into "grey" areas with respect to wrongful intent.

See also: BAIT & SWITCH, CONSUMER FRAUD.

FALSE CLAIMS--fraudulent written claims for payment for goods or services not provided as claimed, to public or private entities.

False claims may involve activities such as:

- presentation of a bogus claim or claimant; e.g., the ghost payroll situation.
- misrepresentation of the qualifications of an otherwise ineligible claim or claimant; e.g., welfare fraud.
- false representation of the extent of payment or benefits to which claimant is entitled, e.g., overtime pay frauds.
- claims for reimbursement for goods and services allegedly provided to non-existent recipients, e.g., Medicaid fraud, by service providers.

The false claim will carry all the trappings of a legitimate claim and is most successfully undertaken by an individual(s) with a thorough-going knowledge of the system being defrauded. The false claim is one of the basic implementing tools of the white-collar thief and can run the gamut from the elaborate computerized creation of fictitious claimants to the simple manipulation of numbers on a time card. False claims will sometimes involve the cooperation of executives or officials of the private or governmental entity to which such claims are submitted.

Violations are prosecuted under both general and specific fraud statutes, e.g., that dealing specifically with false claims submitted to the federal government, larceny, and false pretenses statutes. Such violations are also generally a basis for civil action, whether or not the proof is sufficient to meet the criminal standard of proof.

See also: COMMERCIAL BRIBERY, FRAUDS AGAINST GOVERNMENT PROGRAMS, GHOST PAYROLL, MEDICAID/MEDICARE FRAUD, OVERTIME PAY FRAUD, WELFARE FRAUD.

FALSE STATEMENTS--the concealment or misrepresentation of a fact material to the decision-making process of a government entity, with the result that the government entity accepting the false statement is deprived of the opportunity to decide whether or not to follow up on the situation which a truthful presentation of the situation would have allowed.

The false statement is often the means by which a fraudulent scheme to obtain money or benefit is effected either because (among other things):

- the false statement constitutes the underlying documentation for a false claim; or

- the false statement impedes discovery of the fraudulent scheme; i.e., covers up the fraud. These statements often provide the opportunity for conditioning the victim to unquestioningly accept and approve a false claim.

On the federal level, false statement prosecutions under 18 U.S.C. 1001 have been a major weapon against white-collar crime directed at the federal government. Even where such statutes are not present as part of the arsenal of state statutes, their use for the purposes outlined above will be valuable in showing the manner and means by which frauds were perpetrated, in prosecutions under state general fraud, larceny, and false pretenses statutes.

See also: FALSE CLAIMS, FRAUDS AGAINST GOVERNMENT PROGRAMS, GHOST PAYROLLS.

FRANCHISING FRAUDS--frauds arising out of business opportunity situations in which individuals invest time, talents and money to obtain a business enterprise, relying on others (i.e., the franchiser) to supply at prearranged rates specified goods and services such as necessary business structures, the goods to be sold or materials with which goods can be made, advertising, and an exclusive territorial market or market area for the franchisee's output.

Victims generally invest their major assets in what are fraudulent franchise opportunities.

Frauds in franchises generally arise becuase one or more of the following occurs:

1. Franchisor has no intention of performing on any of his obligations; i.e., the "franchise" is a complete ruse to acquire victim-franchisee's initial investment monies.

2. Franchisor fails to provide promised goods or services essential to success of franchise.

3. Franchisor makes success for franchisee either difficult or impossible by extending too many franchises in a given locale or market area.

4. Franchisor has misrepresented the market or demand for goods/services central to the franchise, or has misrepresented the level of skills needed to realize franchise profitability.

#1 is outright fraud, while #2 - 4 represent variations ranging from fraud to shady dealing, to failure to fulfill contractual obligations.

Franchise frauds are federally prosecuted under the federal mail fraud statute, and under state statutes proscribing frauds, larceny, or false pretenses. In some instances, where success depends not on the victim's own labor, the franchise agreement may be considered a "security," and enforcement may be possible under securities acts in the jurisdiction of the U.S. Securities and Exchange Commission or state securities regulatory agencies.

See also: BUSINESS OPPORTUNITY SCHEMES, CHAIN REFERRAL SCHEMES.

Bibliographic references: 22,23

FRAUDS AGAINST GOVERNMENT BENEFIT PROGRAMS--unlawful application for and receipt of money, property or benefit from public programs designed to confer money, property or benefit under specific guidelines.

Victims are federal, state and local governments, their taxpayers, and qualified, intended beneficiaries of such programs.

Typical kinds of frauds suffered by government programs include:

- misrepresentations of applicants' qualifications concerning program eligibility; e.g., food stamps received by ineligible persons.

- false billing/vouchering in which public programs make good on false claims for services not rendered or for non-existent beneficiaries; e.g., physician's claims under Medicaid programs for patients not treated, or for specific treatments not provided.

- inflated billing/vouchering/claiming, by which public programs are charged more than allowable costs; e.g., housing fraud where cost of construction is inflated so that builder/owner construction is inflated so that builder/owner receives more than total cost of land and buildings and avoids making investment required by law and administrative guidelines.

- embezzlement, by which employees or officials of public programs convert funds, property or benefits to their own use (often via their custodial, fiduciary or programmatic relationship to the program), e.g., licensed dispensers of food stamps converting funds to their own use.

- misuse of properly obtained funds, etc. in which money, property or benefit conferred under very specific guidelines concerning end use, are received and utilized for unauthorized ends; e.g., receipt of federal loan funds (such as student educational loans) with failure to use such for specified purposes.

These frauds are prosecutable under specific enforcement sections of statutes setting up government programs, as well as statutes proscribing false claims, false statements, and conspiracy. They will also be violations of general fraud and larceny statutes, on the state level.

See also: EMBEZZLEMENT AND FIDUCIARY FUNDS, FALSE CLAIMS, FALSE STATEMENTS, MEDICAID/MEDICARE FRAUD, WELFARE FRAUD

Bibliographic references: 19,86,87

FUNERAL FRAUDS--class of guilt inducement frauds relying for success on the emotional stress of victims who have lost, or are about to lose loved ones through death.

Victims are the relatives or friends of deceased or terminally ill persons.

Funeral related frauds often take the form of consumer and merchandising frauds and generally involve one or more of the following practices:

- relying on the guilt or anxiety of bereaved relatives. Victims are persuaded to contract for unnecessary or unduly elaborate funeral services or merchandise.

- billing for funeral expenses to include charges for services not performed (here fraud artist relies on victim anxiety or guilt to preclude memory of whether service was performed or not and/or to preclude victim's challenge of the bill for payment.)

- services or goods in connection with burial are represented as legally required, when in fact they are not.

- contracts are made for future provision of goods or services in connection with funeral and burial arrangements which fraud operator has no intention or no capacity to provide; e.g., sale of non-existent cemetary plots.

Since many such abuses fall into "grey areas" of consumer fraud and misrepresentation, state attorneys-genneral and consumer protection agencies often undertake to provide civil mediation remedies. In addition, the U.S. Federal Trade Commission has expressed considerable interest in fraudulent activities in this area.

See also: CONSUMER FRAUD, GUILT-INDUCEMENT FRAUD, MERCHANDISING FRAUD.

Bibliographic references: 53,85

GHOST PAYROLLS--form of false claim in which fictitious employees are added to a payroll and payments to these employees revert to the payroll manipulator(s). Fictitious employees are commonly referred to as "ghosts."

Victims are generally public and private entitites responsible for honoring payroll claims. Often the ghost payroll is a device used to defraud government programs designed to provide employment for the unemployed or disadvantaged. This is closely related to welfare and unemployment insurance frauds. This device can also be used in cost-plus contracts to cheat govern mental entities, or by managers of sub-units in private enterprises to steal from their parent organizations.

A variation on the ghost payroll is the overtime pay fraud in which false claims are made with respect to overtime work by bonafide employees.

Prosecution on the federal level would be under mail fraud, conspiracy, false claim and false statement statutes. On the state level, such prosecution would be under general fraud, false pretenses, and larceny statutes.

See also: FALSE CLAIMS, FRAUDS AGAINST GOVERNMENT PROGRAMS.

GUILT INDUCEMENT FRAUDS--frauds perpetrated via the tactic of inducing guilt or anxiety in the victim concerning his or her relationship or obligations to another person who is significant to victim (i.e., a child, parent, spouse).

Victims are individuals who, susceptible to the guilt or anxiety induced by the fraud operator, are persuaded to part with money or property in the belief that the questioned transaction will atone for any "shortcomings" or fulfill "obligations" they have toward another.

Because guilt inducement is a major tactic used to secure voluntary victim action, it cuts across many fraud areas. A few examples of the dynamics of such frauds are noted below:

- Encyclopedia salesmen induce victims to enter into purchase contracts for books having suggested to victim that imminent scholastic failure of children can be expected if such purchase is not made--here a merchandising fraud is consummated by the offender's capacity to induce parental anxiety in victims.

- Children of deceased are persuaded to purchase elaborate and unnecessary funeral arrangements construed by the fraud operator to constitute a "decent" burial. The implication in such funeral frauds is that failure to buy the most expensive items, or close checking of the details of bills are tantamount to lack of affection or respect for the deceased

- Unnecessary and imprudent expenditures for life insurance are made by many wage earners to whom it is suggested that failure to subscribe to such policies constituted a failure to one's spouse and family.

- Self-improvement merchandise and facilities are marketed to victims on the basis of such guilt inducements as "you owe it to your spouse to be as (lovely, manly, successful, etc.) as you can be" or "you can only be a failure if you fail to take advantage of opportunities to improve your (looks, job, speaking ability, etc.)".

Depending on the level and quantity of misrepresentations involved in such frauds, remedies will range from criminal prosecutions (mail fraud, state general fraud statutes, etc.) to regulatory or administrative measures in federal, state and local levels to enjoin deceptive practices, compel reimbursement of victims, etc.

See also: FUNERAL FRAUDS, SELF-IMPROVEMENT FRAUDS.

HOME REPAIR OR IMPROVEMENT FRAUDS--frauds arising out of the provision of goods and services in connection with the repair, maintenance or general improvement of housing units.

Victims are generally homeowners but may also include public agencies or programs which subsidize and/or underwrite home purchase and ownership.

Home repair or improvement frauds include the following practices:

- shoddy or incompetent workmanship.
- sale of over-priced or unfit materials or services for home repair projects.
- failure to provide services or goods paid for by customer.
- submission of false claims for materials or work not provided.
- misrepresentation of the need for particular materials or services to be performed.
- misrepresentations or concealment of the costs of credit, or of the nature of leins securing the payment obligations.

The victim may be told that the home is in violation of building codes or in a condition substandard to the rest of the neighborhood, endangering the value of the home or the safety of the victim's family.

These violations are prosecutable under a broad range of statutes including mail fraud, statutes aimed at fraud against the federal government, state general fraud statutes, local licensing laws, including those regulating door-to-door solicitations. This is a major area for administrative and mediational activities on the part of attorneys general offices, municipal consumer protection offices, etc.

See also: CONSUMER FRAUD, MERCHANDISING FRAUDS, REPAIR FRAUD.

Bibliographic references: 52

INSIDER SELF-DEALING--benefiting oneself or others in whom one has an interest by trading on privileged information or position.

Insider self-dealing is reputed to have been the cause of approximately half the bank failures in the United States since 1960.

Typical violative situations include those where a corporate officer or director trades in the stock of his company on the basis of inside informa- tion as to prospective profits or losses; bank officers lending money to themselves or businesses in which they have an interest; corporate execu- tives or purchasing officials setting up suppliers of goods and services to contract with their companies, etc.

For nature of enforcement remedies, see also: ABUSE OF TRUST, BANKING VIOLATIONS, COMMERCIAL BRIBERY, SECURITIES VIOLATIONS.

INSURANCE FRAUD--fraud perpetrated by or against insurance companies.

Victims may be the clients or stockholders of insurance companies or the insurer itself.

Insurance fraud breaks down into the following categories and subclasses:

1. Frauds perpetrated by insurers against clients/stockholders include the following deliberate and intentional practices:

   - failure to provide coverage promised and paid for when claim is made.

   - failure to compensate or reimburse properly on claims.

   - manipulation of risk classes and high-risk policy holder categories.

   - embezzlement or abuse of trust in management of premium funds and other assets of insurance companies.

   - twisting--illegal sales practices in which insurer persuades customers to cancel current policies and purchase new ones from it.

2. Types of frauds perpetrated by insureds against insurance providers:

   filing of bogus claims for compensation or reimbursement, multiple claims for same loss from different insurers.

   inflating reimbursable costs on claim statements.

   payment of bribes or kickbacks to local agents to retain coverage or coverage in improper risk category.

   failure to disclose information or false statements made in application for insurance.

Cases are often developed by insurance company investigators or state insurance departments and referred to investigative and prosecutive agencies. Federal prosecutions are generally under the mail fraud statute; state and local prosecutions under general fraud laws, larceny statutes, etc. Where the frauds are committed against insurers, assistance may be obtained from the Insurance Crime Prevention Institute (ICPI), Westport, Connecticut, an industry investigative group supported by over 40 nationwide insurers.

See also: ABUSE OF TRUST, FALSE CLAIMS.

Bibliographic references: 11,20,31,34,36,38,42,52,61,73,77

INVESTMENT FRAUDS--frauds in which victims, induced by the prospect of capital growth and high rates of return, invest money in imprudent, illusory or totally bogus projects or businesses.

Investment frauds generally victimize those with a pool of liquid or convertible assets, ranging from retirees or near-retirement age people; widows or widowers, to high-income professionals and businessmen.

Hallmarks of many such frauds are:

- higher than average promised rates of return.

- developmental nature of investment object, i.e., project or business is not a mature entity

- sales made by strangers, i.e., through boiler rooms.

- generalized definition of nature and scope of project, lack of detailed plans by which progress might be observed.

- object or site of investment geographically remote or distant from investors.

- failure to fully disclose facts material to investor prior to his commitment of money.

- non-registration with U.S. Securities and Exchange Commission and comparable state regulatory agencies.

- promise of special advantages, e.g., tax shelters.

Examples of such frauds are too numerous to include here. They are generally violations of special statutes such as the federal Securities Acts enforced by the U.S. Securities and Exchange Commission, state securities regulatory laws enforced by state agencies, the mail fraud statute, and state general fraud, larceny, and false pretenses statutes. Where land frauds are involved, the U.S. Department of Housing and Urban Development and state agencies which require full disclosure filings will have enforcement jurisdiction. In this area of enforcement, state and local investigatory and prosecutive agencies can anticipate major support and assistance from federal agencies which have overlapping or parallel enforcement interests.

See also: LAND FRAUD, PONZI SCHEMES, PYRAMID SCHEMES, SECURITIES FRAUD.

Bibliographic references: 8,11,42

LAND FRAUD--a type of investment fraud which involves sale of land, based on extensive misrepresentations as to value, quality, facilities, state of development.

Victims are usually individuals buying land for retirement, investment, or both simultaneously.

Land frauds usually consist of one or more of the following practices. The sale of land or of interest in land:

- to which seller has no present title or claim of right; i.e., seller cannot properly transfer title or interest to buyer as represented at the time of sale;

- about which a misrepresentation or failure to disclose a material fact has occurred;
- at inflated or unjustified prices based on misrepresentations to purchaser;
- on the promise of future performance or development which the seller neither intends to provide nor can reasonably expect to occur. Misrepresentations usually involve presence of utilities, water, roads, recreational facilities, credit terms, etc.

Such frauds have been perpetrated for decades, and resulted in numerous successful prosecutions on both federal and local prosecutive levels, as well as in extensive civil actions by regulatory agencies which have resulted in both extensive restitution to victims and options to cancel improvident purchases. Federal prosecutions are undertaken under the mail fraud statute, and it may be anticipated that there will be increasing prosecutions for failure to comply with recently enacted registration and disclosure laws under the jurisdiction of the U.S. Department of Housing and Urban Development; there are parallel state registration and disclosure laws. Local prosecutions have been undertaken under general fraud laws, false advertising, and larceny statutes. There is substantial federal-state-local cooperation in this enforcement area.

See also: INVESTMENT FRAUD

Bibliographic references: 42,52,58,66,84

LANDLORD-TENANT FRAUDS--unlawful practices involving the leasing or renting of property.

Common fraud practices by landlords include:

- keeping two sets of books, i.e., tax violations.
- schemes to avoid return of security deposits.
- rental of property to which one has no title claim of right.
- deliberate and persistent violations of safety and health regulations, and failure to provide heat, services, etc.

These white-collar crimes are usually misdemeanors, and violations of local ordinances. Frauds such as schemes to cheat tenants out of their security deposits should be prosecutable under state's general fraud laws.

LOAN OR LENDING FRAUD--unlawful practices arising out of the lending or borrowing of money.

Victims may be financial institutions, the stockholders of financial institutions, or borrowers.

Loan frauds generally involve either the failure to disclose relevant information which would bear on the extension or granting of a loan, or the provision of false information, or both.

When perpetrated by the lender, loan frauds may take the form of:

- lending to oneself through ghost accounts, or
- lending to friends or entities in which one has an interest.

- commercial bribery, approving loans to those who would not qualify as borrowers, i.e., exchange for kickbacks or other considerations.
- advance fee schemes, by which borrowers remit money to secure a loan which is not forthcoming or for which no payment was necessary.

When perpetrated by borrowers, loan frauds may take the form of:

- false statements by which loan to which one is not entitled is fraudulently obtained.

  improper use of legitimately obtained loans, where improper use was intended at the time the loan application was made.

- larceny by false pretenses, by which loan is obtained with no intention of repayment.

A separate and important dimension of loan fraud involves the misuse or misrepresentation of items of collateral and collateral accounts.

These frauds are prosecutable under federal statutes proscribing mail fraud, banking frauds, securities frauds, program frauds (such as those involving construction or repair loans which are federally guaranteed), etc. They are also prosecutable under general state fraud laws, false pretenses statutes, and larceny statutes.

See also: ABUSE OF TRUST, BANKING VIOLATIONS, COLLATERAL FRAUDS, FALSE STATEMENTS.

Bibliographic references:

MEDICAID/MEDICARE FRAUD--fraudulent practices arising in connection with the receipt or provision of health care services under government financed programs.

Such frauds are nearly always perpetrated by health care providers (both professionals and facility operators) against the government(s) financing the programs and/or the intended beneficiaries of such programs.

Specific Medicaid/Medicare fraud practices include:

- pingponging--referring patients to other doctors in a clinic in order to claim reimbursements for their "consultation" rather than for bona-fide patient treatment or observation.

- upgrading--billing for services not provided.

- steering--sending patients to a particular pharmacy, medical lab, etc., for required prescriptions or services, and receiving kickbacks therefrom.

- shorting--delivering less medication, e.g., pills, than prescribed while charging for full amount.

- procurement abuses--establishment of supply/purchase arrangements with firms which pay kickbacks to health care facilities or which are owned by those controlling the facility itself.

- false claims--submission of claims for which payment from government for patients that do not exist, or were never seen or treated.

These violations are prosecutable under federal fraud statutes, including mail fraud, false claim, and false statement statutes, as well as specific statutes in legislation authorizing such programs. Since many such programs are administered through state agencies and involve use of state funds, state general fraud, false pretenses, and larceny statutes will also be applicable.

See also: COMPETITIVE PROCUREMENT ABUSE, FALSE CLAIMS, FRAUDS AGAINST GOVERNMENT BENEFIT PROGRAMS, KICKBACKS.

Bibliographic references: 82,83,86,87

MEDICAL FRAUDS--unlawful activities arising out of the provision and sale of bogus, highly questionable or dangerous medical services, cures, or medications.

Victims are often individuals who have been given little hope of recovery or improvement by traditional medical establishments and desperately seek any promise of ameliorating their conditions. Also victimized are persons who are poorly informed and thus vulnerable to claims made by medical fraud artists, often in such areas as beauty treatments, cosmetics, etc.

Medical frauds generally include one or more of the following abuses:

- quackery--false representation of oneself as a legally trained and licensed health care professional.

- fake cures--sale of bogus or highly questionable "cures" for specific illnesses or diseases.

- misrepresentations of medication--misrepresentations as to the therapeutic value of medications, and/or omissions made regarding known side effects of medications.

- misrepresentations of treatment--false statements made with regard to the therapeutic value of a particular treatment protocol, with regard to its degree of "acceptance" or bonafide medical practice; and/or omissions of material information concerning known side effects of treatment that would affect patient's choice of treatment program.

Such frauds may operate through misrepresentations made to victims themselves, as well as to regulatory agencies such as the U.S. Food and Drug Administration. In the latter case the misrepresentations may involve the nature of test results or the methodology or procedures involved in conducting such tests.

Federal enforcement has been dominant in this field, through the mail fraud prosecutions, Food & Drug Administration efforts, and U.S. Federal Trade Commission proceedings. Local quacks should, however, be open to prosecution or control under general fraud statutes, larceny and false pretenses statutes, and vigorous exercise of licensing powers with respect to health and beauty services.

Bibliographic references: 11,18,44,52,82,83

MERCHANDISING FRAUDS--an umbrella term for a broad variety of consumer frauds involving misrepresentations inducing the victims to purchase merchandise, which either is not as represented or which in fact will never be delivered to them.

The frauds usually involve one or more of the following aspects:

- representation that the item is sold at lower than usual price, whereas it is in fact sold at the usual retail price or higher.

- misrepresentation as to the quality or utility of the merchandise.

- misrepresentation as to the ultimate price, or credit terms.

- misleading information as to warranties, cancellation of transaction, returnability of merchandise, and validity of "money back guarantees."

- solicitation of money with no intention to deliver the merchandise promised.

- "Bait & Switch" frauds.

Victims customarily buy from door-to-door salesmen or are entrapped when they respond to newspaper, magazine, radio or TV advertisements. Examples of such frauds include door-to-door magazine subscriptions sales, hearing-aid frauds, bulk sales of items falsely represented to be at wholesale prices (i.e., freezer food sales), and false sales (where items sold are falsely represented to be priced at less than regular prices, or sold pursuant to closeout of a business or replacement of inventory).

Enforcement with respect to these frauds has been successfully undertaken at federal, state, and local levels. Laws invoked have included federal mail and wire fraud statutes, the U.S. Federal Trade Commission Act, general state fraud and false advertising statutes, and local licensing laws governing door-to-door sales and solicitations.

See also: CONSUMER FRAUDS

NURSING HOME ABUSES--a variety of frauds perpetrated by individuals who provide institutional nursing and convalescent care to patients, particularly the aged.

Victims of such frauds are the patients of such facilities, their families, and/or governmental entities who sibsidize the cost of care provided to eligible patients.

Forms of nursing home fraud abuses include:

- unlawful conversion or attachment of patients' assets.

- false claims to patient, family or government entity regarding services delivered.

- false statements in license application or renewal.

- maintenance of fraudulent records as to general or overhead costs of operation of facilities, as a basis for false claims to governmental entities.

- receipt of kickbacks from facility suppliers.

- employment of inadequate or unqualified staff in violation of licensing guidelines.

These frauds are prosecutable under federal false claim and false statement statutes, and state fraud laws. They generally require careful and painstaking audits to separate out extensive self-dealing, kickback arrangements, and concealments through sophisticated accounting techniques, etc.

See also: COMPETITIVE PROCUREMENT ABUSES, EMBEZZLEMENT AND FIDUCIARY FRAUDS, FALSE CLAIMS, FRAUDS AGAINST GOVERNMENT PROGRAMS, MEDICAID/MEDICARE FRAUD.

Bibliographic references: 81

PATENT FRAUD--a form of self-improvement scheme which most closely resembles vanity publishing frauds.

In patent frauds, individuals are solicited through newspaper advertisements, etc. to send "patentable" ideas or gadgets to fraud operator for "evaluation by experts." The "evaluation" of course usually involves a fee, or at least "further processing" of the submission may involve a fee, thus an advance fee situation evolves. The fraud operator generally has neither the intention nor the capacity to develop or process a patentable item.

For further information on remedies, etc., see also: ADVANCE FEE SCHEMES, SELF-IMPROVEMENT SCHEMES, VANITY PUBLISHING SCHEMES.

Bibliographic references: 11,72

304

PENSION FRAUDS AND ABUSES--thefts and fraudulent conversions of pension fund assets either by trustees, employers or employees.

Frauds perpetuated by trustees: violators of fiduciary duty in management of pension fund monies by:

- poor investments tied to self-dealing or commercial bribery.

- embezzlement.

Such fraud victimizes those who have contributed to the fund as those intend ing to benefit from it.

Frauds perpetuated by employees: accrual of abnormal overtime, etc., to form an inflated base period on which pension payment level is to be established (very often in local public sector employment situations). Victims are other employees whose potential benefits are reduced by fraud of their peers or bankruptcy of fund, as well as employer contributors to the pension plan.

Victims are employees who have relied on promised future benefits.

Prosecutions in this white-collar crime area have shown patterns of questionable union-employer agreements to permit widespread trustee fraud. Major violations have been prosecuted under the federal mail fraud statute, and this area is considered one in which there are major white-collar crime/ organized crime interrelationships.

See also: ABUSE OF TRUST, EMBEZZLEMENT AND FIDUCIARY FRAUDS, COMMERCIAL BRIBERY, FALSE CLAIMS.

PIGEON DROP OR POCKETBOOK DROP--one of a large variety of street con games regularly perpetrated on gullible victims.

It is a scheme in which the victim is persuaded to withdraw a large sum of cash from a bank account in order to show good faith or financial responsibility regarding the sharing of a "discovered" cache of money with two other persons (who are con artists). In the course of the con, both the "discovered" money and the victim's "good faith" money disappear as do the con artists.

Victims may be anyone, since perpetrators of this fraud have a remarkable ability to disarm their victims. Keys to the pigeon drop con are:

- the con artists to do not appear to be associated or know each other in any way.

- a pocketbook, envelop, etc., is "found" by one of the confederates, and it contains a sizeable amount of money. no owner ID, and the suggestion that the money is illicitly generated, i.e., a gambler's proceeds, etc.

- an agreement to share the money is made with the victim showing "good faith" (i.e., putting up money) by those involved. (Alternatively, a deal is made for all to put up money in a pool to be held by victim.)

- a switch is made while the victim is distracted, and his or her money is stolen by one of the confederates.

Street cons of this type are generally prosecuted under state fraud, false pretenses, and larceny statutes. Police in most jurisdictions have had experience with one or more such street con games.

Bibliographic references: 7,54

POLLUTION AND ENVIRONMENTAL PROTECTION VIOLATIONS--Many abuses in the environmental area involve more than violations of specific environmental/ pollution control statutes and orders. White-collar crime type abuses in this area consist primarily of the making or submitting of false statements concerning the degree of compliance with statutes and regulations for pollution control; and in order to cover up violations or lack of compliance with environmental standards. Falsification of test or sample data designed to measure compliance with standards represents another form of white-collar violation in this area.

See also: FALSE STATEMENTS

Bibliographic references: 19,74

PONZI SCHEMES--this is a general class of frauds in which the fraud operator uses money invested by later investor/victims to pay a high rate of return on the investments of earlier victims whose money he has already appropriated instead of making investments represented to them. Such schemes must inevitably collapse because it is mathematically impossible to continue them indefinitely. The length of time they can continue will depend upon the promised rate of return to investors, the amount of money the fraud operator takes out for himself, and the costs of inducing victims to part with their money (e.g., sales commissions). Many such frauds have cheated victims of millions of dollars; some have operated over a period of years.

Ponzi elements are to be found in many varieties of investment frauds, under different guises and in different variations; e.g., long-term investments, short-term business financing, etc.

These schemes have been federally prosecuted under the mail fraud statute, and as securities violations investigated by the U.S. Securities and

Exchange Commission. On the state level they would be violations of general fraud, false pretenses, and larceny statutes.

See also: INVESTMENT SCHEMES

Bibliographic references: 75

PRICE FIXING--illegal combinations by sellers to administer the price of a good or service depriving customers of a competitive marketplace, restraining competition and maintaining an artificial price structure.

Victims are customers of such combinations who are deprived of freely determined prices for the goods and services they purchase. Secondary victims may be competitors of the firms participating in the price fixing agreement.

Often when one thinks of price fixing, one thinks of a large nationwide conspiracy between industrial giants. While this is part of the problem, it is equally probable that many price fixing arrangements occur at the local level. For example, in Virginia the practice of a local bar association that set the price for title searches was held to be unlawful. In other locally-prosecuted cases, druggists have been adjudicated for fixing prices on prescription drugs.

Price-fixing violations are most often the subject of federal enforcement efforts, but are also proscribed by many state anti-trust statutes.

See also: ANTI-TRUST OFFENSES, RESTRAINT OF TRADE.

Bibliographic references: 37

PROCUREMENT AND CONTRACTING ABUSES--see COMPETITIVE PROCUREMENT ABUSES.

PUBLIC/OFFICIAL CORRUPTION--white-collar crime which generally falls into the category of abuse of trust-type violations involving commercial bribery, collusion with bid-rigging, avoidance of the competitive process in connection with the purchase of goods and services by governmental entities, self-dealing in connection with governmental purchases or grants of franchise to use public property, real estate variances, etc.

Most public corruption has its parallel in private sector. Thus conflict of interest is the public equivalent of Insider Self-Dealing; and there is little distinction between public and commercial bribery situations particularly where they overlap, such as in the government procurement area.

These violations are federally prosecuted under federal mail fraud and organized crime statutes. On the local level there are numerous statutory ---secution. involving bribery, taking of kickbacks, perjury, etc

See also: ABUSE OF TRUST, COMMERCIAL BRIBERY, COMPETITIVE PROCUREMENT FRAUDS, FRAUDS AGAINST GOVERNMENTAL PROGRAMS.

Bibliographic references: 2,52,65,67,76

PYRAMID SCHEME--the commercial version of the chain letter scheme, used by fraud operators in the selling of phony distributorships, franchises, and business opportunity plans.

See also: CHAIN REFERRAL SCHEMES, FRANCHISING FRAUDS, INVESTMENT FRAUDS.

Bibliographic references: 5,11,49,70

REFERRAL SALES SCHEMES--see CHAIN REFERRAL SCHEMES, MERCHANDISING SCHEMES.

REPAIR FRAUD--a form of consumer fraud involving repairs or maintenance services performed on consumer goods.

Such white-collar crime schemes generally involve:

- overcharging for services performed.

- charging for services and parts not used.

- performing services or repairs not wanted or needed.

- failing to perform services or repairs promised.

This is a major area for pro-active investigations, particularly decoy techniques (See Chapter IV, at page 176 of this manual). Where a sufficient pattern of deliberate violations have been developed, or the decoy technique successfully implemented, there have been convictions under state general fraud laws.

See also: CONSUMER FRAUD.

Bibliographic references: 89

RESTRAINT OF TRADE--actions, combinations or schemes which interfere with unfettered marketplace transactions. Examples are: price fixing, bribery and kickbacks for commercial advantage, interference with competitive bidding processes, dictation of price structure to customers or dealers; exclusive buying arrangements.

While the best known statutes in this area are federal in scope, many abuses occur in local jurisdictions and are subject to state or local remedies, especially when interstate commerce is not involved.

Many organized crime activities, aimed at monopolizing local markets to provide certain services or merchandise, may also involve restraints of trade and state anti-trust statutes should be reviewed to determine their applicability in such situations.

See also: COMMERCIAL BRIBERY, COMPETITIVE PROCUREMENT ABUSES, PRICE FIXING.

Bibliographic references: 28,37

SCAM--See BANKRUPTCY FRAUD.

SECURITIES FRAUD--fraudulent activities involving the sale, transfer, or purchase of securities or of money interests in the business activities of others.

Victims are generally securities investors who are not aware of the full facts regarding transactions they enter into.

Abuses cover a broad range, and can include, for example, situations where:

- businesses or promoters seek to raise capital unlawfully or without proper registration and oversight.

- securities of no value are sold, or are misrepresented to be worth far more than their actual value.

- purchasers are not advised of all facts regarding securities, and/or failure to file appropriate disclosures with federal and state regulatory agencies.

- insiders use special knowledge to trade in securities to the disadvantage of the general public which lacks such knowledge.

- broker-dealers and investment advisers act for their own benefit rather than for the benefit of their clients.

- false information is provided to security holders and the investing public in financial statements published or filed with securities regulatory agencies, or by payments to financial writers or publications

- manipulation of the price of securities by purchases and sales occurs in stock exchange or over-the-counter markets.

- there has been a failure to file registration or other reports with federal and state regulatory agencies.

Law enforcement agencies should be alert to the fact that securities violations potentially exist whereever investors rely on others to manage and conduct the business in which an investment is made. It is not necessary that there be any formal certificates such as stocks and bonds. Any form of investment agreement is potentially a "security."

This field is one where there is vigorous federal enforcement by the U.S. Securities Exchange Commission, and many outstanding examples of expert and zealous enforcement by state regulatory agencies. It is also an area where much support to local investigations is supplied by regional offices of the U.S. Securities and Exchange Commission.

See also: ADVANCE FEE SCHEMES, BOILER ROOMS, FALSE STATEMENTS, INSIDER SELF-DEALING, INVESTMENT FRAUDS.

Bibliographic references: 8,17,20,33,47,48,77,80

SELF-IMPROVEMENT SCHEMES--frauds which appeal to victims' desires to improve themselves personally or financially, by the acquisition of social or employment skills.

Schemes in this category tend to run on a continuum from improving purely personal/social skills and attributes to those tied to an individual's employment opportunities. On the personal end of the scale are the dance studio or charm school schemes; on the employment end of the scale are fraudulent job training schemes and advance fee employment agencies.

Somewhere in the middle are modeling agencies which purport both to improve the "person" and his other employment prospects; also courses on improving one's image or ability to communicate with others. Some business opportunity schemes which hold out the prospect of financial improvement plus "being a respected community businessman" also fall into this category by appealing to victim's desire to improve his or her finances and life style.

These abuses have been prosecuted under mail fraud and state fraud statutes, curbed by the U.S. Federal Trade Commission, and have also been the subject of enforcement efforts based on state and local legislation, licensing codes, and other codes governing the operation of schools or educational settings.

See also: BUSINESS OPPORTUNITY SCHEMES, EMPLOYMENT AGENCY FRAUDS, TALENT AGENCY FRAUDS, VANITY PUBLISHING.

Bibliographic references: 11,72

"SEWER" SERVICE--a term of art used to describe the kinds of activity noted below.

Many merchandising, home repair, and other frauds rely on the use of litigation for ultimate collections of proceeds of the fraud. Likewise, many enterprises which are not strictly speaking fraudulent, e.g., those which sell much overpriced merchandise on credit, similarly depend upon litigation or the threat of litigation to squeeze money from victims.

In both these situations devices are often adopted to fraudulently deprive victims of the opportunity to defend against such litigation--usually by not informing them that litigation has been initiated against them (i.e., dropping the summons or subpoena "down the sewer"). This is accomplished, usually, by false affidavits, filed in court, that a summons and complaint were served on the victim. Sometimes the litigation plaintiff is aware of the practice, sometimes he closes his eyes to what the process server is doing; in other instances the process server is making false affidavits to collect the fee for non-existent service, without the knowledge of the plaintiff or his attorney.

Such violations have been federally prosecuted for violation of the 1866 Civil Rights Act, but state violations are clearly present where false affidavits are filed in court.

Bibliographic references: 19

SHORT WEIGHTING OR LOADING--purposeful shorting of the volume or quantity of a cargo, accompanied by a false claim (invoice) demanding payment for the full amount.

Such frauds are easiest to perpetrate where the cargo is of such nature or bulk that it is difficult for the receiver to detect shortages. The reverse of the short weighting/loading fraud is often used as a modus operandi for diversions (thefts) of cargo. In this situation a transport vehicle is purposefully overloaded; the overage is not recorded (false statement by omission); and the overloaded amount forms the basis of kickbacks to scheme operators by the recipients of the shipments (often fences of stolen goods). Manipulation of the size or volume of loads must always be accompanied by false claims or false statements, since accompanying documentation or invoices do not reflect the fraudulent changes in the load size.

This violation involves either a false claim to a customer, or a plain and simple theft from the shipper. Since insiders are frequently involved, it will often involve commercial bribery, kickbacks, etc., as well as federal violations involving interstate shipment of stolen property.

See also: WEIGHTS AND MEASURES VIOLATIONS.

TALENT AGENCY SCHEMES--see SELF-IMPROVEMENT FRAUDS, VANITY PUBLISHING SCHEMES.

TAX AND REVENUE VIOLATIONS--perpetrated with the intent to deprive a taxing authority of revenues to which it is entitled or of information it needs in order to make a judgment regarding revenues to which it is entitled, or to avoid admission of involvement in illicit, though profitable, business activities.

Tax frauds may be perpetrated through the filing of false returns--as in personal income tax frauds; through the bribery of public officals--as may occur in property tax assessment frauds; or in the failure to file appropriately--as with an organized crime-figure who may not be concerned with avoiding tax liability but rather with revealing the sources of his taxable income. Many white-collar crimes obligate the offender to commit tax fraud because of illicitly obtained monies he does not wish to report, i.e., assets due to bribes, larcenies, kickbacks, or embezzlement proceeds. Common crimes, especially of a business nature, also result in tax violations: bookmaking, fencing of stolen goods (both income and sales tax abuses).

Tax avoidance through false statements may be a component of otherwise legitimate business enterprises, especially in areas of business and occupation taxes, inventory taxes, and sales taxes. Individuals and businesses will also seek to avoid or evade excise taxes; e.g., on cigarettes, substitution of low-taxed home heating oil for higher-taxed diesel fuel for trucks, etc.

Tax violations are usually prosecuted under special federal, state and local tax statutes.

Bibliographic references: 4,10,35,41,45,46,69

VANITY PUBLISHING SCHEMES--schemes which involve eliciting fees from individuals on the promise of promoting their creative "talents" (real or imaginary), or assisting them in the development of said "talent."

Such frauds rely upon the vanity of the victim (i.e., his or her belief that s/he has a creative talent that has not as yet been discovered.) Generally these schemes relate to creative endeavors in which clear performance standards regarding the talent are not available and are often a matter of taste, such as literary publishing, song writing, etc.

The scheme operator will imply a promise of national advertising, book reviews, distribution, special marketing services--but not so concretely that he will be held to any implied promise. The victims usually invest heavily, and lose both their money and their hopes--what they are left with are a few copies of a printed and scored song arrangement, or a number of copies of books which established book review publications have not troubled to look at because of their publishing source.

It should be kept in mind that there is a legitimate private publishing market. General principles of fraud analysis should be applied to determine whether or not the line has been crossed in ways which make misrepresentations fraudulent.

See also: SELF-IMPROVEMENT SCHEMES, TALENT AGENCY SCHEMES.

Bibliographic references: 11

WEIGHTS AND MEASURES VIOLATIONS--abusive practices involving the cheating of customers by failure to deliver prescribed quantities or amounts of desired goods. These violations usually involve false statements or claims in which the victim has relied on seller's representation of the delivered quantity in remitting higher payment.

Examples of such white-collar crimes are:

- gas pump meter manipulation to show more gas pumped than received by customer.

- butcher's thumb on the meat scale.

- odometer rollbacks in auto sales.

These frauds are most successful where one victim cannot easily verify weights or measuring devices himself, or where victim has no reason to question the seller's claim or statement; i.e., when products sold are bottled or packaged.

These abuses are usually detected on inspection by local agencies' personnel and prosecuted or enforced as violations of local ordinances. Purposeful, intentional, and continued activity of this kind should be considered as possibilities for violations of general fraud, false pretenses, and larceny statutes.

See also: SHORT WEIGHING OR LOADING.

Bibliographic references: 30

WELFARE FRAUD--abuses associated with government income and family subsidy programs.

Government welfare programs are always exploited by a small number of applicants who apply for benefits to which they are not entitled, or continue to claim eligibility when they no longer meet the established criteria for such aid.

Receipt of monies from claimants by officials processing welfare claims represents another dimension of this fraud area. Such monies may be solicited as kickbacks in exchange for inflated claims filed; as bribes to certify claimants who are ineligible or to avoid reporting claimants' ineligibility, or as extortion for processing claims to which recipient is fully eligible. In some cases non-existent recipients ("ghosts") may be created to fraudulently siphon money out of such programs.

These violations are enforced under both specific provisions of welfare legislation, and under general fraud statutes. Where federal funds are involved, there may be overlapping federal/state enforcement jurisdiction.

See also: FRAUDS AGAINST GOVERNMENT BENEFIT PROGRAMS.

WORK-AT-HOME SCHEMES--**see** BUSINESS OPPORTUNITY SCHEMES, FRANCHISE FRAUDS,
SELF-IMPROVEMENT FRAUDS.

APPENDIX C (Part 2)

BIBLIOGRAPHY OF WHITE-COLLAR CRIME
REFERENCE SOURCES

The reference sources listed below constitute a selected bibliography on white-collar crime and related abuses. They are divided into two lists. The first list contains sources of information on specific crimes for the investigator. Each of the references in this first list is preceded by a number and is keyed to items in the glossary above. The second list contains reference sources of a general nature which can provide the investigator with background and orientation information in the white-collar crime area. These latter sources are not numbered and are included to provide white-collar crime units with a general reference list. All of the references in this selected bibliography are in the public domain. Most can be found in public, university, or law school libraries. Others are available from the U.S. Government Printing Office, the Law Enforcement Assistance Administration, or the public agency or professional group which published them.

315

I. REFERENCE SOURCES RELATED TO SPECIFIC CRIMES

1. Allen, B. "Embezzler's Guide to the Computer," <u>Harvard Business Review</u>, 53:79, July, 1975.

2. American Bar Association. <u>Preventing Improper Influences on Federal Law Enforcement Agencies</u>. (A Report of the American Bar Association Special Committee to Study Federal Law Enforcement Agencies), 1976.

3. "Bait Advertising Scheme Held Violation of New York False Advertising Statute," <u>Columbia Law Review</u>, 59:958-961, June, 1959.

4. Balter, Henry G. "Plea Bargaining and the Tax Fraud Syndrome," <u>Taxes</u>, 52:333, June, 1974.

5. "Battling the Biggest Fraud: Pyramid Operations," <u>Time</u>, July 16, 1973, p. 51.

6. "Be Wary of Phony Business Brokers," <u>Changing Times</u>, November, 1955, pp. 29-32.

7. Bigham, B. "Pigeon Drop: The Con Game Aimed at Older Women," <u>Retirement Living</u>, 15:36-37, September, 1975.

8. Black, Hillel. <u>The Watchdogs of Wall Street</u>. New York: Morrow, 1962.

9. Bowley, G. F. "Law Enforcement's Role in Consumer Protection--Consumer Protection Symposium," <u>Santa Clara Lawyer</u> 14:447, Spring, 1974.

10. Caplin, Mortimer. "The I.R.S. Racketeers, and White Collar Crime," <u>American Bar Association Journal</u>, 62:865, July, 1976.

11. Carey, Mary, and George Sherman. <u>A Compendium of Bunk, or How to Spot a Con Artist</u>. Springfield, Ill.: Charles C. Thomas, 1976.

12. Cressey, Donald R. <u>Other People's Money: A Study in the Social Psychology of Embezzlement</u>. Belmont, California: Wadsworth, 1971.

13. "Crime in the Suites: C. Arnholt Smith's Fraud Involving U.S. National Bank," <u>Forbes</u>, 116:16, August 15, 1975.

14. "Criminal Law: Oklahoma Credit Card Crime Act of 1970--Dr. Leary I Presume?", <u>Oklahoma Law Review</u>, 28:622, Summer, 1975.

15. DeFranco, Edward J. <u>Anatomy of a Scam: A Case Study of a Planned Bankruptcy by Organized Crime</u>. Washington, D.C.: U.S. Government Printing Office, 1973.

16. DeWeese, J. T., "Trojan Horse Caper--and Assorted Other Computer Crimes," <u>Saturday Review World</u>, 3:10, November 15, 1975.

17. Dirks, Raymond L. and Leonard Gross. <u>The Great Wall Street Scandal</u>. New York: McGraw Hill, 1974.

18. Ducovny, Amram M. The Billion Dollar Swindle: Frauds Against the Elderly New York: Fleet Press Corporation, 1969.

19. Edelhertz, Herbert. The Nature, Impact, and Prosecution of White-Collar Crime. Washington, D.C.: U.S. Government Printing Office, 1970. Stock #027-000-00063-1.

20. "Equity Funding, Anatomy of a Swindle," Fortune Magazine, August, 1973.

21. Federal Trade Commission. Beware of "Bait and Switch" and Phony Business Opportunities.

22. Federal Trade Commission. Franchise Business Risks. Consumer Bulletin No. 4.

23. Federal Trade Commission. Franchising. Report of Ad Hoc Committee on. 1969.

24. Federal Trade Commission. Guides Against Bait Advertising. Adopted November 24, 1959.

25. Federal Trade Commission. Guides Against Debt Collection Deception. Adopted June 30, 1965, as amended June 14, 1968.

26. Federal Trade Commission. Truth in Lending and the Advertisement of Real Estate Credit. Division of Special Projects, Staff Guide.

27. Finch, James H. "Espionage and Theft Using Computers," Assets Protection, Winter, 1976, pp. 32-38.

28. Geis, Gilbert. "Deterring Corporate Crime," in Corporate Responsibility, Ralph Nader and Mark Green, eds., New York: Grossman, in press.

29. Givens. "Roadblocks to Remedy in Consumer Fraud Litigation," Case Western Law Review, 24:144, 149-150, 1972.

30. Gordon, Leland J. Weights, Measures, and the Consumer. Third National Survey of State Weights and Measures Legislation, Administration, and Enforcement. (By mail from CU, 256 Washington St., Mt. Vernon, NY 10550), 1969.

31. Grimes, John A. "Equity Funding: Fraud by Computer," American Federationist, 80:7, December, 1973.

32. Hoover, J. Edgar. "Investigation of Fraudulent Bankruptcies by the FBI." New York Certified Public Accountant, 32:187-94, March, 1962.

33. Hutchison, R. A. "Looting of I.O.S.," Fortune Magazine, 87:126-130, March, 1973.

34. I.A.C.P. Training Key #241. Insurance Fraud. A publication of the Professional Standards Division, Gaithersburg, Md., 1976.

35. "Income Tax Evasion: Dealing with IRS Special Agents and Prosecutors," Criminal Law Bulletin, 10:437, June, 1974.

36. Insurance Crime Prevention Institute, A Primer on Insurance Fraud, (1971),
     (from the Insurance Crime Prevention Institute, 21 Charles St., Westport,
     Conn. 06880).

37. Kefauver, Estes. In a Few Hands--Monopoly Power in America. Baltimore,
     Md.: Penguin Books, 1965.

38. "Kicking Back on Title Insurance: There Are a Few Defenders, But Outlawing
     the Practice is a Tough Political Job," Business Week, April 13, 1974,
     p. 97.

39. Kossack, Nathaniel E. and Sheldon Davidson. "Bankruptcy Fraud: The Unholy
     Alliance Moves In," Credit and Financial Management, 68:20-24, 68:28-32,
     April, 1966, and May, 1966.

40. Kossack, Nathaniel E. "Scam: The Planned Bankruptcy Racket," New York
     Certified Public Accountant, 35:417-423, June, 1965.

41. Kostelanetz, Boris. Tax Frauds. New York: Practising Law Institute,
     1975.

42. Kwitney, Jonathan. The Fountain Pen Conspiracy. New York: Alfred
     Knopf, 1973.

43. Leibholz, Stephen W. and Louis D. Wilson. Users Guide to Computer Crime.
     Radnor, Pa.: Chilton Book Company, 1974.

44. Lewis, Howard and Martha. The Medical Offenders. New York: Simon and
     Schuster, 1970.

45. Lofts, Robert L. and Nancy C. Tax Crimes: Evasion of Another's Tax and
     Defenses. Washington: Tax Management, 1973.

46. Maltz, Michael D., Herbert Edelhertz and Harvey H. Chamberlain. Law
     Enforcement Guide: Combatting Cigarette Smuggling. Washington, D.C.:
     U.S. Dept. of Justice, 1976. (From the Organized Crime Desk, Enforcement
     Division, Office of Regional Operations, Law Enforcement Assistance Admin-
     istration.)

47. Mathews, Arthur F. Enforcement and Litigation Under the Federal Securities
     Law. New York: Practising Law Institute, 1975.

48. Mathews, Arthur F. "Criminal Prosecutions Under the Federal Securities
     Laws and Related Statutes: The Nature and Development of SEC Criminal
     Cases," The George Washington Law Review, 39:901, July, 1971.

49. Maxa, Rudy. Dare to be Great. New York: Morrow, 1977.

50. McKnight, Gerald. Computer Crime: How a New Breed of Criminals is Making
     Off With Millions. New York: Walker, 1974.

51. Menkus, Belden. "Computerized Information Systems are Vulnerable to Fraud
     and Embezzlement," CPA Journal, 43:617-619, July, 1973.

52. Miller, Charles A. Economic Crime: A Prosecutor's Hornbook. A Project of the National District Attorneys Association, July, 1974.

53. Mitford, Jessica. The American Way of Death. New York: Simon and Schuster, 1963.

54. Nash, J. Robert. Hustlers and Con Men: An Anecdotal History of the Confidence Man and His Games. New York: M. Evans, distributed by Lippincott, 1976.

55. National Association of Attorneys General, Committee on the Office of Attorney General. State Antitrust Laws and Their Enforcement, 1974.

56. National Better Business Bureau, Inc. Debt Adjuster--Boon or Burden? Unregulated Pro-rating Companies Are Subject of Many Complaints. New York, 1955.

57. National Association of Credit Management. Preventing Business Fraud. New York, 1966.

58. "New Mexico's War on Land Frauds," Business Week, November 17, 1975, p. 49-50.

59. New York State Legislature. Joint Legislative Committee on Charitable and Philanthropic Agencies and Organizations. Report. Legislative Document No. 26, Albany, N.Y., 1954. Report. Legislative Document No. 70, Albany, N.Y., 1955.

60. "Official Report From Washington--Antitrust and the Proposed Revision of the Federal Criminal Law," ABA Antitrust Law Journal, 43:393, 1974.

61. O'Ryan, Liam. "How Insurance Firms Fight Fraudulent Accident Claims," Parade Magazine, September 19, 1976, pp. 24-26.

62. Parker, Donn P. Crime by Computer. New York: Charles Scribners Sons, 1976.

63. Parker, Donn P. "Profile of a Computer Criminal," Data Management, July, 1973, pp. 32-34.

64. Parker, Donn P., Susan Nycum, and S. Stephen Oüra. Computer Abuse. Menlo Park, California: Stanford Research Institute, 1973.

65. Pashigian, B. P. "On Control of Crime and Bribery," Journal of Legal Studies, 4:311, June, 1975.

66. Paulson, Morton C. The Great Land Hustle. Chicago: Henry Regnery Co., 1972.

67. Pennsylvania Crime Commission. Report on Organized Crime. Office of the Attorney General, 1970.

68. Pratt, Lester A. Bank Frauds, Their Detection and Prevention. New York: Ronald, 1965.

69. President's Commission on Law Enforcement and Administration of Justice. Task Force Report: Crime and Its Impact--An Assessment. Washington, D.C. U.S. Government Printing Office, 1967.

70. "Prohibiting Pyramid Sales Schemes: County, State, and Federal Approaches to a Persistent Problem," Buffalo Law Review, 24:877, Spring, 1975.

71. Randall, Donald A. and Arthur P. Glickman. The Great American Auto Repair Robbery. New York: Charterhouse, 1972.

72. Reid, Robert H. American Degree Mills. Washington, D.C.: The American Council on Education, 1959.

73. Robertson, Wyndham. "Those Daring Young Con Men of Equity Funding," Fortune, August, 1973, pp. 80-85.

74. "The Role of Michigan's Attorney General in Consumer and Environmental Protection," Michigan Law Review 72:1030, 1974.

75. Russell, F. "Bubble, Bubble, No Toil, No Trouble: C. Ponzi's Investment Swindles," American Heritage, 24:74-80, February, 1973.

76. Skinner, Samuel K. "Corruption," in Report of the National Conference on Organized Crime. Washington, D.C.: U.S. Department of Justice, Law Enforcement Assistance Administration, October, 1975, pp. 50-52.

77. Soble, Ronald L. and Robert E. Dallos. The Impossible Dream. The Equity Funding Story: The Fraud of the Century. New York: G. P. Putnam's Sons, 1975.

78. U.S. Congress. House Committee on Government Operations. Crimes Against Banking Institutions: Eighteenth Report (88:2), H. Rep. No. 1147. Washington, D.C.: U.S. Government Printing Office, February 20, 1964.

79. U.S. Congress. House. Committee on Government Operations. Subcommittee on Legal and Monetary Affairs. Crimes Against Banking Institutions: Hearing, October 15, 1963. (88:1.) Washington, D.C.: U.S. Government Printing Office, 1963.

80. U.S. Congress. House. Select Committee on Crime. Conversion of Worthless Securities into Cash. Washington, D.C.: U.S. Government Printing Office, 1973. Stock #5271-00339.

81. U.S. Congress. Senate. Special Committee on Aging. Subcommittee on Long Term Care. Nursing Home Care in the U.S.: Failure in Public Policy. Supporting Paper No. 2, Drugs in Nursing Homes: Misuse, High Costs, and Kickbacks. Washington, D.C.: U.S. Government Printing Office, January, 1975.

82. U.S. Congress. Senate. Special Committee on Aging. Subcommittee on Frauds and Misrepresentations Affecting the Elderly. Frauds and Quackery Affecting the Older Citizen: Hearings, January 15-17, 1963. 3 pts. (88:1) Washington, D.C.: U.S. Government Printing Office, 1963.

83. U.S. Congress. Senate. Special Committee on Aging. Subcommittee on Frauds and Misrepresentations Affecting the Elderly. Health Frauds and Quackery: Hearings, 4 pts. (88:2). Washington, D.C.: U.S. Government Printing Office, 1964.

84. U.S. Congress. Senate. Special Committee on Aging. Subcommittee on Frauds and Misrepresentations Affecting the Elderly. Interstate Mail Order Land Sales: Hearing, May 18-20, 1964. 3 pts. (88:2). Washington, D.C.: U.S. Government Printing Office, 1964.

85. U.S. Congress. Senate. Special Committee on Aging. Subcommittee on Frauds and Misrepresentations Affecting the Elderly. Preneed Burial Services: Hearing, May 19, 1964. (88:2) Washington, D.C.: U.S. Government Printing Office, 1964.

86. U.S. Congress. Senate. Special Committee on Aging, Subcommittee on Long-Term Care. Medicare and Medicaid Frauds. 4 pts. Pt. 1, Hearing, September 26, 1975. Part 2, Hearing, November 13, 1975. Part 3, Hearing, December 5, 1975. Part 4, February 16, 1976. Washington, D.C.: U.S. Government Printing Office.

87. U.S. Congress. Senate. Special Committee on Aging. Subcommittee on Long-Term Care. Fraud and Abuse Among Practitioners Participating in the Medicaid Program--A Staff Report. Washington, D.C.: U.S. Government Printing Office, August, 1976.

88. U.S. Congress. Senate. Select Committee on Small Business. Criminal Redistribution Systems and Their Economic Impact on Small Business. Based on Hearings before the Committee May 1 and 2, 1973, April 30 and May 2, 1974. Washington, D.C.: U.S. Government Printing Office, 1974.

89. Vaughan, Diane and Giovanna Carlo. "The Appliance Repairman: A Study of Victim-Responsiveness and Fraud," Journal of Research in Crime and Delinquency July, 1975, pp. 153-161.

II. GENERAL REFERENCE SOURCES

American Bar Association. "A Symposium, White-Collar Crime," The American Criminal Law Review, Summer, 1973.

Bailey, F. Lee, and Henry Rothblatt. Defending Business and White Collar Crime, Federal and State. Rochester, N.Y.: Lawyers Co-op Publishing Company, 1969.

Blum, Richard. Deceivers and Deceived. Springfield, Ill.: Thomas, 1972.

Butler, Robert N. "Why Are Older Consumers So Susceptible?", Geriatrics, December, 1968, pp. 83-88.

Caplovitz, David. "The Merchant and the Low Income Consumer," in The White-Collar Criminal, edited by Gilbert Geis, New York: Atherton Press, 1968.

Caplovitz, David. The Poor Pay More: Consumer Practices of Low-Income Families. New York: Free Press of Glencoe, 1963.

Carey, Mary and George Sherman. A Compendium of Bunk or How to Spot a Con Artist. Springfield, Ill.: Thomas, 1976.

Carper, Jean. Not with a Gun. New York: Grossman Publishers, 1973.

Chamber of Commerce of the United States. White Collar Crime, Everyone's Problem, Everyone's Loss. 1974.

Chamber of Commerce of the United States of America. Deskbook on Organized Crime. 1972.

Clinard, Marshall B. The Black Market: A Study of White Collar Crime. Montclair, N.J.: Patterson Smith, 1972 (paperback edition).

Coates, Joseph F. "The Future of Crime in the United States from Now to the Year 2000," Policy Sciences, 3:27-45, 1972.

Cressey, Donald R. Theft of the Nation: The Structure and Operation of Organized Crime in America. New York: Harper and Row, 1969.

Curnow, David P. "Economic Crimes: A High Standard of Care," Federal Bar Journal, 35:21, 1976.

Curtis, S. J. "Focus on the Future: A Look at Business Crime Today and Tomorrow," Police, 8:25-27, November-December, 1963; 20-24, January-February, 1964.

Edelhertz, Herbert. The Nature, Impact and Prosecution of White-Collar Crime. Washington, D.C.: U.S. Government Printing Office, 1970. Stock #027-000-00063-1.

"FBI Investigation of Fraud," Journal of Accountancy, 120:34-39, July, 1965.

Federal Trade Commission Staff Report. Economic Report on Food Chain Selling Practices in D.C. and San Francisco. 1969.

Finn, Peter and Alan R. Hoffman. Exemplary Projects: Prosecution of Economic Crime. Washington, D.C.: U.S. Government Printing Office, 1976.

Geis, Gilbert. "Criminal Penalties for Corporate Criminals," Criminal Law Bulletin, August, 1972, pp. 377-92.

Geis, Gilbert and Herbert Edelhertz. "Criminal Law and Consumer Fraud: A Sociolegal view," American Criminal Law Review, 11:989, 1973.

Geis, Gilbert. "Victimization Patterns in White Collar Crime," in Victimology Vol. 5, Exploiters and Exploited: Dynamics of Victimization, I. Drapkin and E. Viano, Eds., Lexington, Mass.: D. C. Heath, 1975, pp. 89-105.

Geis, Gilbert. The White Collar Criminal. New York: Atherton Press, 1968.

Geis, Gilbert. "White-Collar Crime," in Handbook of Criminology, Daniel Glaser, ed., New York: Rand McNally, in press.

George, B. James, Jr. White Collar Crimes: Defense and Prosecution. New York: Practising Law Institute, 1971.

Gibney, Frank. The Operators. New York: Harper and Brothers, 1960.

Glick, Rush and Robert S. Newsom. Fraud Investigation Fundamentals for Police Springfield, Ill.: Charles C. Thomas, 1974.

Hartung, Frank E. "The White-Collar Thief," in Delinquency, Crime, and Social Process, D. R. Cressey and David A. Ward, eds., New York: Harper and Row, 1969.

Horn, J. "Portrait of an Arrogant Crook: Studying White-Collar Criminals and Their Victims," Psychology Today, April, 1976.

Jester, Jean C. An Analysis of Organized Crime's Infiltration into Legitimate Business. Huntsville, Texas: Institute of Contemporary Corrections and the Behavioral Sciences, Sam Houston State University, 1974.

Kahn, E. J. Fraud. New York: Harper and Row, 1973.

Kahn, E. J. Fraud: The U.S. Postal Inspection Service and Some of the Fools and Knaves It Has Known. New York: Harper and Row, 1973.

Kwan, Quon Y. and others. "The Role of Criminalistics in White Collar Crime," Journal of Criminal Law, Criminology, and Police Science, 62:437, 1971.

Langway, L. and P. Moreland. "Patent Hustle: Idea Promoters Cited by the FTC for Consumer Fraud," Newsweek, September 8, 1975.

Lipson, Milton. On Guard: The Business of Private Security. New York: Quadrangle/The New York Times Book Co., 1975.

323

Maurer, David W. The Big Con. New York: Bobbs Merill Co., 1962.

Maurer, David W. The American Confidence Man. Springfield, Ill.: Thomas, 1974.

Miller, Charles A. Economic Crime: A Prosecutor's Hornbook. A project of the National District Attorneys Association, July, 1974.

Morgenthau, Robert M. "Equal Justice and the Problem of White Collar Crime," The Conference Board Record, August, 1969, pp. 17-20.

Nash, J. Robert. Hustlers and Con Men: An Anecdotal History of the Confidence Man and His Games. New York: M. Evans, dist. by Lippincott, 1976.

National Association of Attorneys General. Prosecuting Organized Crime, 1974.

National Association of Attorneys General. "Help, Help! Or Why FTC Seeks Aid of the Attorneys General in Combating Consumer Deception and Unfair Competition," by Gale P. Gotschall, September 2, 1966. Reprinted: Congressional Record, September 30, 1966: 23729-30.

National District Attorneys Association. Fighting the $40 Billion Rip-Off: An Annual Report from the Economic Crime Project, U.S. Dept. of Justice, L.E.A.A., 1976.

National Retired Teachers Association/American Association of Retired Persons. Proceedings of the National Forum on the Consumer Concerns of Older Americans. Washington, D.C.: Consumer Office, NRTA/AARP, 1975.

Newman, Donald J. "White Collar Crime," Law and Contemporary Problems, 37:735.

Office of Consumer Affairs. Executive Office of the President. Consumer Education Bibliography. Washington, D.C.: U.S. Government Printing Office, September, 1971.

Office of the United States Attorney General, Southern District of New York. A Handbook on How to Combat Crime in the Business World. December, 1972.

Ogren, Robert W. "The Ineffectiveness of the Criminal Sanction in Fraud and Corruption Cases: Losing the Battle Against White-Collar Crime," American Criminal Law Review, November, 1973.

President's Commission on Law Enforcement and Administration of Justice. Task Force Report: Organized Crime. Washington, D.C.: U.S. Government Printing Office, 1967.

President's Commission of Law Enforcement and Administration of Justice. Task Force Report: Crime and Its Impact--An Assessment. Washington, D.C.: U.S. Government Printing Office, 1967.

Prior, James T. "White Collar Crime: Nemesis of Business," New Jersey Business, 20:30, September, 1973.

Reckless, Walter C. The Crime Problem. New York: Appleton-Century-Crofts, 1973, 5th edition. (Chapter 13: White Collar Crime.)

"The Role of California's Attorney General and District Attorneys in Protecting the Consumer," University of California Davis Law Review, 4:35, 1971.

"The Role of Michigan's Attorney General in Consumer and Environmental Protection," Michigan Law Review 72:1030, 1974.

Rothschild, David and Bruce C. Throne. "Criminal Consumer Fraud: A Victim Oriented Analysis," Michigan Law Review, March, 1976, pp. 661-708.

Seymour, Whitney. "Social and Ethical Considerations in Assessing White Collar Crime," American Criminal Law Review 11:821, 1972.

Steele, Eric H. "Fraud, Dispute, and the Consumer: Responding to Consumer Complaints," University of Pennsylvania Law Review, 123:1107-86, May, 1975. Reprinted: Research Contributions of the American Bar Foundation, No. 4, 1975.

Sutherland, Edwin H. White Collar Crime. New York: Holt, Rinehart, and Winston, 1961.

Tompkins, Dorothy Campbell. White Collar Crime--A Bibliography. Berkeley, California: Institute of Governmental Studies, University of California, Berkeley, 1967.

U.S. Department of Commerce. Crimes Against Business, A Management Perspective. Proceedings of Seminars Held in Los Angeles, California, February 3, 1976, and San Francisco, California, February 5, 1976. Washington, D.C.: U.S. Government Printing Office, May, 1976.

"White Collar Crime: Huge Economic and Moral Drain," Congressional Quarterly, May 7, 1971.

APPENDIX D

The Seventh Basic Investigative Technique
Analyzing Financial Transactions in the
Investigation of Organized Crime and White
Collar Crime Targets

by

Richard A. Nossen

THE SEVENTH BASIC INVESTIGATIVE TECHNIQUE

Analyzing Financial Transactions
in the
Investigation of Organized Crime
and
White Collar Crime Targets

Author:
Richard A. Nossen, Consultant,
Criminal Justice Systems—White Collar Crime
Investigative Techniques

I

FOREWORD

This handbook, entitled, The Seventh Basic Investigative Technique, was prepared to meet repeated recommendations made formally and informally by key speakers, panel members, workshop group leaders and participants at the October, 1975 National Conference on Organized Crime. Their recommendations strongly urged the Federal Government to develop training materials geared to the needs of law enforcement officials in the area of tracing financial transactions entered into by organized crime and white collar crime figures.

The handbook highlights an approach to the investigation of organized crime and white collar crime targets by criminal investigators that was introduced to and enthusiastically received by state and local law enforcement officials who attended a series of LEAA regional conferences on organized crime beginning in 1970 at Zion, Illinois, and culminating at the February, 1972, conference at San Diego, California.

The handbook was prepared by Mr. Richard A. Nossen, a Criminal Justice Systems Consultant, who, while serving as Assistant Director of the Intelligence Division and in other subordinate positions with the U. S. Internal Revenue Service, developed and presented the concept of applying financial investigation techniques to criminal investigations at the series of organized crime training conferences mentioned in the preceding paragraph.

This publication, which is another direct outgrowth of the proceedings of the National Conference on Organized Crime, is but one of many attempts being made by LEAA to meet their commitment to local law enforcement, mandated in the primary objectives of the NCOC, i.e.,

"To present the current state-of-the-art in organized crime control for the information and education of state and local criminal justice and public organizations whose activities and support are necessary in controlling the problem of organized criminal activity nationwide."

The handbook will accordingly be distributed to all NCOC participants and will be included as an appendix to the Investigator's Manual presently being prepared by the Battelle Memorial Institute under an LEAA grant. It will also be available in the library of the National Institute of Law Enforcement and Criminal Justice.

It is our sincere hope that this latest investigative tool, added to the arsenal of other training materials developed and furnished to law enforcement officials by LEAA, will lead to further successes in our mutual efforts to control Organized Crime and White Collar Crime in the United States.

Richard W. Velde
Administrator

TABLE OF CONTENTS

TABLE OF CONTENTS

CHAPTER I

Introduction To The Seventh Basic Investigative Technique

For countless years, criminal investigators have relied on six basic investigative techniques to solve crimes; i.e., (1) the development of informants, (2) use of undercover agents, (3) laboratory analysis of physical evidence, (4) physical and electronic surveillance, (5) interrogation, and (6) where permitted by law, wiretapping. Each of these techniques has resulted in varying degrees of success.

The purpose of this handbook is to introduce to criminal investigators, on a broad scale, an investigative tool, a seventh basic investigative technique, used primarily in the investigation of violations of the Federal income tax laws. This tool, if properly applied, can greatly enhance the success of the investigation of cases where illegal profits and a greed for wealth are the principle motives of the violators.

Excluding crimes of passion, it is difficult to isolate a motive for crime other than monetary gain. Racketeers who violate the narcotic laws, engage in hijacking, fencing, shylocking, gambling, prostitution rings, etc., as well as white collar type criminals engaged in more subtle crimes such as commercial bribery, political corruption, etc., are motivated by the same common denominator — a desire for financial gain and the power that it commands.

It follows, therefore, that if money is the primary motive behind the crimes committed by both racketeer and white-collar type criminals, the use of the Seventh Basic Investigative Technique must be added to the skills of criminal investigators to ensure optimum success in their ultimate prosecution.

All too often in the past, criminal investigators have been reluctant to broaden the scope of their investigations into the financial area, thereby sacrificing the potential evidentiary value of leads that may have been successfully developed if properly explored. This reluctance is understandable, and was caused, in part, by an inhibition that has existed for years among criminal investigators that financial transactions, for the most part, were difficult to investigate unless the investigators had an accounting background. Rather than take positive action to overcome this inhibition, many criminal investigators took a negative approach and merely dismissed the need to investigate financial leads by rationalizing their minimal evidentiary value.

1

As a result of this general reluctance to probe the financial activities of the racketeer — white collar crime element, an attitude has developed among criminal investigators that if the six basic investigative techniques do not result in a successful investigation, drop the investigation or, perhaps, turn the information over to IRS; in the mistaken belief that IRS agents have a monopoly on the capabilities necessary to develop evidence relating to financial transactions.

On the contrary, it is the writer's experience, shared by many others with similar investigative backgrounds, that all criminal investigators, at the Federal, state and local level, can and, when appropriate, should investigate financial leads and analyze financial transactions in the same competent and professional manner as demonstrated by their development of interrogation skills, networks of informants and the overall application of investigative innovativeness that they have so ably utilized in the successful investigation of organized crime and white collar crime cases in the past.

The following chapters in the handbook, therefore, were developed to provide journeymen criminal investigators with the tools necessary to explore, develop and carefully follow financial transactions engaged in by the targets of their investigations with complete confidence that they will soon master the technique. While the application of these techniques is not expected to wipe out the racketeer-white collar type criminal element engaged in crimes that are "money motivated," there is every reason to believe that, properly used, the "seventh basic investigative technique" can and will become another major weapon in the control of organized and white collar crime.

In studying the following chapters, it is imperative to keep in mind the primary objective of all criminal investigators; that is, to develop adequate credible evidence against targets that will not only convince prosecutors that prosecutive action is warranted; but will enable them to successfully present the evidence to grand juries and to the Courts.

It is the author's view, based on his own experience and on his association with judges and prosecutors throughout the United States over a period of more than two decades, that they are far more favorably impressed with evidence, such as that reflected in the following chapters of this Handbook, than with speculation that many investigators, at all levels of Government, have too often engaged in for too long, using

2

such tired old phrases as A is "tied in" with B and C "meets frequently" with D; all of which adds up in the minds of prosecutors as so much trivia.

It takes <u>evidence</u> to get a conviction, and in the area of today's organized and white collar type crimes, the need to gather evidence of targets' financial transactions has become critical.

For the purposes of this Handbook, the title, criminal investigator, includes all Federal, state and local investigative personnel charged with responsibility to investigate violations of criminal statutes, who have <u>not</u> utilized investigative accounting techniques in the investigation of financial crimes; including, but not limited to, agents of the Department of the Treasury and the Department of Justice at the Federal level, as well as investigators on the staffs of state attorneys' general, county district attorneys' investigators hired by or assigned to grand juries and crime commissions and members of state, county and city police departments.

CHAPTER II

Application of the Net-Worth-Expenditures Principle

Definition

Before explaining how the net worth-expenditures principle can be used in the investigation of racketeer and white collar crime targets, it is necessary to clearly define the principle.

The net worth-expenditures principle, as used in this handbook, is a mathematical computation designed to determine the total accumulation of wealth and annual expenditures made by an individual. The principle has been used for many years by the U. S. Internal Revenue Service for the purpose of determining taxpayers income tax liabilities, primarily in those instances where no books or records of income and expenses have been maintained by taxpayers from which a determination of tax liability could be made.

The use of this principle by the IRS in making a civil determination of taxpayers' income, has been upheld by the U. S. Supreme Court. The principle has also been upheld by the Supreme Court when used to establish one of the elements of proof of criminal tax fraud, i.e., that a taxpayer has, in fact, understated his income, upon which an additional tax is due and owing.

The net worth and expenditures computation, when used by IRS to determine tax liabilities for either civil or criminal purposes, is complex. However, the complexity is caused not by the net worth principle, itself, but by the fact that the computations must be made, taking into account the highly complex tax laws. In other words, adjustments have to be made to ensure that tax liabilities, computed by the application of the net worth principle, take into account the effect of the receipt, by taxpayers, of non taxable, or partially taxable income.

The use of the net worth and expenditures principle by criminal investigators for the purpose outlined herein is not as complex and can be developed with comparative ease. It can be applied effectively in criminal investigations without regard to the tax laws, whatsoever.

Application

The net worth-expenditures principle can be applied, when appropriate, to: (1) gather intelligence, (related to financial transactions), (2) enhance the successful interrogation of a target, (3) corroborate other evidence of a crime for the purpose of presenting facts to, (a) the district attorney for his consideration, (b) a grand jury, or (c) a trial jury, or to the Court in the event of a bench trial, (4) assist in determining whether a target is engaged in other crimes, (5) determine havens where a target may be hiding assets, and, (6) to identify or locate assets for restitution or collection of fines.

The computation can be presented in two formats. One is commonly referred to as a "Net worth-Expenditure Schedule;" the other is perhaps more readily recognized as a schedule of "Source and Application of Funds." Either format will produce, essentially, the same result: The net worth format should normally be used when a target's spending habits appear to include the acquisition and disposal of real estate, jewelry, furs, bank accounts, life insurance policies having a cash value and periodic reductions of mortgage loans. The source and application of funds schedule is normally used when a target's expenditures have been of a more transient nature, such as for high personal living expenses.

Illustrations of both schedules, based on the same hypothetical practical exercise, are contained in the following chapter.

CHAPTER III

Practical Exercise

Factual Situation

Target "A" has been identified over a period of years as being involved in major fencing operations. While he has been the subject of frequent investigations he has successfully avoided indictment. His ownership of a retail furniture store, which investigators are convinced is a cover, has successfully shielded his fencing operation. A warehouse, allegedly maintained as a storage facility for furniture and other merchandise related to his retail operation, is located so as to make physical surveillance difficult. Allegations and raw intelligence have failed to meet the test for probable cause to obtain a search warrant.

One of the investigators assigned to Intelligence has gained the confidence of Target "A's" bookkeeper, who informed the investigator that the Target's furniture store is generating only nominal profits; that she has access to copies of his annual profit and loss statements and balance sheets for the past four years prepared by the Target's accountant and overheard the Target inform his accountant that the profit and loss statements of the furniture store operation reflected his sole source of income. She voluntarily furnished the investigator with copies of the profit and loss statements and balance sheets for the years 1972 through 1975.

The profit and loss statements disclosed net profits of $14,000, $16,250, $11,750 and $14,375 for the years 1972 through 1975, respectively. The balance sheets disclosed a balance in the Target's capital account of $15,000 for each of the years 1972 through 1975, respectively. No additional investments were made since the Target made his initial investment in the business in 1972. Earnings, reflected above, have been withdrawn from the business each year.

A realistic factual background accordingly exists which would warrant the application of investigative resources to explore the "Seventh Basic Investigative Technique."

Investigative Steps

Through physical surveillance the investigator observes the Target enter Bank "A". Upon making inquiry at the bank, the investigator learns that the Target has a commercial account and safe deposit box and that he obtained a Bank Americard through the same bank.

7

Safe Deposit Box

The investigator obtained a copy of the safe deposit box contract filed with the bank by the Target at the time he applied for the safe deposit box rental. The contract, shown below, (Illustration 1), not only discloses a physical description of the Target and an exemplar of his handwriting, but contains other pertinent background information as well:

Illustration 1

No.	
SAFE DEPOSIT-INDIVIDUAL	
LESSEE	
DEPUTY	
DATE OF CONTRACT	RENT $
PASSWORD	
	LESSEE
	DEPUTY
	DEPUTY

Illustration 1

_____ 19 _____ hereby designate

and appoint _____

as _____ deputy and agent, to have access to the box covered by this contract. To take and remove from or add to the contents thereof, and have full and absolute control over the same, hereby waiving any liability of the lessor, arising out of the exercise, by the said deputy, or any of the powers herein contained.

_____
Lessee

_____
Lessee

Deputy

Witness: _____

_____
Address of Deputy

The Appointment Of The Above Deputy Is Hereby

Revoked _____ 19 _____

_____
Lessee

Witness: _____

_____ 19 _____ hereby designate

and appoint _____

as _____ deputy and agent, to have access to the box covered by this contract. To take and remove from or add to the contents thereof, and have full and absolute control over the same, hereby waiving any liability of the lessor, arising out of the exercise, by the said deputy, or any of the powers herein contained.

_____
Lessee

_____
Lessee

Deputy

Witness: _____

_____
Address of Deputy

The Appointment Of The Above Deputy Is Hereby

Revoked _____ 19 _____

_____
Lessee

Witness: _____

Identification

Name	Name	Name
Residence	Residence	Residence
Phone	Phone	Phone
Firm	Firm	Firm
Address	Address	Address
Phone	Phone	Phone
Mothers Maiden Name	Mothers Maiden Name	Mothers Maiden Name
Color Of Hair	Color Of Hair	Color Of Hair
Color Of Eyes	Color Of Eyes	Color Of Eyes
Height	Height	Height
Weight	Weight	Weight
Remarks	Remarks	Remarks

Each time an individual enters his safe deposit box, he is required to sign an entry slip, (Illustration 2), shown below:

Illustration 2

ENTRY SLIP

The undersigned lessee or authorized deputy desires access to safe deposit box.

Signature

_____
Lessee or Deputy

Booth No.	Attended By	Box No.

14-0007

The entry slip discloses the date and time of day that an individual enters his safe deposit box. It is usually stamped on the reverse side in order that the individual's signature can be identified. This information can be of inestimable value to an investigation since the dates of entry into a safe deposit box may reconcile with the dates of other cash financial transactions. (This will be illustrated in subsequent paragraphs). The information can also be used by an investigator to contradict a target's alibi as to his whereabouts during a key interrogation or by a prosecutor during cross examination of a target at trial.

The record of entries into a safe deposit box should, accordingly, be obtained on every target whose financial transactions are being investigated and those targets on whom "financial intelligence" is being gathered.

The record retention period for safe deposit box entries varies among banks. However, many banks continue to retain the records well beyond the scheduled destruction date due to the limited storage space they require and the cost of manpower to meet record destruction schedules. In any event, the information should be obtained as quickly as possible; as soon as a target is placed under financial investigation or identified as a suspect on whom intelligence is to be gathered.

10

The record of entries by the target into his safe deposit box, for the purpose of this exercise, is shown in Illustration 3 below: (This particular bank's entry record form provides for a four year record, however, only two years are illustrated below).

Illustration 3

BOX NO.																NAME OF LESSEE																	

RECORD OF VISITS — SAFE DEPOSIT

REMINGTON RAND   131   CAT. NO. 1-1321.2   KP 28476

1974	1	2	3	4	5	6	7	8	9	10	11	12	13	14	15	1974	16	17	18	19	20	21	22	23	24	25	26	27	28	29	30	31	T
JAN																JAN																	
FEB																FEB																	
MAR																MAR																	
APR																APR																	
MAY																MAY																	
JUNE												✔				JUNE																	
JULY																JULY																	
AUG																AUG																	
SEPT															✔	SEPT																	
OCT																OCT																	
NOV																NOV																	
DEC																DEC																	

1975	1	2	3	4	5	6	7	8	9	10	11	12	13	14	15	1975	16	17	18	19	20	21	22	23	24	25	26	27	28	29	30	31	T
JAN																JAN																	
FEB																FEB						✔											
MAR																MAR						✔											
APR					✔											APR																	
MAY																MAY								✔									
JUNE																JUNE	✔				✔							✔					
JULY		✔														JULY																	
AUG																AUG																	
SEPT																SEPT																	
OCT																OCT																	
NOV																NOV																	
DEC																DEC																	

	1	2	3	4	5	6	7	8	9	10	11	12	13	14	15		16	17	18	19	20	21	22	23	24	25	26	27	28	29	30	31	T

Checking Account

Illustration 4, shown below, is a copy of the signature card relating to the target's checking account. This card, again, furnished the investigator with an exemplar of the target's handwriting as well as background information of interest.

Illustration 4

PERSONAL DDA SIGNATURE CARD

☐ JOINT
☐ INDIVIDUAL

_____
ACCOUNT NUMBER

Please STAMP Bank Name Here

1	Account Name	SEAL
2	Account Name	SEAL
	Social Security Number	SEAL

I (we) the above-signed, have been provided with and have read the rules and regulations of Bank governing this account and agree to be bound by the provisions thereof, and as they shall, from time to time, be amended by the Bank.

If two or more signatures appear above, each agrees that all moneys, checks and other instruments for payment of money at any time deposited in this account are and will be their joint property during their joint lives and upon the death of either of them the entire right, title and interest therein shall vest absolutely in the surivior; that at any time the balance in this account shall be subject to withdrawal, transfer or other disposition, in whole or in part, by either of them, or the duly constituted attorney of either of them without duty of inquiry on your part; that payment to, or by order of, either of them, or the duly constituted attorney of either of them, shall be full discharge to you for such payment, whether the other be living, incompetent or deceased; that you shall be authorized to make payment in accordance with the terms hereof, not withstanding any notice or demand which may be given by or on behalf of either of them to the contrary. The Bank is authorized to off-set the balance, without notice, against the indebtedness of any one or more of us to the Bank; and to send all statements, notices and vouchers to the address from time to time furnished the Bank.

| Date Opened | Opened by | Approved by | Branch |
| Amount of Initial Deposit | Type of Deposit | | Reference Checked |

• **PLEASE PRINT**

☐ SEND MAIL TO ☐	Home Address	City, State, Zip Code		Telephone & Area Code
	Employer		Position	Yrs. there
	Employer's Address	City, State, Zip Code		Telephone & Area Code

Bank Reference		Other Reference	
Account Number	Type of Account		Telephone Number
Street Address		Street Address	
City State Zip Code		City State Zip Code	

Personal I.D.	
Driver's License Number	State
Charge Account Number	Type

Illustration 5, shown below, is a copy of the target's monthly bank statement for the month of June, 1975, which was also obtained from the bank. (Copies of the statements showing "year end" bank balances for the years 1972 through 1975 were also obtained for the purpose of completing the net worth computations. While they are not included as Illustrations, they show balances in the amounts of $300, $1100, $3600, and $4300 at the end of the years 1972 through 1975, respectively).

Illustration 5

CHECKING STATEMENT

Beginning Date	Ending Date	Account Number	Dial	For Information Regarding Your Account
6-2-75	6-30-75	00-000-000	788-2823	

TARGET

Balance Last Statement	We Have Added			We Have Subtracted			Resulting	Items Enclosed
	Number	Deposits Totaling	Number	Items Totaling		Service Charge	In A Balance Of	
933 83	3	26 500 00	10	26 021 00		1	1412 83	10

CK = Check DB = Other Debts CR = Other Credits SC = Service Charge BA = BankAmericard Charge
LS = List DP = Deposit MC = Miscellaneous Charge (—) = Overdrawn Account BC = Blue Chip Charge

Date	Checks/Debits	Checks/Debits	Deposits/Credits	Balance
6/6	200.00		400.00	1133.83
6/6			1100.00	2233.83
6/9	175.00			2058.83
6/12	90.00			1968.83
6/13	110.00			1858.83
6/16			25000.00	26858.83
6/17	80.00			26778.83
6/18		25000.00		1778.83
6/20	18.00			1760.83
6/23	93.00			1667.83
6/24	185.00			1482.83
6/26	70.00			1412.83

The bank statement discloses that the Target made a $25,000 deposit on June 16, 1975.

A comparison of the dates of large deposits and withdrawals shown on the Target's bank statement with the dates of entries by the Target into his safe deposit box, shows that he entered his safe deposit box on the same day that he made the $25,000 deposit to his commercial bank account.

The "inference" that the Target removed $25,000 in currency from his safe deposit box and deposited it to his bank account is supported by an examination of the bank's microfilm copy of the Target's deposit slip, (shown below in Illustration 6), which shows that the $25,000 deposit was made with currency.

Illustration 6

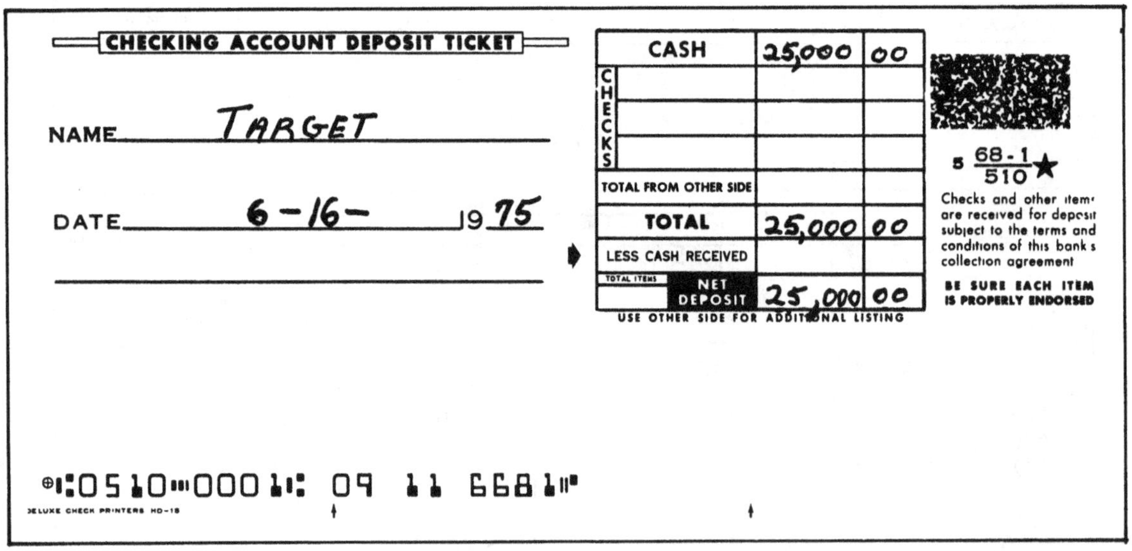

CHECKING ACCOUNT DEPOSIT TICKET

NAME TARGET

DATE 6-16- 1975

CASH	25,000	00
CHECKS		
TOTAL FROM OTHER SIDE		
TOTAL	25,000	00
LESS CASH RECEIVED		
TOTAL ITEMS / NET DEPOSIT	25,000	00

USE OTHER SIDE FOR ADDITIONAL LISTING

5 68-1/510

Checks and other items are received for deposit subject to the terms and conditions of this bank's collection agreement

BE SURE EACH ITEM IS PROPERLY ENDORSED

⑆0510⑆000 1⑆ 09 11 6681⑈

DELUXE CHECK PRINTERS HD-18

A schedule, comparing the dates of large bank deposits and with-drawals, as well as the dates and amounts of all other large financial transactions, with the dates of entries into a target's safe deposit box should _always_ be made. Among other things, it assists the investigator in establishing a possible pattern engaged in by a target in making financial transactions and, as mentioned earlier in this chapter, can be used during the investigatory interrogation process as a psychological tool to demonstrate how much the investigator already knows about the target or during trial for a variety of purposes.

Illustration 5 also shows that $25,000 was withdrawn from the Target's bank account on June 18, 1975.

The investigator obtained a microfilm copy of the Target's check from the bank, (see Illustration 7 below).

Illustration 7

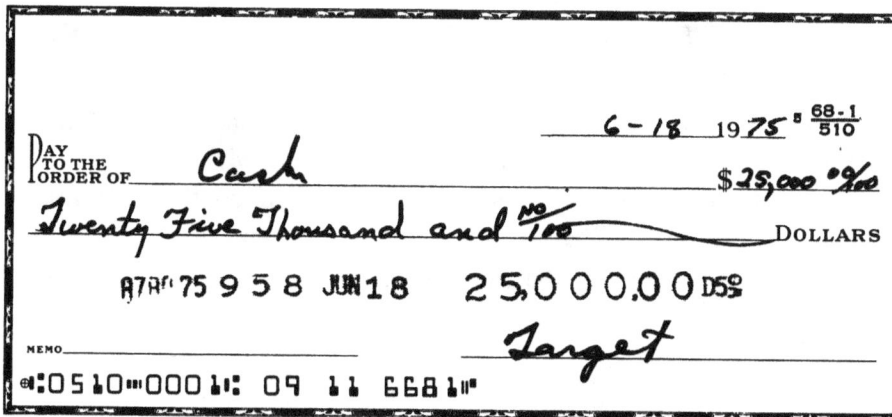

The code numbers and date, stamped on the face of the check shows that it was cashed by the Target.

All banks use a series of codes or symbols, which they usually stamp or imprint on the face of a check to show that it was "cashed." The codes used by some of the major banks in principal geographic areas are shown in Illustration 19, Chapter IV.

The next logical investigative step, in an attempt to trace the dis-position of the $25,000, is to examine the bank's "cashier's check" records. _A cashier's check can be purchased from any bank in most any amount. The check is issued by the bank on its own funds and is signed_ by one of the bank's officers. At the time of purchase the bank inserts the date and the name of the payee.

Cashier's checks are used frequently by the racketeer and white collar crime element in the mistaken belief that their expenditures may escape detection since the names of the purchasers do not appear on the face of the checks. Cashier's checks have the added advantage to the criminal engaged in large financial transactions, (legal and illegal), of avoiding carrying large amounts of currency, usually a high risk element when dealing with their own kind.

Cashier's checks, of course, _can_ be traced. Purchasers _can_ be identified. But _only_ if the investigator is thorough, touches all bases, and makes the necessary inquiries to determine if a target has used the cashier's check technique in an attempt to conceal his expenditures.

In the example in this chapter the investigator made the necessary inquiries and learned that the Target purchased three cashier's checks on June 18, 1975, in the amounts of $10,000, $10,000 and $5,000, payable to Stockbroker "A".

The bank teller's "daily proof sheet," an internal record of the bank, shows that the cashier's checks were purchased with currency.

One of the three checks is shown below and on the following page in Illustration 8. (There is no need to illustrate all three of the checks as they all contain the same endorsement as explained in the following paragraph).

BANK "A"	1- 59198
	June 18, 1975 $\frac{68-750}{560}$

PAY TO THE ORDER OF Stockbroker "A" $10,000.00

Ten Thousand and no/one-hundredths   DOLLARS

CASHIER'S CHECK   AUTHORIZED SIGNATURE

Cashier

⑈0560⑈0750⑈   009 697⑈0⑈

DELUXE CHECK PRINTERS - LH (1)

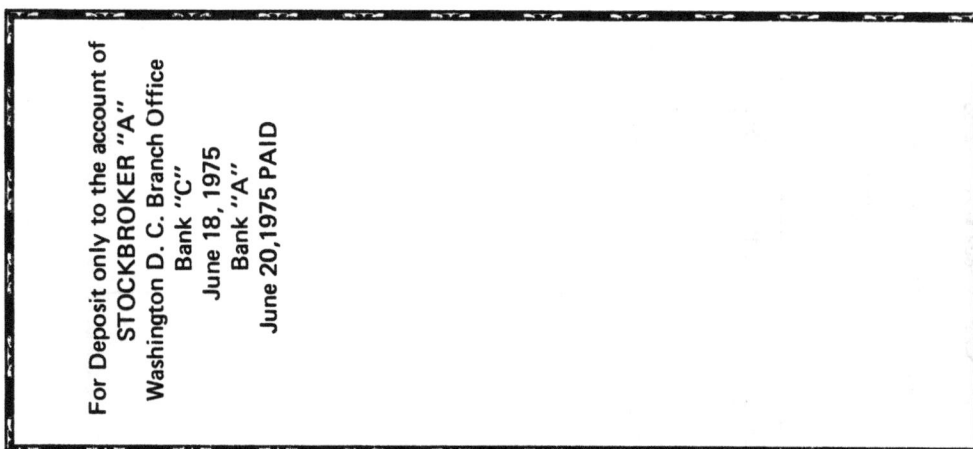

For Deposit only to the account of
STOCKBROKER "A"
Washington D. C. Branch Office
Bank "C"
June 18, 1975
Bank "A"
June 20,1975 PAID

DELUXE CHECK PRINTERS - LH (1)

Illustration 8

Security Account

The endorsements on the back of each of the three checks show that they were deposited at Bank "C" in Washington, D. C., into the account of Stockbroker "A", a nationwide stock and bond brokerage firm which has an office in Washington, D. C. (See Illustration 8, above).

The investigator places a telephone call to a Washington Metropolitan Police Department Intelligence Unit contact and asks him to find out, through his information sources, whether or not the Target has an account at Stockbroker "A" and, if so, to get copies of his monthly security account statements for the past four years.

The Washington, D. C., police contact learns that the Target opened an account with Stockbroker "A" in June, 1975. He mailed copies of the Target's signature card and his June statement to the investigator. (June, 1975, was the only month to date that the account reflected any activity). A copy of the June monthly statement is shown in Illustration 9 on the following page.

Period ENDING JUNE 30, 19__   TARGET "B"

YOUR ACCOUNT NUMBER
247630

STATEMENT OF YOUR SECURITY ACCOUNT WITH
STOCKBROKER "B"

MEMBERS NEW YORK STOCK EXCHANGE AMERICAN STOCK EXCHANGE
TORONTO STOCK EXCHANGE AND OTHER LEADING STOCK AND COMMODITY EXCHANGES

KINDLY MENTION YOUR ACCOUNT NUMBER WHEN REFERRING TO THIS STATEMENT OR OTHER TRANSACTIONS.

DATE	QUANTITY Bought or Received	QUANTITY Sold or Delivered	DESCRIPTION	PRICE OR SYMBOL	AMOUNT DEBITED (CHARGED) TO YOUR ACCOUNT	AMOUNT CREDITED TO YOUR ACCOUNT	BALANCE (BY TYPE OF ACCOUNT)
6 19			Check			10,000.00	10,000.00
6 19	100		ABC Corp.	100	10,000.00		-0-
6 20			Check			10,000.00	10,000.00
6 20	100		ABC Corp.	100	10,000.00		-0-
6 23			Check			5,000.00	5,000.00
6 23	200		DEF Corp.	25	5,000.00		-0-

KINDLY DIRECT INQUIRIES CONCERNING THIS STATEMENT TO THE OFFICE WHICH SERVICES YOUR ACCOUNT   SEE REVERSE SIDE FOR ADDRESS AND TELEPHONE NUMBER

LEDGER

FOR DESCRIPTION OF TYPE OF ACCOUNT AND EXPLANATION OF SYMBOLS USED, SEE REVERSE SIDE.

Illustration 9

18

The signature card is not illustrated in the handbook since it is similar, in most respects, to the checking account signature card shown in Illustration 4. It, however, again offers the investigator an opportunity to obtain a handwriting exemplar and to acquire other significant background information about the Target.

The June statement (Illustration 9) furnishes the Investigator with significant information. The statement is similar in many respects to a monthly bank statement and can be easily analyzed. It is necessary to keep in mind only a few simple rules. These rules are explained in detail in Chapter IV, Sources of Information.

In this instance, the Target deposited a $10,000 check to his account with Stockbroker "A" on June 19, 1975, (the first of the three cashier's checks — Illustration 8) which gave him a $10,000 "credit" balance in his account.

The next entry reflects that the Target purchased 100 shares of the ABC Corporation on June 19, 1975, at $100 per share. His account was charged, (debited), accordingly. Since the Target had already placed $10,000 in his account, his "balance is "0.""

The Target made two additional purchases as shown in Illustration 9; an additional 100 shares of ABC Corporation at $100 per share on June 20, 1975, and 200 shares of DEF Corporation at $25 per share on June 23, 1975. The purchases were paid with the remaining two cashier's checks.

The June statement does not reflect any sales of stock by the Target.

For the purpose of this exercise it is assumed that the Target did not engage in any other stock transactions during the years in question and that the above securities were physically retained by the broker for the Target. Further information regarding the impact on "net worth and expenditures" and "source and application of funds" schedules, caused by the sale or delivery of securities to the Target, is contained in pages 33-34 in this Chapter.

Purchase of Automobiles

At an early stage of any criminal investigation, an investigator ordinarily checks motor vehicle registration records to obtain an identification of a Target's automobile. The investigator's interest should be enlarged to include the identification of the car dealer and a determination of the cost of a target's automobiles, those of his girl friend, and the nature of the funds used to pay for them. It is not at all unusual to discover that a target finances the purchase of his own automobile and pays cash (usually currency) for his girl friend's automobile. His motivation may range from concealment of the latter purchase from his wife or merely to impress his girl friend. In any event, appropriate employees of automobile dealers (finance officers, salesmen, bookkeepers, etc.) are a valuable source of information concerning the spending habits of a target and a close liason should be maintained with them. While transactions of this nature are unusual, they _do_ occur, at most _all_ automobile dealers, and usually are made by individuals of interest to criminal investigators.

For the purpose of this exercise, State motor vehicle records show that the Target is the registered owner of a 1975 Cadillac El Dorado and that the automobile is titled in the name of Bank "B". Inquiries at Bank "B" disclose the name of the Cadillac dealer from whom the automobile was purchased, and the fact that the Target made a loan from the bank to purchase the automobile. In addition, by being thorough, the investigator learns that the Target also has a savings account and a mortgage loan at Bank "B". (Details concerning the savings account and mortgage loan will be covered in subsequent paragraphs).

He also learns that the Target has purchased cashier's checks from time to time at Bank "B" and he made arrangements to obtain further information concerning the checks at a later date.

After noting the balance due on the automobile loan as of the end of 1975 ($3,000), the investigator made inquiries at the Cadillac agency and learned that, in addition to purchasing his El Dorado, he also purchased a Chevrolet Caprice for his girl friend.

Copies of the invoices relative to the purchases of the El Dorado and Caprice are shown in Illustrations 10 and 11 respectively, on the following pages.

Illustration 10

CAR INVOICE

CADILLAC COMPANY

06488

CADILLAC

	DESCRIPTION OF MOTOR VEHICLE	TERMS OF TIME CONTRACT
DATE March 10, 1975		
		FINANCE COMPANY
SOLD TO	MAKE CAD ** ELDORADO	
TARGET	YEAR 1975	PAYMENTS OF $
	MOTOR NUMBER C809671	EACH PAYABLE ON THE DAY
	SERIAL NUMBER G8R38880	OF EACH MONTH BEGINNING
	MODEL ELDORADO "r 410"	SUMMARY OF INSURANCE COVERAGE
		FIRE $ TERM
	BODY STYLE Tudor	THEFT $ NONE TERM
	IGN KEY Same 6168072	COMPREHENSIVE $ TERM
	TRUNK KEY	COLLISION—UPSET $ TERM
		P D & P.L $ TERM
	NEW GREEN	COMPANY – BROKER – AGENT
SALESMAN TELEPHONE	CAR TRADED 1973 Chev	N/A

OPTIONAL EQUIPMENT AND ACCESSORIES		
DESCRIPTION PRICE	BASIC PRICE OF CAR	
	TRANSPORTATION	
	OPTIONAL EQUIPMENT AND ACCESSORIES	13,500.00
	ALL OTHER CHARGES	
	TITLE OR SALES TAX	Included
	PERSONAL PROPERTY TAX	in purchase
Included in purchase price	INSPECTION FEE	price
	REGISTRATION FEE	
	CERTIFICATE OF TITLE	
	NOTARIAL AND RECORDING FEES	
	OTHER (ITEMIZE)	
	CASH SALE PRICE	13,500.00
	DEPOSIT	5,000.00
	CASH ON DELIVERY	2,500.00
	TRADE-IN ALLOWANCE	
	TOTAL CASH PRICE BALANCE	6,000.00
	TOTAL COST OF INSURANCE	-0-
	CREDITOR'S LIFE INSURANCE	-0-
	AMOUNT OF FINANCE CHARGE	-0-
	TOTAL TIME PRICE BALANCE DUE Bank	
	FROM THE PURCHASER "B"	6,000.00

THE OR SALES & REYNOLDS CO. DAYTON, OHIO   LITHO IN U.S.A.

NO LIABILITY INSURANCE INCLUDED

21

Illustration 11

CAR INVOICE

CADILLAC COMPANY

06488

DATE March 10, 1975	**DESCRIPTION OF MOTOR VEHICLE**
SOLD TO	
Target's Girl Friend	

DESCRIPTION OF MOTOR VEHICLE

MAKE   Chev Caprice

YEAR   1975

MOTOR NUMBER   C7057689

SERIAL NUMBER   SA150697864

MODEL   Caprice

BODY STYLE   Tudor

IGN KEY   Same   47689736

TRUNK KEY

NEW USED

CAR TRADED   None

ESMAN   TELEPHONE

TERMS OF TIME CONTRACT

FINANCE COMPANY

EACH PAYABLE ON THE   DAY
OF EACH MONTH BEGINNING

SUMMARY OF INSURANCE COVERAGE

FIRE $		TERM
THEFT $	NONE	TERM
COMPREHENSIVE $		TERM
COLLISION—UPSET $		TERM
P D & P.L $		TERM

COMPANY — BROKER — AGENT

N/A

OPTIONAL EQUIPMENT AND ACCESSORIES

DESCRIPTION	PRICE

Included in purchase price

BASIC PRICE OF CAR	
TRANSPORTATION	
OPTIONAL EQUIPMENT AND ACCESSORIES	6,500.00
ALL OTHER CHARGES	
TITLE OR SALES TAX	Included
PERSONAL PROPERTY TAX	in purchase
INSPECTION FEE	price
REGISTRATION FEE	
CERTIFICATE OF TITLE	
NOTARIAL AND RECORDING FEES	
OTHER (ITEMIZE)	
CASH SALE PRICE	6,500.00
DEPOSIT	
CASH ON DELIVERY	6,500.00
TRADE-IN ALLOWANCE	-0-
TOTAL CASH PRICE BALANCE	-0-
TOTAL COST OF INSURANCE	-0-
CREDITOR'S LIFE INSURANCE	-0-
AMOUNT OF FINANCE CHARGE	-0-
TOTAL TIME PRICE BALANCE DUE FROM THE PURCHASER	

NO LIABILITY INSURANCE INCLUDED

The first invoice shows that the Target paid $13,500 for the El Dorado; received a trade-in allowance of $2,500 for his 1973 Chevrolet, (which he had also purchased at the same dealer in 1972 for $4,500); made a cash down payment of $5,000 (in currency); and financed the balance at Bank "B".

The second invoice shows that the Target paid $6,500 for the Caprice, that no trade-in was involved, and that the Target paid for the car with currency. The invoice also showed that the automobile was titled in a name later identified by the investigator as the Target's girl friend.

A subsequent re-check of State motor vehicle records showed that both of the above cars are still registered to the Target and his girl friend in 1976. This "re-check" is necessary to prove continued ownership, the importance of which is explained on Pages 33-34.

Savings Account

Since the Target's account reflected only nominal activity, the investigator made a transcript of the dates and amounts of all deposits as well as noting year end balances for the purpose of completing the net worth computations (There were no withdrawals from the account). While the transcript is not included as an "illustration," it shows balances of $200, $2100, $7400, and $9200 at the end of the years 1972 through 1975, respectively.

Cashier's Checks — Bank "B"

After obtaining the transcript of the Target's savings account the investigator strikes a bonanza. While only two cashier's checks were purchased by the Target at Bank "B", each check led to significant financial transactions as follows:

Travelers Cheques

The first of the two checks, in the amount of $20,000, was purchased on September 15, 1974, and was made payable to and endorsed by Bank "A", the bank referred to on Pages 7-16 where the Target maintained his safe deposit box and checking account. Inquiries at Bank "A" revealed that the Target used the proceeds of the cashier's check to purchase American Express Travelers Cheques in the amount of

$20,000 (200 checks of $100 denomination). (The investigator made a note on his transcript of the Target's entries to his safe deposit box at Bank "A" that he entered his safe deposit box on the same day that he purchased the $20,000 cashier's check).

The investigator listed the serial numbers of the cheques contained on the bank's retained copy of the sales record, (Illustration 12, below):

Illustration 12

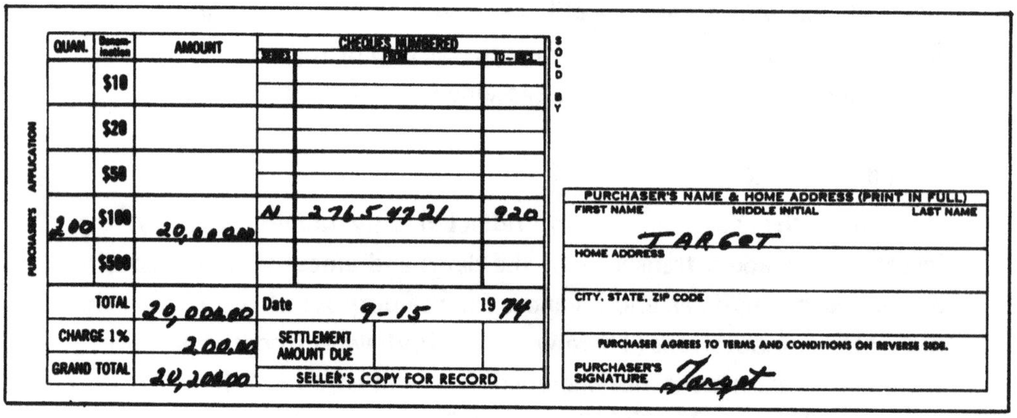

The investigator obtained copies of the cancelled travelers cheques from the American Express Company. (Further information on how to obtain copies of redeemed travelers cheques, record retention periods, etc., is contained in Chapter IV, Sources of Information).

The investigator studied the endorsements on the 200 checks and made a transcript showing the names of the payees filled in by the Target, the endorsements appearing on the reverse side and the dates that they were negotiated. The transcript confirmed intelligence obtained from other sources that the Target, having scored heavily in his fencing activities in 1974, celebrated his "business" successes by taking two trips with his girl friend; one to Acapulco and one to the French Riviera in the Fall of 1974. The nature of the expenditures ranged from airline tickets, expensive hotel bills and restaurants, to purchases at a variety of boutiques. These expenditures, all of which represent personal living expenses, are taken into account in the "net worth and expenditures" and "source and application of funds" computations on pages 28-30 of this chapter.

Fur Coat

The second cashier's check, in the amount of $5,000, was purchased on March 21, 1975. The endorsement was made by an exclusive Furrier. Information obtained from the Furrier confirmed the fact that he had received the check from the Target in payment for a full length Tourmaline mink coat. He identified a picture of the Target's girl friend as the recipient of the coat and gave the investigator the name of the insurance broker to whom he had mailed a copy of an appraisal on the coat at the request of the Target.

Diamond Ring

The investigator contacted a representative of the insurance company referred to in the preceding paragraph and learned, not only that insurance was still in force on the mink coat, (which proves continued ownership for the purposes outlined on pages 33-34), but also that the Target has insured a man's two karat diamond ring for $5,000, effective May 23, 1975, and that the policy was still in effect. He also advised the investigator that the appraisal was prepared by Jewelry Store "A". The investigator subsequently contacted the owner of Jewelry Store "A", a small but exclusive operation specializing in custom design jewelry. The owner confirmed that he sold the Target a $5,000 diamond ring on July 3, 1975; that he remembers the transaction very well, since the Target paid for the ring with fifty $100 bills. The investigator subsequently checked the date of payment with his transcript of safe deposit box entries and, again, noticed the correlation between the date of entry and the date of payment.

Condominium Apartment

An examination of Bank "B's" mortgage loan records by the investigator disclosed that the Target purchased a condominium apartment, where he presently resides, in June, 1973. A copy of the "purchaser's settlement sheet," included among other papers in the bank's loan file, shows that the Target paid $65,000 for the apartment unit, made a cash down payment of $25,000, and borrowed the remaining $40,000 from Bank "B". A copy of the Target's mortgage loan payment record, obtained from Bank "B", shows that the mortgage loan balances on December 31, 1973, 1974 and 1975 were $37,500, $27,500 and $17,500 respectively. The loan records disclosed, in addition to making the required monthly payments of $450, (an expenditure wholly inconsistent with the Target's alleged sole source of income from his furniture store), he made additional principal payments on the mortgage of $1,750, $8,500 and $8,000 in 1973, 1974, and 1975, respectively.

In the event that the investigator had not discovered the existence of the mortgage loan at Bank "B", he would have made inquiry at the County Courthouse in the county where the Target was known to reside. An examination of the County land records, which are open to examination by the public, would have disclosed not only the date and description of the property purchased by the Target, but the purchase price and the name of the lender as well. The purchase price can easily be determined by the investigator by noting the amount of "grantors' tax" or "documentary" or "transfer" stamps attached to the deed of trust. This tax, which varies by state, usually is assessed within a range of $1.00 to $1.25 per $1,000 of the purchase price. The name of the lender would be included in the body of the deed of trust "note," a copy of which is also in the file.

Examination of county land records should be routinely made by an investigator when a decision has been made to subject a target to a financial investigation. It should cover a period of years at least equal to those in which the target is suspected of being involved in an illegal activity not reflected by his known sources of income.

While the names of the various records and the types of filing systems vary from state to state, they are not difficult to examine and, in all instances, assistance from personnel in the appropriate county courthouse offices is available.

The need to prove continued ownership of the property during the years involved in the computation for this exercise, (as explained on pages 33-34), is met by (1) the fact the county records do not show a transfer of the property out of the name of the Target as of December 31, 1975, and (2) the fact that the mortgage loan is being paid timely and has an existing balance as of December 31, 1975.

Results of Inquiries to Date

At any point, during the course of completing the "Seventh Basic Investigative Technique," that it appears to the investigator that a "test check" of results should be made, it can be accomplished by using either of two basic formats as explained in Chapter II. Both formats are illustrated on the following pages and reflect merely an arithmetical summary of the evidence of expenditures made by the Target.

Source and Application of Funds Format

This title has many synonyms, including, "Statement of Resources Received and Applied," "Statement of Application of Funds," "Expenditures Statement," or, in the vernacular, "Where Did It Come From — Where Did It Go." They are all appropriate for the purposes of the investigator. The format is also highly flexible and can be presented by using a variety of different schedules. There is no right or wrong way. The decision on how to present the evidence in schedule form should be made solely on the basis of which format is most easily understood.

The Source and Application of Funds Format is illustrated on the following page (Illustration 13).

SOURCE AND APPLICATION OF FUNDS

FUNDS APPLIED:	1973	1974	1975	Page No.
Increase in Checking Account Balance	$ 800	$ 2,500	$ 700	13
Increase in Savings Account Balance	1,900	5,300	1,800	23
Down Payment on Apartment	25,000			25-26
Purchase of Securities:				
ABC			20,000	16-19
DEF			5,000	16-19
Purchase of Cadillac (Down Payment)			5,000	19-23
Purchase of Chevrolet			6,500	19-23
Purchase of Diamond Ring			5,000	25
Purchase of Fur Coat			5,000	25
Purchase of Travelers Cheques		20,000		23-24
Reduction of Mortgage on Apartment	2,500	10,000	10,000	25-26
Reduction of Loan on Cadillac			3,000	20
TOTAL FUNDS APPLIED	$30,200	$37,800	$62,000	

SOURCE OF FUNDS:				
Income from Furniture Store	$16,250	$11,750	$14,375	7

INCOME FROM UNIDENTIFIED				
SOURCES	$13,950	$26,050	$47,625	

Illustration 13

Net Worth and Expenditures Computation

There are few, if any significant variations in describing the title of this format. The schedules used to make the computation are basically the same.

While its use is rather common it is sometimes considered more difficult to explain. However, as indicated earlier in a discussion of the format of the Source and Application of Funds Statement and in Chapter II, the investigator should use whichever computation and format is, in his judgement, most easily understood.

The Net Worth and Expenditures Statement Format is illustrated on the following page (Illustration 14).

NET WORTH AND EXPENDITURES COMPUTATION

ASSETS	12/31/72	12/31/73	12/31/74	12/31/75	Page No.
Checking Account — Bank A	$ 300	$ 1,100	$ 3,600	$ 4,300	13
Savings Account — Bank B	200	2,100	7,400	9,200	23
Condominium Apartment		65,000	65,000	65,000	25-26
Furniture Store — Capital Investment	15,000	15,000	15,000	15,000	7
Securities:					
200 Shares ABC				20,000	16-19
200 Shares DEF				5,000	16-19
Automobiles:					
1973 Chevrolet	4,500	4,500	4,500	-0-	19-23
1976 Cadillac				13,500	19-23
1976 Chevrolet				6,500	19-23
Diamond Ring				5,000	25
TOTAL ASSETS	$20,000	$87,700	$95,500	$143,500	
LIABILITIES					
Mortgage-Condominium Apt.		$37,500	$27,500	$17,500	25-26
Automobile Loan				3,000	20
TOTAL LIABILITIES	-0-	$37,500	$27,500	$20,500	
Net Worth	$20,000	$50,200	$68,000	$123,000	
Less Net Worth Prior Year		20,000	50,200	68,000	
Increase in Net Worth		$30,200	$17.800	$ 55,000	
Add: Identified Personal Expenses:					
Loss on Trade in of 1973 Chevrolet				$ 2,000	19-23
Travelers Checks			$20,000		23-24
Fur Coat				5,000	25
TOTAL EXPENDITURES		$30,200	$37,800	$ 62,000	
Income from Furniture Store		16,250	11,750	14,375	7
INCOME FROM UNIDENTIFIED SOURCES		$13,950	$26,050	$ 47,625	

Illustration 14

Additional Living Expenses

Other living expenses, such as food, medical care, clothing, interest, taxes, contributions, etc., have not been taken into account in the foregoing practical exercise. Evidence of expenditures of this nature would, of course, further increase the amount of unexplained source or sources of income expended by the Target and would, accordingly, give the investigator and/or prosecutor greater leverage in applying the various techniques suggested earlier in this Handbook. If information concerning day to day living expenditures is readily available to the investigator, it should be obtained and documented in a manner similar to the other expenditures illustrated in the practical exercise.

Expenditures of this nature can be critical to the value of the overall computations if the total expenditures over and above known sources of income in any of the years in question are nominal. However, if the excess of expenditures in each of the years in question is sufficient to clearly demonstrate a pattern of expenditures well beyond the Target's legitimate sources of income, there is no need to expend additional investigative time to prove additional expenditures of this nature.

A principal source of information to prove additional living expenses is the several national credit card companies which have grown immensely in recent years. One of these companies, Bank Americard, was mentioned briefly in the opening pages of this chapter. As of the end of the first quarter of 1976, Bank Americard listed 7,058 participating banks and 31.8 million cardholders; second only to Master Charge who listed 7,483 participating banks and 37.4 million cardholders.

Further information concerning Bank Americard and other similar companies is contained in Chapter IV, Sources of Information.

Impact of Cash on Hand on Computations

In computing the amount of income derived by the Target from unexplained sources in the examples shown on pages 28 & 30, three factors, cash on hand, gifts or inheritances and loans were intentionally not taken into account. Their impact can best be explained at this stage of the practical exercise after the computation has been completed.

There are, primarily, only four explanations that can be made by a target when confronted by the results shown in the previous computations. He can allege that the expenditures made in excess of his available income from his legitimate sources were made with cash accumulated in and retained from prior years. He can also allege that he received gifts of cash from friends. He can further allege that he borrowed cash from friends and that said loans remain unpaid. Or, he can claim that he inherited cash or other property which he converted to cash.

These attempts to explain away evidence of other sources of income are not difficult to disprove because the explanations are usually false. If the explanations are, in fact, false, the Target is literally forced to state that the funds allegedly received from others or saved from prior years were in currency, since he cannot point to any documentary evidence to substantiate his claims. For example, if he placed the funds in his checking or savings accounts, or if he received cashier's checks or securities, or jewelry which he later converted to cash, etc., there would have to be at least some written record to substantiate his claim. The fact that the explanation relates to "currency" is, therefore, the best indicator to an investigator that the explanation is false.

If the Target identifies the individual or individuals from whom he allegedly received cash gifts or loans (probably others engaged in illegal activities) he subjects them to the same investigative perils as he is currently facing. He may, by the very fact of identifying them, finger other potential targets; some of whom may warrant an investigation of their financial activities; particularly if, by some remote chance, there is a degree of validity to the Target's explanation. In effect, the investigative emphasis could conceivably shift, perhaps to a target at a higher echelon.

If the Target claims to have inherited money in prior years and allegedly used those funds to make the expenditures during the years in question, there are public probate records available in local courthouses, enabling an investigator to check out the validity of such claims.

Assuming that some or all of the countermeasures taken by the investigator are not productive for any of a variety of reasons, there are ample sources of evidence available to an investigator to negate most all of the claims outlined above. Most of this evidence can and should be obtained during the course of the inquiries previously made by the investigator, and which have already been discussed in this chapter.

For example, while making inquiries at the banks the investigator should have routinely requested copies of financial statements submitted to them by the Target. These statements, which vary in form, and are universally required when applying for a loan, require the applicant to list his cash holdings as well as cash in banks and other assets. The applicant must also list his liabilities.

The absence of any disclosure of cash on hand in a financial statement or the absence of any indication of money owed to individuals, tends, in and of itself, to negate previously referred to allegations of cash on hand and cash loans.

The analysis of the Target's entries to his safe deposit box may also assist the investigator in overcoming the "cash" allegations made by the Target. In questioning the Target as to the dates on which he received gifts, inheritances or loans, and where he placed the funds for safekeeping, it may well be shown that the Target did not enter his safe deposit on the dates or even near the dates that he claimed to have received the cash.

There are other types of information available to negate any attempts to explain away the source of funds used to make the expenditures referred to in the exercise by alleging the existence of an accumulation of cash from prior years. They include public records disclosing judgements arising from non payment of debts, a poor work record, nominal living standards, testimony of relatives, girl friends, etc.

The principle point to keep in mind is that during the interrogation process, when the Target is confronted with the evidence of his inordinate expenditures,

1. He has been surprised. He is faced with the reality that the investigator knows he is spending substantially more funds than he can account for from legitimate sources.

2. He is trying to avoid incriminatory statements that will disclose his fencing activities.

3. His attempts to explain away the expenditures are, in all probability, a complete fabrication, hastily and, as a result, poorly conceived, and

4. As he attempts to make plausible explanations he becomes even more "off balance" and is more vulnerable to the application of skilled interrogation techniques designed to bring out the Target's fencing activities, which is, after all, the primary objective of the application of the "Seventh Basic Investigative Technique."

Continued Ownership of Assets

In making the preceding computations it should be kept in mind that it is not only necessary to prove that a target acquired an asset, (stocks, land, automobiles, etc.) but, that he either disposed of it during one of the years involved in the computation, or retained the asset throughout the years in question.

For example if the Target, in the exercise in Chapter III, sold an asset during any of the years in question, he would have funds available to make other expenditures. If the investigator gathers evidence of the other expenditures and adds them to the expenditures previously determined, the result would be that the Target would have been erroneously charged with having spent the same money twice. For example, if the Target sold his DEF stock on August 1, 1975, which he had purchased in June, 1975, and used the $5,000.00 proceeds to buy a diamond ring in September, 1975 for $5,000.00, his net expenditures for the year would be only $5,000.00.

However, if it can be established that the Target still owned the DEF stock at the end of the year, and purchased the diamond ring in

September of the same year, his net expenditures would then be $10,000.00.

The need, therefore, to determine whether or not the Target kept or sold his stocks is obvious. In the example illustrated in this handbook, continued ownership of the stocks was assumed. However, if the Target had taken delivery of the stocks, other evidence of continued ownership (or sale) would have had to be obtained by the investigator. The best sources of information would be the appropriate corporations' transfer agent, usually a bank. The transfer agent maintains a record on each stockholder's holdings, which includes the number of shares owned, the certificate numbers, the dates of acquisition, and the full name in which the shares were issued. The transfer agents records will also show the surrender or cancellation date of all certificates.

The name of a Corporation's transfer agent can be obtained from either the Corporation, Moodys or Standard and Poor's.

Continued ownership of the other assets referred to in Chapter III has already been commented on in the appropriate paragraphs in Chapter III, i.e., Automobiles, Page 23, Fur Coat and Diamond Ring, Page 25 and Condominium Apartment, Page 26.

Summary

While, during the course of the preceding exercise, the Target may appear to have undergone a series of wholly unnecessary manipulations of cash, they were not at all unusual. The transactions reflect the actions of an individual who is attempting to conceal the nature of his financial activities, hoping to avoid leaving a trail. They constitute the actions of a guilt ridden individual, taken primarily to hide the proceeds of his illegal activities. The very nature of their circuitous route, once discovered by the investigator, can, among other things, contribute significantly to a successful interrogation.

The degree to which the computations should be perfected should depend on the manner in which the information is to be utilized. If its use is to, initially, be limited to interrogation of a target, there is no need to tie down every loose end to a mathematical certainty. If, however, it appears that the computation has potential for assisting a prosecutor in presenting a case to a grand jury or during the course of trial, then, by all means, the computations should be perfected. Assistance from investigative financial analysts and/or others with similar backgrounds should be utilized for this purpose if this type of resource personnel are available.

CHAPTER IV

Sources of Information

Introduction

This handbook does not include a comprehensive list of sources of information available to an investigator. That is not its purpose. Nor is it necessary to do so, since basic instruction in this area, as well as all other basic investigative techniques, are included in the curricula of most law enforcement training academies. In addition, most, if not all, investigators have had considerable experience in cultivating a broad variety of information sources.

The sources of information included in this handbook are, accordingly, limited primarily to those necessary to trace financial transactions that have an impact on the "net worth and expenditures" computations; the so-called "Seventh Basic Investigative Technique."

Some of the sources of information utilized in tracing financial transactions have already been explained in Chapter III during the development of the practical exercise and will not be repeated in this chapter. Only those sources of information which require further explanation will be discussed herein. They relate, primarily, to bank records, stockbrokers' records, travelers cheques, and records of the major credit card companies.

Authority to Obtain Information

During the course of presenting investigative accounting techniques to literally thousands of state and local criminal investigators at organized crime seminars throughout the United States the author has encountered, during the early stages of his presentations, not a reluctance to apply the suggested techniques, but sincere questions challenging the ability or the right of criminal investigators to obtain information from banks and other business organizations without subpoena power. Invariably, after comprehensive discussions with the groups, the author was readily able to overcome these concerns. It is hoped, therefore, that the following paragraphs will, likewise, overcome any undue concern among those criminal investigators who will be studying the contents of this handbook about their ability to successfully obtain all of the information necessary to make the computations illustrated in Chapter III, and more.

A considerable part of the evidence, necessary to make the computations illustrated in Chapter III, is readily available to criminal investigators, either from public records, such as those located in county courthouses, or, under certain circumstances, from city, county, state and Federal agencies.

Subpoena power, when available through the courts, grand juries, legislative bodies, crime commissions and other administrative groups, should be fully utilized. However, adequate sources of information should be independently developed to the fullest extent possible.

Of major importance, however, when developing sources of information, criminal investigators should not concentrate solely on developing informants among the criminal element or from sources often referred to as "street" sources, whose credibility is so often found to be highly questionable.

Criminal investigators should broaden the scope of this powerful investigative technique and develop informants and cooperative individuals among the white collar groups who may have knowledge of a target's financial activities, as well as among the white collar criminal's associates. In other words, develop sources of information among those individuals in the financial community where the profits from a target's illegal activities are actually expended. Keep in mind that one of the most important keys to solving crimes, motivated by a greed for money, lies with the development of evidence of the disposition of the fruits of the crime . . . . . . money. In developing sources of information among those in the financial community, criminal investigators should keep in mind that the automobile dealers, furriers, jewelry store owners, boutique operators, banks, etc., are all looking to the law enforcement officer for protection from the criminal element, not just from those who commit crimes of violence, but from those who commit financial crimes as well. The criminal investigator, therefore, literally has his foot in the door in creating a cooperative relationship with the business community.

In developing sources of information within the financial community, investigators should employ the same high standards of conduct, to ensure that Federal, state and local statutes are not violated, as those employed in developing information from all other sources.

BANK RECORDS

A cursory review of the practical exercise in Chapter III clearly shows that one of the most important sources of information, necessary to successfully employ the Seventh Basic Investigative Technique, is the nation's banks.

The purpose of the following paragraphs, therefore, is to familiarize criminal investigators with certain bank records in greater detail than previously explained in Chapter III.

Internal Bookkeeping Procedures

It is not the purpose of this chapter, or any other chapter in this handbook, to explain to criminal investigators the intricacies of internal banking bookkeeping procedures. It would be impractical, detract from the objectives of the handbook, and would serve no useful purpose.

Internal banking record keeping practices and procedures are not only complex, but are changing constantly, due, primarily, to the further sophistication of computer technology. The nation's banks are moving steadily toward an "electronic funds transfer" system which will eliminate the use of checks. Such a system would automatically transfer money from the account of a purchaser to the account of a seller. The familiar "paper trails" would, accordingly, disappear. These and other electronic innovations would make any attempt to explain internal record keeping procedures of banks obsolete by the time the handbook is printed.

Retention of Records

Of greater importance to the criminal investigator than the electronic advances being made by banks in keeping records is the knowledge and assurance that they do not need to familiarize themselves with intricate internal record keeping procedures of banks in order to obtain the types of information necessary to their investigations. The criminal investigator does need to know, however, that records of customers' transactions, regardless of their complexity, are maintained and are retained. The retention of said records is mandatory in accordance with the provisions of Titles I and II of Federal Public Law 91-508, the Financial Record Keeping and Currency and Foreign Transactions Act.

U. S. Treasury regulations, implementing Public Law 91-508, provide, in part, that an original, microfilm, or other copy or reproduction of most demand deposits (checking account) and savings account records must be retained for five years. The records must include:

1. Signature cards
2. Statements, ledger cards or other records disclosing all transactions; i.e., deposits and withdrawals.
3. Copies of customers' checks, bank drafts, money orders, cashier's checks drawn on the bank, or issued and payable by it.

In addition, banks must retain for a two-year period all records necessary to:

1. Reconstruct a customer's checking account. The records must include copies of customer's deposit tickets.
2. Trace and supply a description of a check deposited to a customer's checking account.

All of the above requirements apply only to checks written or deposits made in excess of $100.00. It should be noted, however, that most banks find that it is cheaper to microfilm all pertinent records, including those checks and deposits in amounts of less than $100.00, rather than sort out their records into two categories. Therefore, if a particular transaction of less than $100.00 appears to be of particular interest to an investigator, there is a strong likelihood that the necessary records to identify the transaction are, in fact, available.

The regulations further provide that whatever system banks use to photocopy or microfilm checks, drafts or money orders, both sides of the checks must be reproduced unless the reverse sides are blank.

The regulations also provide that banks maintain their records in such a manner so that they can be made available, upon request, within a "reasonable period of time."

Public Law 91-508 provides for civil and/or criminal penalties for willful violations of the law or the regulations summarized, in part, above.

Detailed information concerning Public Law 91-508 can be obtained by requesting from the U. S. Department of The Treasury, a publication prepared by the Office of the General Counsel and issued in June, 1972, entitled "Currency and Foreign Transactions Reporting Act — Statute, Regulations, and Forms."

Requests should be addressed to the Deputy Assistant Secretary (Enforcement), The Department of the Treasury, Washington, D.C., 20220.

Recognizing "Cashed" Checks

As stated in Chapter III, all banks use a series of codes or symbols to indicate on the face of a check the nature of its disposition. Of particular interest to the police investigator are those checks, either drawn on a target's checking account, or received by a target from others, which have been cashed.

Illustration 15 below shows the "cashed" code used by one of the major banks in the Mid-Atlantic States. It is one of the most commonly used codes, and is stamped on the face of cashed checks.

Illustration 15

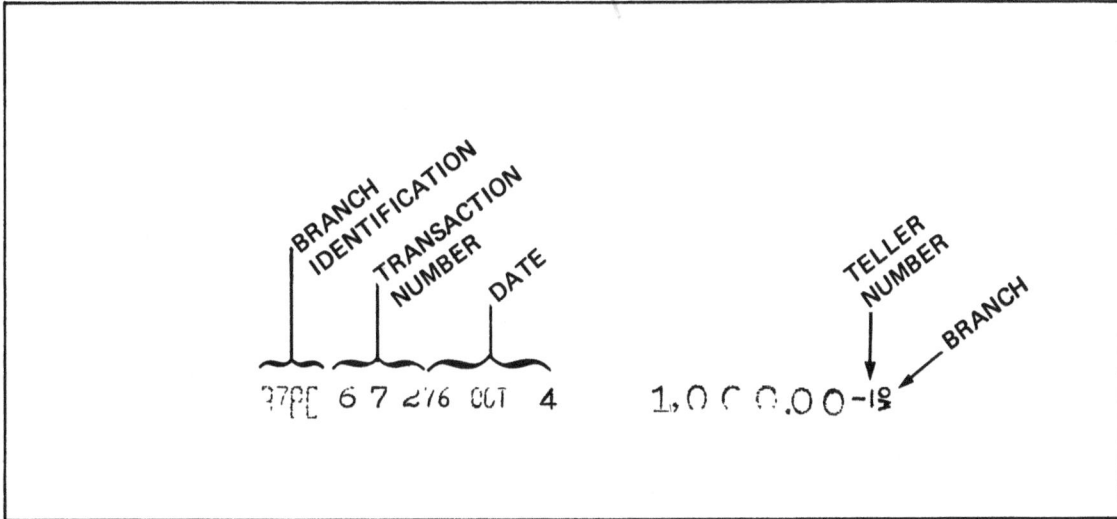

Other examples of "cashed" codes used by banks are shown in Illustration 16 below: (In each instance the codes are stamped on the face of checks.)

Illustration 16

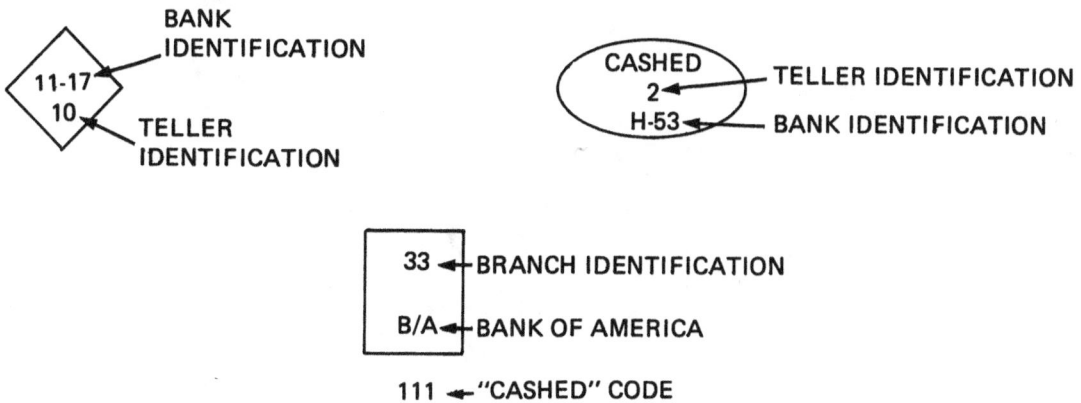

No attempt has been made to include in this handbook "cashed" codes of all banks due to the variety of codes used. This information can, however, be readily obtained by making appropriate local inquiries.

Bank Identification Symbols

All checks printed for banking institutions contain a series of numbers in the upper right hand corner on the face of the checks. These numbers represent an identification code developed by the American Banker's Association and are usually referred to as the "ABA Transit Number." See Illustration 17 below:

Illustration 17

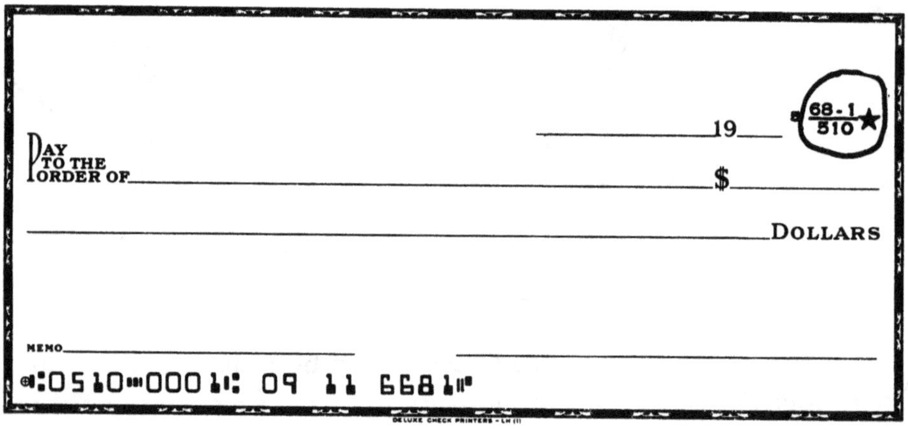

The "ABA Transit Number" Identification Code is illustrated below: (Illustration 18)

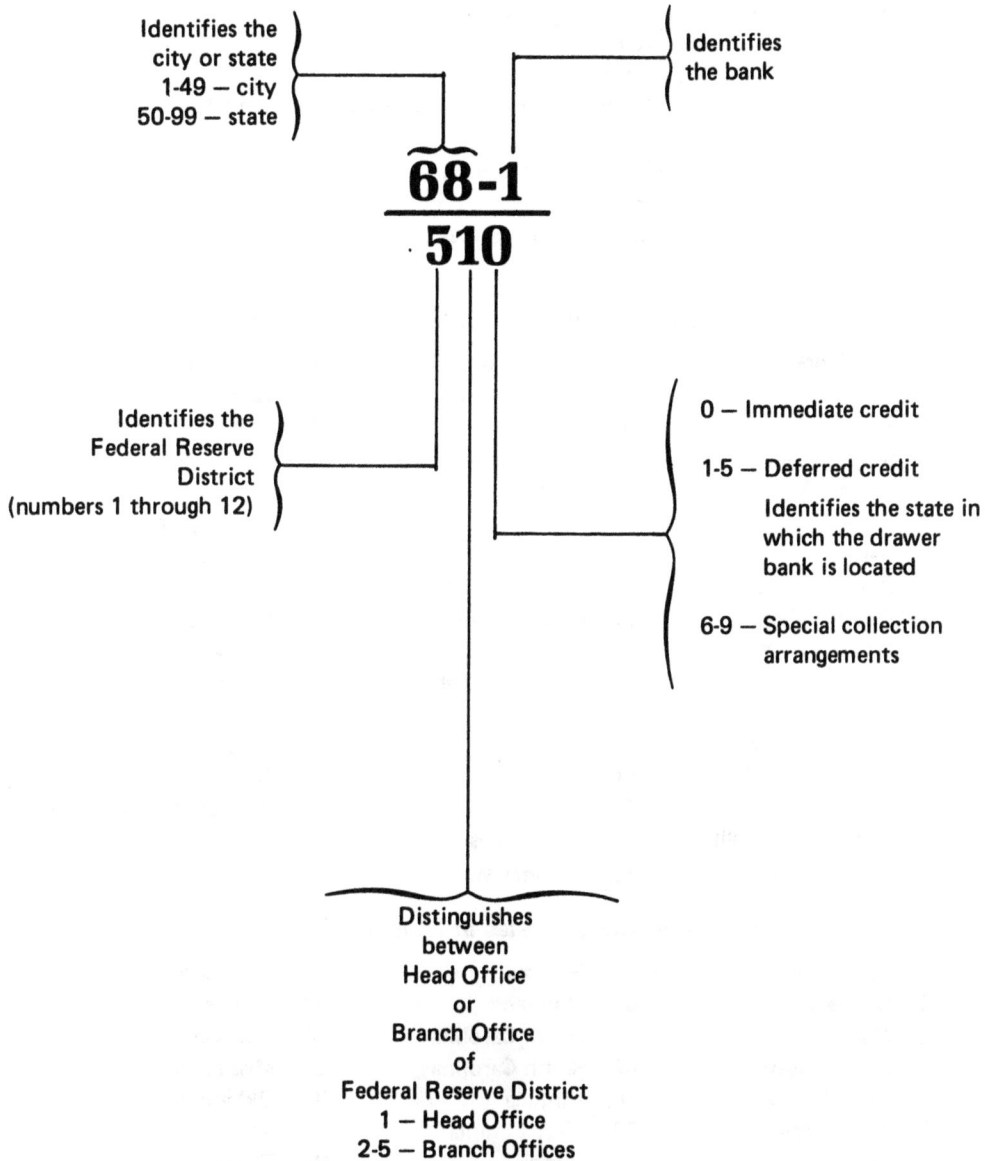

Identifies the city or state
1-49 — city
50-99 — state

Identifies the bank

68-1 / 510

Identifies the Federal Reserve District (numbers 1 through 12)

0 — Immediate credit

1-5 — Deferred credit

Identifies the state in which the drawer bank is located

6-9 — Special collection arrangements

Distinguishes between Head Office or Branch Office of Federal Reserve District
1 — Head Office
2-5 — Branch Offices

Illustration 18

A complete listing of the ABA Numerical System Identification Code is contained on the following two pages. (Illustration 19)

Illustration 19

THE NUMERICAL SYSTEM
of The American Bankers Association
Index to Prefix Numbers of Cities and States

Numbers 1 to 49 inclusive are Prefixes for Cities.

Numbers 50 to 99 inclusive are Prefixes for States.

Prefix Numbers 50 to 58 are Eastern States.

Prefix Number 59 is Alaska, American Samoa, Guam, Hawaii, Puerto Rico, and
   Virgin Islands.

Prefix Numbers 60 to 69 are Southeastern States.

Prefix Numbers 70 to 79 are Central States.

Prefix Numbers 80 to 88 are Southwestern States.

Prefix Numbers 90 to 99 are Western States.

Prefix Numbers of Cities in Numerical Order

1. New York, N. Y.	18. Kansas City, Mo.	35. Houston, Texas
2. Chicago, Ill.	19. Seattle, Wash.	36. St. Joseph, Mo.
3. Philadelphia, Pa.	20. Indianapolis, Ind.	37. Fort Worth, Texas
4. St. Louis, Mo.	21. Louisville, Ky.	38. Savannah, Ga.
5. Boston, Mass.	22. St. Paul, Minn.	39. Oklahoma City, Okla
6. Cleveland, Ohio	23. Denver, Colo.	40. Wichita, Kan.
7. Baltimore, Md.	24. Portland, Ore.	41. Sioux City, Iowa
8. Pittsburgh, Pa.	25. Columbus, Ohio	42. Pueblo, Colo.
9. Detroit, Mich.	26. Memphis, Tenn.	43. Lincoln, Neb.
10. Buffalo, N. Y.	27. Omaha, Neb.	44. Topeka, Kan.
11. San Francisco, Calif.	28. Spokane, Wash.	45. Dubuque, Iowa
12. Milwaukee, Wis.	29. Albany, N. Y.	46. Galveston, Texas
13. Cincinnati, Ohio	30. San Antonio, Texas	47. Cedar Rapids, Iowa
14. New Orleans, La.	31. Salt Lake City, Utah	48. Waco, Texas
15. Washington, D. C.	32. Dallas, Texas	49. Muskogee, Okla.
16. Los Angeles, Calif.	33. Des Moines, Iowa	
17. Minneapolis, Minn.	34. Tacoma, Wash.	

Prefix Numbers of States in Numerical Order

50. New York	64. Georgia	82. Colorado
51. Connecticut	65. Maryland	83. Kansas
52. Maine	66. North Carolina	84. Louisiana
53. Massachusetts	67. South Carolina	85. Mississippi
54. New Hampshire	68. Virginia	86. Oklahoma
55. New Jersey	69. West Virginia	87. Tennessee
56. Ohio	70. Illinois	88. Texas
57. Rhode Island	71. Indiana	89. . . . .
58. Vermont	72. Iowa	90. California
59. Alaska, American	73. Kentucky	91. Arizona
Samoa, Guam,	74. Michigan	92. Idaho
Hawaii, Puerto	75. Minnesota	93. Montana
Rico & Virgin	76. Nebraska	94. Nevada
Islands	77. North Dakota	95. New Mexico
60. Pennsylvania	78. South Dakota	96. Oregon
61. Alabama	79. Wisconsin	97. Utah
62. Delaware	80. Missouri	98. Washington
63. Florida	81. Arkansas	99. Wyoming

Illustration 19

ROUTING SYMBOLS (IN ITALICS) OF BANKS THAT ARE MEMBERS OF THE FEDERAL RESERVE SYSTEM

ALL BANKS IN AREA SERVED BY A FEDERAL RESERVE BANK OR BRANCH CARRY THE ROUTING SYMBOL OF THE FEDERAL RESERVE BANK OR BRANCH

FEDERAL RESERVE BANKS AND BRANCHES

1. Federal Reserve Bank of Boston Head Office — $\frac{5-1}{110}$

2. Federal Reserve Bank of New York Head Office — $\frac{1-120}{210}$

   Buffalo Branch — $\frac{10-26}{220}$

3. Federal Reserve Bank of Philadelphia Head Office — $\frac{3-4}{310}$

4. Federal Reserve Bank of Cleveland Head Office — $\frac{0-1}{410}$

   Cincinnati Branch — $\frac{13-43}{420}$

   Pittsburgh Branch — $\frac{8-30}{430}$

5. Federal Reserve Bank of Richmond Head Office — $\frac{68-3}{510}$

   Baltimore Branch — $\frac{7-27}{520}$

   Charlotte Branch — $\frac{66-20}{530}$

6. Federal Reserve Bank of Atlanta Head Office — $\frac{64-14}{610}$

   Birmingham Branch — $\frac{61-19}{620}$

   Jacksonville Branch — $\frac{63-19}{630}$

   Nashville Branch — $\frac{87-10}{640}$

   New Orleans Branch — $\frac{14-21}{650}$

7. Federal Reserve Bank of Chicago Head Office — $\frac{2-30}{710}$

   Detroit Branch — $\frac{9-29}{720}$

8. Federal Reserve Bank of St. Louis Head Office — $\frac{4-4}{810}$

   Little Rock Branch — $\frac{81-13}{820}$

   Louisville Branch — $\frac{21-59}{830}$

   Memphis Branch — $\frac{26-3}{840}$

9. Federal Reserve Bank of Minneapolis Head Office — $\frac{17-8}{910}$

   Helena Branch — $\frac{93-26}{920}$

10. Federal Reserve Bank of Kansas City Head Office — $\frac{18-4}{1010}$

    Denver Branch — $\frac{23-19}{1020}$

    Oklahoma City Branch — $\frac{39-24}{1030}$

    Omaha Branch — $\frac{27-12}{1040}$

11. Federal Reserve Bank of Dallas Head Office — $\frac{32-3}{1110}$

    El Paso Branch — $\frac{88-1}{1120}$

    Houston Branch — $\frac{35-4}{1130}$

    San Antonio Branch — $\frac{30-72}{1140}$

12. Federal Reserve Bank of San Francisco Head Office — $\frac{11-37}{1210}$

    Los Angeles Branch — $\frac{16-16}{1220}$

    Portland Branch — $\frac{24-1}{1230}$

    Salt Lake City Branch — $\frac{31-31}{1240}$

    Seattle Branch — $\frac{19-1}{1250}$

NATIONAL CREDIT CARDS

Bank Americard

In the opening paragraph of the "Investigative Steps" section of Chapter III, mention was made that the investigator learned that the Target had obtained a Bank Americard at Bank "A".

No further mention was made of the Bank Americard in the practical exercise until the closing pages of the Chapter under the sub-heading, "Additional Living Expenses." It was suggested that further investigative effort and expense to prove additional living expenses should not be undertaken unless such proof was needed to establish a clear pattern of expenditures beyond a target's legitimate sources of income.

In the event that additional evidence of living expenses is needed, one of the best sources of information is Bank Americard and similar credit card systems.

Records of purchases made by Bank Americard holders are retained on microfilm by participating banks. The record retention period varies according to the record retention policies of member banks. It should be noted that all records relating to customers who have used their accounts, or those of others, in a fraudulent manner, are retained permanently.

Since the records of purchases are stored in facilities maintained by each of the member banks, no attempt is being made to list the location of Bank Americard storage centers in this handbook due to the large number of participating banks. This information can be readily obtained on a local basis.

Illustration 20 below is a sample monthly statement issued to card holders by Bank Americard.

Illustration 20

The first four digits of the account number located in the upper left hand corner of the statement identify the name of the member bank. The statement clearly shows the potential value of this source of information, not only to prove expenditures for the purpose of making the computations demonstrated in Chapter III, but as a general source of leads, target contacts, whereabouts on given dates, etc.

Master Charge

Records of purchases made by Master Charge Credit Card holders are also retained on microfilm by participating banks. The record retention period varies according to the record retention policies of said banks.

As stated in the above paragraphs relating to Bank Americard, record storage facilities are maintained by each of the member banks. Therefore, it would be impractical to attempt to include in this publication locations of all record retention centers.

The Master Charge company is presently in the process of converting their record keeping system which, when implemented, will provide card holders with a monthly statement format similar to Bank Americard. It will replace the present system in which copies of charge tags are returned to customers.

45

American Express

Records of purchases made by American Express Credit Card holders are retained on microfilm for at least six years. Requests for copies of monthly statements, if circumstances require making a formal request, should be directed to the American Express Company, Box 13779, Phoenix, Arizona 85002.

The monthly statement issued to card holders by the American Express Company is similar in format to the statement issued by Bank Americard.

TRAVELERS CHEQUES

American Express

Cancelled American Express Travelers Cheques are retained for a period of six years and one month in storage facilities located in Piscataway, New Jersey. The cheques are filed serially by date of redemption, not by issue date. Requests for copies of paid cheques should be directed to the American Express Company, American Express Plaza, New York, New York 10004.

Citibank of New York

Cancelled Citibank travelers cheques are also filed, serially, by date of redemption, rather than by issue date. Requests for copies of paid cheques should be directed to the Citibank Travelers Cheque Refund Department, P. O. Box 2202, F.D.R. Station, New York, New York 10022.

Bank of America

Cancelled Bank of America travelers cheques are also filed, serially, by date of redemption, rather than by issue date. Requests for copies of paid cheques should be directed to the Bank of America Check Corporation, Attention: Claims Department, Fifth Floor, 1 — Powell Street, San Francisco, California 94102.

Analyzing Customer Security Account Statements

The following rules are applicable in analyzing a target's security account statement.

Illustration 9, originally referred to in Chapter III, is repeated on page 48 for easy reference with relation to the following explanations.

When a target purchases stock there would be entries in all of the following columns:
1. "Bought or Received" column
2. "Description" column, where the name of the security would be listed.
3. "Price or Symbol" column, where the purchase price per share would be listed.
4. "Debit" column, the amount of the purchase charged to the Target's account.

When a target sells stock there would be entries in all of the following columns:
1. "Sold or Delivered" column
2. "Description" column, where the name of the security would be listed.
3. "Price or Symbol" column, where the sales price per share would be listed.
4. "Credit" column, the proceeds from the sales credited to the Target's account.

When a target purchases stock he has the option of taking "delivery" of the certificates from the broker or leaving them in the broker's custody.

If he takes delivery of the certificates the number of shares would be noted in the "Sold or Delivered" column and the date column would show the date of delivery. In addition there would be <u>no</u> entry in the "price or symbol" column. If there was a price in the "price or symbol" column, the entries would reflect a sale rather than a delivery.

If there are no entries indicating "delivery" of the securities, they are, in fact, being held by the broker and the target is in what is commonly referred to as a "long" position. Usually the broker will list at the bottom of the target's December statement a summary of his "long" position, i.e., a listing of the number of shares of each stock being held for the target.

Period
ENDING
June 30, 1975

TARGET "A"

YOUR ACCOUNT NUMBER
247630

STATEMENT OF YOUR SECURITY ACCOUNT
WITH

STOCK BROKER "A"

MEMBERS NEW YORK STOCK EXCHANGE   AMERICAN STOCK EXCHANGE
TORONTO STOCK EXCHANGE AND OTHER LEADING STOCK AND COMMODITY EXCHANGES

KINDLY MENTION YOUR ACCOUNT NUMBER WHEN REFERRING TO THIS STATEMENT OR OTHER TRANSACTIONS.

DATE	QUANTITY Bought or Received	QUANTITY Sold or Delivered	DESCRIPTION	PRICE OR SYMBOL	AMOUNT DEBITED (CHARGED) TO YOUR ACCOUNT	AMOUNT CREDITED TO YOUR ACCOUNT	BALANCE (BY TYPE OF ACCOUNT)
6 19			Check			10,000.00	10,000.00
6 19	100		ABC Corp.	100	10,000.00		-0-
6 20			Check			10,000.00	10,000.00
6 20	100		ABC Corp.	100	10,000.00		-0-
6 23			Check			5,000.00	5,000.00
6 23	200		DEF Corp.	25	5,000.00		-0-

KINDLY DIRECT INQUIRIES CONCERNING THIS STATEMENT TO THE OFFICE WHICH SERVICES YOUR ACCOUNT   SEE REVERSE SIDE FOR ADDRESS AND TELEPHONE NUMBER

LEDGER

FOR DESCRIPTION OF TYPE OF ACCOUNT AND EXPLANATION OF SYMBOLS USED, SEE REVERSE SIDE

CHAPTER V

Summary

The law enforcement profession has been literally inundated over the past several years with so-called advanced training programs, seminars, etc., sponsored by Federal, state and local agencies, private industry, foundations, etc., at which instructors, introduced as highly experienced experts in the field of surveillance, undercover techniques, interrogation and other criminal justice subjects, proceed to offer to their "students" a course of instruction that, on occasion, has been so basic that their presentations are received with laughter and, at times, outright indignation.

This author has attempted to avoid such a mistake in this publication. His prior experience in making presentations similar to the material outlined in this handbook at Organized Crime Conferences and before other law enforcement groups over a period of several years has made it patently clear that (1) basic criminal investigative techniques are taught at the basic schools conducted by the various law enforcement agencies, where they should be, and (2) as stated in greater detail in Chapter I, criminal investigators at all levels of government have already acquired considerable experience in the application of criminal investigation techniques; in many cases, far beyond that of some of the so-called "expert" instructors.

Therefore, what the author is suggesting is that criminal investigators no longer need continued training in the basic "state of the art." Rather, they should expand their areas of expertise by utilizing the Seventh Basic Investigative Technique wherever appropriate. In the interrogation process, therefore, where the technique may enhance results, criminal investigators should develop a line of questioning with which they are personally comfortable, using all of the psychological approaches that they have already mastered over the years, but redesigned to confront targets with the fact that they have been spending money at a rate far in excess of the funds available to them from legitimate sources year, after year, after year.

If a target breaks, then perhaps the seventh technique will have contributed to the success of the interrogation. If an interrogation fails, the investigative efforts will not have been in vain. The information gathered relating to a target's financial transactions should automatically go into the department's intelligence system, and, where appropriate, should be disseminated to cooperating law enforcement information networks. The information may, as a result, lead to the detection of other crimes, identify havens where a target may be hiding assets, or lead to the identification or location of assets for restitution or collection of fines.

Some of the information may become the missing link in a future investigation of a target or an investigation of one or more of his associates. Its availability to a district attorney may enhance his presentation before a grand jury or during a future trial of a target or one or more of his associates.

The investigative concepts outlined in this handbook are certainly no panacea in solving the Organized and White Collar Crime problems in the United States. However, if the application of these concepts contribute to the successful investigation of only one significant case each year in each of the 50 states or in each of the major metropolitan areas of the United States, the efforts of everyone associated with the development and application of the Seventh Basic Investigative Technique will have paid handsome dividends.

One of the ultimate goals of everyone engaged in the criminal justice system is to control organized crime and white collar crime in the United States. It is the sincere belief of the author that the application of the Seventh Basic Investigative Technique can play, at least, some small part in achieving our mutual objective.

www.ingramcontent.com/pod-product-compliance
Lightning Source LLC
Chambersburg PA
CBHW080410270326
41929CB00018B/2972